<deconstructing web graphics>

■ Words: Lynda Weinman
■ Design: Ali Karp

Deconstructing Web Graphics

By Lynda Weinman

Published by: New Riders Publishing
201 West 103rd Street
Indianapolis, IN 46290 USA

Printed in the United States of America 1 2 3 4 5 6 7 8 9 0
ISBN: 1-56205-641-7

This book was produced digitally by Macmillan Computer Publishing and manufactured using 100% computer-to-plate technology (filmless process), by Shepard Poorman Communications Corporation, Indianapolis, Indiana.

Publisher: Don Fowley
Publishing Manager: David Dwyer
Marketing Manager: Mary Foote
Managing Editor: Carla Hall

Deconstructing Web Graphics Credits

Project Editor
Laura Frey

Technical Editor
Bill Weinman

Associate Marketing Manager
Tamara Apple

Acquisitions Coordinator
Stacey Beheler

Administrative Coordinator
Karen Opal

Cover Designer
Bruce Heavin

Cover Production
Aren Howell

Book Designer
Ali Karp

Production Manager
Kelly Dobbs

Production Team Supervisor
Laurie Casey

Production Analysts
Jason Hand
Bobbi Satterfield

Production Team
Joe Millay
Elizabeth Shott

Proofreader
Megan Wade

Indexer
Sharon Hilgenberg

■ Lynda Weinman. (photo: Douglas Kirkland)

About the Author

Lynda Weinman writes full-time for a living now, but in the past has been a designer, animator, magazine contributor, computer consultant, instructor, moderator, and lecturer. She lives in California with her seven-year-old daughter, two cats, one snake, and five computers. She teaches Web Design, Interactive Media Design, Motion Graphics, and Digital Imaging classes at Art Center College of Design in Pasadena, California. Lynda has a monthly column in *The Net Magazine*, and contributes regularly to *MacUser*, *Step-by-Step Graphics*, *New Media*, and *Full Motion* magazines. She likes the Web so much, she even has a domain for her name:

■ http://www.lynda.com

Lynda, get a life!

■ Lynda, daughter Jamie, and Bruce.

■ Lynda, and artist Bruce Heavin. (photo: Bart Nagel)

■ Jamie (who asked if she could be her "real age" in the next book). (Only those who have Lynda's other book, *Designing Web Graphics*, will understand!)

Lynda's Acknowledgements

To **all the people** who let me profile and interview them for this book. Who took time away from their busy lives and provided answers to my persistent questions. Who acted in the spirit of the Web and freely shared their knowledge.

To **Bruce Heavin**, who painted this book's amazing cover. Who painted my last book's amazing cover. Who won my heart in the process—first through his art, and later through his friendship, unparallelled supportiveness, and love.

To **Jamie**, who watched her mommy write another book in between all the other things that happened to her this year: loosing her two front teeth, becoming encyclopedic about whales, getting a color printer for her computer, and finishing first grade.

To **my brother Bill**, who edited all the programming examples in this book. Who turned into the WebMonster and maintained his sister's Web design mailing list and Web site when he was really too busy with his own work to have that kind of time. Who gave her love and encouragment and support, and became closer to her than when they were growing up together.

To **Ali Karp**, whose re-design of *Deconstructing Web Graphics* was everything we wanted: clean, unimposing, and utilitarian. Who beta tested the book, and offered invaluable insights and suggestions. Who, above all, was a treasured friend and unselfish collaborator.

To **David Dwyer**, who reminded me to interject my teaching skills when I was overwhelmed by the scope of this book. Who understands big things, like the importance of this medium and the value of enduring relationships.

To **Mary Thorpe**, who made everything work when I couldn't. Who made the greatest food, took Jamie to the coolest places, and warmed our home with her big smile and bigger heart.

To **Crystal Waters**, who wrote her own book while I wrote mine (*Web Concepts and Design*/New Riders; plug plug, plug plug). Who kept me laughing, listened to my moaning, and most importantly, made me listen to hers.

To **my teaching assistants** this term at Art Center, who kindly watched after their absent-minded professor and helped me as I juggled too many things: **Joeseph Paguirigan**, **Wendy Polek**, and **Shane Rebenschied** — three very talented designers and all-around great people.

To **my students at Art Center**, who gave me more than they knew. Who inspired me and who will be missed as I venture into a full-time writing career.

To **the rest of my family**, who missed me and put up with me "working on my book" all the time.

To **my friends**, who missed me and put up with me "working on my book" all the time.

To the overwhelming number of **people who e-mailed** me to say they liked my first book, *Designing Web Graphics*. Who gave me the encouragement to write another book.

To the emergence of the **World Wide Web**, which inspired a lot of very smart people to come together and figure out a lot of very hard things. Which changed communication as we knew it, and empowered individuals to publish their own information and visuals in a worldwide forum.

To **New Riders Publishing** and all the people there, who have supported me while writing *Deconstructing Web Graphics*. Who took a risk, trusted me, and didn't stop me from breaking a lot of their rules. Especially to **Don Fowley**, New Riders' fearless leader, who has everyone's respect for his insight and vision, including mine.

■ Jamie and Lynda. (photo: Douglas Kirkland)

■ Lynda with book designer, Ali Karp.

contents at a glance

1 Hot Hot Hot 1

2 DreamWorks Interactive SKG 17

4 Sony Music Online 53

5 @tlas 71

11 Construct 181

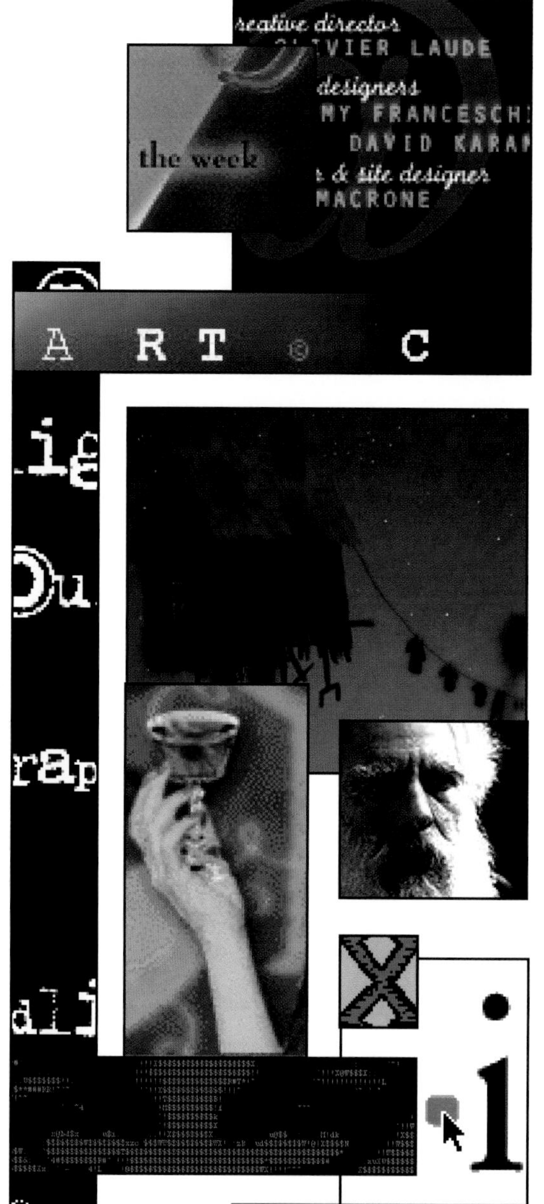

Introduction

what this book is about

Most of us looking to design Web sites—especially those who are already designing Web sites—have a healthy appetite for new knowledge, resources, ideas, tips, and techniques. Due to the fast-paced development cycles of the Web, newcomers and experienced Web designers alike are finding the need to educate themselves on a regular basis.

Even though Web publishing is one of the fastest growing areas in digital design, there are few rules, standards, or clear-cut job definitions. Anyone claiming to be a Web design expert has been doing it for two or three years at the most.

The overwhelming number of Web designers I've encountered learned to design Web pages by studying other people's Web pages. Reverse-engineering sites in order to understand what has already been done is a proven approach to learning how to do this kind of work.

As long as the Web continues, there will always be more to discover about it; that's why it has captivated so many of our imaginations and pioneering efforts. I have observed many site designers inventing the same wheel over and over. This book attempts to pool together helpful tips and solutions that will spare everyone the wasted time of solving something that's already been thought of.

HTML, CGI, VRML, Java, JavaScript...

Though many of us are new to programming HTML tags, one savior is the opportunity available in most Web browsers to view or copy anyone's source code. Checking out a well-designed page's source code tells part of the story, but not all. If you don't understand what the HTML tags are doing, it's sort of like trying to learn a foreign language by reading a book written in it. Some things might be obvious, but most of it won't be.

Part of what this book does is to walk readers through HTML code, while demystifying and describing key concepts. Through the generosity of the programmers who created code for the sites included in this book, many other compiled scripts and applets, such as CGI scripts, Java, and VRML, that would normally be hidden from view are also presented and deconstructed.

Beyond deconstructing HTML tags and code, I found it fascinating that no two Web designers or programmers had the same background or area of expertise. The Web is far too young for a standardized path to exist for learning how to do this type of work. Because we are in uncharted territory, it is even more important to see how others solve the same problems that we are encountering or will encounter.

My intent was to do more with this book than offer insight into a Web site's HTML. I wanted to hear stories of how these pages were designed, what problems and solutions were encountered, who made them and how they learned how, and what software they used. I think seeing work in context of each site's goals and technical limitations can often be more meaningful than studying an abstract principle in a computer book or technical manual.

Web Graphic Tips and Techniques

In addition to relating the stories behind the sites profiled in this book, I switched into teacher mode in order to describe what techniques were used, and reconstruct them as step-by-step tutorials. By studying the experiences and techniques of Web designers in this book, it should be possible to avoid some of the frustration and painful mistakes that Web design often incurs.

This book is written from my perspective as a visual designer. It is intended to be useful to anyone interested in understanding how sophisticated Web sites are created. I've found it easier to find resources about the programming end of the Web (HTML, Java, VRML, CGI, and so forth) but have found very little information on the visual design side. In my opinion, issues such as how to make the graphics, make them interesting and load quickly, and transfer them from print, video, and other mediums, have great importance to the success of a Web site and deserve to receive their own focused attention.

The Philosophy of this Book

There is a digital revolution going on around us, and the rules are new to everyone. It used to be that you could define yourself as just a writer, an illustrator, a typographer, a layout artist, a programmer, a musician, or an interface designer, and that was enough. A medium like the Web merges all these separate disciplines into one integrated communication medium, and it's enough to make a single individual easily feel overwhelmed. There are a few super-humans who do it all well, but they are the exception, not the rule.

It's my belief that books about the Web should help people find their way through unfamilar territory, without intimidation or information overload. I write and teach in a very direct style with the intent to avoid fluff, hype, and unnecessary technical jargon.

What You'll Find in *Deconstructing Web Graphics*

When I was writing my first book, *Designing Web Graphics*, I intended for it to include a gallery of successfully designed sites, but ran out of time and room. This second book is more than a gallery or an assemblage of HTML code written by experts. It is my attempt to lend a single, informed voice that carefully walks readers through all the confusing factors of Web design—from content, programming, and management to visual design techniques.

Deciding Which Sites to Profile

I chose the sites reviewed in this book based on my own taste and aesthetics. These are sites that I admired and was curious to learn more about. I'm sure there are many other worthy sites that I could have chosen from, as well as many more that will exist in the future. For this reason, I hope you will visit my site at: ■ http: //www.lynda.com/decon/ to find links to these and other sites that are not presented in this book.

The process of writing *Deconstructing Web Graphics* served as a perfect vehicle to address many advanced topics that extended beyond the scope of my first book, *Designing Web Graphics*. I see these two books as companions to each other—the first book offers a thorough explanation of image and media preparation and creation. This second book, *Decontstructing Web Graphics*, approaches the same subject by using a different paradigm of looking to others for inspiration and technique.

Some of the Things You'll Find in this Book

- Profiles of Web designers and programmers
- Visual examples of their finished pages
- An explanation of their HTML and scripts
- A behind-the-scenes look into planning their sites
- A behind-the-scenes look into the preparation of their artwork
- A synopsis of the problems and solutions that relate to their pages
- A review of tools and resources they used to create their pages
- Tips and techniques used and developed by these Web designers

How this Book Works

This book does not have to be read in a linear order. Certain concepts are introduced in earlier chapters and then referenced in later chapters. Whenever crossover information occurs, the other chapters are noted.

This book has Notes, Tips, Step-by-Steps, and Deconstructions. Each of these types of components are flagged with a red box and are easy to find throughout the book. There's no penalty for skimming the book and picking up random ideas and tips. It was written and designed intentionally to make that possible.

What the Chapters Cover

History in the Making?

If you are new to the Web, as you are reading this book you may find yourself amazed at how much work goes into a Web site. Designing for the Web is not an easy panacea or way to get rich quick. It takes lots of hard work to make a successful site, and there is a lot of specialized information to learn before you can dance the professional Web design dance. It's best to start with your own home pages, experiment there, and try to find a job or internship with a company where you can learn and get paid at the same time. Even experts learn all the time—not knowing everything in this field is the norm, not the exception!

There is one guarantee I can make—everything in this book will eventually change or become outdated. My book designer Ali Karp called out of the blue one day to say, "Lynda! I had a funny thought! You thought you were writing a computer help book, but did you realize you're also writing a history book? Years from now people will look at *Deconstructing Web Graphics* to study the early days of Web construction." Though it hadn't occured to me that I was creating a historical document, I think Ali is right, and that it's going to be amazing to remember these primitive days back when the Web first began.

I believe that even if tags change and the Web environment changes, it's still educational to read about how people work through today's roadblocks. In a field where new problems arise with every new feature, the process of solving a problem is as valuable as having the answer to it. In other words, troubleshooting problems is part of a Web designer's life and work. It's almost as important to understand how to solve problems as it is to have the answers to them.

Bad Links and Mistakes

It's inevitable that some of the links listed in this book will change or be removed. This book represents a snapshot in time, and time moves forward—especially on the Web! If you encounter a link that doesn't work, be sure to visit my site at: ■ http://www.lynda.com/decon/ to find out where it has gone. I keep an updated list of sites that I think are inspirational, and will publish any eratta or changes to this book there, long before a second printing could ever address the changes.

Contacting the Author

I hope the information presented here serves as a valuable resource to artists, programmers, clients, and hobbyist who seek to understand the inner workings of Web page design. Authoring for the Web is not an easy road, but I suspect you will find it a fascinating one. This book is dedicated to all those who have paved the way of the Web so far, and to all those who will come along after and make it even better.

I can't promise to answer everyone, but I always welcome comments and feedback related to this and my other books.

■ My email address is lynda@lynda.com.

■ New Riders Publishing

The staff of New Riders Publishing is committed to bringing you the very best in computer reference material. Each New Riders book is the result of months of work by authors and staff who research and refine the information contained within its covers.

As part of this commitment to you, the NRP reader, New Riders invites your input. Please let us know if you enjoy this book, if you have trouble with the information and examples presented, or if you have a suggestion for the next edition.

If you have a question or comment about any New Riders book, there are several ways to contact New Riders Publishing. We will respond to as many readers as we can. Your name, address, or phone number will never become part of a mailing list or be used for any purpose other than to help us continue to bring you the best books possible.

You can write us at the following address:
New Riders Publishing
Attn: Publisher
201 W. 103rd Street
Indianapolis, IN 46290

If you prefer, you can fax New Riders Publishing at:
(317) 581-4670.

You can also send electronic mail to New Riders at the following Internet address:
■ ddwyer@newriders.mcp.com

NRP is an imprint of Macmillan Computer Publishing.
To obtain a catalog or information, or to purchase any
Macmillan Computer Publishing book, call (800) 428-5331.

Thank you for selecting *Deconstructing Web Graphics*!

Hot Hot Hot
low-bandwidth design

What this chapter covers:

- **Advantages to Working with Aliased Graphics**
- **Converting Existing Images to Web Graphics**
- **Examples of Basic HTML**
- **Forms Processing HTML and CGI**

http://www.hothothot.com Hot Hot Hot was one of the earliest examples of low-bandwidth-conscious design. It looked great and loaded fast. Even two years later (an eternity in Web design years) the site still looks good and performs impeccably. It succeeds on so many levels—great illustrations, wonderful color choices in a limited palette, and universal accessibility to all browsers. This site is an excellent example of what can be done by using economy of color and size, without sacrificing beauty, quality, or performance.

Web Design Firm: Presence

URL: http://www.hothothot.com

Type of Site: Retail

Server (at launch): SPARCstation LX

Operating System: 4.1.3

Server Software (at launch): NCSA server 1.0

Webmaster/Information Design: Mike Kuniavsky

Illustrator and Art Direction: Yeryeong Park

CGI Programming: Mike Lazarro

Production Design Hardware: Macintosh, Scanner

Programming Hardware: Macintosh

Design Software: Photoshop

From Retail Store to Web Catalog

Monica and Perry Lopez own the popular Pasadena-based retail store, Hot Hot Hot, which markets exotic and hard-to-find hot sauces. In June of 1994, Monica was accidentally locked out of her store and got to talking with one of her customers who was waiting outside. That customer, Tom Soulanille, was in the process of starting a Web design firm that came to be called Presence. Monica decided to be his first client, and the rest, as they say, is history.

Those were the days of Mosaic, before Netscape and Internet Explorer. There were all kinds of browsers then, just like now, and everyone's goal was to make the site visible and easy regardless of the browser. It's amazing that even today, their site is accessible from any browser, and its clear interface and ease of use is an oasis in a sea of confusing sites using newer technology for technology's sake.

Given the store's novelty, the challenge was posed: how does one translate merchandising gourmet hot sauces to a Web site mail-order catalog? No one imagined the Hot Hot Hot site would ultimately account for 23% of the Lopez's total sales and would bring the owners numerous magazine articles and talk show appearances. When the Hot Hot Hot site was formed, there were no other business models like it. Their pioneering efforts are now models for others to follow and learn from.

Creating Illustrations for Hot Hot Hot

Presence hired independent graphic designer Yeryeong Park to art direct the site, even though she had never designed for the Web until this project. Yeryeong is a graduate of Art Center College of Design, where she majored in Graphics and Packaging. She was chosen based on the strength of her illustration and print graphics portfolio. It took a synergy of Yeryeong's design talents, and experienced Webmaster Mike Kuniavsky's understanding of Internet constraints to arrive at the perfect blend between excellent images and Web-savvy file sizes.

For budget reasons, the Hot Hot Hot owners chose to work with Yeryeong's black and white illustration style. The idea was to keep Yeryeong's time down to a minimum so her talents could be used most effectively, and others could color her work based on her instructions.

All of the artwork created for the site was generated using tools of traditional pen and ink on paper and vellum. Even though Yeryeong was an experienced digital artist, the hand-drawn style of the illustrations for the site were best created using traditional tools.

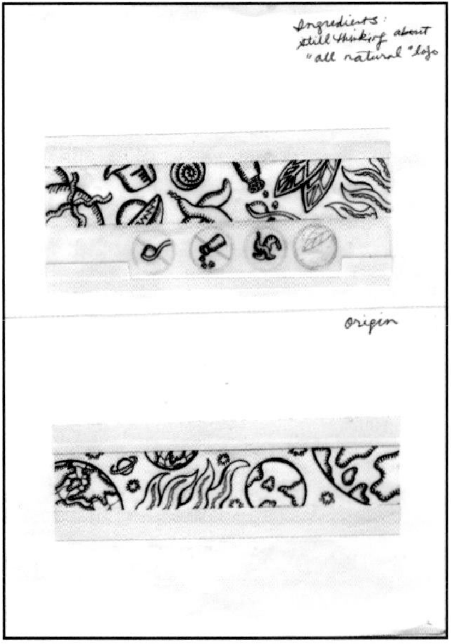

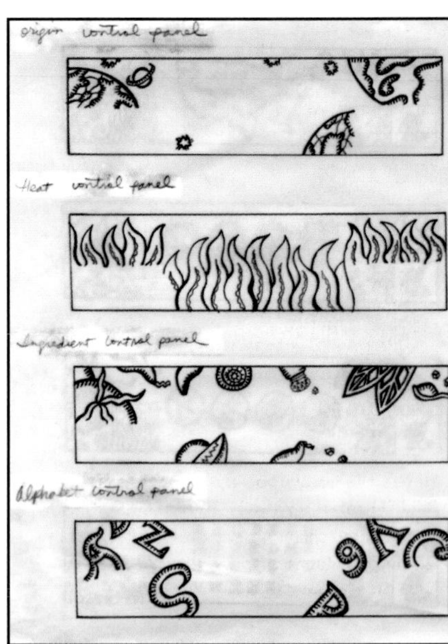

Original sketches were made with pencil, pen, and ink on vellum paper. After illustrations were scanned, they converted easily to line art that could be colored with the computer.

Setting and Reaching Target Goals for File Sizes

Presence information designer and Webmaster Mike Kuniavsky's goal was to keep all the images on a page no larger than a total of 30k. A major purpose of the site was to make the graphics accessible to all browsers, and fast downloading and viewing speed was critical.

Mike discovered that GIFs were much smaller if the graphics weren't anti-aliased and used limited color palettes. Small file sizes were achieved by converting Yeryeong's black and white drawings to aliased artwork. This was accomplished by scanning the originals in black and white instead of grayscale. Yeryeong and Mike arrived at a limited color palette of seven carefully chosen colors. These combined techniques yielded impressive results as each individual file ranged from 3.5k–9k after being saved in the GIF file format.

Anti-aliased example. This image is 21.3k. Using anti-aliased images on the site would have made pages over three times larger and taken three times longer to download!

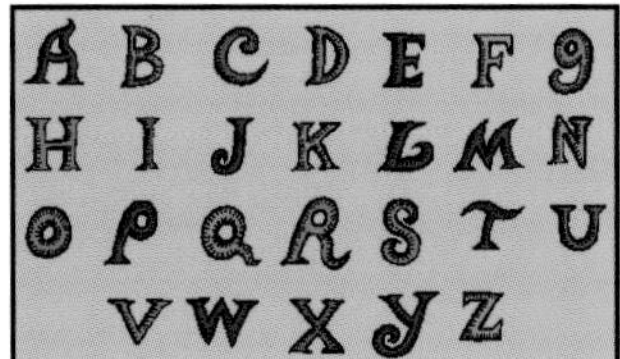

Aliased version: Here's the same graphic created as an aliased image instead. It is significantly smaller at 6.4k.

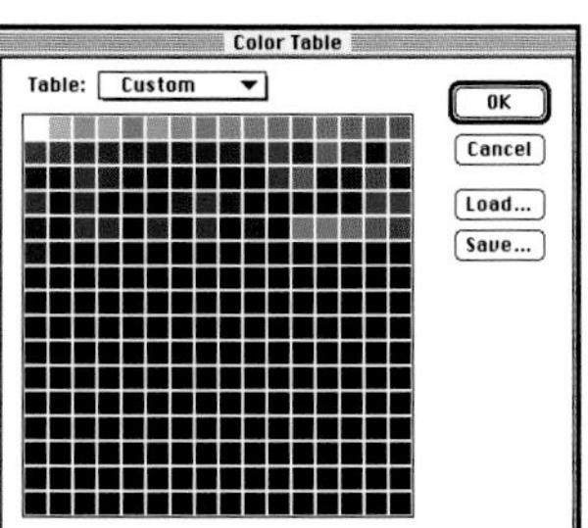

Here's the color look up table (CLUT) for the anti-aliased graphic. Notice how many more colors anti-aliasing produces than its aliased counterpart that follows. Anti-aliasing requires extra colors, and therefore creates larger file sizes.

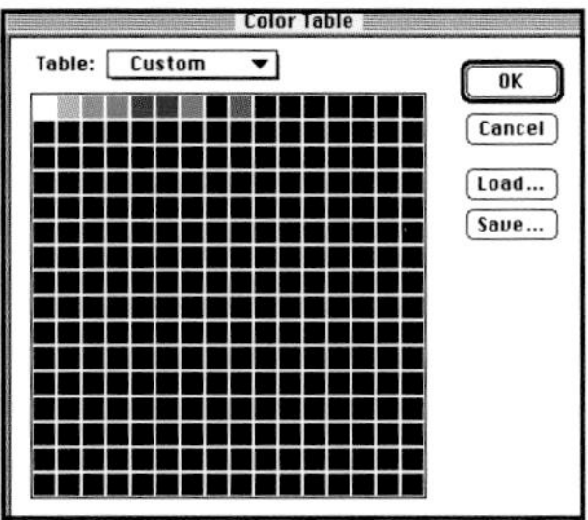

The color look up table for the aliased graphic is much smaller, and so is the file size.

Using aliased graphics and only seven colors, the total size of this Web page is only 30k!

■ tip

Keeping File Sizes Small by Today's Standards

Today, one could follow the same principles Mike employed to reduce file size. For a GIF file, there are several things that can contribute to making images small. Color-depth, which describes how many colors are used in the document, is one factor. By using only eight colors, the color depth of the images on the Hot Hot Hot site was only 3-bit.

Sometimes, aliased graphics look bad. It should be noted that Yeryeong's illustration style was perfect for aliased graphics. In the event that you have graphics that require anti-aliasing, you can still experiment with reducing bit-depth. In Photoshop, when colors are indexed (a term used for converting from RGB/24-bit color images to 256 color images), it's possible to change the settings to any number you want to try. Experimenting with different values will let you determine how low you can take the bit-depth of an image and still maintain acceptable image quality. You can always try a large bit-depth reduction and if it looks bad, undo the change and try another setting. File size directly relates to download speed. Though the connection speed of your audience will vary widely, an accepted measurement used by many Web designers is that 1k of data will equal one second of download time. Therefore, the Hot Hot Hot site limit of 30k per page equates to a :30 per page download for the average viewer.

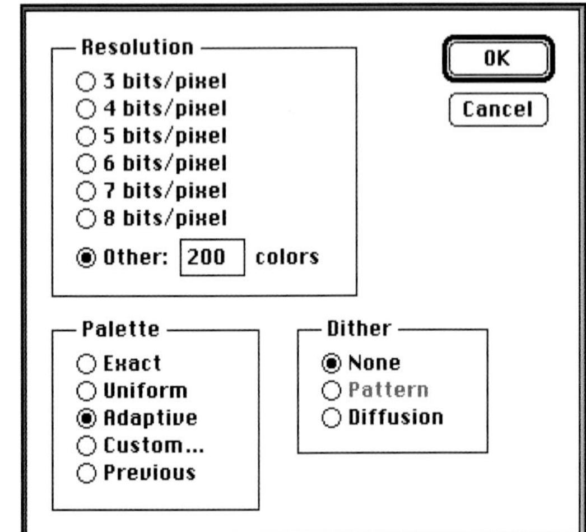

You can enter custom numbers in the Indexed Color dialog box in Photoshop and make lower bit-depth images. This can significantly reduce file size.

The Production Process: Scanning the Illustrations

Yeryeong's illustrations were scanned in at 800 dpi (though Presence has since discovered the same quality can be obtained from scanning at 150–300 dpi instead) as black and white line art, with no grays. By scanning at a high resolution, extra information was captured that would later become essential when setting up the color fills. The scans were then reduced to a standardized size of 6"×1.25" at 72 dpi. This process of scanning large and then shrinking the files actually lends more definition to the resulting images than if they had been scanned in 1:1.

step-by-step

Converting a Grayscale Anti-Aliased Image to a Bitmap Aliased Image

If you have an existing grayscale document, and want to try to save file size and see how it looks in black and white with aliased edges instead, it's easy to do in Photoshop.

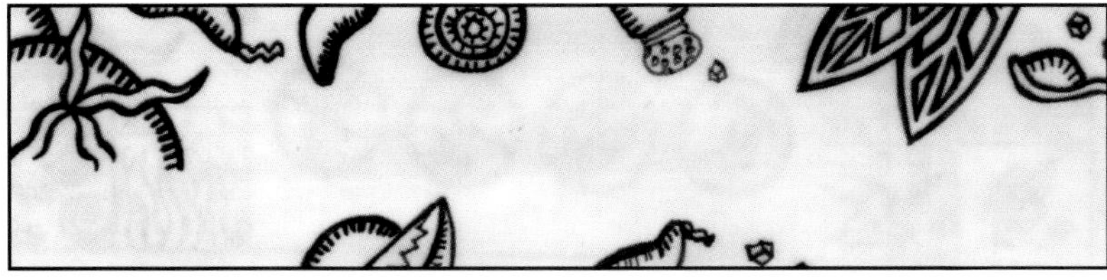

Step 1: In Photoshop, open the image that was scanned originally in grayscale.

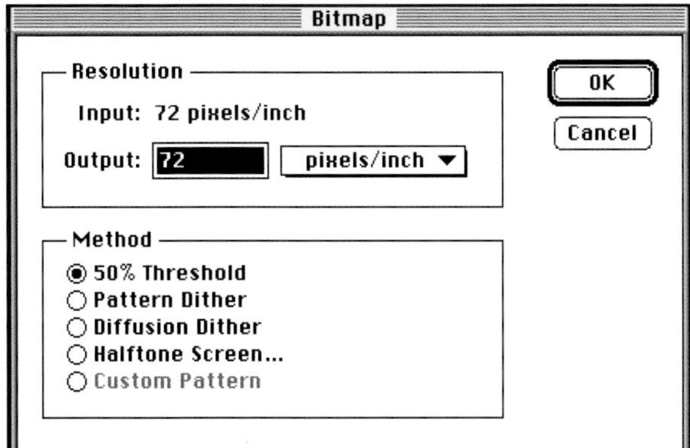

Step 2: Under the Mode menu, select Bitmap, and choose a 50% Threshold Method at 72 pixels/inch.

Step 3: Converting the grayscale image to bitmap creates an aliased image. It can be filled with color using the Photoshop Paint Bucket Tool, set to a tolerance of 1 with anti-aliasing unchecked.

tip

Aliased Photoshop Tools

By double-clicking on the magic wand or paint brush tool, the Options palette opens automatically. You can turn Anti-aliasing off and set Tolerances. Tolerance settings of 1 should be used for anti-aliased fills and selections.

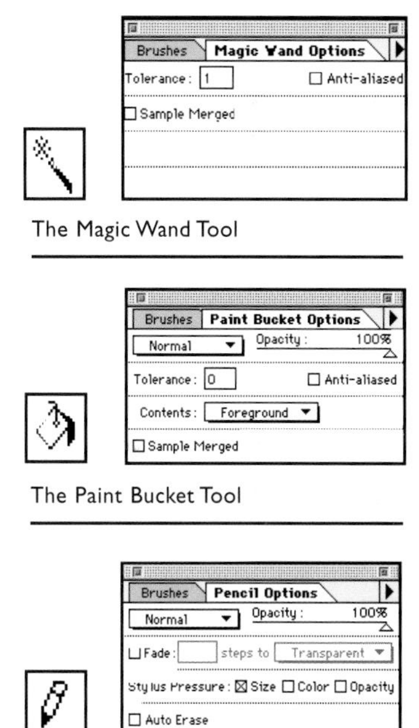

The Magic Wand Tool

The Paint Bucket Tool

The Pencil Tool

Filling Regions of an Aliased Graphic with Solid Color

Due to the nature of Yeryeong's illustrations, with the fine hatched linework, it was a challenge to color the images in Photoshop. There were lots of areas that had to be retouched in order to create regions that didn't leak when filled with color. Yeryeong supplied tissue overlays in colored pencil that dictated what regions of an illustration were filled with what colors. This freed her to do illustrations while production artists at Presence did the time-consuming color fill work.

Mike had to do a lot of touch-ups, and worked with Photoshop's magnifying glass to zoom way into the image. He used the magic wand set to a level 1 tolerance to select areas to fill and used the aliased pencil tool to close areas that leaked when using the aliased bucket tool for color fills.

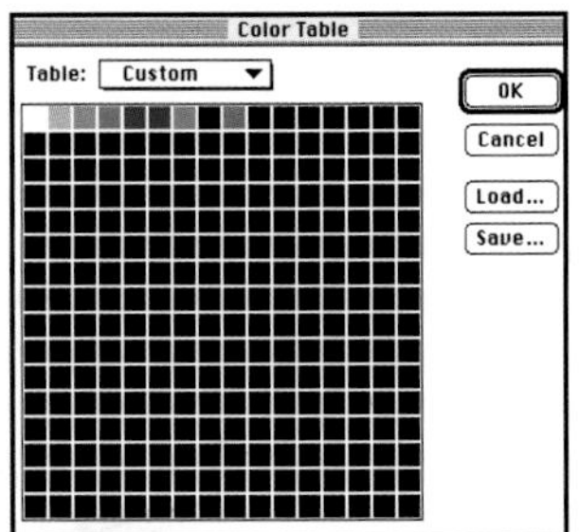

This is Yeryeong's eight color palette. She chose colors that combined warm and cold hues, and offered good contrast. She tried to pick color combinations that would work well together or in groups of three. Notice how there are also primary and secondary colors. A primary, such as red, has companion secondaries in two shades of orange. This palette was chosen by an artist well-trained in color theory, and the site is immeasurably enhanced by her choices.

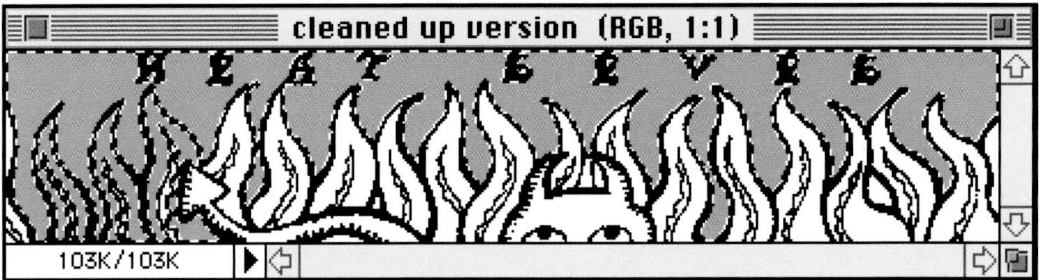

Using Photoshop's magic wand at a tolerance setting of 1, notice the leaks on the left side of this image. Leaks are caused by breaks in the lines, which cannot be seen at a 1:1 magnification.

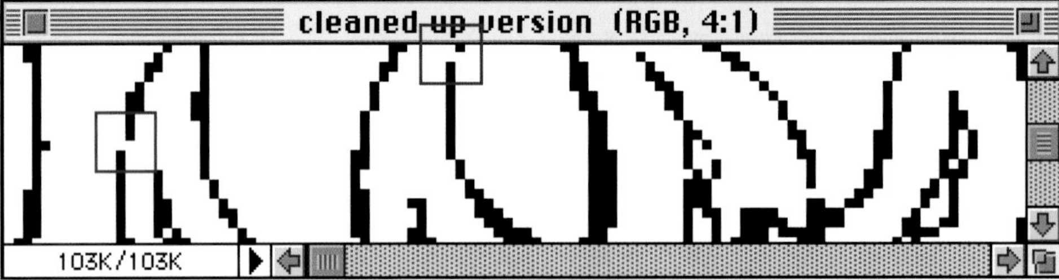

Here's a close-up of the original art, showing that a break in the line at the left side of the image will cause a leak to a filling region.

Working with Browser-Safe Colors

When the Hot Hot Hot site was developed in 1993, no one knew about browser-safe colors. The browser-safe color chart was first identified, published, and described in detail in my first book, *Designing Web Graphics* in early 1996.

Browser-safe colors are colors that the browser uses whenever it's launched on a computer that's limited to a 256 color display. Many computer owners don't own color cards that go higher than 256 colors, so artwork that was developed to be viewed in millions of colors is often converted to 256 by the browser, unbeknownst to the originator of the artwork. Web browsers, such as Netscape, Internet Explorer, and Mosaic use fixed palettes of the system colors. For example, on a Mac those 256 colors would be the system palette. On a Windows 95 machine, those 256 colors would be the native Windows 95 color palette.

The browser-safe colors are composed of 216 colors that are shared between the Mac, Windows, and Windows 95 system palettes. Each platform reserves 40 of its own custom colors that are not present on all platforms. By eliminating the 40 colors that vary and sticking to colors from the 216 browser-safe color palette, your images will not dither on 256 color systems.

Dithering occurs when a computer can't display the exact colors of your document. For an example of dithering, see what happened to the Hot Hot Hot graphics on a 256 monitor when viewed within Netscape. The solution to avoiding unwanted dithering would be to redefine the colors, using browser-safe choices. I used the browser-safe palette to refill the color regions. The palette is availabe from my Web site at ■ www.lynda.com. The results show how the image will no longer dither if the colors are choosen from the browser-safe color chart.

It behooves sites that use illustrations that contain a lot of solid colors to honor the same colors as the browser palette, so that unsightly dithering can be avoided.

Using the browser-safe palette on photographs is totally unnecessary, because the browser will convert the photograph to its palette and the resulting dithering is far less objectionable than within a solid color illustration. Examples of this are demonstrated on my site, at ■ www.lynda.com.

The dots present inside this image are examples of dithering, which is what happens when an image is composed of colors outside of the browser-safe color palette amd viewed within a browser on a 256 color system.

Here's an example of the image viewed from a 256 color display within Netscape, substituting colors from the browser-safe CLUT. Fortunately, the color substitutes are so similar that Yeryeong's wonderful color choices could be accurately preserved.

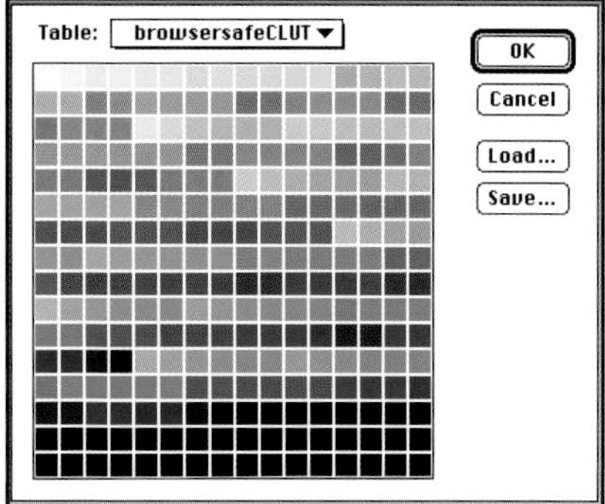

This is the browser-safe color look up table (CLUT). It is composed of 216 colors that are shared between Mac and PC/Win/Win95 Web browsers. Choosing colors from this palette will ensure that your image will not dither. See the Browser-Safe Color Chart in the Appendix.

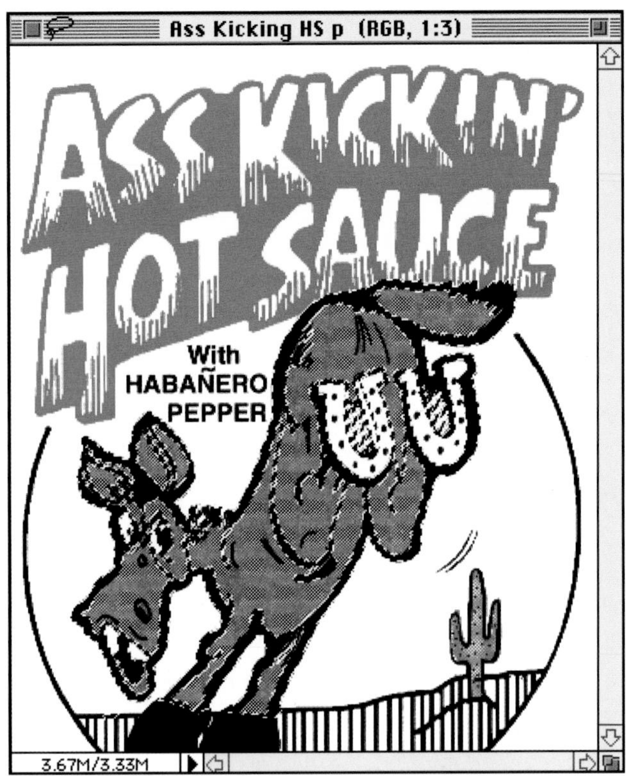

Notice the moirés inside the donkey. This is a result of scanning an original source image that was printed with a dot pattern, and is a common occurance when scanning from any printed source, such as a catalog, magazine, or book. Mike edited the image at an enlarged scale and reduced it to a thumbnail for the final image, seen below.

The finished graphic was simplified, with the moiré pattern removed and filled with a solid color. The type was also removed from the original because it was unreadable within the small Web graphic.

Converting Printed Material to Digital Files

Besides generating custom illustrations for the site, everyone thought scanning the actual hot sauce label art would make a great visual for the order form section. Scanning in labels proved to be a bit more challenging than originally expected, however.

When labels are printed, dot screens are used. This would be true of any type of printed source artwork, whether the artwork originated from labels or a printed catalog, magazine, or book. After screened artwork is scanned, moirés occur, yielding unsightly scans that are unusable.

Mike had to individually edit each scanned label image to eliminate the moirés. He used Photoshop's masking and selection tools to do the job. By isolating and selecting the areas that had the moirés and scanning problems, he was able to fill them with solid colors or simple gradients, using colors derived from the labels themselves.

Besides the problems with moirés, other problems surface when working with detailed images that need to be converted to small Web graphics at 72 dpi. Many of the details of printed artwork get lost after the resolution and size is scaled down to Web standards. In addition to removing moirés in the artwork, Mike also simplified complex images by removing patterns and fine-print type using the eraser tools. He spent close to an hour on each label using this technique to ensure that the resulting images would be clean and simple.

Today, the techniques used by Mike are still the only solution for dealing with moirés and converting high-resolution images to low-resolution Web images. Details such as small print are unreadable at small images sizes created at 72 dpi. If you are working on a site that requires images to be scanned from a catalog or printed material, expect to spend a lot of extra time hand-editing and cleaning up the images for 72-dpi Web display.

Photoshop Selection and Masking Tools

In order to isolate areas of the labels, Mike used selections, masks, and cloning techniques. An entire book could be written on this subject, but here are some tips to help you with selections, masks, and cloning in Photoshop:

Selection Tools

Selection tools create "marching ants" around areas that are selected. An area must first be selected before it can be filled or altered. Different tools are right for different selection tasks.

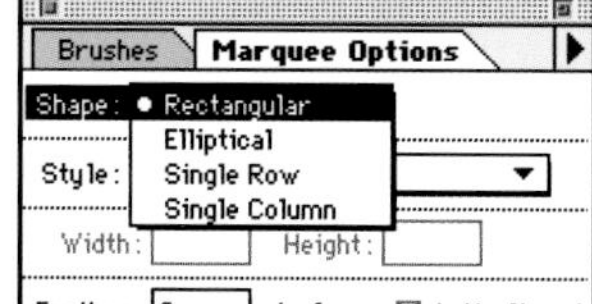

The Marquee tool is good for areas that are rectangular in nature. It can be toggled to create elipses by double-clicking on it to open the Marquee Options window.

Brushes | Lasso Options
Feather: 0 pixels ☐ Anti-aliased

The Lasso tool is great for selecting irregular shapes. Try holding the Option key on Macs or the Control key on PCs to create a "rubber-band" effect of straight lines. The Lasso can be set to not anti-alias in the Lasso Options window by leaving the box unchecked.

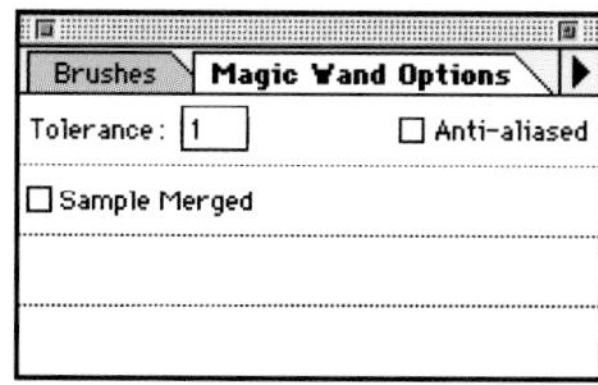

The Magic Wand tool is good for selecting areas based on color and brightness. The tolerance level dictates how many colors it will select.

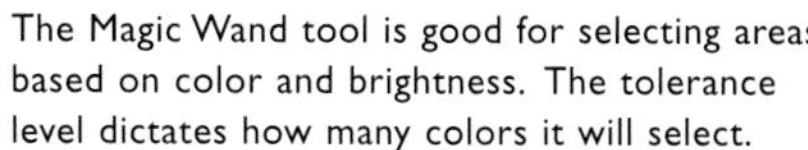

■ step-by-step

Creating a Quick Mask

Sometimes, none of the selection tools work for a complex shape. That's where Quick Masks can come in handy. Quick Masks are used when you want to paint a selection.

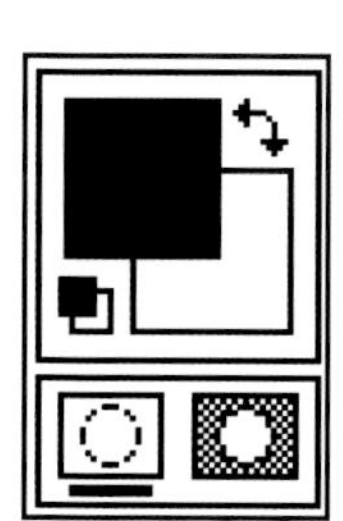

Step 1: Make sure your foreground color is set to black. Select a brush to paint with.

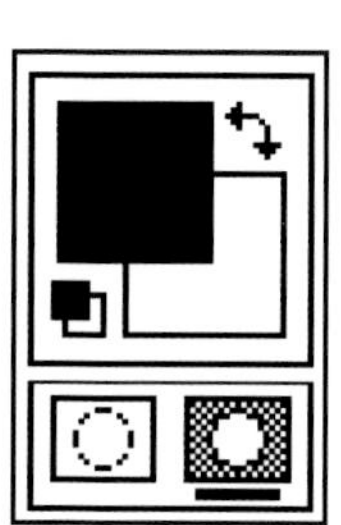

Step 2: Click on the Quick Mask icon located at the bottom of the tool bar. When you paint it will use a red transparent color.

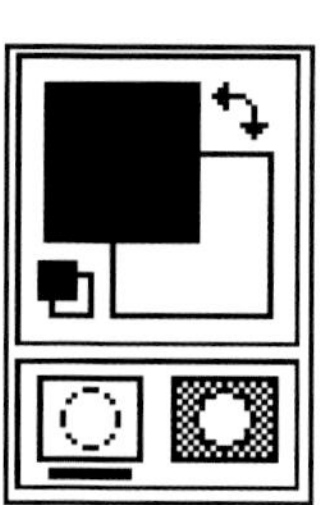

Step 3: After you're happy with the selection you've painted (hint: paint with white to erase any mistakes) click on the left Quick Mask icon. This converts the painting to a selection.

Basic HTML

What does it take to make a site that works on all graphic Web browsers? Solid background colors, alignment to the left, and GIFs only. Sounds boring? It is, but this site doesn't suffer for it. The moral of the story? It's not fancy HTML that makes a good site, it's good content and presentation that makes a good site. What follows is the deconstruction of Hot Hot Hot's simple HTML commands.

Opening Screen HTML

```
1  <HTML>
2  <HEAD>
3  <TITLE>HotHotHot!</TITLE>
   </HEAD>
4  <BODY BGCOLOR="#FEAD00">
5  <IMG SRC="/i/hot/elements/combination.gif"
6  ALT="HotHotHot"><p>
7  <H2>The Net's Coolest Hot Shop</H2>
8  We have one of the largest collections of
   international hot sauces for you to discover; best
   of all it's here, online and always available.
9  <P>
10 <BR>
11 <H1>
12 <A HREF="/g/p/hot/holiday/__0d14e302/index.html">
   Gifts of Fire!
   <IMG SRC="/i/hot/elements/holiday.gif"></A></H1>
   <p>
13 <H3>Sauces organized by:</H3><BR>
   <A HREF="/g/p/hot/heat/__0d14e302/index.html">
   <IMG src="/i/hot/elements/heat.gif"
   alt="Heat"></A><br>
   <A HREF="/g/p/hot/origin/__0d14e302/index.html">
   <IMG src="/i/hot/elements/origin.gif"
   alt="Origin"></A><br>
   <A HREF="/g/p/hot/ingredients/__0d14e302/index.html">
   <IMG src="/i/hot/elements/ingredients.gif"
   alt="Ingredients"></A><br>
   <A HREF="/g/p/hot/alphabet/__0d14e302/index.html">
   <IMG src="/i/hot/elements/alphabet.gif"
   alt="Alphabet"></A><P>
```

Opening Screen: This is the first page of Hot Hot Hot's site ■ http://www.hot.presence.com/g/p/__4f051092/hot/h3-home.html. It contains basic tags that exist in most HTML documents. Study this deconstruction for an overview understanding of HTML structure.

■ tags

Opening Screen HTML Deconstruction

1 <HTML> All HTML documents must begin with this tag and close with the </HTML> end tag.

2 <HEAD> Header information, such as the title of the document, must be contained within <HEAD> and </HEAD>.

3 <TITLE> This tag causes the title of the document to appear within the title bar. </TITLE> closes the title tag.

4 <BODY BGCOLOR> Instructs the browser to include a background color. In this example the hexadecimal value of "FEAD00" is creating a mustard orange color. The <BODY BGCOLOR> always follows the title and head tags. The </BODY> tag should always be used once the text within an HTML document is finished. Color values are always spelled out by their hexadecimal equivalent of RGB values within HTML documents.

5 <IMG SRC> The image source tag instructs the browser to display an image.

6 <ALT> The alt tag instructs the browser to display whatever text is specified if it cannot display the image. This is useful for older browsers and browsers with an option to disable graphics.

7 <H2> A header tag for second-level headers. In some browsers (such as Netscape), it causes the text within it to be sized larger than normal text and be in bold. It must be closed at the end using a </H2> tag.

8 When there is no header <Hx> tag, the text displays in a default font at a default size with no linking or style proper ties.

9 <P> Indicates the beginning of a paragraph.

10
 Causes a line break.

11 <H1> A header tag that specifies a first-level header. In some browsers (like Netscape) it causes the text within it to be sized larger than normal text and be in bold. Note that Netscape displays <H1> headers in a larger font size than <H2> headers. Other browsers, like NCSA Mosaic, allow the user to configure a different font and size for each level of header.

12 <A HREF> An anchor and hypertext reference tells images and text to be hyperlinks to other files. In this case the text "Gifts of Fire" and the image source "holiday gift" both link to another HTML page called "index.html." The "index.html" file is nested within other directories, hence the slashes before the file.

13 <H3> A header tag that specifies a third-level header. Note that Netscape displays <H3> headers in a smaller font size than <H2> headers.

The CGI–Forms Processing

The Hot Hot Hot site wouldn't be nearly as successful or interactive if it weren't possible to order the products on-line. In order to add orderform funtionality, additional programming was required.

CGI, Common Gateway Interface, is used to extend the capabilities of a Web site. CGI requires knowledge of a programming language. Many different languages may be used to program CGI; some of which are Perl, C/C++, sh, and Applescript.

Because CGI runs on a server, in order to run or test CGI, you must have an active Web server. This is not the case with HTML, which can be tested from a local hard drive. In order to write CGI, you need to first become experienced with writing in a programming language and the process of uploading and installing programs on your Web server. You will not be able to write and test CGI programs on your local hard drive.

In the case of the Hot Hot Hot site, CGI was used to process the orderforms. Forms involve a two-fold process: First to write the forms-based controls (text fields, buttons, etc.) into the HTML code, and second to add the processing and database functionality to the buttons through using CGI.

It's outside the scope of this book to teach you how to write CGI programs. In practice, most visual designers team up with programmers to add CGI and forms processing functionality to a site. For those of you who are interested in learning about CGI here are some resources:

The original and authoritative CGI site
- http://hoohoo.ncsa.uiuc.edu/cgi/

Marc Hedlund's CGI FAQ
- http://www.best.com/~hedlund/cgi-faq

Bill Weinman's online resource for *The CGI Book*
New Riders Publishing ISBN:1-56205-572-2
- http://www.cgibook.com

step-by-step

How the Forms Work on the Hot Hot Hot Site

The HTML coding for buttons is the easy part. Adding the functionality is a whole different enterprise, one best suited to an experienced programmer. Mike Lazarro programmed the CGI using the programming language C++. At the time, C++ was chosen because it was the most powerful language available. Today, a CGI programmer has the choice to use C++, Perl, or Applescript.

Presence developed a custom CGI and database program that they called "Guppy." Guppy enabled them to modify the contents of their HTML pages according to user input. Here's a step-by-step recounting of what the Guppy CGI enabled them to do:

Step 1: When a Hot Hot Hot visitor clicks on an order button, several things happen at once. The order button simply reads "Select," but within the HTML, much more is going on.

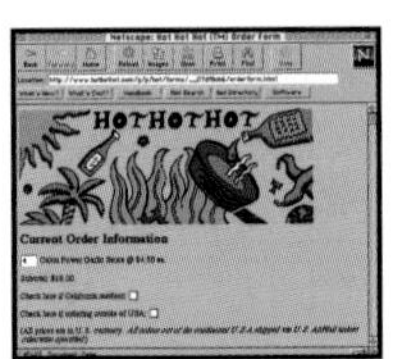

Clicking on the Select button brings up a more detailed screen.

Step 2: If the customer selects multiple items, the order process is repeated. When the customer is finished with each selection, the customer is shown how many items they've ordered. The customer can continue ordering, and each time, this process is repeated. Eventually a list of items is assembled, and when ready, the buyer clicks on a form button that reads "Billing Information." From there, the buyer is prompted to enter his or her mailing, shipping, and credit card information.

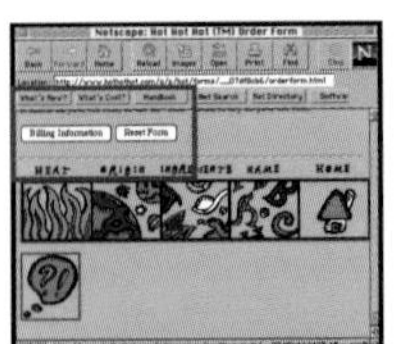

Clicking on Billing Information triggers a more detailed screen. Clicking on Reset Form clears the form completely.

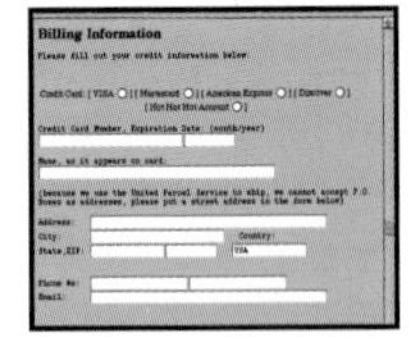

The Billing Information form is where the order gets finalized, and the results are faxed electronically to the Hot Hot Hot store.

Step 3: When all the billing information is assembled, the data gets processed by the CGI script, and an electronic fax is generated that gets sent to the store.

Forms Processing HTML

The following three screens explain the HTML used for Hot Hot Hot's forms processing screens. A custom CGI was used (not shown) that interfaced with the following HTML.

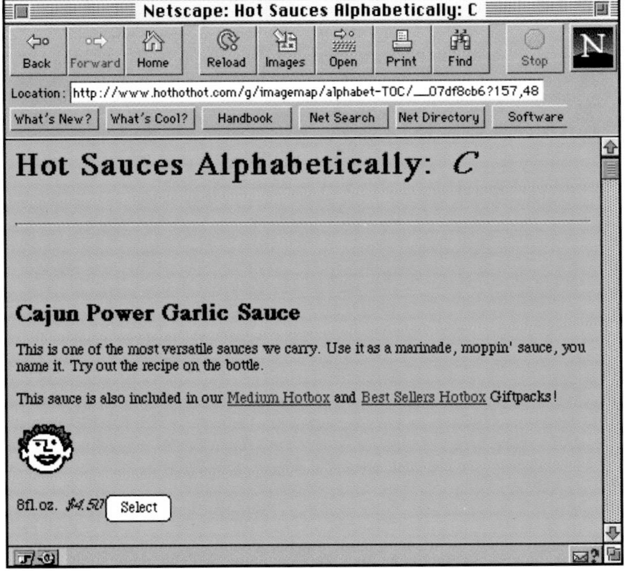

The selections screen found at: ■ http://www.hot.presence.com/g/imagemap/alphabet-TOC/ __3fa6590a?154,44

Selections Screen HTML

```
  <H1>Hot Sauces Alphabetically: <EM>C</EM><p></h1>
  <hr>
1 <A name=="Cajun_Power_GarlicS"></a>
  <IMG src="/i/hot/elements/vertical-half-inch.gif"
  alt="">
  <H2>Cajun Power Garlic Sauce</H2>
  This is one of the most versatile sauces we carry.
  Use it as a marinade, moppin' sauce, you name it.
  Try out the recipe on the bottle.<P>
  This sauce is also included in our
  <A  HREF="/g/p/hot/holiday/07df8cb6/hotbox.html#HB-
  medium">Medium Hotbox</A> and
  <A HREF="/g/p/hot/holiday/07df8cb6/hotbox.html#HB-
  bestsellers">Best Sellers Hotbox</A> Giftpacks! <P>
  <IMG SRC="/i/hot/icons/icon-medium.gif" ALT="MEDIUM">
2 <FORMACTION="/g/p/hot/forms/_07df8cb6/orderform.html"
3 METHOD="POST">
  8fl.oz. <EM>$4.50</EM>
4 <INPUT TYPE="hidden" NAME="saucename" VALUE="Cajun
  Power Garlic Sauce">
  <INPUT TYPE="hidden" NAME="subaction"
  VALUE="additem">
5 <INPUT TYPE="submit" VALUE=" Select ">
  </FORM>
```

■ tags

Selections Screen Deconstruction

1 <A NAME> indicates an anchor tag is in effect for a NAME. Using an anchor tag means that a link is set. In this case, the anchor is linked to a NAME, instead of an external image or URL. When this link is activated, the browser will take the customer to the exact spot in the HTML document where "Cajun Power GarlicS" is found, instead of to the top of the page.

2 A <FORM ACTION> initiates the beginning of a form tag. The ACTION attribute specifies where to send the data from the form.

3 A <FORM ACTION> must also include a METHOD. In this case the POST method has been employed. There are two METHOD types—GET and POST. The difference is the GET method sends the form data as part of the URL, and it has a limit to how much data it can process. The POST method sends the data in the body of a message from the browser. Programmers choose between the two methods depending on how much data there is, and whether they want users to be able to bookmark the URL with the data in it.

4 Forms require an <INPUT TYPE> tag within the HTML. In this example, the input type is "hidden." This means that the data won't be displayed by the browser, but the information submitted will supply context to the CGI program. The VALUE field gives the form information about what product the user requested.

5 The "Select" button is an <INPUT TYPE="submit">. There are actually two other input types attached to the same button, but both are labled <INPUT TYPE="HIDDEN">, which makes them invisible to the end viewer. A "submit" input type generates a button that a user can push. The VALUE=" Select " tag is generating a button with the word Select printed on it. A "hidden" input type enables information to be passed to the CGI script without the user seeing it. In this case, the "hidden" input types submit information about the product's name and instructs it to add this item to the buyer's list.

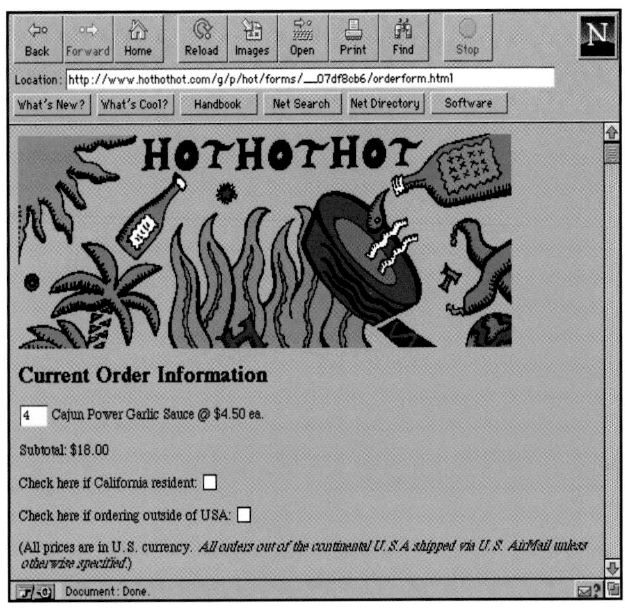

The sauce name screen found at: ■ http://www.hot.presence.com/g/p/hot/forms/__3fa6590a/orderform.html

Sauce Name Screen HTML

```
1 <img src="/i/hot/elements/combination.gif"
  alt=""><p>
  <FORM ACTION="/g/p/hot/forms/orderform2.html
  _0f839631"
  METHOD="POST">
  <INPUT TYPE="hidden" NAME="subaction" VALUE="update">
  <H2>Current Order Information</H2><P>
  <INPUT TYPE="text" NAME="itemq0" VALUE="4" SIZE="3">
  Cajun Power Garlic Sauce @ $4.50 ea.
  <P>
  <P>
  Subtotal: $18.00<P>
2 Check here if California resident: <INPUT
  TYPE="checkbox"
  NAME="taxable_resident" VALUE="Y"><p>
  Check here if ordering outside of USA: <INPUT
  TYPE="checkbox"
3 NAME="intl_resident" VALUE="Y"><p>
  (All prices are in U.S. currency. <em>All orders
  out of the continental
  U.S.A shipped via U.S. AirMail unless otherwise
  specified.</em>)<P>
```

■ tags

Sauce Name Screen Deconstruction

1 This is the code that's enabling a customer to enter the quantity of items they want to order.

2 An INPUT TYPE="checkbox" generates a box in the form that can be checked on or off.

3 The VALUE=Y lets the CGI know that a checked box means "yes."

■ note

HTML for Buttons within Forms

The HTML required for forms is fairly easy, and is possible to program without any programming knowledge, other than HTML. Here's a breakdown of HTML required to generate buttons within forms.

checkboxes

```
input type=checkbox
```

radio buttons

```
input type=radio
input type radio name=checked
```

buttons

Submit Query Reset

```
input type=submit
input type=reset
```

custom type within the button

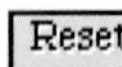

Gum? What's that?

```
input type=submit value="Billing information"
```

pull-down menus

```
<select><option selected>Gum? What's that?
</select>To create scrolling menus:<select>
<option>1-2 <option>3-4 <option>5-6
<option selected>Gum? What's that?
</select>
```

Billing Information

Please fill out your credit information below:

Credit Card: [VISA ○] [Mastercard ○] [American Express ○] [Discover ○]
[Hot Hot Hot Account ○]

Credit Card Number, Expiration Date: (month/year)

Name, as it appears on card:

(because we use the United Parcel Service to ship, we cannot accept P.O. Boxes as addresses, please put a street address in the form below)

Address:
City: Country:
State,ZIP: USA

Phone #s:
Email:

Shipping Information (If Different)

Name:

(because we use the United Parcel Service to ship, we cannot accept P.O.

The billing information screen found at: ■ http://www.hot.presence.com/g/p/hot/forms/orderform2.html/__3fa6590a

Billing Information Screen HTML

```
   <H2>Billing Information</H2>
   <pre>
   Please fill out your credit information below:<P>
1  <TABLE BORDER=0><TR><TD>
   Credit Card:  [ VISA <INPUT TYPE="radio" NAME="card-
   type"
   VALUE="VISA">] [ Mastercard <INPUT TYPE="radio"
   NAME="cardtype"
   VALUE="MC">]  [ American Express <INPUT TYPE="radio"
   NAME="cardtype" VALUE="AE">] [ Discover <INPUT
   TYPE="radio"
   NAME="cardtype" VALUE="DISC">]</TD></TR>
2  <TR><TD COLSPAN=2><CENTER>[ Hot Hot Hot Account
   <INPUT
   TYPE="radio" NAME="cardtype"
   VALUE="ACCOUNT">]</CENTER></TD>
3  </TR></TABLE><P>
   Credit Card Number, Expiration Date: (month/year)
   <INPUT TYPE="text" NAME="cnum" VALUE=""
   SIZE="30"><INPUT
   TYPE="text" NAME="expdate" VALUE="" SIZE="10"><br>
   Name, as it appears on card:
   <INPUT TYPE="text" NAME="b_name" VALUE=""
   SIZE="50"><P>
   (because we use the United Parcel Service to ship,
   we cannot accept P.O.Boxes as addresses, please
   put a street address in the form
   below)<p> Address:<INPUT TYPE="text"
   NAME="b_address"
   VALUE="" SIZE="50">       City:
   <INPUT TYPE="text" NAME="b_city"
   VALUE="" SIZE="28">    Country: State,ZIP:
   <INPUT TYPE="text"
   NAME="b_state" VALUE="" SIZE="15"><INPUT TYPE="text"
   NAME="b_zip" VALUE="" SIZE="10">
   <INPUT TYPE="text"
   NAME="b_country" VALUE="USA" SIZE="15"><P>
   Phone #s:  <INPUT TYPE="text" NAME="b_phone"
   VALUE=""
   SIZE="20"><INPUT TYPE="text" NAME="b_altphone"
   VALUE=""
   SIZE="20">      Email:
   <INPUT TYPE="text"
   NAME="b_email" VALUE=""
   SIZE="50"><P>
   </pre>
```

■ tags

Billing Information Screen Deconstruction

1 Tables are being used on this page for aligning the Credit Card entries. The <TABLE BORDER=0> indicates that tables are being used, with an invisible border. <TR> stands for table row, meaning a row is beginning, and <TD> stands for table data, meaning the content within the table will follow. When the data content ends within a row, ending tags are required: </TR> and </TD>.

2 COLSPAN=2 indicates that the content that follows will take up the space of two columns within the table.

3 </TABLE> indicates that the table is completed.

■ site summary

Hot Hot Hot

What makes the Hot Hot Hot site so successful? Small graphics, beautiful illustrations, a simple interface, and effective processing forms. Here are some lessons to learn from this site:

- Retail Web sites have the potential to contribute significant extra revenue for retailers.
- Hire an experienced illustrator to lend a distinctive look to your site. Don't be concerned about whether the illustrator is Web-savvy or not, team her/him up with an experienced HTML programmer who understands Web graphic file preparation and you'll get the best of both worlds.
- Using simple HTML tags that work on all browsers does not automatically mean your site has to be boring.
- Aliased graphics produce much smaller file sizes than anti-aliased graphics.
- Aliased graphics do not automatically lower the production value of a site.
- Using browser-safe colors can eliminate unwanted dithering on 8-bit (256-color) display systems.
- Whenever artwork is scanned from a printed source it introduces moirés and noise from the dot pattern. These scans must be masked and reworked for Web delivery.
- Scanning at higher resolution, and resampling to 72-dpi, can sometimes generate a better looking result than scanning at 72-dpi to begin with.
- Including forms on a site requires the use of CGI scripting, as well as HTML form tags.

DreamWorks Interactive SKG

browser-safe colors & seamless patterns

What this chapter covers:

- **Customizing Type in Photoshop and Illustrator**
- **Interlacing Browser-Safe Colors for Hybrid Variations**
- **Creating Clean Transparent GIFs**
- **Making Custom Brushes**
- **Painting with Photoshop Layers**
- **Creating Seamless Tiles**

http://www.dreamworksgames.com The DreamWorks Interactive SKG Web was still in prototype stage and had not yet gone online at the time this chapter was written. Designed by two supremely talented illustrators—Don Barnett and Bruce Heavin, the site uses custom typography, transparency, custom brushes, computer-painted illustrations, and custom mixed browser-safe colors to achieve its distinctive appearance.

Web Design Firm: DreamWorks Interactive SKG

URL: http://www.dreamworksgames.com

Type of Site: Prototype for Interactive Multimedia Company

Art Direction and Illustration: Don Barnett and Bruce Heavin

Development and Production Platform: Macintosh

Software: Photoshop, Illustrator

About the DreamWorks Web Design Team

Don Barnett and Bruce Heavin were classmates in the illustration department at Art Center College of Design and both graduated in 1993. Neither of them touched computers for the purpose of creating images until their final year in art school. This allowed them to focus on learning design, painting, and illustration. For them, the computer was simply another tool to add to their image-making repertoire.

Bruce had worked a little bit on the Web before the DreamWorks project, having designed graphics for a magazine-based Web site and a series of personal pages for self-promotion. He also did extensive color palette research and design work on my first book, *Designing Web Graphics*; including painting the cover for that (and this) book using traditional media (acrylics and crayon). When he began the DreamWorks project Bruce did not know a word of HTML.

Don knew even less. In fact, he had barely even seen the Web when this project began. Neither of them were worried about being inexperienced Web designers. In fact, they decided to disregard all the known limitations of the Web at first and concentrate on what they knew best; design, image making, and concepts. Their freedom with the site's design in the beginning of the process didn't stop them from honoring Web file size and color constraints when the time came to make final Web graphics.

Developing Storyboards, Concepts, and Flowcharts

Don and Bruce spent six weeks storyboarding and concepting the DreamWorks site. This might seem like an inordinate amount of time to many clients and employers, but the results speak for themselves. Building a Web site is a lot like making a movie, something that DreamWorks co-founder Steven Spielberg fortunately appreciated. Don and Bruce were grateful to

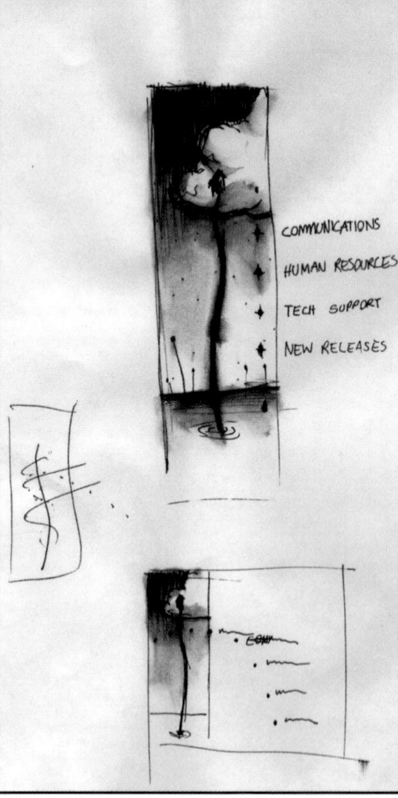

Don Barnett and Bruce Heavin created hundreds of sketches and color studies before making final artwork for the site. Their first priority was to develop a solid direction.

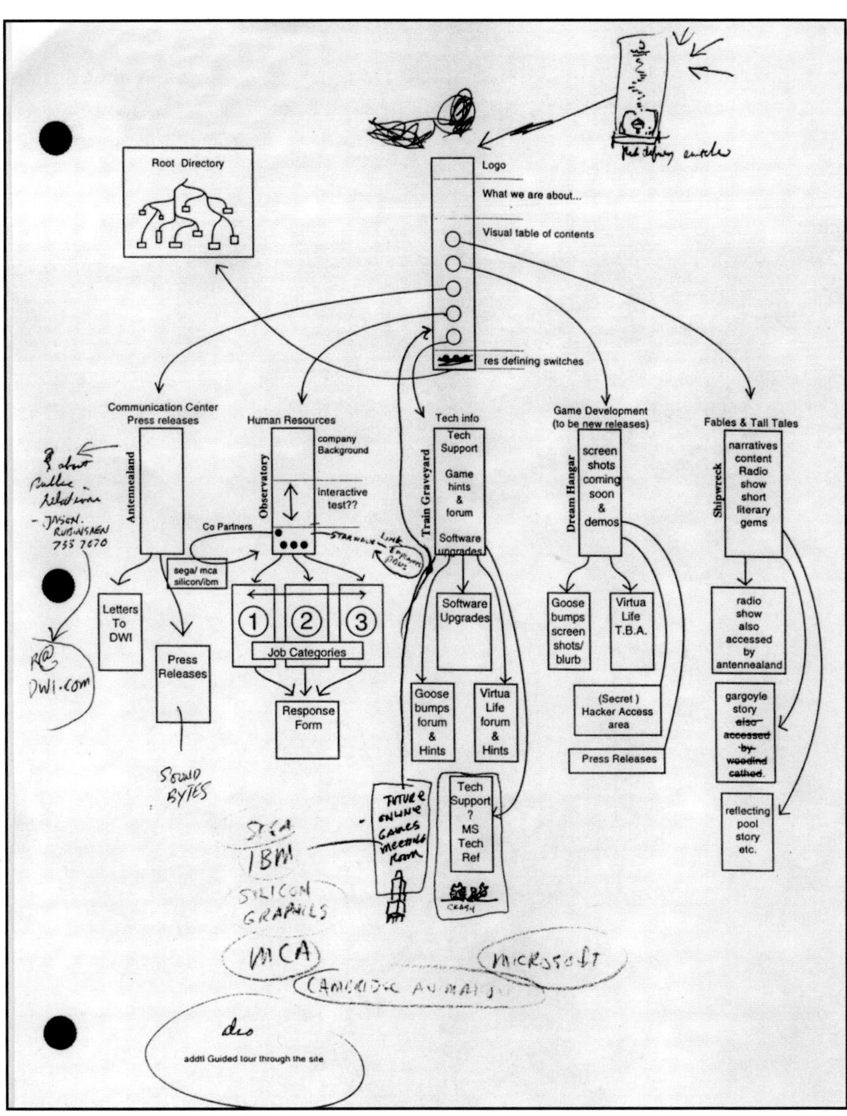

The working flowchart for the DreamWorks site. It details the navigation from screen-to-screen, and was created in Illustrator. It changed often, and this is simply one version of it in progress.

have the freedom to work the way they knew best, and to find a client that understood the value of their methods.

While the site was in development, Don and Bruce created hundreds of sketches and color studies. They made a couple of finished color images for demonstration purposes only, but their true concern was to have a solid direction before going forward with finished images.

The depiction of dreams inspired the theme for most of Don's and Bruce's ideas. They tried to imagine what it would be like to navigate through dreams; images of trains, clouds, stars, ships, shipwrecks, bobbins, machinery, construction scaffolding, tracks, fishing line, poles, ramshackle houses, smoke, spirals, uncertainty, and fantasy were the visual metaphors for the environment they chose to create.

Another challenge to the Web designer, besides getting the storyboards and concepts planned, is understanding how the information will flow and what order it will be viewed in. Having a working flowchart is a critical step in the process, even though the flowchart model is certain to change frequently.

Blueprints for the Web

A Web designer's job is many-fold. Beyond creating the artwork, there are many other challenges. One of these challenges is client presentation. Never underestimate the importance of keeping your client well-fed with evidence of your hard work.

Don and Bruce decided to turn their sketches into literal blueprints. Every page on the site eventually had a blueprint representation. The blueprints were made in Photoshop by taking the original sketches and inverting them. The blue cast was added by setting the Layer Opacity slider and the Compositing mode to Screen.

After seeing the success of their blueprint technique, Don and Bruce chose to make the blueprints an actual part of the site, as artwork for the Low Resolution section. The blueprint images were saved as JPEGs, in order to create small file sizes.

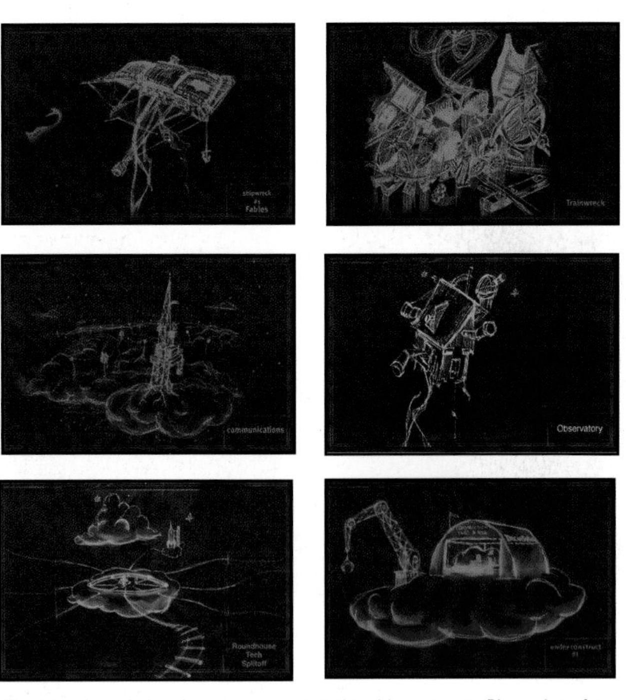

The storyboard sketches were converted to blueprints in Photoshop for presentation purposes.

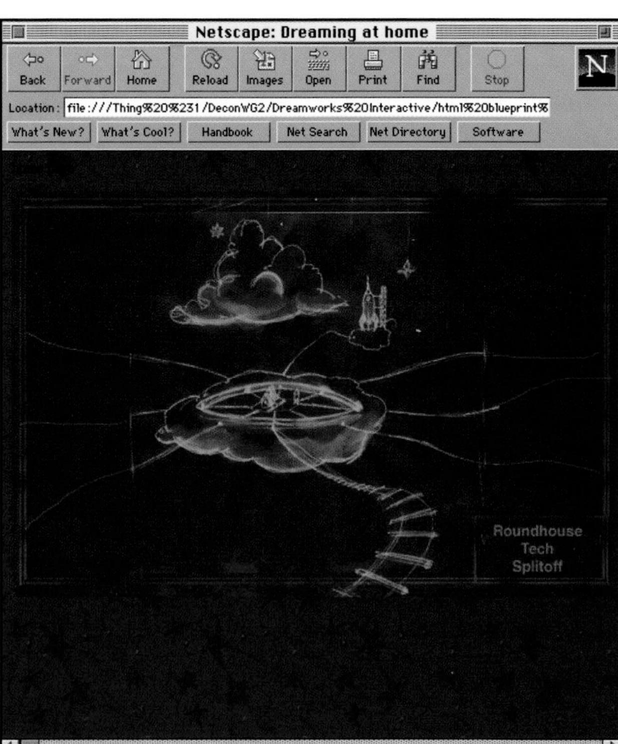

The blueprints were inserted into HTML documents, and became a set of pages for the Low Resolution portion of the site.

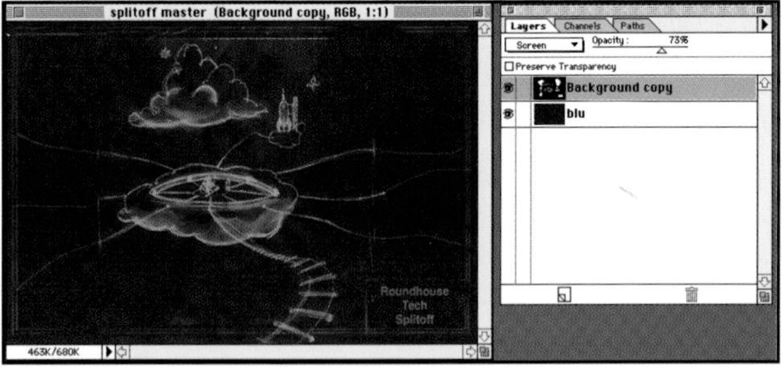

The original sketch was scanned, inverted, and put on the top layer with a custom opacity setting in "Screen" Mode. Screen Mode enabled the blue layer underneath to influence the blacks in the composite. This created a set of uniform blueprints, all with the same "look" from source files that originated from scans of varying lightness, created on different kinds of papers, that used different sketching styles and pens.

Three versions of pages were made for the DreamWorks Interactive site. The Low Resolution pages used the storyboards for each page in blueprint format. The High Resolution version included full-color images and animated GIFs, and the Text Only version was made for browsers that don't support images at all, such as Lynx.

Interlacing Color with the Browser-Safe Palette

Making the final images required fitting the concepts that had been storyboarded so carefully into the Web environment. Even though Don and Bruce decided to ignore the Web's limits while brainstorming on ideas, that didn't mean they intended to lose sight of their medium when it came time to make final art.

Both Don and Bruce understood the importance of making a Web site that would look good on 256-color systems. Because Bruce was instrumental in identifying the browser-safe colors for my first book, *Designing Web Graphics*, he, more than anyone, understood the palette and the need to honor it.

The colors in the browser-safe palette, however, were simply not appropriate for the aesthetic Don and Bruce were seeking. Don, who had worked with 256-color environments and palettes for several years in his multimedia work with Microsoft, came up with a plan that involved mixing the browser-safe colors, which would produce hybrid variations.

Don took three colors from within the browser-safe palette and created a pixel-by-pixel pre-mixed pattern. This technique allowed him to use colors for the background of his pages that did not look like colors found in the browser-safe palette, but that in effect still were. This new hybrid optically-mixed color palette has all the same advantages of the browser-safe color palette. These colors will not shift hue across platform or dither unexpectedly. Yay!

This is the example of a solid color not found within the browser-safe chart. It's still browser-safe however, because it's formed out of checkerboarded pixels made with source colors from the correct palette.

Here's a close-up of the checkerboarding. Don Barnett took three colors from within the browser-safe palette and alternated them, pixel by pixel. At this magnified view, it's obvious, but at 1:1 it appears as an optical mixture of a different color.

Examples of hybrid variations that Don Barnett designed for the DreamWorks site. The optical mixture is made pixel-by-pixel in Photoshop using browser-safe colors.

■ step-by-step

Making Seamless Tiles

Creating pages that look fully textured without uploading tons of high memory graphics to your Web site is possible through a technique called tiling. The <body background> tag allows Web page authors to insert a tiny image, and have the image repeat indefinitely over the Web page, regardless of how big or small the end viewer's monitor is.

The following is the HTML required to load a background tile into a Web page:

```
■ <body background="toc.gif">
```

Any artwork can be the source for a patterned background tile. Making the tile appear to have no seams is the tricky part! Don used the Offset filter set to Wrap Around in Photoshop to achieve the seamless pattern he used on the DreamWorks pages. Here's a step-by-step look into his construction process:

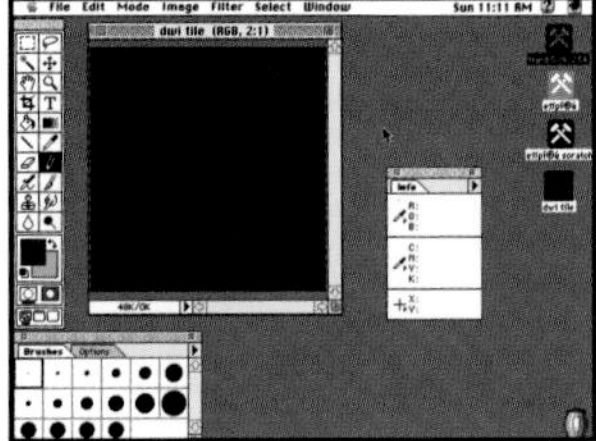

Step 1: Don began with a solid field of browser-safe color, and blew up his 128x128 pixel image to 200 percent by using the Magnifying Glass tool.

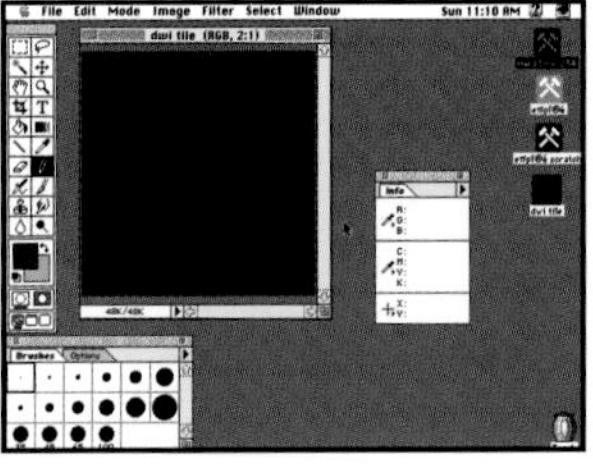

Step 2: He drew his first spiral using the aliased pencil tool. Anti-aliasing adds a lot of unnecessary file size to the final image, and the tile looked fine using aliased drawing tools instead.

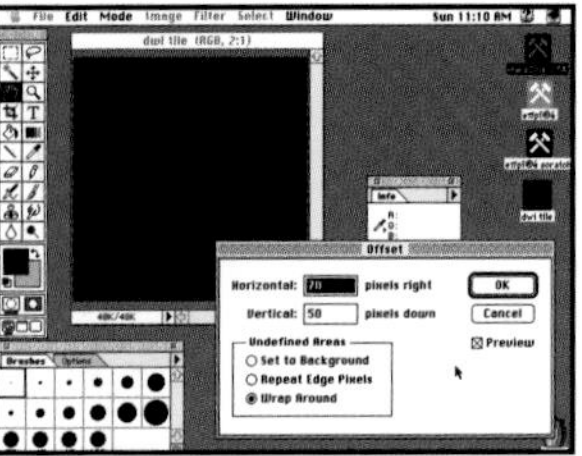

Step 3: Using the Offset filter under the Filter menu in Photoshop is key to creating seamless tiles. This enabled Don to work on all the areas of the tile graphic, to make sure the extreme edges matched up with each other.

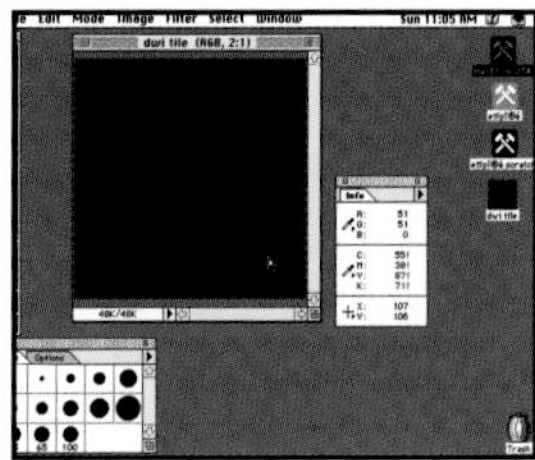

Step 4: By using the offset tile repeatedly, Don was able to continue to make the seams of the tile line up and match.

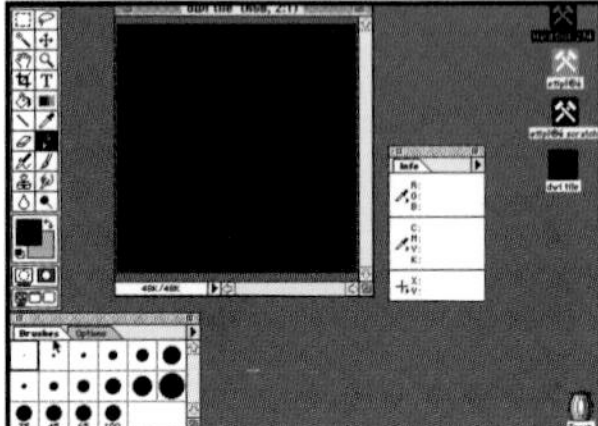

Step 5: Don added more shapes to the areas that were empty, making sure there were no gaps that would break the illusion of seamlessness.

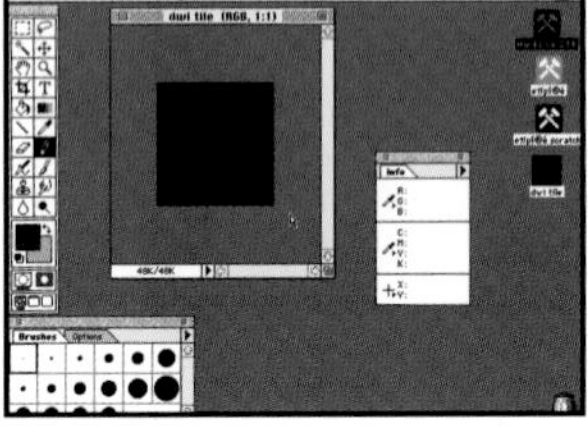

Step 6: He added the dots and used the Offset filter repeatedly to make sure he distributed them evenly over the tile.

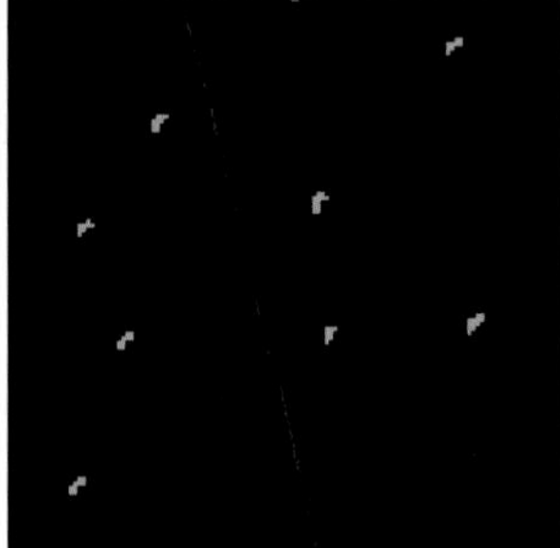

Step 7: The finished 128x128 tile was saved as a GIF. It is only 2.3k and has only five colors!.

What is the Offset Filter, Anyway?

The Offset filter ships with every version of Photoshop and is found at the bottom of the Filters menu in the Other category. The Offset filter takes any image and moves it according to pixel values that can be typed in. It has three important options: Set to Background, Repeat Edge Pixels, and Wrap Around. In the Set to Background mode, the background color within Photoshop is left behind as the image moves. In Repeat Edge Pixels, the background color of the actual image is left behind as the image moves. In the Wrap Around option, the part of the image that gets cut off on one edge appears on the opposite edge.

The Offset filter is invaluable in making seamless repeating background tiles for the Web. If you set the option to Wrap Around, the filter shows the area of the edge that would produce a seam or obvious repeating pattern. If you study Don's steps, you'll see that by repeatedly offsetting his image he was able to draw a pattern in the areas where the unwanted seams would normally be.

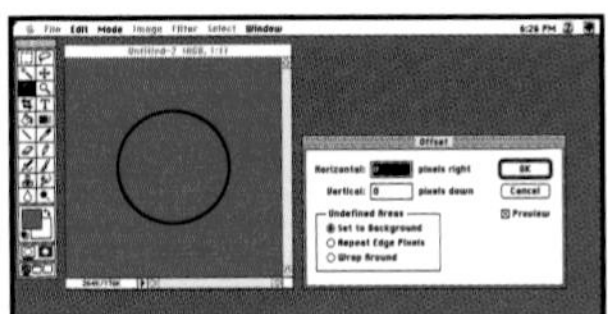

When the Repeat Background Color option is set, you will not see the edges that will appear with seams in the final tile.

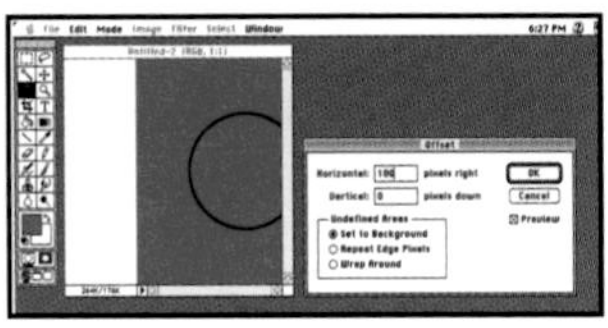

It doesn't matter what value you enter, the Offset filter will move the image by that many pixels.

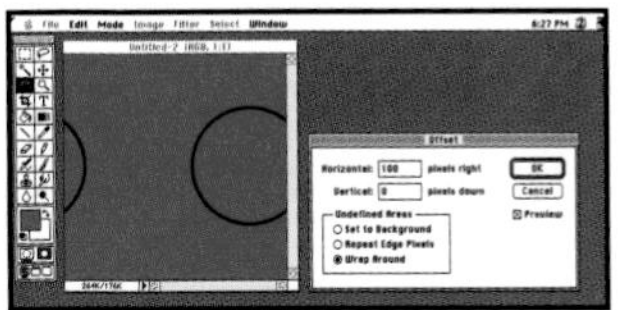

Using the Wrap Around feature, the part of the image that's been moved appears at the opposite edge. This is how you can see where to paint in order to eliminate obvious seams.

■ step-by-step

Checking the Repeating Pattern in Photoshop

It's one thing to know how to make a seamless tile, but another thing to see it repeated over a large area. It's important to know how to preview the pattern before posting it to the Web.

Don always previewed his tiles in Photoshop before finishing them for the Web. This enabled him to check to see if there were any noticeable repeats in the tiling of the pattern. In Photoshop, the way to preview a pattern follows:

Step 1: Open your finished tile and under the Select menu, choose Select All.

Step 2: Under the Edit menu, choose Define Pattern.

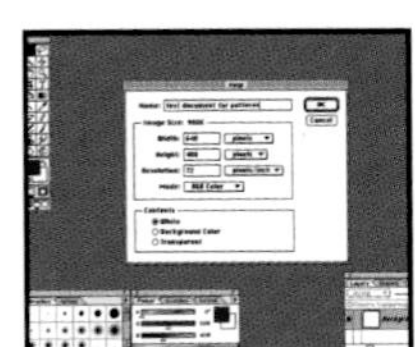

Step 3: Create a larger document that represents the size of your Web page. Any size will work, but if you don't have a page size in mind try 640x480 pixels.

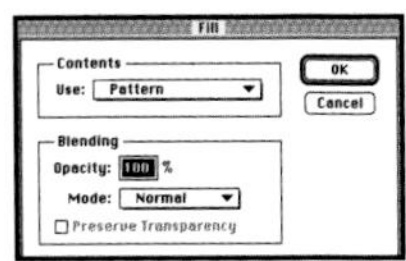

Step 4: Under the Edit menu, choose Fill. Within the Fill dialog box in the Contents section, choose Use Pattern. The blending modes should be set at 100% opacity and normal.

■ Here is the finished result tiled in a large Photoshop document. Notice how you cannot see any seams in the pattern.

Custom Painting Techniques Using Photoshop

Although both Don and Bruce were extremely comfortable painting with traditional pens and brushes, they chose to create all the artwork for the DreamWorks site on the computer using Photoshop.

One of their favorite techniques was to apply layers using the various Photoshop modes. This allowed for sections of the artwork to superimpose realistically, in order to create the look of lighting or depth.

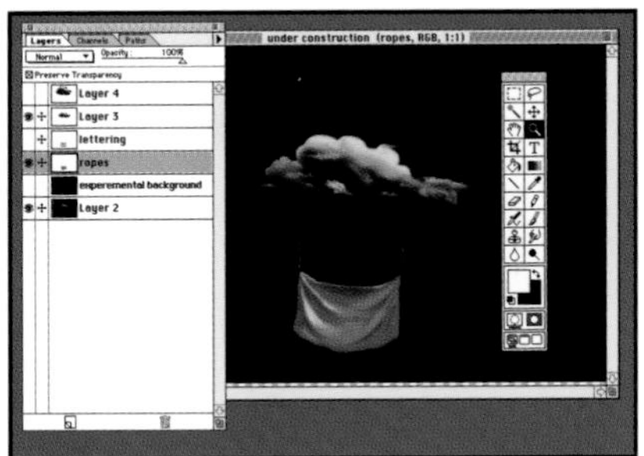

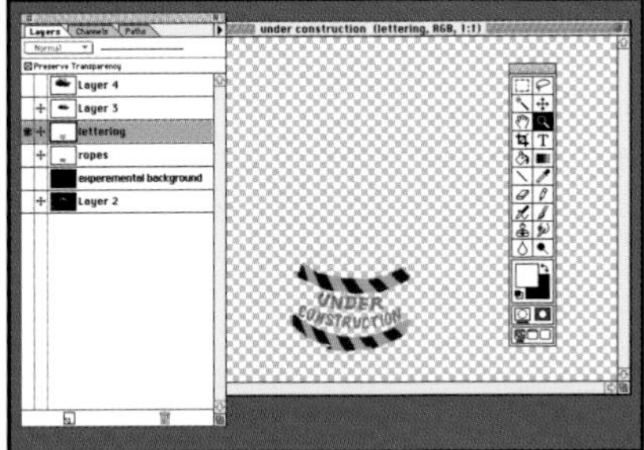

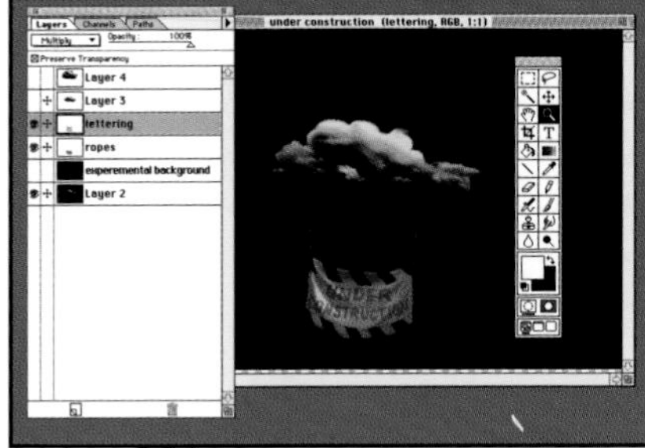

These three Photoshop files demonstrate how the Multiply mode added a sense of realism to the final image. The left image shows the painted flag. The middle image shows the layer with the lettering on it. Notice how flat it looks there. In the third example, where the layer has been added to the first using Multiply, all the folds in the fabric show through with great realism.

Another technique used on the site was to create custom brush sets in Photoshop for painting purposes. Bruce created an angled brush for the shingles on the rooftop of the opening screen. Don created a custom brush set that was used for the links on the mines in the gallery page shipwreck scene. Custom brushes were used in general to get into tight spots, create angled strokes, and wedge shapes for tight corners.

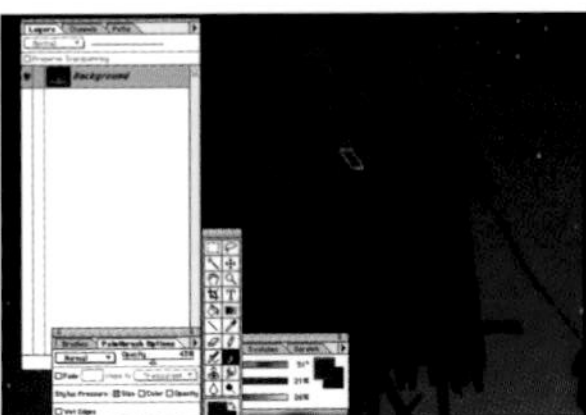

The angled brush, used with a pressure-sensitive stylus, enabled Bruce Heavin to quickly lay in the roof shingle shapes.

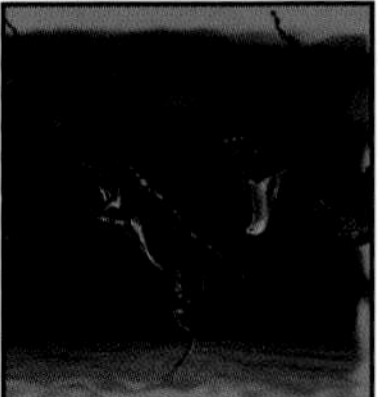

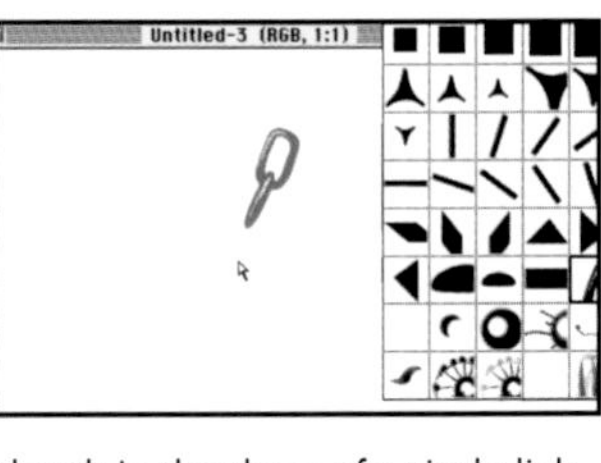

Don Barnett created one brush in the shape of a single link, and set the spacing so he could quickly create the linked chain on the floating mines. He would occasionally draw an individual link by hand to eliminate any appearance of pattern repetition.

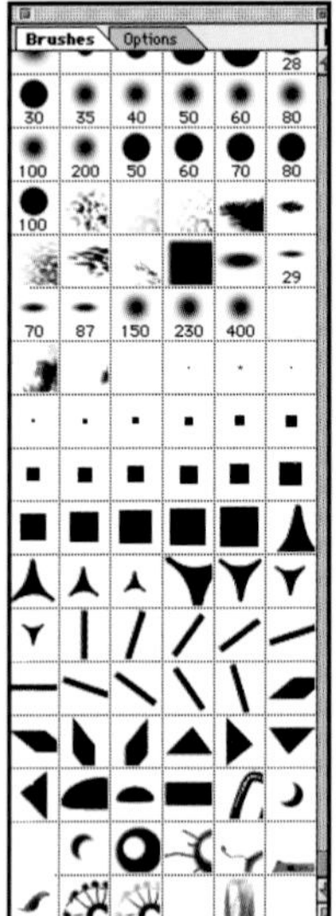

Don Barnett's custom brush set was used for angled brushes and wedge shapes.

■ step-by-step

How to Create a Custom Brush

Creating a custom brush is fairly simple in Photoshop. Create a shape, select it, go to the upper right hand pop-up menu arrow in the Brush Palette and choose Define Brush. This automatically puts the shape into the Brush Palette. Brush sets can be saved, loaded, and appended to other brush sets using the same pop-up menu arrow.

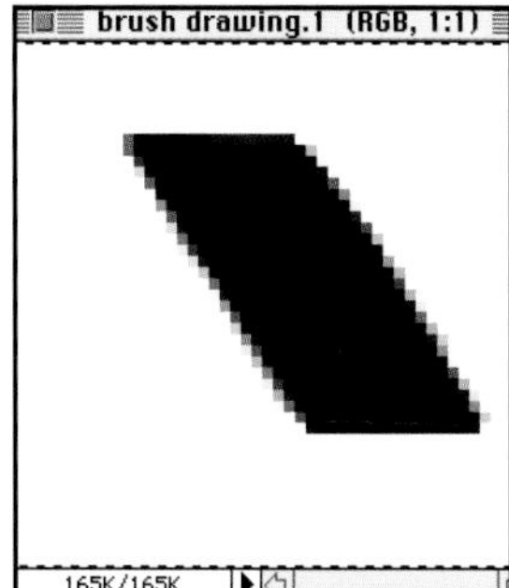

Step 1: Create a shape for the brush in grayscale or color. Color will be converted to grayscale once the brush is defined. Select the image.

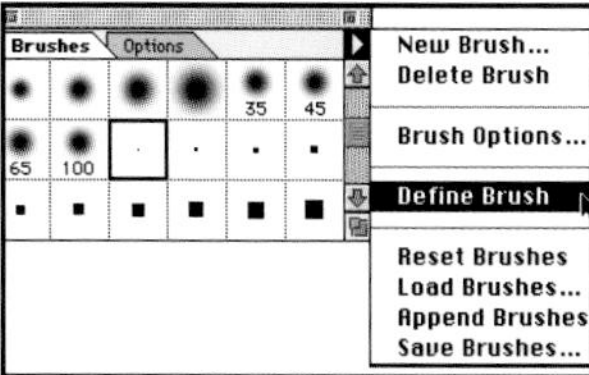

Step 2: Using the upper right-hand pop-up arrow in the Brush Palette, choose Define Brush.

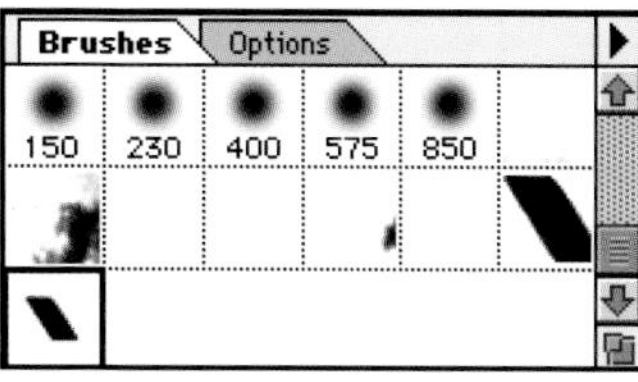

Step 3: This puts the selected image into the brush set for permanent use.

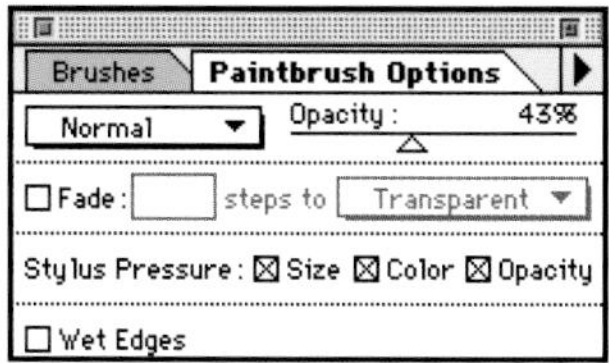

Step 4: Using a pressure-sensitive stylus and tablet, with the Stylus Pressure set to change according to Size, Color, and Opacity, Don and Bruce were able to get organic-looking results from using a repetitive custom brush shape.

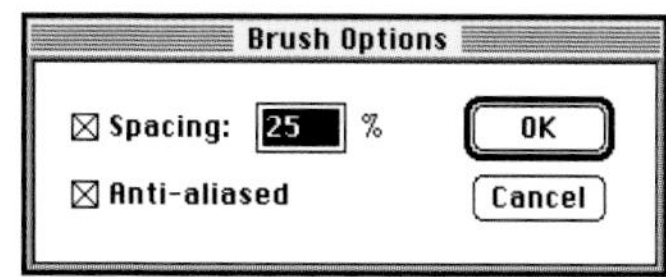

Step 5: By double-clicking on any custom brush, this Brush Options palette opens. Spacing can affect how often the brush is repeated. It can be set to make patterns, such as dotted lines, or making the link shapes look to be attached to each other.

Creating Custom Text in Illustrator

Photoshop is a great image editing program, but it has very poor text handling capabilities. Illustrator, on the other hand, is not a great image editing program, but has great text handling. Together, they make the perfect program!

Don Barnett set the type for the front screen of the DreamWorks site in Illustrator, using its text on a path tool. He created the curves in Illustrator, and when satisfied, applied text to the shapes. Next, Don copied the Illustrator typography and pasted it into Photoshop.

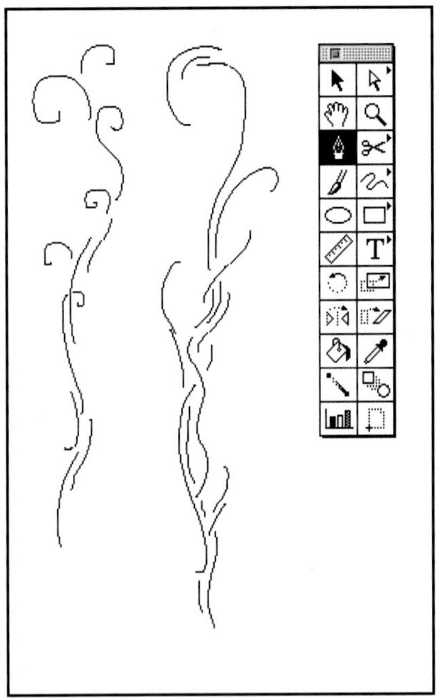

Don created some different curve sets before arriving at the final shapes.

The Type-Along-a-Path tool enables you to click on a Bezier curve and type along it. After the curve is used for a type path, it disappears and all that remains is the type along a custom path.

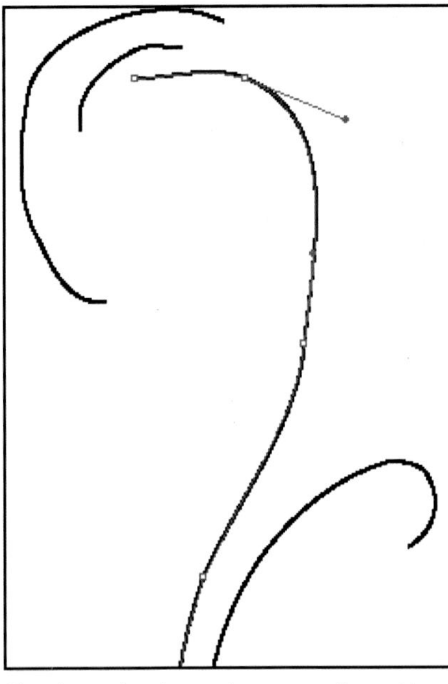

The shapes for the smoky text are formed by "Bezier" curves. Bezier is a type of mathematical curve.

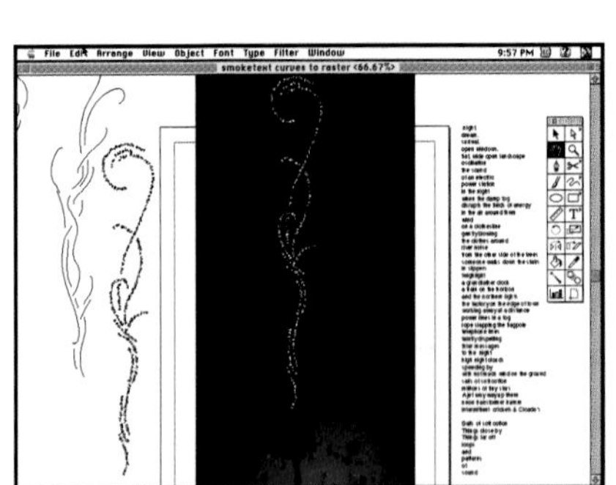

The Illustrator document with the type set on top of a for-position-only (FPO) image of the house. Placing the image behind the Illustrator scene helps ensure registration between the Illustrator and Photoshop files.

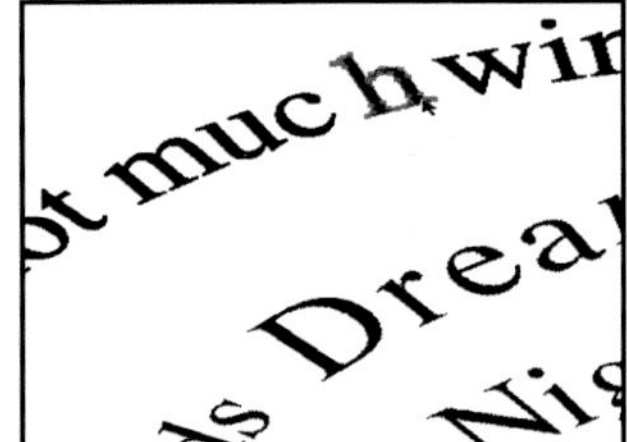

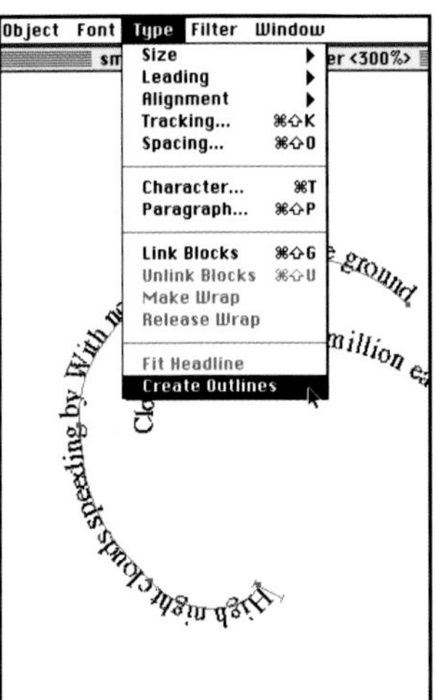

Don converted the text to outline-type before exporting it to Photoshop. This allowed for individual letters to be moved and positioned, and for making minor adjustments easier than reflowing the text along the curve.

Don placed a 72 dpi image of the house and background into Illustrator and set the curved type on top of it. Placed images must be saved first in EPS format, and appear in Illustrator as 8-bit preview files, hence the banding in the Illustrator template. The placed image is used for-position-only (FPO). Using a placed image at 72 dpi ensures that the scale of the typography will translate appropriately when the image is brought into Photoshop.

The Illustrator file was brought back into Photoshop, where it could be converted to a bitmap. Because Don intended to save the final graphic in a combination of GIFs and JPEGs (explanation follows), he needed to work with bitmap images.

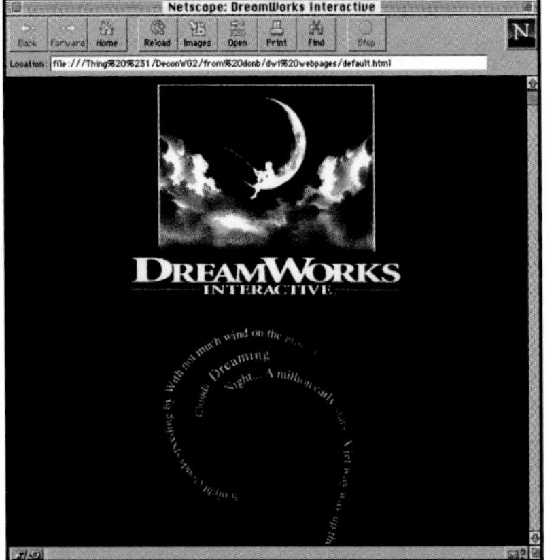

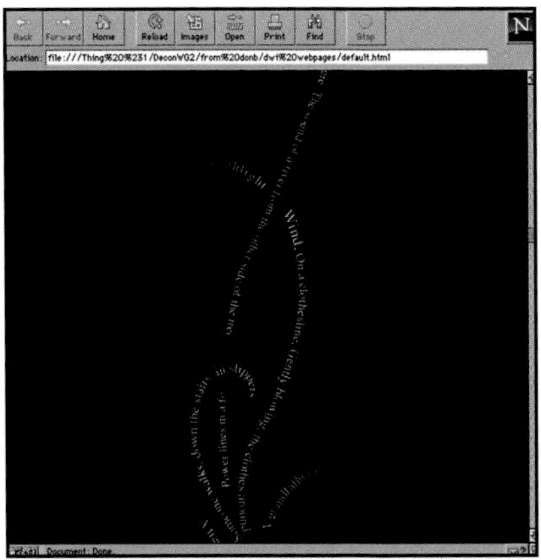

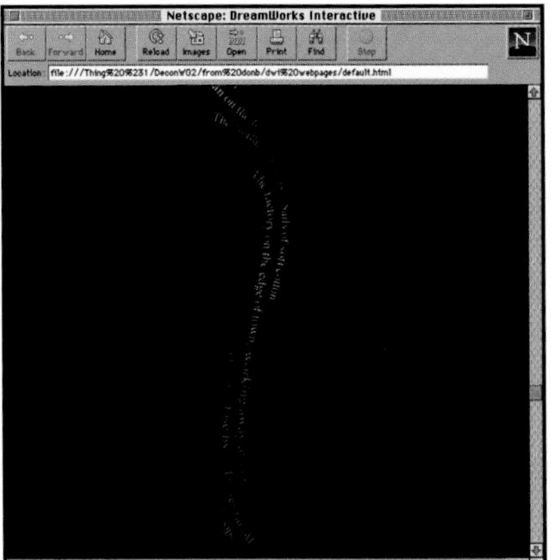

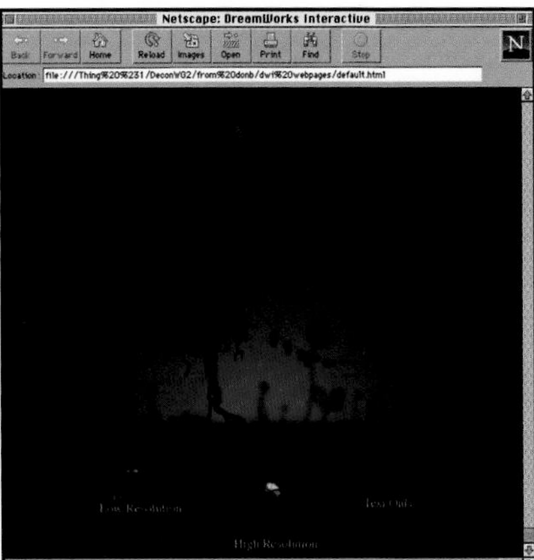

After the Illustrator documents are converted to Photoshop files and saved as GIFs and JPEGs, the custom type forces the page into a long vertical shape. It takes four screenfuls of graphics to scroll to the bottom of the DreamWorks site.

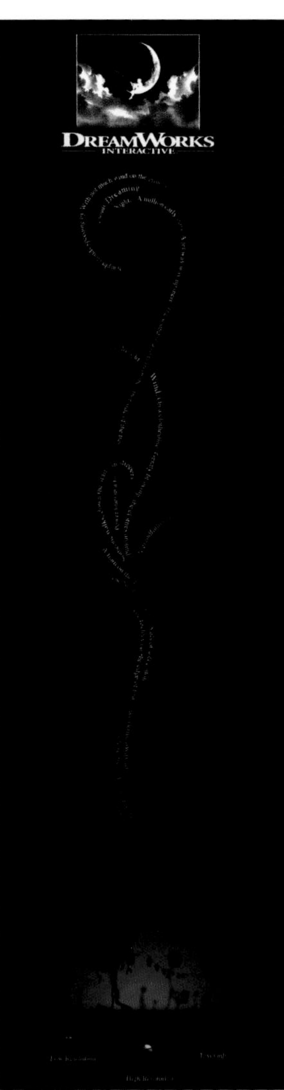

The long opening-page graphic viewed as a single screen.

Converting Illustrator Documents to Photoshop Documents

Illustrator is a Postscript drawing program that was invented for printing purposes. Postscript artwork is resolution-independent, meaning that it prints at whatever resolution the printer does. A linotronic printer will print a higher resolution version of an Illustrator document than a laser printer will. Its resolution is completely flexible, and not specified by the image format.

Photoshop documents, on the other hand, are bitmap documents. Bitmaps are composed of pixels at a fixed resolution. Both GIF and JPEG file formats are bitmap-based. In order to work with Illustrator files in Photoshop, they must be converted to bitmaps.

To bring an Illustrator file into Photoshop, it should first be saved as a standard Illustrator document. It can then be selected, copied, and pasted into Photoshop to function there as a bitmap. If you use this technique, a Paste dialog box appears asking if you want to paste as pixels or paste as paths. For Don's purpose, pasting as pixels was chosen because he wanted to use the Illustrator file as a Photoshop layer. Paths are usually used for print graphic purposes, and are not accurate enough for the tiny letterform shapes of Don's graphic.

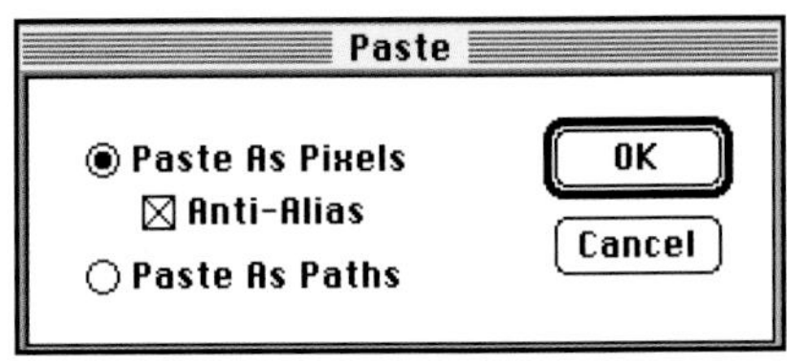

Choose Paste as Pixels when pasting Illustrator selections into Photoshop.

■ tip

Using Cropmarks for Registration

The file could have also been opened in Photoshop, using the Open command under the File menu. When you attempt to Open an Illustrator document into Photoshop, the Rasterize Illustrator Format dialog box appears. This effectively does the same thing as pasting with pixels, except takes up less RAM because the clipboard is not needed.

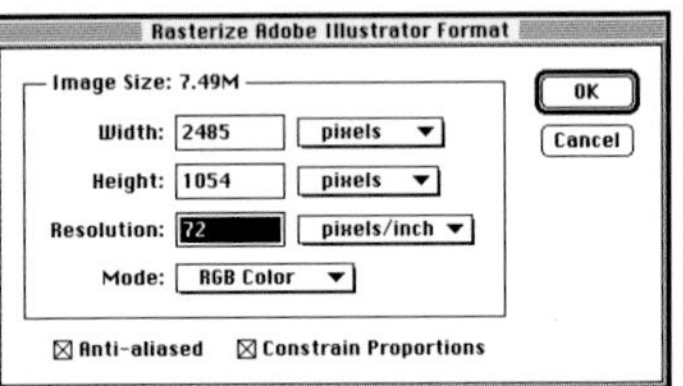

The size at which the image opens within Photoshop is dictated by how the original Illustrator file was created. Illustrator files can either be saved with or without cropmarks. Examples follow that demonstrate the difference cropmarks make with registration.

By using cropmarks in Illustrator, designers can specify exact control over the size of the image before opening in Photoshop. This can be very useful in maintaining registration between the two programs.

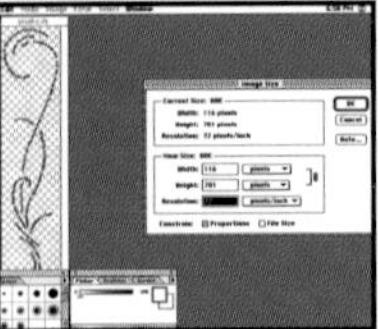

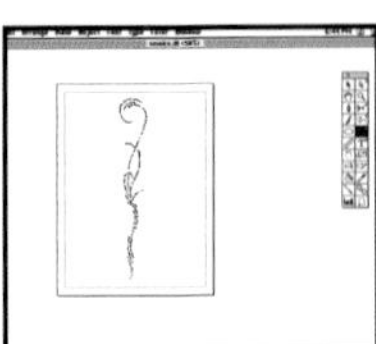

If you don't set cropmarks in Illustrator before saving, after the image is opened in Photoshop it defaults to being cropped tightly around the bounding shape of the Illustrator image.

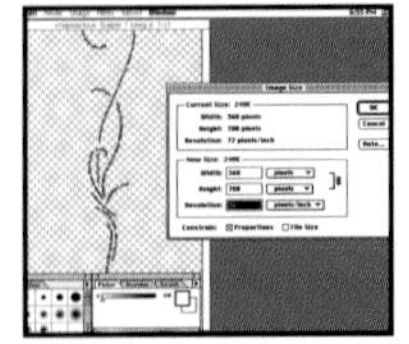

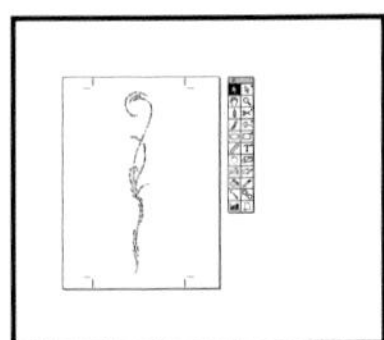

Here's an example of cropmarks set in Illustrator. When a document that has cropmarks is opened in Photoshop it assumes the size around the cropmarks, not the default bounding shape of the image.

■ step-by-step

Setting Cropmarks

Step 1: In Illustrator, drag out a rectangle in the size of the cropmarks you want. Hint: Keep the Info Palette open to see the size of the rectangle as you're dragging.

Step 2: With the rectangle selected, choose Cropmarks under the Objects Cropmarks, Make menu.

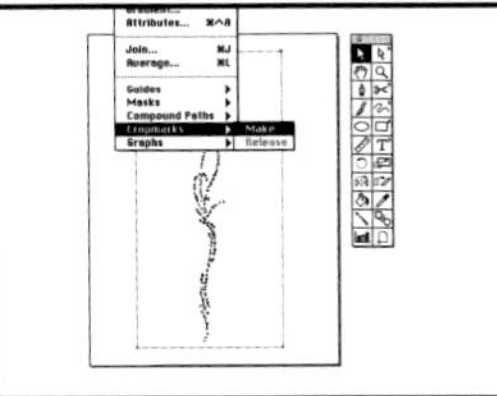

Step 3: Cropmarks will appear.

Step 4: Save the file as a native Illustrator file.

Painting Illustrator Type

After the file was in Photoshop, Don set the Illustrator type on its own layer against black. He was able to use the Dodge and Burn tools to lighten and darken the text image. At the base of the type, he used the Smudge tool to cause it to blend with the smoke.

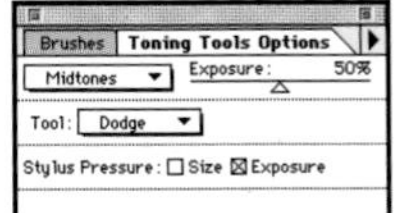

Don used the Dodge tool to lighten the type.

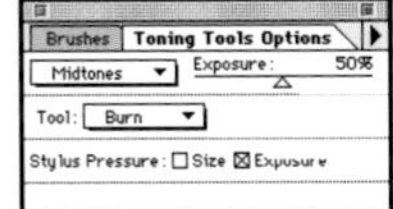

Don used the Burn tool to darken the type.

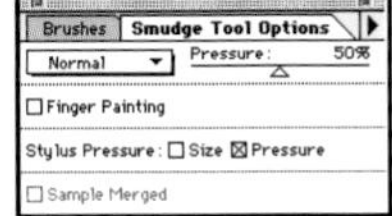

Don used the Smudge tool to blend the type into the smoke.

Here's an example of the painted type. Notice how it changes from being brighter, darker, and smudged in different places. This was accomplished with the Dodge, Burn, and Smudge tools in Photoshop.

Scanning a Custom Alphabet

Don Barnett created all the custom lettering for the site by hand, drawing it first with pen on paper, and then scanning the images. He scanned them at very high resolution so he could touch up the letterforms and then insert them into the Web images.

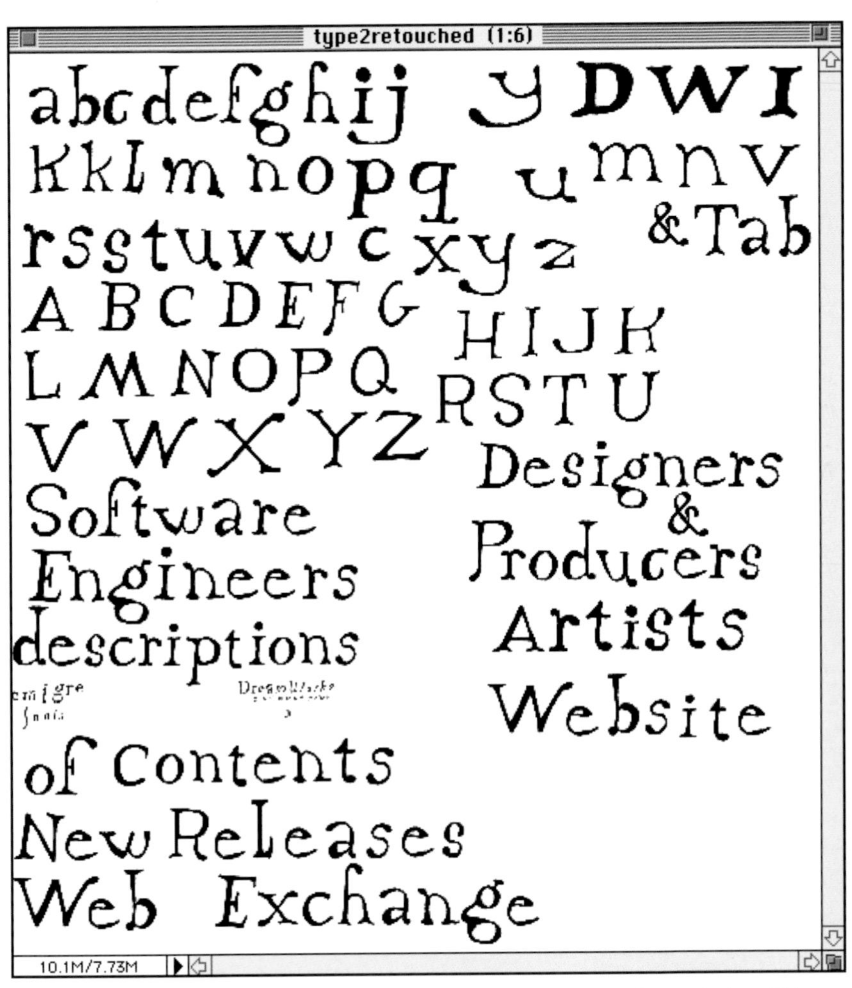

The type was scanned in at 600 dpi, which created huge images that could be touched up. This shows the file at a 1:6 ratio.

Here's the same image 1:1 in Photoshop. Don was able to retouch any corrections at this scale, then reduced the files to 72 dpi for the final Web pages.

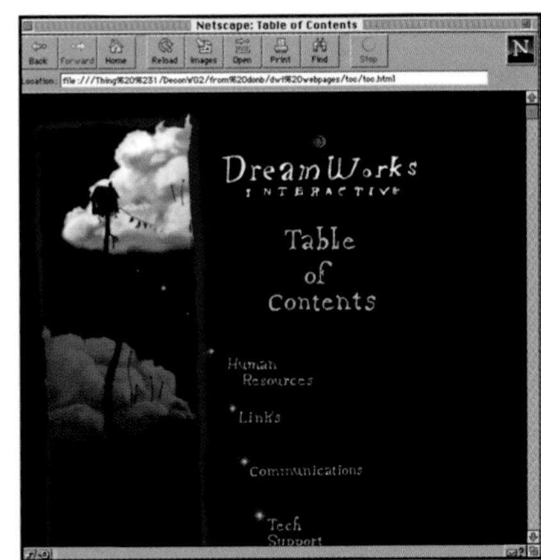

Here's a sample screen that shows Don's typography on a finished Web page.

■ step-by-step

Creating Transparent GIFs for Type and Graphics

The transparent GIF format creates image files that have been assigned to have specific areas set to disappear. This is useful for generating files in irregular shapes that will layer over background images, such as the spiral background on the Table of Contents page.

Don began with a layered Photoshop file where he previewed the way the screen would ultimately look. He prepared his images very carefully because they contained anti-aliased edges and glows. Working with anti-aliased and diffused artwork is very tricky when trying to achieve clean, one-color transparency masking effects. Don used glows and anti-aliasing for his type and stars, but put that artwork on top of an aliased black background so one-color transparency would work without fringing.

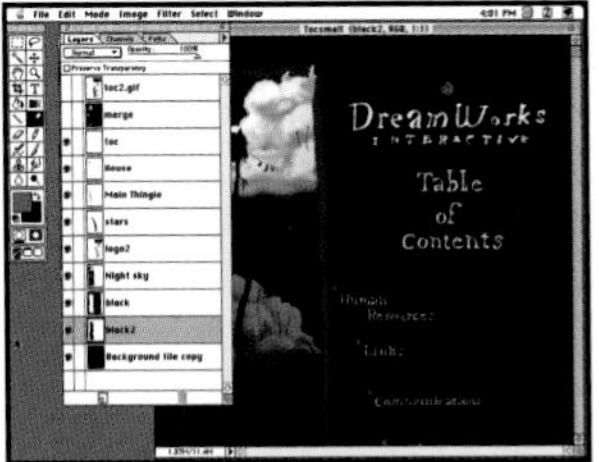

The layered Photoshop document where Don previsualized the Web page before creating final elements.

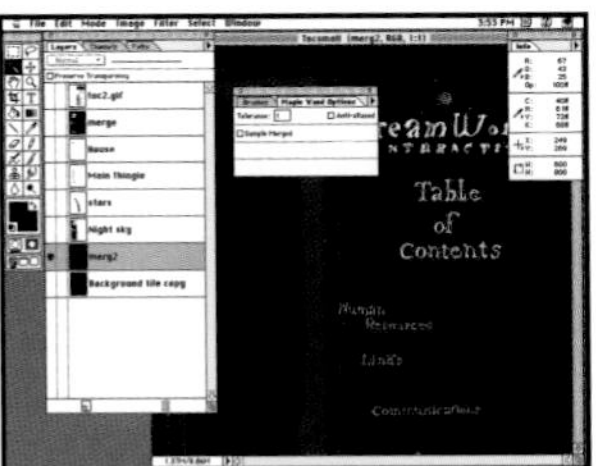

Step 1: He turned on layers that forced the background to black in order to select the type with an aliased edge. He used the magic wand tool at a tolerance setting of 1, without anti-aliased checked to select and delete the background color. It was very important that the edge of a transparent graphic be aliased instead of anti-aliased, in order to avoid fringing.

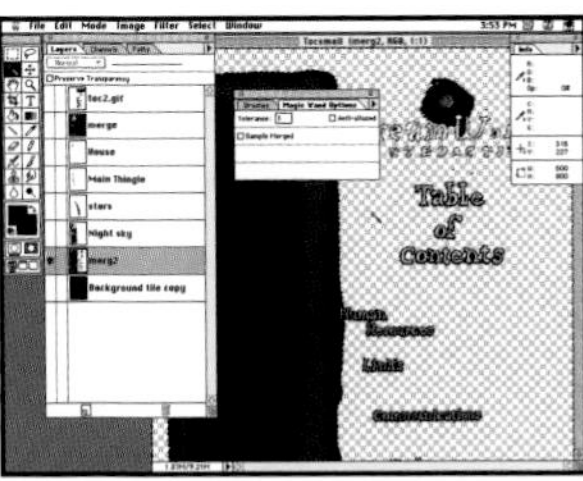

Step 2: Once the aliased selection was made, he deleted the background.

Step 3: He created an alpha channel in the Channel Palette to define the rectangular bounding region of the transparent image. (More on alpha channels follows in the section after Transparency.)

Step 4: By loading the alpha channel selection, he was able to preplan exactly where all the elements from this graphic would be cropped. The transparent GIF section was easily separated from the rest of the graphic.

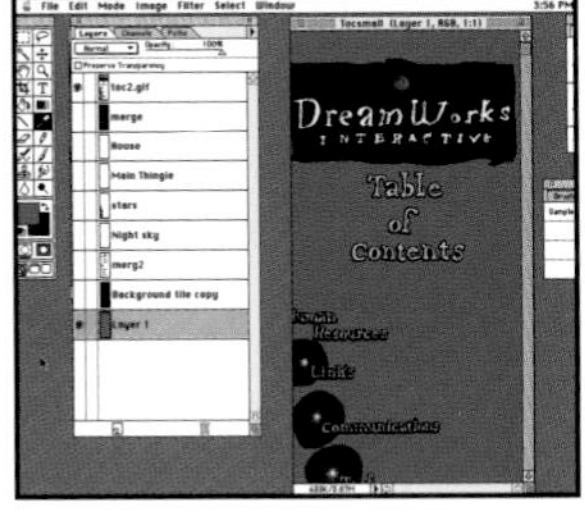

Step 5: Don chose to insert a lavender background into the back layer, which would make the background easy to isolate when setting transparency. He had to index the colors first, so the file could be saved as a GIF.

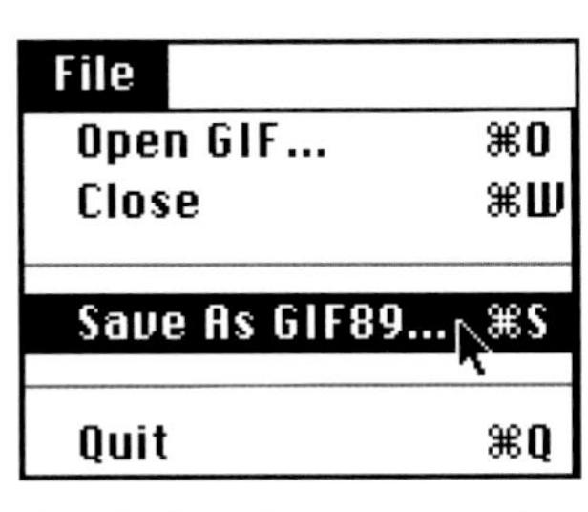

Step 6: Once the transparent color was established, he saved the file as a GIF89, which is the technical name for a transparent GIF.

Preparing Files Properly for Transparent GIFs

The process of making a transparent GIF is fairly straightforward. There are many programs and plug-ins that assist with this procedure and make generating the transparent GIF files relatively easy. It's preparing the original images properly for clean looking transparency that is more tricky.

GIF transparency only allows for a single color to drop out. This is a vey limited transparency scheme, because artwork with soft glows and anti-aliased edges can't be masked with good looking results when limited to a one color mask. The nature of anti-aliased and soft edged artwork is that it must blend over more than one color. So when the mask is limited to one color, as in transparent GIFs, the blended edges are left with an unwanted residual outline. This unwanted effect is called a fringe or halo.

The solution is to create aliased graphics, or graphics that have no anti-aliasing. The graphics with aliased edges will look terrible by themselves, but are much better looking than anti-aliased graphics once composited using one color GIF trasparency on a Web page. Creating aliased graphics is the result of working with tools in Photoshop that can be set to turn anti-aliasing off. These tools are the Pencil, the Eraser, the Paint Bucket, and the Magic Wand.

Most digital artists are accustomed to making artwork with anti-aliased edges.

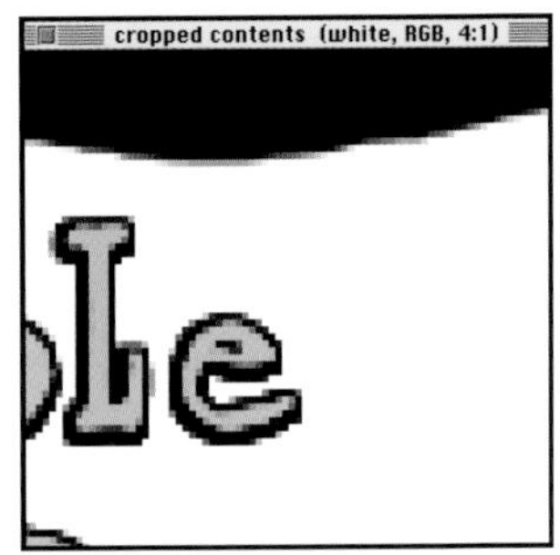

This is an example of what anti-aliasing looks like close-up. Notice how it blends to the white.

The blending to white is exactly what's causing the unattractive fringe around the artwork in this example.

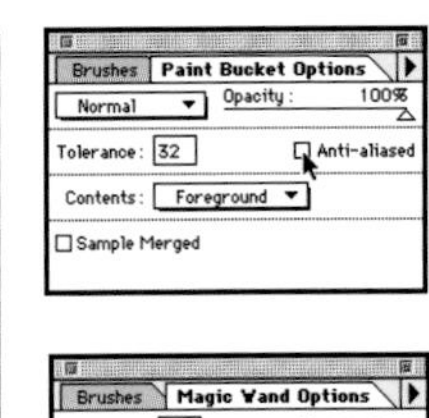

Examples of turning the anti-aliasing option off with the Paint Bucket and Magic Wand tool in Photoshop. Pencil and Eraser tools have aliased brushes as part of their default settings.

By itself, the aliased graphic looks awful; you can see the jaggies.

Notice how the outer edge of this file is jaggy. That's what aliasing looks like—jagged pixels with no blending. Note how Don anti-aliased the interior elements, like the type, but left the dark edge aliased.

The final composite looks perfect. No fringing or halos!

■ step-by-step

Using Alpha Channels for Cutting Apart the Images

Because Don created all the original artwork as Photoshop layered documents, the task to separate the individual images for perfect registration on a Web page was not a small one.

For this purpose, Don used a series of alpha channel selections within Photoshop. An "Alpha Channel" is an intimidating sounding word for masks that are stored permanently within the layered documents. Every time you use a selection tool in Photoshop, such as the Magic Wand, Marquee, or Lasso, you are using an alpha channel without knowing it. Alpha channels are nothing more than selections that are saved and stored in the Layer Palette for repeated use.

The selection region is represented within an alpha channel by a grayscale image. The whites in the alpha channel indicate what is active within the selection, and the blacks indicate what is masked out. Levels of gray within an alpha channel represent levels of transparency, with light grays leaning more towards opacity and dark grays leaning more towards transparency.

By keeping a permanent record of the mask for the different regions within his Photoshop documents, Don was able to ensure precise registration when cutting apart the individual files for GIF and JPEG preparation.

Alpha Channels are created by following these steps:

Step 1: Create a selection using any combination of selection tools.
Step 2: Under the Select Menu, choose Save Selection.
Step 3: Go to the Channels Palette to view the results.

Alpha Channels are accessed by following these steps:

Step 1: Under the Select Menu, choose Load Selection.
Step 2: The selection will appear within the Photoshop layer's screen.
Step 3: You can now edit the image within the selection. In Don's case, he loaded the selection and then chose Crop.

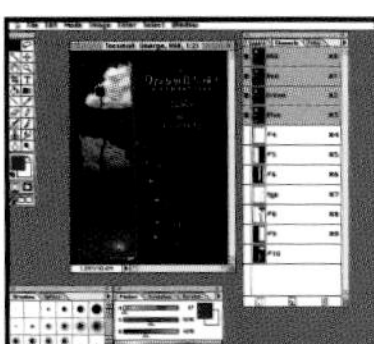

■ Here's a document that Don wanted to cut apart into two perfectly aligned vertical strips. He wanted to make the left side a JPEG, and the right side a transparent GIF.

Step 1: Don created a selection of the crop he wanted. He would later make this side of the Photoshop document a transparent GIF.

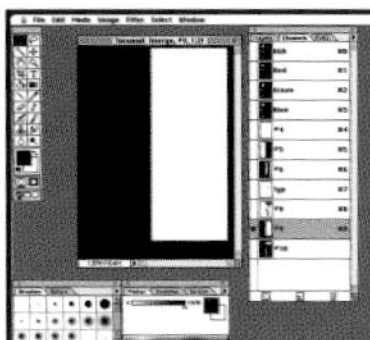

Step 2: Under the Select Menu, Don chose "Save Selection." By saving the selection as an alpha channel, Don could access this selection region whenever he needed to.

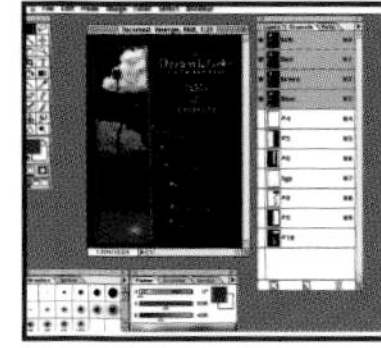

Step 3: Don created a mirror image of the selection by "Loading" the first alpha channel he made, and choosing "Inverse" under the Selection Menu.

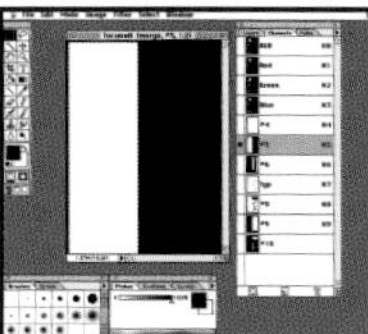

Step 4: Under the Select Menu, Don chose "Save Selection" for the second shape. You can view the black and white "alpha channel" by switching over to the Channels Palette.

Choosing Optimum Web-based Compression for the HTML Pages

The Opening Screen and the Table of Contents Screen might look like single images, but they actually consisted of several separate pieces of artwork. This was done for compression purposes, because the pages included images that would be best saved in both GIF and JPEG formats. Each of these images are found within the HTML below as separate <img src> tags.

■ tags

Opening Screen
Graphic File Formats Deconstruction

The HTML alignment of the images that make up the seamless opening page are held together by simply letting them fall next to each other. An alternative method would be to hold them in place using tables, as in the HTML deconstruction shown in Chapter 5, "@tlas." This would eliminate the possibility of the images moving around if the browser window were re-sized.

```
   <HTML><TITLE>DreamWorks Interactive</TITLE><HEAD>
   <BODY bgcolor=000000 text=ffffcc></BODY><center>
   <A HREF="toc/toc.html">
1  <img src="dwilogo.gif" alt="[DreamWorks
   Interactive Logo]" border=0><br>
   <A HREF="toc/toc.html">
2  <img src="smoke.gif" alt="[TypeSmoke]"
   border=0><br>
3  <img src="smoke2.jpg"
   alt="[TypeSmoke2]"border=0><br>
4  <img src="home.jpg" alt="[home]" border=0><br>
5  <img src="lores.gif" alt="Low Res]"border=0>
6  <img src="space.gif" border=0>
7  <img src="hibobb.gif" alt="hi Res]"border=0>
   <A HREF="toc/toc.html">
8  <img src="space.gif" border=0>
9  <img src="texony.gif" alt="text only ]"border=0><br>
10 <img src="hires.gif" border=0></A></center></HTML>
```

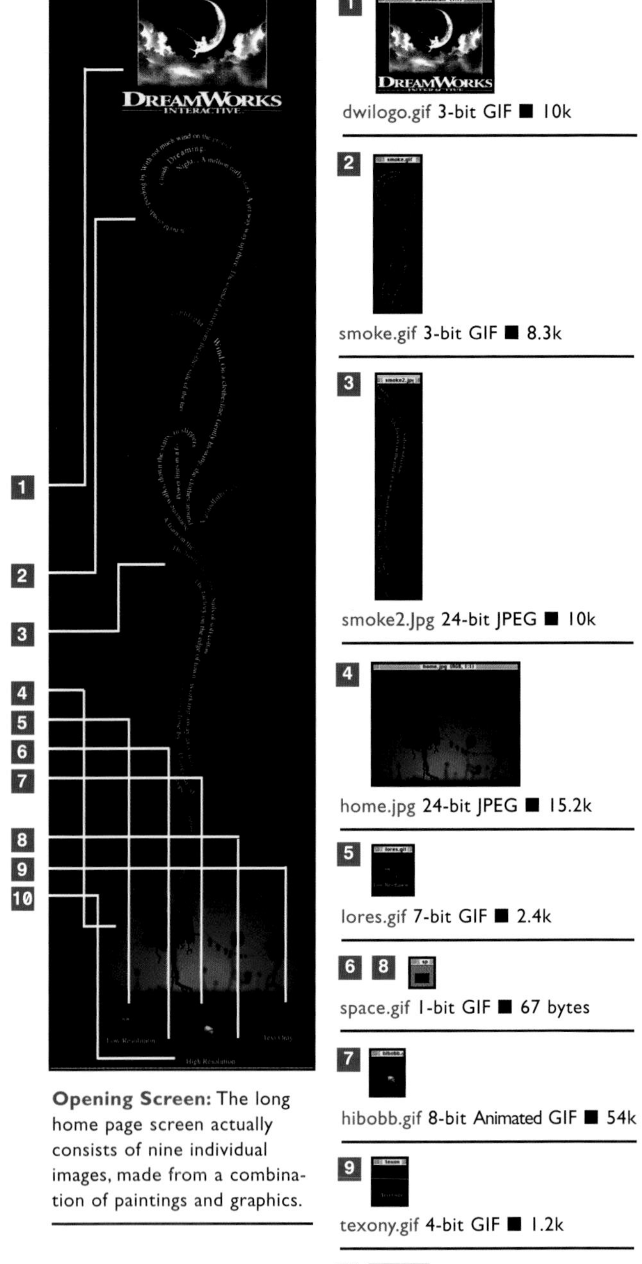

Opening Screen: The long home page screen actually consists of nine individual images, made from a combination of paintings and graphics.

Generally, GIF compression is best used for graphics such as type, images with areas of flat color, or hard defined edges. JPEG is best suited for photographic or continuous-tone images, such as illustrations and paintings. By separating the images, Don and Bruce were able to optimize each file with its own bit-depth and compression settings. This made for the smallest possible file sizes for the Web pages.

■ tags

Table of Contents
Graphic File Formats Deconstruction

The Table of Contents page might appear as one graphic, but it actually consisted of several images. The images were saved as separate pieces of art so they could be compressed and handled differently. It has one background tile and two images, the one on the left, and the other transparent GIF on the right.

```
<HTML>
<HEAD><TITLE>Table of Contents</TITLE></HEAD>
1 <BODY bgcolor=1e0c00 background="toc.gif"
text=ffffcc link=ffffcc vlink=ffffcc>
2 <img src="toc.jpg" alt="[toc]">
3 <img src="toc2.gif" alt="[toc2]" align=top>
<br clear=all><p>
<A HREF="../links/links.html">Links to Other
Sites<br><br>
<A HREF="../comm/comm.html">Communication<br><br>
<A HREF="../gallery/gallery.html">Gallery<br><br>
<A HREF="../hr/hr.html">Human Resources<br><br>
<A HREF="../tech/tech.html">Technical
Support<br><br>
<A HREF="../root/root.html">root
directory<br><br></A>
</LEFT>
</HTML>
```

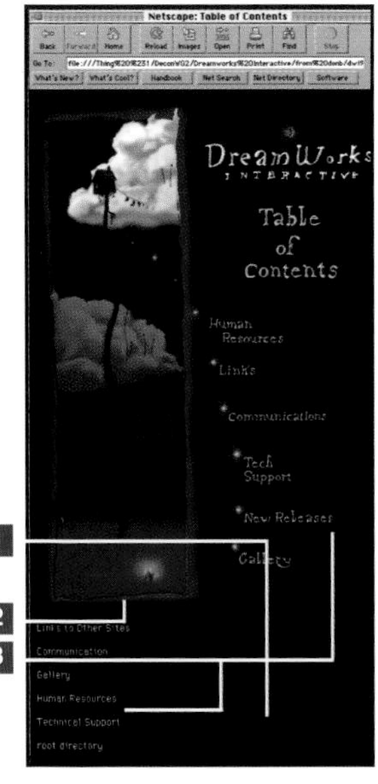

Table of Contents: The table of contents screen, which looks like one seamless image, is actually composed of a tiled background and two individual images.

1 

tocgif 7-bit Trans GIF ■ 20.2k

2 

toc.Jpg 24-bit JPEG ■ 24k

3 

toc2.gif 3-bit GIF ■ 1.5k

■ site summary

DreamWorks Interactive SKG

The DreamWorks site provides an excellent example of combining paintings and graphics on a Web site. The Photoshop painting techniques employed by Don Barnett and Bruce Heavin are valuable tutorials for anyone creating artwork using Illustrator and Photoshop, whether for Web graphics or not. Don Barnett's hybrid browser-safe color discovery is a tremendous gift to anyone wanting to work outside the confines of the browser-safe colors, but who still wants the benefits of using them. This site is respectful of cross-platform compatibility and low-memory graphics without skimping on richly detailed images, quality, or innovation.

■ Storyboarding and concepting a site might take some time, but add a lot of value to the final result.

■ Working with browser-safe color makes sites look acceptable on 256-color displays. By checkerboarding the browser-safe colors, you can create optical mixtures of more than 216 color combinations.

■ Knowing Photoshop well is probably the single most important tool a Web designer can possess. Working with different Photoshop modes, such as Screen and Multiply can add a lot of realism to digital paintings.

■ Creating custom brushes in Photoshop can be a time-saving device over painting repetitive imagery from scratch.

■ When making images for transparent GIFs, aliased edges produce the cleanest possible results. If your image has a fringe or halo around it, chances are you anti-aliased the edges.

■ Don't make large images that use the same compression if it might save space to separate them to optimize each individual image.

Hollywood Records

ascii art and animated GIFs

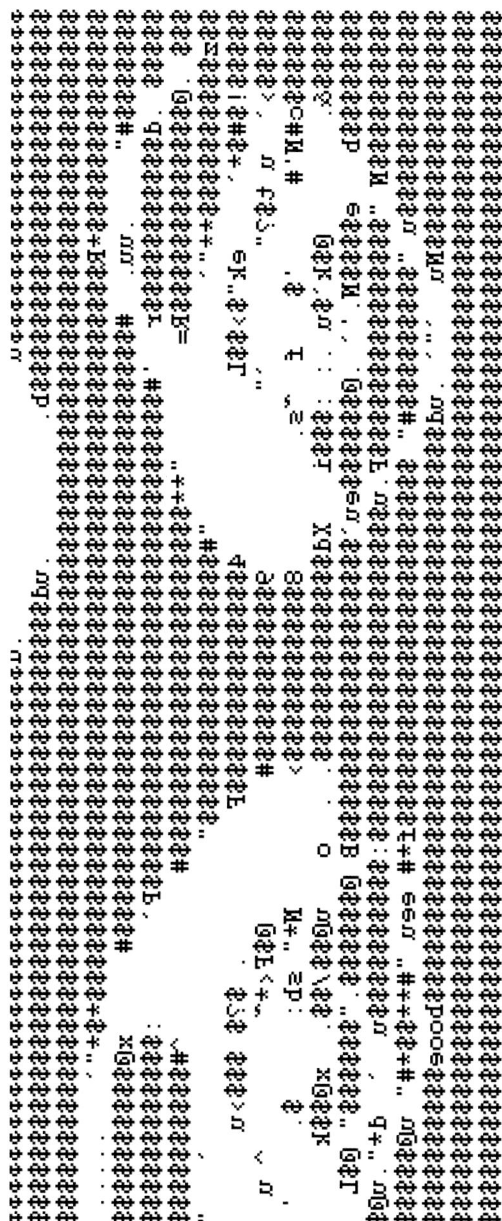

What this chapter covers:

- **How to Plot ASCII Art Paths Using Photoshop**
- **How to Convert GIFs to ASCII Character Paintings**
- **Sprite Animation Using Animated GIFS**

http://www.hollywoodrec.com The low-fi version of Hollywood Records' site was inspired by a nostalgic throwback to the 1970's ASCII art craze, with a 1990's design twist. The site's designers unearthed a treasure of a program called GIFscii that converts GIFs to ASCII character paintings. They throw a couple of other cool tricks into the mix too, such as using Photoshop for saving color palettes and creating animated GIFs that use sprite animation.

Web Design Firm: Disney Online

Client: Hollywood Records

URL: http://www.hollywoodrec.com

Type of Site: Record Company

Server: Sparc 20

Server Software: CERN

Producer: Eric Hardman

Webmaster: Yoshinobo Takahas

Digital Designers: Johnny Rodriguez, Chauncey Cummings, and Alex Lieu

Development and Production Platform: Macintosh

Software: Photoshop, GIFscii, GIFbuilder

ASCII and You Shall Receivscii

It all started innocently enough, with the design team for Hollywood Records' Web site searching for visual themes that would distinguish separate versions of their pages for varying bandwidth demands. The idea of a hi-fi, sci-fi, and low-fi hierarchy surfaced, in order to cater to users with fast connections, all the way down to those viewing with text-only browsers.

Funny that the design for the lowest bandwidth and most minimal browser requirements ended up being the site's most original achievement, but so it goes. Even though the Web is only a few years old, it's already hard to come up with an entire concept that's still original. The idea of doing the low-bandwidth site with ASCII characters, at that time (1994), was original and fresh—and holds up as a great-looking solution to low-bandwidth Web graphics even to this day.

ASCII art uses only text to create graphics, by placing text characters into shapes of pictures. One of the advantages to using ASCII on a site is that it downloads quickly. The ASCII pages for the Hollywood Records site are all below 5k! ASCII-only pages also display on all browsers—including the most rudimentary browsers that don't support graphics at all, like Lynx.

Designing Graphics with ASCII

Probably no one has ever put a high-powered tool like Photoshop to such primitive use as creating ASCII graphics, but that was the first method used to create the low-fi version of the Hollywood Records site.

The process of making the final page was painstaking. Chauncey Cummings, who converted the ASCII to HTML, needed to hand-count each text character to match the placement of Eric's Photoshop file. After he got the pattern laid out, he then inserted the hyperlinks, and went back and forth between his text editor and browser in preview mode to make sure he had inserted the proper number of spaces to achieve the desired design.

Eric Hardman experimented with different type configurations in Photoshop layers.

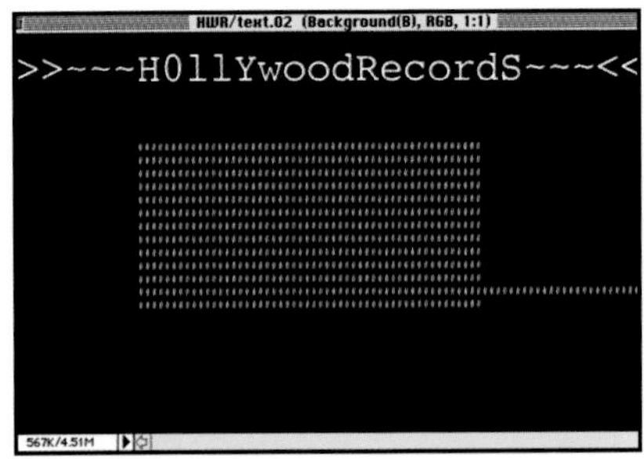

He took one line of type and copied and pasted it repeatedly to form a solid grid.

Using the eraser, he carved out graphic shapes.

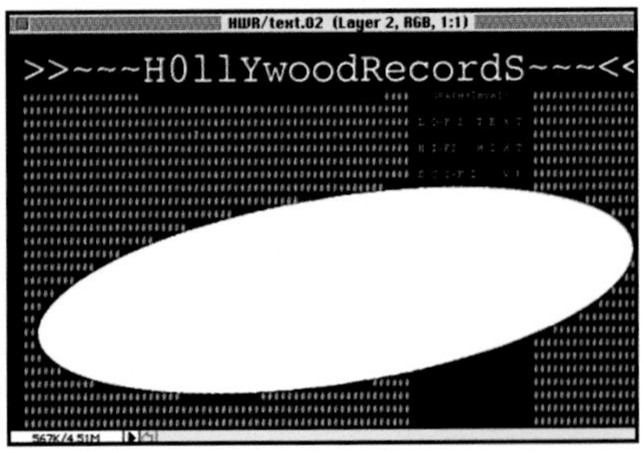

Eric inserted shape templates to use as his erasing guides.

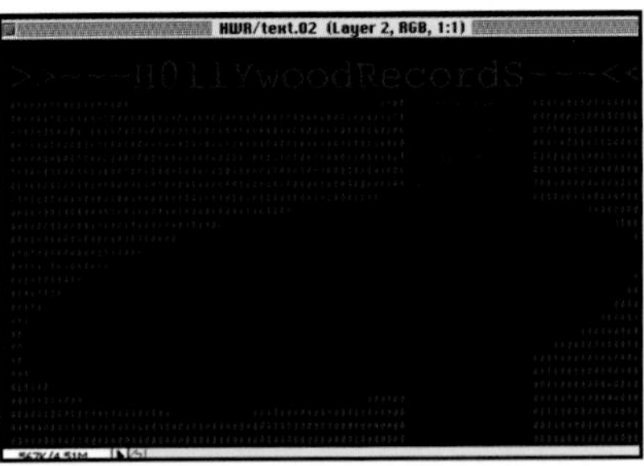

By creating a solid field of green and changing the Mode to darken, he tried several different color treatments.

Eric created the final layout and color scheme using Photoshop as a pre-visualization tool.

Here's the final page in Netscape. The page was prototyped in Photoshop and then coded in HTML. In order to use ASCII art within an HTML page, it's necessary to enclose the ASCII text shapes with the <PRE> and </PRE> tags. That instructs the browser to recognize that the text within those tags is pre-formatted, and should not be word-wrapped like it would with regular HTML text.

Opening Screen HTML

```
<HTML>
<HEAD>
<TITLE>Hollywood Records</TITLE>
</HEAD>
<BODY BGCOLOR="#090301" TEXT="#436E58" LINK="#CF7B42"
VLINK="#323172" ALINK="#ffffff">
<CENTER>
<PRE>
<FONT size=7>>>>>~~~~H011YwoodRecordS~~~~<<<<</Font>
##################
<A HREF="/HollywoodRecords/home.html">H I-F I
G R A F X </A>##
<AHREF="/HollywoodRecords/HollywoodRecordsV.html"> S C I
-F I  V R </A>### H O M E   P A G E ###
<A HREF="/Note"> E M A I L  U S</A>
########################################################
##                     ##################
########################################################
##                     ##########
<A HREF="/Help"> H E L P</A>
########################################################
##                     ##################
########################################################
##                     ##################
########################################################
##                     ##################
########################################################
##                     ##################
##################################################
##################
#########################################
<A HREF="/HollywoodRecords/Roadtrips/RoadtripsL.html">
R O A D T R I P S </A>        ##########
###############################
######
########################
###
###################
##
##############
<A HREF="/HollywoodRecords/Soundtrax/SoundtraxL.html">
S O U N D T R A C K S</A>                         ##
##########
###
#######
####
####
######
##
<A HREF="/HollywoodRecords/Musicians/AcidJazz/AcidJazzL.
html">A C I D  J A Z Z</A>
<AHREF="/HollywoodRecords/Musicians/MusiciansL.html">
M U S I C I A N S </A>      ########
##
############
##
<A HREF="/HollywoodRecords/catalog/catalog.html">  C A T
A L O G</a>             ###############
##
##################
###
<A HREF="/HollywoodRecords/UpComing/UpComingL.html"> W H
A T ' S  N E W </A>
##################
######
##################
###########
######                     ##################
########################
########################
##################
########################################################
#                     ##################
########################################################
#                     ##################
</CENTER>
</PRE>
(c) 1995 Hollywood Records.  All Rights Reserved.
</BODY>
</HTML>
```

■ As you can see, the HTML code looks nothing like the shapes plotted in the finished graphic in Photoshop because the code also includes HTML tags. These tags, such as header and color information, as well as hyperlinks, take up extra spaces for the additional text characters required by the hyperlink <a><href> codes.

Testing HTML files—Going Between Browser and Text Editor

Any kind of text editor works for creating HTML text. First, create the HTML in the text editor and save it as text only with an .html extension at the end of it. Windows 3.1 users are limited to three letter extensions, so .htm will work fine, too.

If you have a browser on your hard drive, you can test the HTML easily by opening the browser, then opening the .html document off your hard drive. The Web page should load and look exactly as it would in final form. If you make a change to the HTML and save it, you can simply press the reload button in the browser and the file updates. Note that if you also include images on the Web page, those files must be located within the same folder directory as the .html file that requests them.

This process is used by most Web designers and offers the opportunity to make minor tweaks and changes while enabling the author to view the file before posting it to a live Web server. Almost all Web browsers have the capability to open a file off your hard drive. This feature is usually found under the browser's File menu.

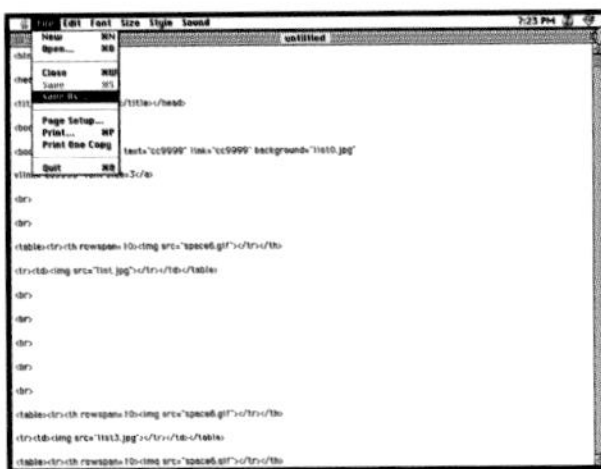

Save the document as a "text only" file, and save it with an .html or .htm extension.

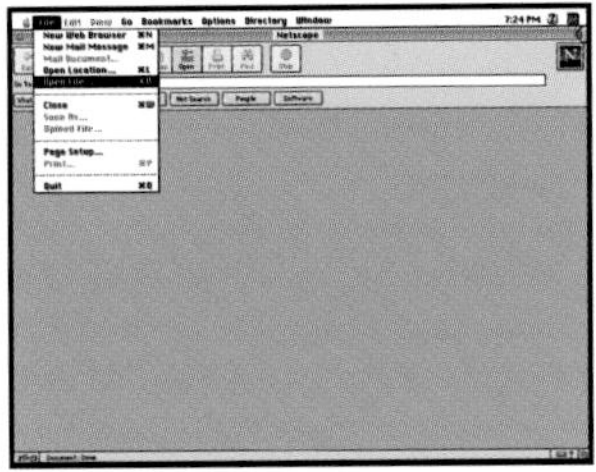

In Netscape, choose Open File and select the .html document. If your HTML requires specific images, make sure they are in the same folder as the text document you open, or that the images are inside a folder that is specified within the HTML, such as "/images'my.jpg."

■ tip

Using Preserve Transparency to Change Color

One way to change the color of the type within Photoshop is to use the Preserve Transparency button on the layer you want to alter. This checkbox effectively turns on a mask and allows whatever content is within that layer to be filled with a different color, while not affecting the other layers.

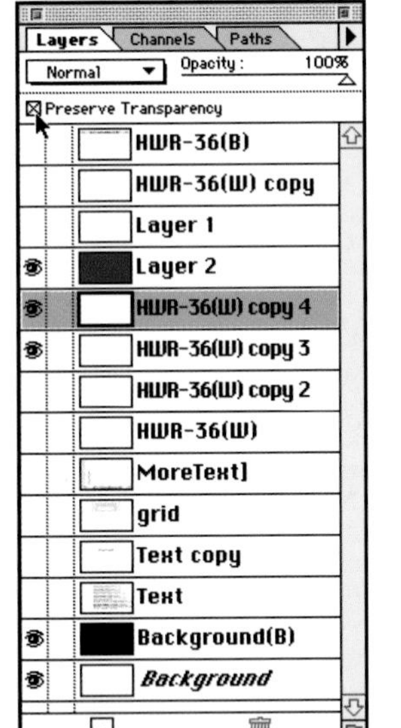

By using the Option+Delete key on a Mac or the Alt+Backspace key on a PC, you can quickly fill with whatever color is set in the foreground color swatch within Photoshop, instead of making an extra trip to the top menu bar to do the same operation. This makes it easy to switch and alter colors, until you arrive at the exact color you like.

Browser-Safe Color Advice

The Hollywood Records site was created before the browser-safe colors were identified. It would have been much better to choose hexadecimal colors from the browser-safe palette, because colors that are outside that palette will shift from platform to platform on 8-bit displays.

Remember, browser-safe colors do not shift between platforms. If you look at the colors chosen within the <BODY> tag of the HTML for Hollywood Records' home page, you will see that they are not browser-safe. Browser-safe colors are always combinations of 0s, Fs, Cs, 3s, 6s, and 9s. FFCC99, for example, is an obvious browser-safe color. The colors chosen on the Hollywood Records site, <BODY BGCOLOR="#090301" TEXT="#436E58" LINK="#CF7B42" VLINK="#323172" ALINK= "#ffffff">, are not browser-safe (except for the FFFFFF).

Also keep in mind that while many designers use Macs to design their work, most end viewers use PCs. There are differences between Macs and PCs that have to do with monitor gamma, which is the contrast and brightness of your monitor. Typically, PC monitors are substantially darker than Mac monitors. Sites with dark text against dark backgrounds tend to loose their contrast and readability when viewed on a PC. In this case, the dark blue VLINK color (323172) becomes unreadable (almost invisible!) against the near black BGCOLOR (090301) when viewed on a PC.

Refer to the browser-safe color charts in the appendix of this book to view the 216 colors that work reliably between platforms. For a much more in-depth explanation of the charts, how to use them, and gamma differences among platforms, consult the chapters "Color Palette Hell" and "Fun with Hex" in my first book, *Designing Web Graphics*.

The colors look one way on a Mac system in 256 colors.

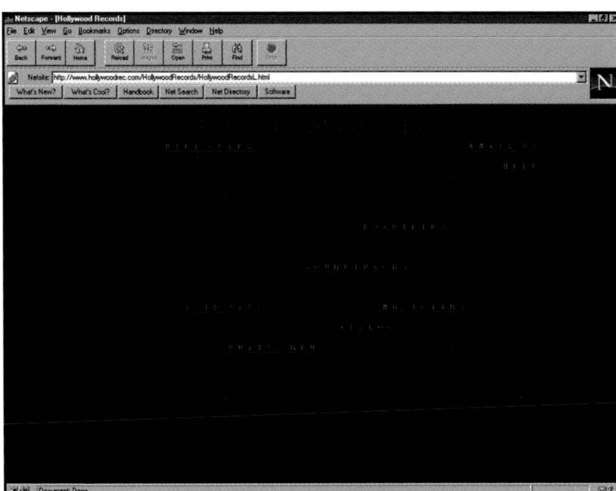

They have shifted on a PC viewed in 256 colors. If browser-safe colors had been used this would not have happened!

Using GIFscii

During the process of painfully creating the ASCII code for the site, Chauncy stumbled across a tiny application called GIFscii on the AOL graphics software library forum that came to the ASCII design process rescue. You can download GIFscii from ■ http://www.erg.cuhk.hk/~stdtadm/freeware/freeware.html. (There's also a program for PCs that functions much like GIFscii. It's called GIFASC.EXE, by Chris O'Donnell 70431.1427@compuserve.com, shareware $15.)

GIFscii is a simple program that translates a GIF image into ASCII characters. It looks to contrast, value, and shape within the source image, and automatically assigns the best possible ASCII characters to that image.

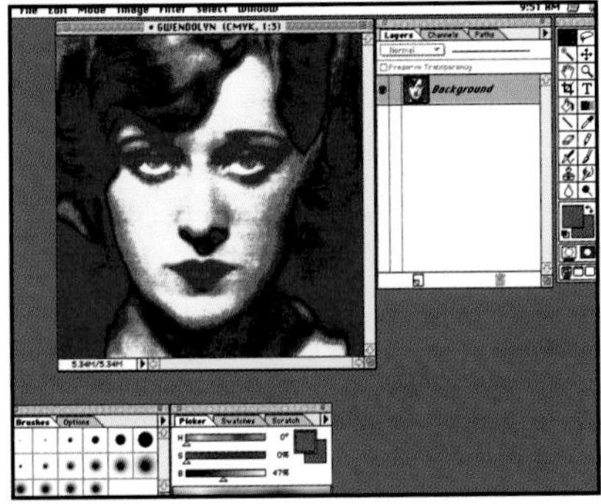

The band Gwen Mar's album cover art in CMYK at print resolution.

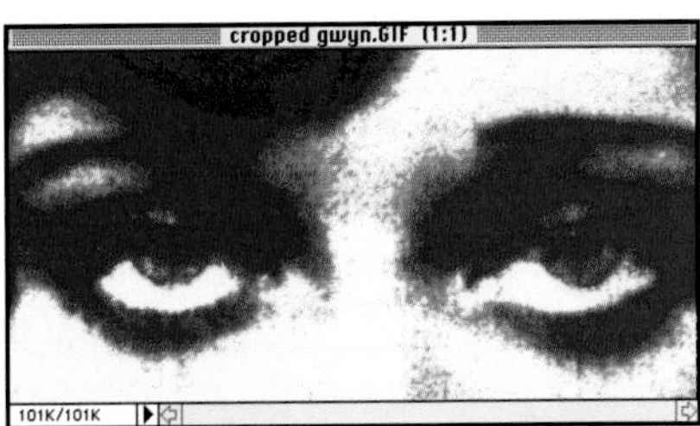

The image was reduced in size, cropped, changed to 72 dpi, reduced to 8 colors in Indexed Color Mode, and saved as a GIF file.

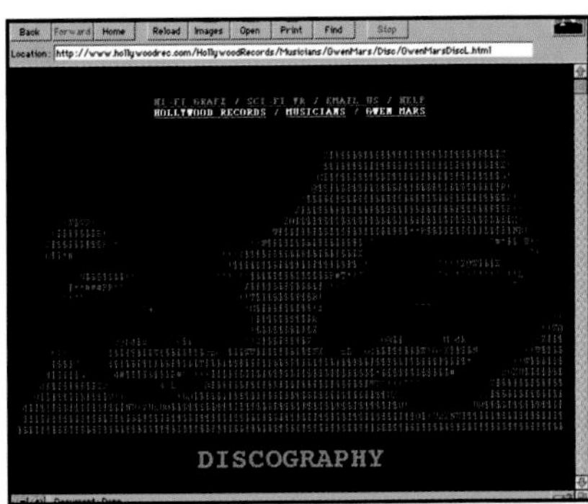

The ASCII art version of the album cover, created with the GIFscii program. The code for this screen is on the following page.

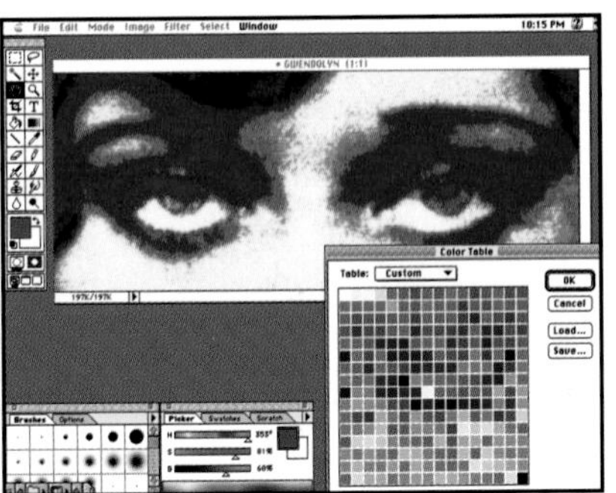

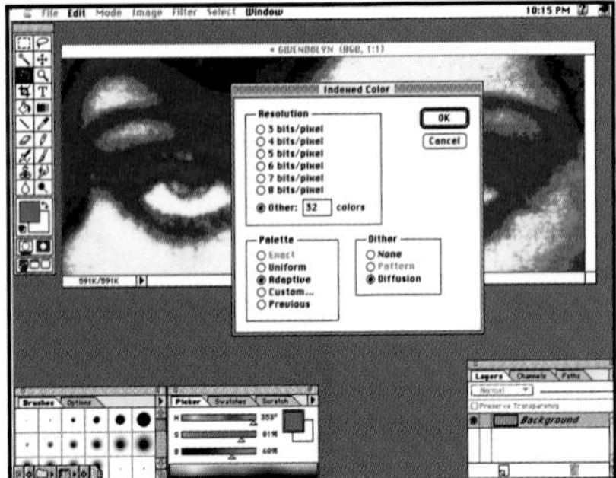

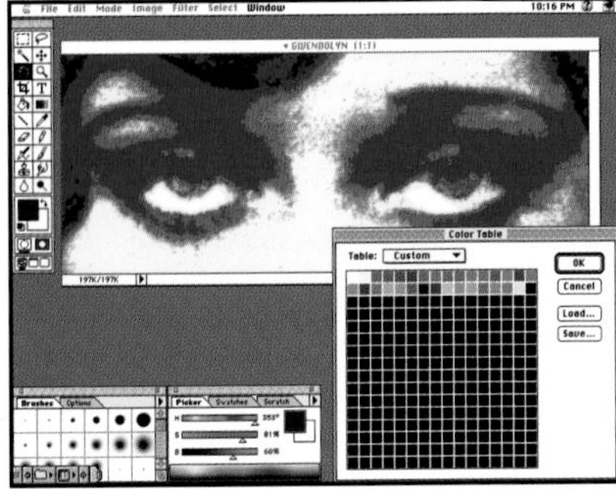

You can change the number of colors in a Photoshop document by typing in your own values when the Index Color dialog box appears. First, change the Mode menu to Indexed Color. Then, type 32 colors into the dialog box. The last image shows the results. GIFscii will have a much easier time converting the graphic to ASCII if there are fewer colors.

```
<HTML>
<HEAD>
<TITLE>GWEN MARS Discography</TITLE>
</HEAD>
<BODY TEXT="#A99A05" LINK="#A99A05" VLINK="#FFFFFF" BGCOLOR="#001000">
<CENTER>
<PRE>
<FONT SIZE=+0>
<B>
<A HREF="/HollywoodRecords/Musicians/GwenMars/Disc/GwenMarsDiscM.html">HI-FI GRAFX</A> /
        <A HREF="/HollywoodRecords/Musicians/GwenMars/GwenMarsV.html">SCI-FI VR</A> /
                <A HREF="/Note">EMAIL US</A> / <A HREF="/Help">HELP</A>
<A HREF="/HollywoodRecords/HollywoodRecordsL.html">HOLLYWOOD RECORDS</A> /
        <A HREF="/HollywoodRecords/Musicians/MusiciansL.html">MUSICIANS</A> /
                <A HREF="/HollywoodRecords/Musicians/GwenMars/GwenMarsL.html">GWEN MARS</A>
</B>
</FONT>
</PRE>
<PRE>
                                          `                X$$$$$$$$$$$$$$$$$$$$$$$$$$$$$$X
                        -.                                :$$$$$$$$$$$$$$$$$$$$$$$$$$$$$$$X!
                                                         .M$$$$$$$$$$$$$$$$$$$$$$$$$$$$$$$&!
                                                        .@$$$$$$$$$$$$$$$$$$$$$$$$$$$$$$$$R!
                                                       !$$$$$$$$$$$$$$$$$$$$$$$$$$$$$$$$$$X!
                                                     :X$$$$$$$$$$$$$$$$$$$$$$$$$$$$$$$$$$$R!!
        .!W$WW!:                                   X@$$$$$$$$$$$$$$$$$$$$$$$$$$$$$$$$$$$$M!
      !$$$$$$$B!:                              :W$$$$$$$$$$$$$$$$$$$$$$$**R$$$$$$$$$$$$$$$NB!.
     X$$$$$$$$$R!!-                       ..!!!W$$$$$$$$$$$$$$$$$$"~                    `"#*$$!W!!
     t$$*#`                              !!!X$$$$$$$$$$$$$$$$$$$$$X:                   :       `~!
    '!`        ...                      !!!$$$$$$$$$$$$$$$$$$$$$$$!!               '!!!X@W$$$X::
        .:U$$$$$$$!!.                  !!!!!!$$$$$$$$$$$$$$$R#T*!~              `~!!!!!!!!!!!!!L
       .!$**###RR!~`~                   '`!!X$$$$$$$$$$$$$$!!!~                     `~ ` ~
       `~!~~                                 !!T$$$$$$$$$$B!.
                     '  ~4.                   !M$$$$$$$$$$!f                 ..~~~
                                              '!$$$$$$$$$$k                                        !!
                                              '!$$$$$$$$$$X                                      '!!W@
                 x@bd$x    ..u$i.      ..:!!X$$$$$$$$X.             u@$$  :   .M!dk            !X$$$
      tX!      :$$$$$$$$W$$$$$$$$xzc $$$WW$$$$$$$$$$$WX!::zB  ud$$$$$$$$W!@!X$$$$N           !!W$$$$
      $$$$W:    `$$$$$$$$$$$$$$$$T$$$$$$$$$$$$$$$$$$$$$$$$$$$$$$$$$$$$$$$$$$$$$$$*`        !!W$$$$$$
     d$$$$$&:    '4#$$$$$$$$$R#" !!!$$$$$$$$$$$$$$$$$$$$$$$$$$$$$$$$*$$$$$$$$$$$$#        :xuXU$$$$$$$
    d$$$$$$$$$$Xx. ' -  . 4!L    !@$$$$$$$$$$$$$$$$$$$$$$$$$$$$$$$$WX!!!!~~~ `          X$$$$$$$$$$$$$
  .@$$$$$$$$$$$$$W!!         `!U@$$$$$$$$$$$$$$$$$$$$$$$$$$$$$$$$$$$$$$UX!            .!$$$$$$$$$$$$$$
 d$$$$$$$$$$$$$$$$$NU!XUxU@$$$$$$$$$$$$$$$$$$$$$$$$$$$$$$$$$$$$$$$$$$$$U!.          :U@$$$$$$$$$$$$$$$
:$$$$$$$$$$$$$$$$$$$$$$$$$$$$$$$$$$$$$$$$$$$$$$$$$$$$$$$$$$$$$$$$$$$$$$$@$!UxXNW$$$$$$$$$$$$$$$$$
$$$$$$$$$$$$$$$$$$$$$$$$$$$$$$$$$$$$$$$$$$$$$$$$$$$$$$$$$$$$$$$$$$$$$$$$$$$$$$$$$$$$$$$$$$$$$$$$$$
</PRE>
<FONT SIZE=+5><B><CODE>DISCOGRAPHY</CODE></B></FONT><P>
</HTML>
```

The ASCII code almost looks identical to the GIFscii data. The GIFscii results are simply inserted between a <pre> and </pre> tag to maintain its original appearance.

■ step-by-step

How to use GIFscii for Web Pages

Step 1: Save an image as a GIF. Important Note: The fewer colors in the original GIF, the better for GIFscii. It will choke on files with 256 colors. A good maximum would be 32 colors, and an even better number would be 8 colors or less.

Step 2: Launch GIFscii.

Step 3: GIFscii will prompt you with: What is the name of the GIF file?

Step 4: Type the name of the file exactly how it appears in the directory. Press the Return key. Note: The GIF image must be stored in the same folder directory as the program GIFscii.

Step 5: GIFscii will generate a lot of automatic data, and then prompt you again: How many columns to create? If you don't specify how many columns, it will create as many columns wide as your image is in pixels. You can either accept the default by pressing Return, or enter a value of how wide you want the resulting ASCII art file to be and press the Return key. You can also press the return key without a specified value and it will default to the width of the image.

Step 6: GIFscii will then prompt you again: How many lines to create? If you don't specify how many lines, it will create as many lines down as your image is in pixels. Enter a value and press the Return key, or just hit Return with no specified value.

Step 7: Press the key "v" (for view) and Return. The image will appear. Copy and paste the image into an HTML editor.

■ GIFscii shortcut commands are case-sensitive and recognize different commands for capital and lowercase of the same letter. Here are other command keys.

```
v = View The Gif
z = Zoom In On The Center
Z = Zoom Out To Normal Size
s = Save to disk
l/L = Pan Left
r/R = Pan Right
u/U = Pan Up
d/D = Pan Down
I = Invert Black/White
c = Decrease Contrast
C = Increase Contrast
b = Decrease Brightness
B = Increase Brightness
A = Animate vt100 Screen Reveal
X = Toggle between min/max ascii sets
Any other character will quit
```

Step 8: Add the header information to the HTML:

```
<HTML>
<HEAD>
<TITLE>Insert the name of your page here</TITLE>
</HEAD>
<BODY BGCOLOR= Insert hex colors for background,
text, links, and so on here >
<PRE>
Insert the pasted GIFscii output here.
</PRE>
</BODY>
</HTML>
```

Step 9: Convert all the illegal HTML ASCII characters to "entities," or replace them with legal HTML characters. Certain ASCII characters cannot display within HTML without being translated to different code. (See the list of entities on page 45.)

Entities and ASCII Art

Certain ASCII characters are reserved in HTML for code functions. If GIFscii automatically produces some of these illegal characters, they will not appear properly within your HTML document.

You can do one of two things to remove illegal ASCII characters from your HTML. Convert the illegal characters to legal characters, or use the entity equivalent of that character. For example, the bracket symbol "<" (without quotes), understandably reserved for HTML tags, would be coded as "<" (without quotes). To the right is a list of more entities:

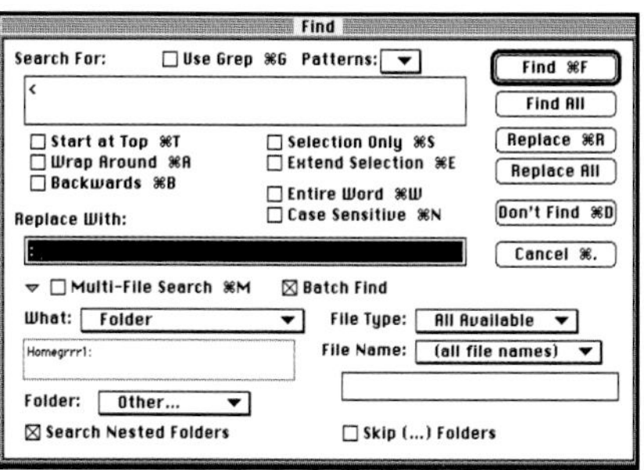

Using a text editor with search and replace functions is the easiest way to convert illegal ASCII characters into characters that will be recognized in HTML. The Hollywood Records' team used BBEdit ■ www.barebones.com, as shown in this example.

Universal Entities

The first four entities are supported by virtually all Web browsers. The rest of them are supported in various combinations by different browsers. The current release of Netscape Navigator (3.0) seems to support them all. This is the first browser I've seen that does.

Description	Numeric	Named Entity
quotation mark	" --> "	" --> "
ampersand	& --> &	& --> &
less-than sign	< --> <	< --> <
greater-than sign	> --> >	> --> >

The Rest of the Entities:

&	&	Ò	Ò	ï	ï	¬	
<	<	Ø	Ø	ñ	ñ		–
>	>	Õ	Õ	ó	ó	®	®
"	"	Ö	Ö	ô	ô	¯	¯
©	©	Þ	fi	ò	ò	°	°
®	®	Ú	Ú	ø	ø	±	±
&Aelig;	Æ	Û	Û	õ	õ	²	2
Á	Á	Ù	Ù	ö	ö	³	3
Â	Â	Ü	Ü	ß	ß	´	´
À	À	Ý	†	þ	fl	µ	µ
Å	Å	á	á	ú	ú	¶	¶
Ã	Ã	â	â	û	û	·	·
Ä	Ä	æ	æ	ù	ù	¸	¸
Ç	Ç	à	à	ü	ü	¹	|
Ð	‹	å	å	ý	‡	º	°
É	É	ã	ã	ÿ	ÿ	»	»
Ê	Ê	ä	ä	¡	¡	¼	π
È	È	ç	ç	¢	¢	½	∏
Ë	Ë	é	é	£	£	¾	≤
Í	Í	ê	ê	¥	¥	¿	¿
Î	Î	è	è	¦	|	×	x
Ì	Ì	ð	›	§	§	Þ	fi
Ï	Ï	ë	ë	¨	¨	÷	÷
Ñ	Ñ	í	í	©	©		
Ó	Ó	î	î	ª	ª		
Ô	Ô	ì	ì	«	«		

Contrast and Brightness in ASCII Art

It's possible to drastically change the results of an image conversion within the GIFscii program by adjusting the contrast and brightness of an image, or painting on the image. Here are some examples of images that were altered in Photoshop and then converted to ASCII art using GIFscii.

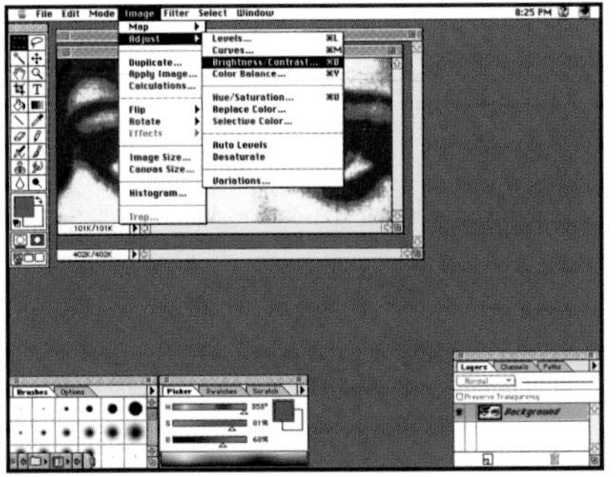

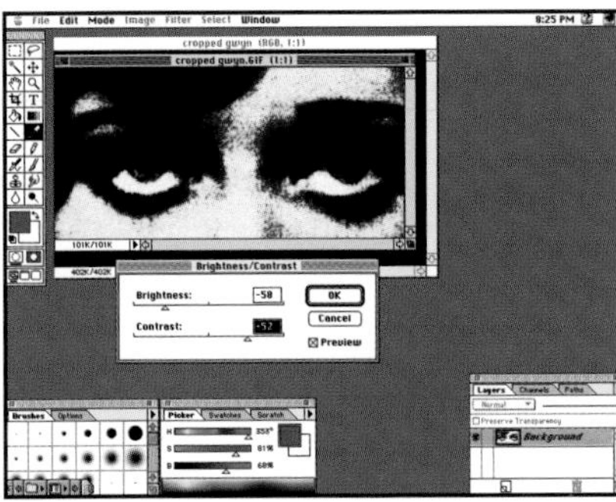

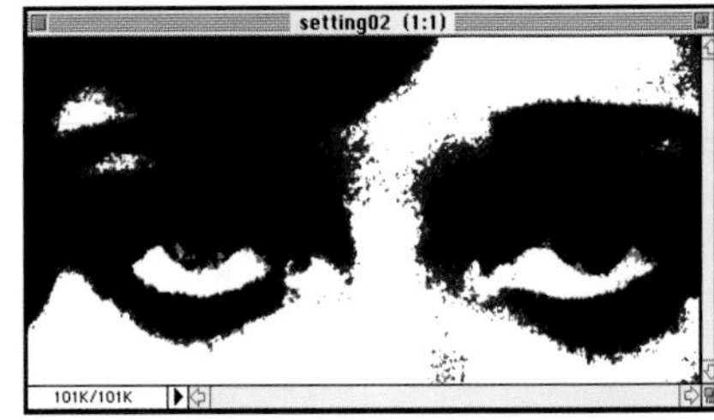

Changing the contrast changes the ASCII.

Photoshop enables you to easily adjust the contrast and brightness of an image. Go to the Adjust menu and select Brightness and Contrast. Playing with the sliders with the preview button checked will enable you to see the results before you commit.

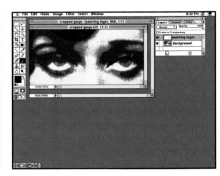

Higher contrast in the original GIF changes the ASCII art that GIFscii generates.

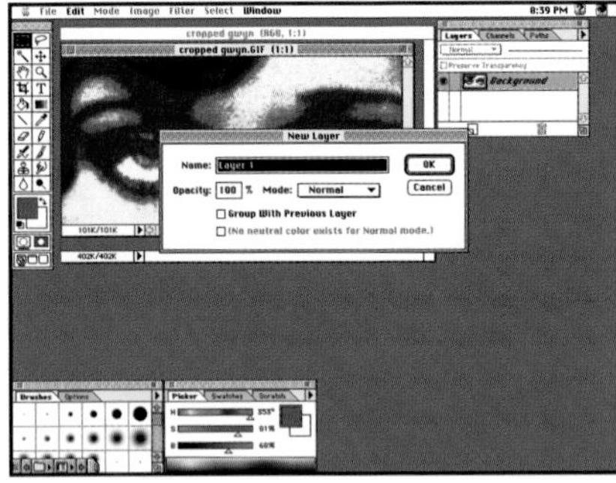

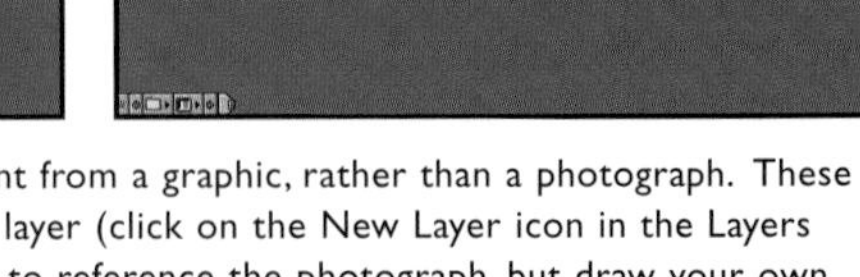

You might also try making a GIFscii document from a graphic, rather than a photograph. These screens show the process of creating a new layer (click on the New Layer icon in the Layers palette) and painting on it. This enables you to reference the photograph, but draw your own image instead on a transparent layer.

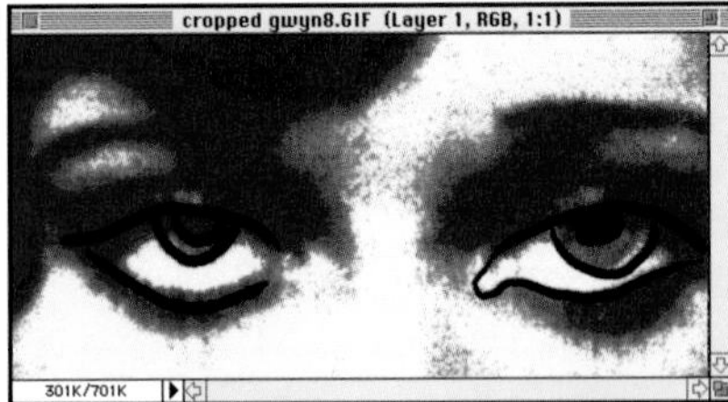

Here's an example that was painted using a transparent layer over the original image in Photoshop. A pressure sensitive stylus was used to get the thick and thin lines.

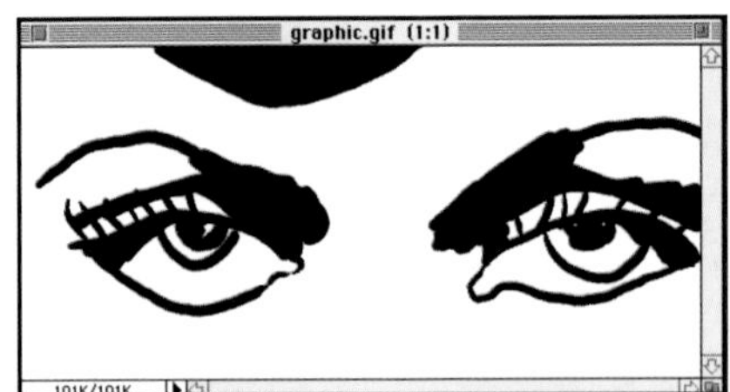

Turn off the layer with the photograph to see the finished painted graphic. Save it as a GIF so GIFscii can do its handiwork!

The finished ASCII art from a high-contrast, more graphical source will read the best.

More Fun with GIFs—Animating with Sprites

The GIF file format is the subject of speculation these days, because a company called Unisys owns the patent on the algorithm that implements the Lempel-Ziv (LZW) compression used in GIF files and has decided to charge a license fee. What this means is that vendors who write programs that create GIF files (and charge money for those programs) must pay a license fee to Unisys. Many predict this will be the demise of GIF as a key file format in Web design, but if that day ever comes many Web designers will miss it sorely.

GIFs can do a few things that other Web graphic image file formats cannot—one being that a single GIF image can actually store multiple images and those multiple images can play back in sequence over the Web. Not all browsers support GIFs with multiple images in them. Multiple images in GIFs have been part of the specification since GIF87a (the original GIF spec developed in 1987). Animated GIFs existed on CompuServe long before the Web. At the time this chapter was written, the only two browsers that supported animated GIFs were Netscape (2.0 and higher) and Microsoft Internet Explorer.

Making animated GIFs is fairly simple with the proper software. Two applications are widely used by most Web designers:

GIFBuilder (Macintosh), by Yves Piguet
■ http://iawww.epfl.ch/Staff/Yves.Piguet/clip2gif-home/GifBuilder.html)

GIF Construction Kit (MS Windows) by Alchemy Mindworks Ltd.
■ http://www.mindworkshop.com/alchemy/alchemy.html)

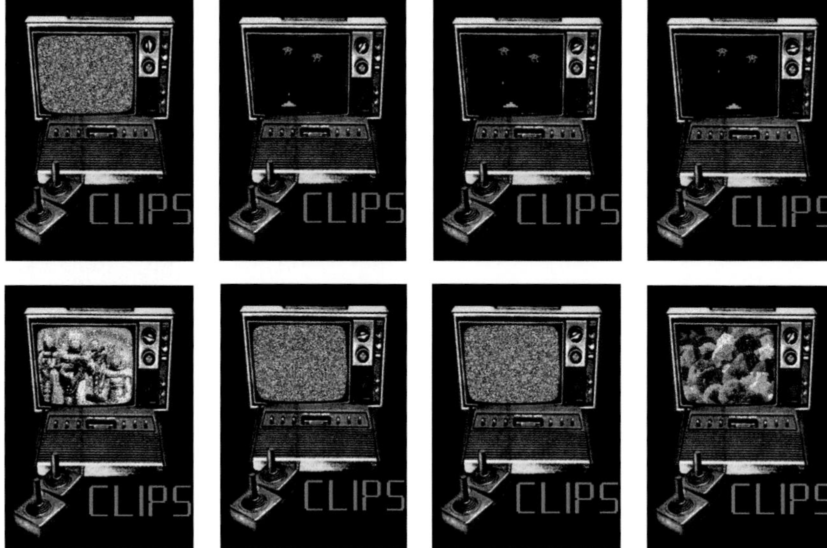

An example of an eight-frame animated GIF produced by Johnny Rodriguez of Disney Online for ■ www.hollywoodrec.com. The background stays stationary while the channel knob rotates as images on the screen flip from video games to television shows.

One of the disadvantages to animated GIFs is that their file sizes can be quite large because they actually store more than one image. When viewed in browsers that support the multi-image format, this is not a problem because the images load individually and display as soon as they load (this is called streaming). This means that even though a subsequent image might be loading, the one before it is already in view, so the download time really only applies to each individual frame of artwork within the multiple image (multi-block) GIF.

The disadvantage to the large file size problem is more apparent in browsers that don't support the multi-block file format. Some of those browsers will load the first frame of the animated GIF, but won't be able to show the other frames. Others load the entire animation before displaying one image, and will then display only the last image. What results is a huge animated GIF file that yields no payoff for being so big because the animation won't play.

It's still important, for this reason, to care about file sizes with animated GIFs. One of the best ways to keep file sizes low is to work with sprite animations, where only the foreground of the GIF changes, and the background is stationary. In this example, the sprite-based version was 74k, while the same animation with full screens changing each frame would have been 224k.

How to Build an Animated GIF Using Sprites and Transparency

The principle of animating sprites follows: instead of full frame images laying on top of each other, sprite animation uses smaller images that overlay on top of a stationary background through using transparency or repositioning.

There's a great example of a sprite animation on the Hollywood Records site. Because the Hollywood Records site is developed on the Macintosh, the design team used the program GIFBuilder. This same sprite-based technique can be used in the PC-based program, GIFConstruction Set for Windows.

In this example, the transparent images were made in a multiple layered Photoshop document where they could be registered to a background, and then saved out as individual files.

You don't have to work with registered files when making animated GIFs. You can also take a small image and move it around in GIFBuilder or GIF Construction Set, which accomplishes the same thing. The idea is you only have to animate what changes, not the static parts, such as a background image.

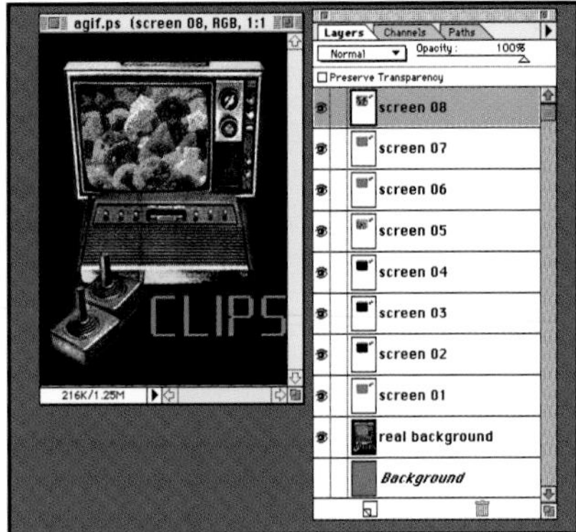

■ The TV screen and channel changer are the only parts of this image that animate. All of the TV screens have been put on separate layers.

Step 1: Put the changing animated frames into a layered Photoshop document. Make sure that the images that change are created against the same background they will be placed over within the final animation. This ensures that the frames will register when the file is converted to play as an animation. [Note: Be sure the images that overlay the background are masked without anti-aliasing. Anti-aliasing introduces fringing along edges of transparent GIFs.]

Step 2: Save this file as a Photoshop 3.0 document. This is an extremely important step. You will be reverting to this file repeatedly.

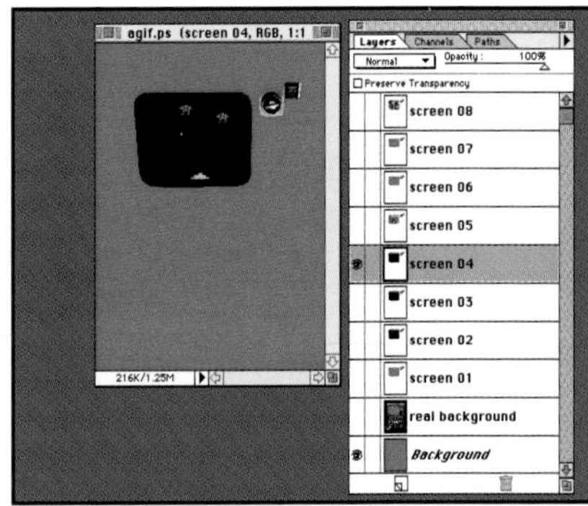

Step 3: Establish a background color that isn't present anywhere else in the image. See how a red layer has been named "background" and put into the bottom position in the layer palette? You can make a background color by selecting a new layer, filling it with a solid color, and positioning it at the bottom of the stack. This color will later serve as a mask to convert the document to be a "transparent" GIF in a future step.

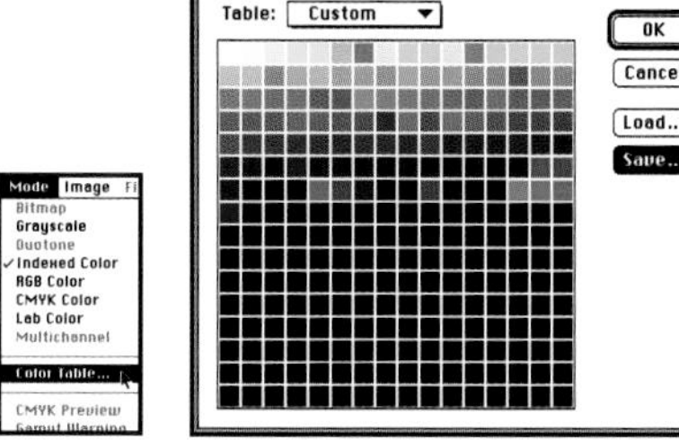

Step 4: Convert the Photoshop document to Indexed Color mode, making sure that all the colors present within all the layers of the document are visible. This step is for the purpose of creating a color palette only. A color palette, otherwise known as a color look up table (CLUT), assigns colors to an image. It's critical that every frame of this sequence of images share the identical palette, and this is the first step to ensure that it does. Save the color table by first converting the image to Index Color Mode. Then, under the Mode menu, select Color Table. You can name and save the color table in the dialog box that appears. It doesn't matter where you store it on your hard drive, just put it someplace safe, so you remember where to retrieve it from. The color table is being saved so it can be loaded into GIFBuilder when these frames are completed and imported.

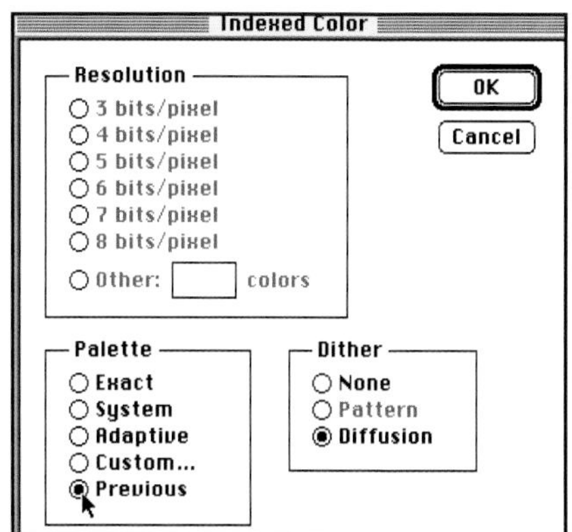

Step 5: Turn on the first layer in the sequence, and change the Mode to Indexed Color. You will be asked to flatten the document. Click yes, and the Index Color Window will appear. Be sure to click the Previous button. This loads and applies the color table palette you established in Step 4. [Note: If you shut down between steps 4 and 5, or have an unexpected system crash, click on Custom, instead of Previous. This allows you to re-load the color table you saved in Step 4.]

Step 6: Under File, choose Save a Copy and choose the CompuServe GIF format. Save the file with the number 01 after the title name. For example: A01.GIF (It's a good idea, even on systems that allow otherwise, to name your GIFs with the .GIF extension, A01.GIF, A02.GIF). Some software applications will require it, especially those earlier versions for the Windows platform.

Step 7: Under the File menu, choose Revert to Saved. This replaces the flattened Indexed Color document with the original Photoshop layered document. The goal is to save all the layers following the instructions from Steps 5 and 6. You should end up with a folder of GIFs that are numbered sequentially, such as A01.GIF.GIF, A02.GIF, A03.GIF. It's critical that the names be identical except for the changing numbers, and that the numbers accurately reflect the order of the animating files.

Step 8: Save the background as a CompuServe GIF, and name it to be the first file. For example: A00.GIF.

■ note

Transparent GIFs

The GIF89a specification actually allows for each frame of the animation to have its own color palette, called a local palette. However, there are two distinct disadvantages to using this technique.

1: The file size will increase and suffer accordingly.
2: Netscape 2.0 doesn't support local palettes and applies the palette only to the first image of the entire animation, which can cause unwanted palette shifting. Currently, only Netscape 3.0 renders multi-palette GIFs correctly.

Step 9: Open GIFBuilder. Each image can be loaded individually, or you can drag and drop all the files into the project window and they will appear in order.

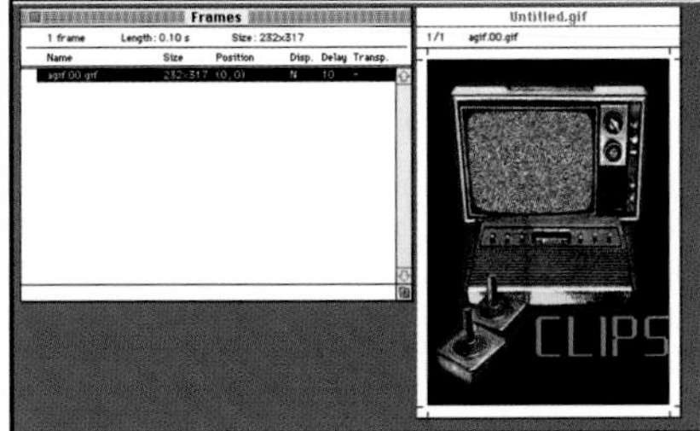

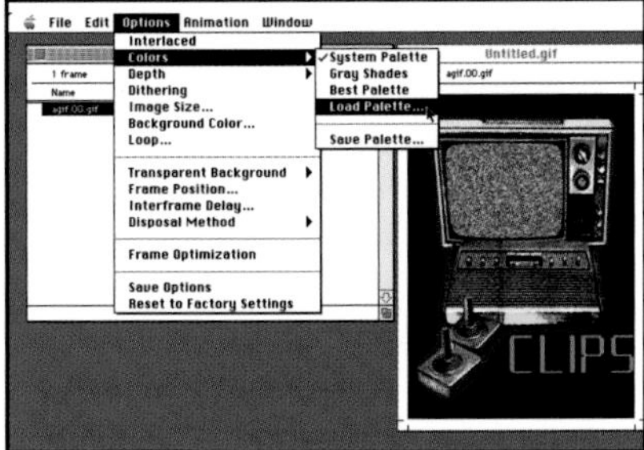

Step 10: You might notice that the colors within the artwork look skewed. That's because you need to load the color table saved in Step 4. Select Load Palette under the Option Color menu and open the CLUT you saved in Photoshop in Step 4.

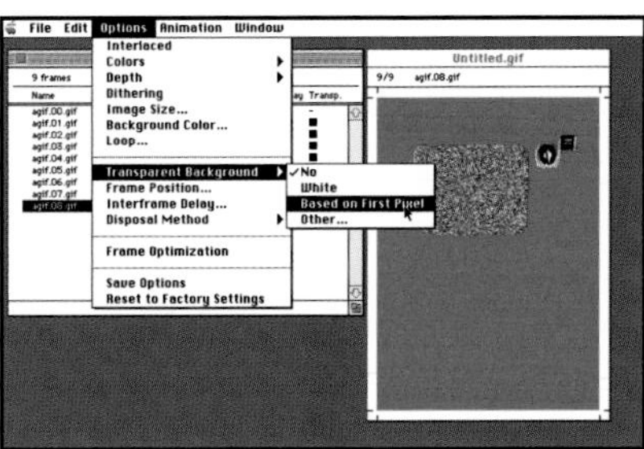

Step 11: Select all the frames that you want to become transparent by holding down the shift key. Under Options, choose Transparent Background, Based on First Pixel. Here's where the red background comes in handy. If you had left the background to this frame white (by setting the transparency to that color), it would have affected other white areas within the image. That's why you pick a color for the background of the transparent frames that doesn't exist elsewhere within the images.

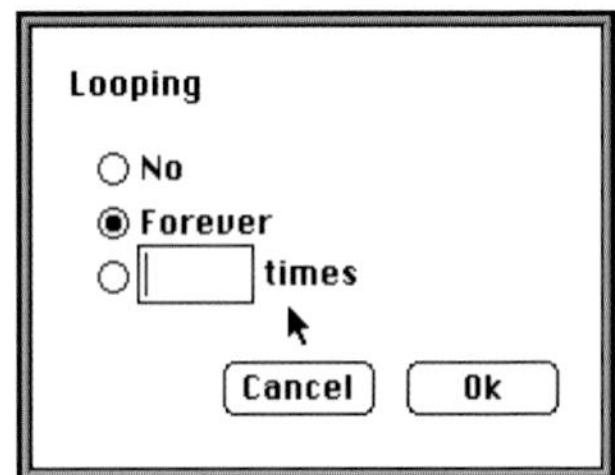

Step 12: If you want the animation to loop, Choose Options, Loop and a dialog box will appear that enables you to set the number of repeats. [Note that specifying the number of repeats (as well as setting delay times) does not work with some beta versions of Netscape 2.0.] Some people like their image to play once only, others want their image to play indefinitely. It's a personal choice. Unlike Server Push (as described in Chapter 8, "Server Push: levi.com"), the number of repeats will have no effect on the server's load. The looping is all happening off the end-user's hard drive, which is great because it doesn't tie up the Internet connection, tax the server, or require the use of CGI scripts, like Server Push.

Step 13: Under the File menu, choose Save As and name the finished multi-block GIF. If you want to test it, you can select Start under the Animation menu.

■ note

Image Maps and Animated GIFs

You can also use an animated GIF as the source for a link or an image map, using the exact same HTML as required for non-animating GIFs. For information related to image maps, refer to Chapter 5, "@tlas."

■ note

Inserting the Animated GIF into the HTML

```
<img src="myanimatedgiffile-
name.gif">
```

Putting the animated GIF into an HTML document is the same as putting any GIF into an HTML document. That's the beauty of animated GIFs!

Steps for PC Users [GIF Construction Set]

To bulild an Animated GIF using Sprites and Transparency on a PC running Windows or Windows 95, replace steps from Step 9 on with the following:

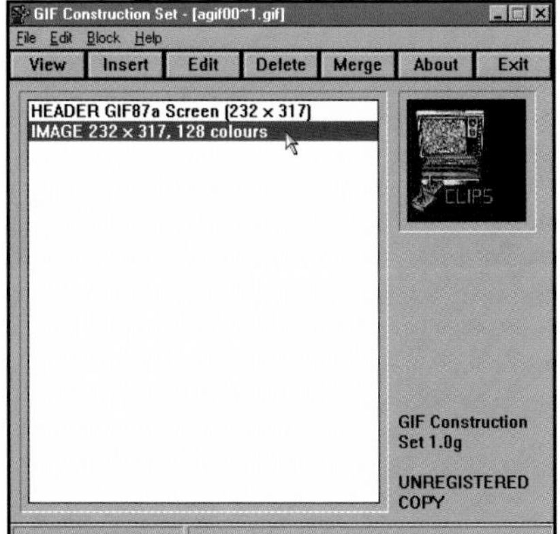

Step 9a: Launch GIF Construction Set, and load the first image of the animation.

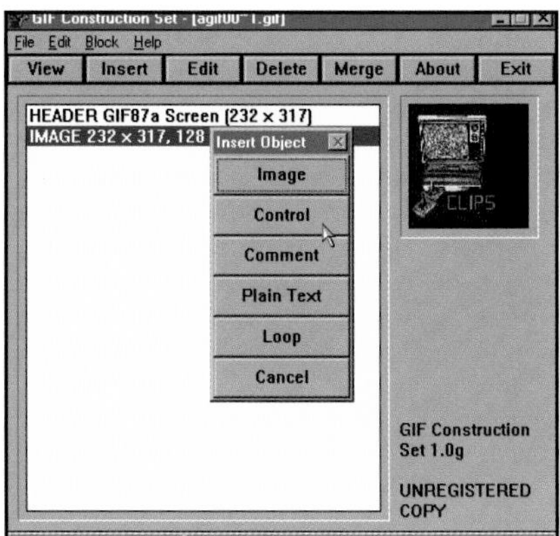

Step 10a: For each of the remaining images, insert a control block and then the image. Press the Insert button, and you will see the Insert Object dialog box. Press the Control button for a control block, and press the Image button to load an image.

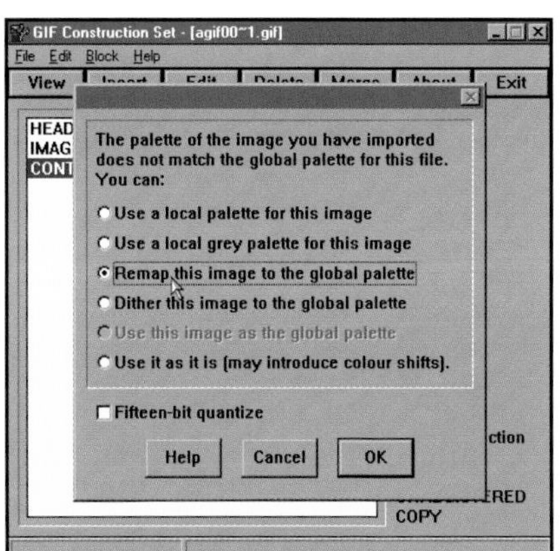

Step 11a: After you load each image, you will be asked what palette to use for that image. Because all of these images were created with the same palette, choose "Remap this image to the global palette." This will ensure that all the images use the same palette, which keeps the file small and prevents palette flicker when displayed.

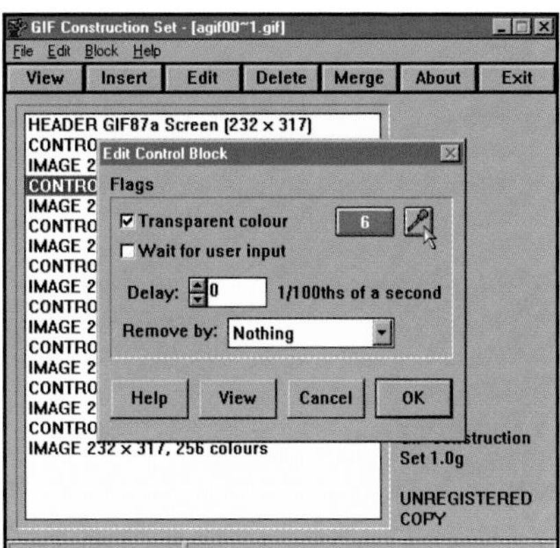

Step 12a: After you load all of your images, your display should look like this. Now go back to each of the control blocks (except the first one, if you have one there), and double-click to edit the information in them. [Note: The control block for each image is the one before the image.]

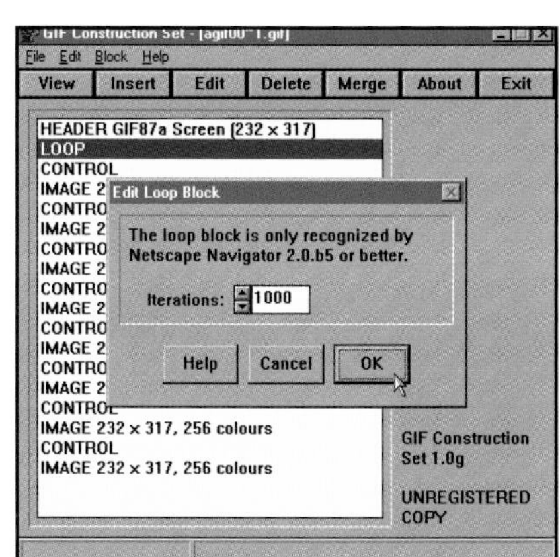

Step 13a: Select the Transparent Color checkbox, then choose the dropper tool and select the color for transparency. The color will show up in the button to the left of the dropper tool. This is also the dialog where you would select any delays you want between frames.

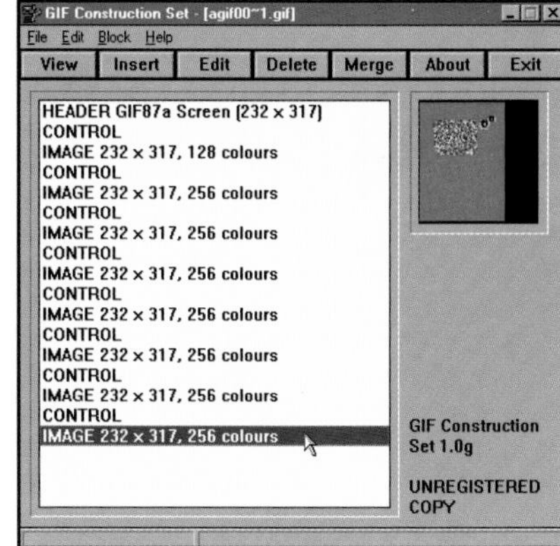

Step 14a: Finally, when you have all of your control blocks set up, you can insert a looping block (looping is a Netscape extension to the GIF specification) by pressing the Insert button and selecting Loop. Keep in mind that the number in this box is the number of times the animation will loop after it has already displayed once. (To display the animation twice, enter a 1 here.)

■ site summary

Hollywood Records

The Hollywood Records site is a hub of fresh ideas and an excellent source of simple techniques for economical Web design methodologies. Here's a summary of what you can learn from their efforts:

■ If you want to use ASCII art, convert all the illegal ASCII characters in HTML to entities or other characters. This can be done with a search-and-replace-enabled text editor.

■ Be sure to use browser-safe colors for ASCII art unless you're willing to accept color shifting across different platforms.

■ The Preserve Transparency feature in Photoshop is an excellent way to change colors on layers quickly.

■ When creating GIF89a animations, using sprites and transparency will produce much smaller file sizes.

Sony Music Online

dynamic pages using lowsrc

What this chapter covers:

- **Black and White Photo Techniques**
- **Designing for Double-Loads: the LOWSRC Trick**
- **Photographic Collage Methods**
- **Working with Simple JavaScript and HTML**

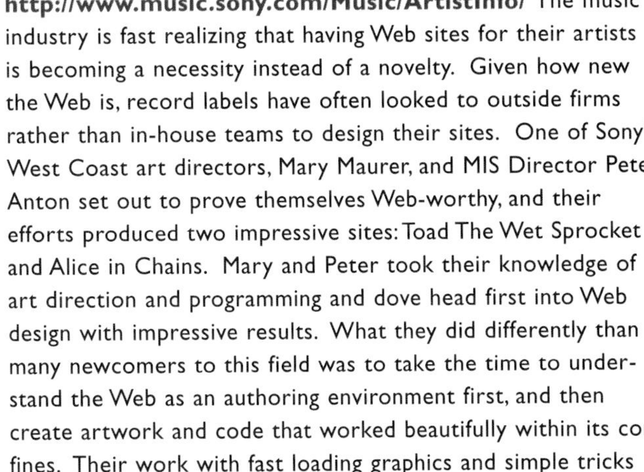

http://www.music.sony.com/Music/ArtistInfo/ The music industry is fast realizing that having Web sites for their artists is becoming a necessity instead of a novelty. Given how new the Web is, record labels have often looked to outside firms rather than in-house teams to design their sites. One of Sony's West Coast art directors, Mary Maurer, and MIS Director Peter Anton set out to prove themselves Web-worthy, and their efforts produced two impressive sites: Toad The Wet Sprocket and Alice in Chains. Mary and Peter took their knowledge of art direction and programming and dove head first into Web design with impressive results. What they did differently than many newcomers to this field was to take the time to understand the Web as an authoring environment first, and then create artwork and code that worked beautifully within its confines. Their work with fast loading graphics and simple tricks with two frame animations should inspire others to follow in their footsteps.

Client: Sony Music Online

URL#1: http://www.music.sony.com/Music/ArtistInfo/Toad/

URL#2: http://www.music.sony.com/Music/ArtistInfo/AliceInChains/

Type of Site: Music Industry

Server: Sun Spark

Operating System: Unix

Server Software: Solaris

Art Director: Mary Maurer

Webmaster: Peter Anton

Software: Photoshop, DeBabelizer, GIFBuilder, WebMap

From Graphics Packaging to Web Packaging

When Mary Maurer, a Los Angles-based Senior Art Director for Sony Music (and person responsible for Toad The Wet Sprocket's packaging and graphics), saw an unofficial site created for the band, a bulb went off. The notion of creating an official site became a pursuit that she shared with Peter Anton, the (then) MIS Director for Sony Records. It seemed that Peter had been aching to get his HTML feet wet too, and the two proceeded to pitch the idea of an official Toad Web site to Sony, who had usually gone out of house for Web design up to that point. Sony accepted their proposal, and the two set on a course that proved very rewarding—especially rewarding in light of the promotion it earned Peter, as the Director of New Media for Sony Music!

Getting approvals and finding the look and feel for a band's identity would normally be a big part of the design process in other circumstances. Mary felt very lucky because she already knew the band's tastes well, after having overseen the production on their two album covers and associated packaging for the past five years. Before begining their site, she looked around the Web for inspiration and didn't care for much of what she saw. Everything looked so computerish, and so predictable and it mostly served to teach her what she didn't want to do.

Mary turned to Peter to ask what the technical limitations were related to creating artwork for the site. Peter told her about low bandwidth graphics and speed considerations, and how fewer colors in images could make the graphics smaller. This fit in well with Mary's plan, who was looking to do something much more along the lines of the "Toad" aesthetic anyway. She wanted something homey and handmade, and decidedly un-computerish in look and feel.

Mary understood well that the graphics had to be small and load fast from her own explorations of the Web. She found herself annoyed at long wait times and wanted to do anything within her power to avoid them. But she also wanted big graphics. Her goal was to fill the screen with custom artwork—not create something disjointed that looked pieced together using boxy images and HTML-based text.

Mary, with Peter's help, arrived at the style of the site. Everything, with few exceptions, was created in black and white. Because most of the artwork was created in only these two colors she was able to make the dimensions of her graphics large while the file sizes remained small.

The opening page of Toad The Wet Sprocket aims for a homemade look and a fast load.

This GIF is only 16.4k, even though it's huge (580×374) by Web standards. It takes a small amount of disk space and downloads quickly because it only contains four levels of gray (3-bit). The same image, if 256 levels of gray (8-bit) had been used would have been 38k, almost 3 times larger!

Continuing with the limited color idea, Mary chose to use red as a contrasting accent color for hypertext and key images. She chose the Fonthaus font "Trixie" for its rough-around-the-edges appearance. By varying the size of the font, she was able to achieve a more friendly and less precise appearance.

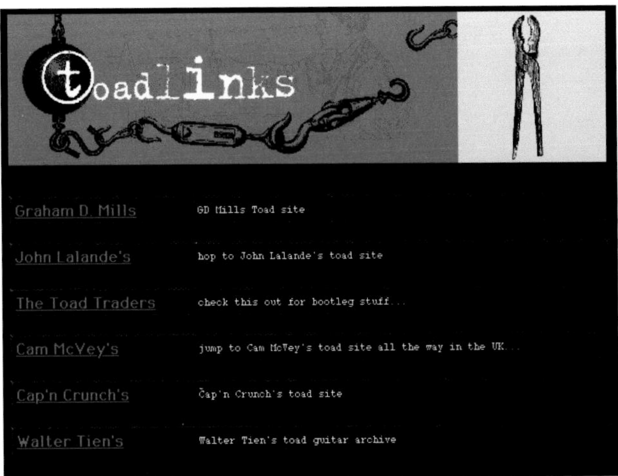

Red was used as an accent color against the stark black and white of the rest of the site. It was used for link colors and certain key graphics.

With the success of Toad under their belts, Mary and Peter moved next to design a site for Alice in Chains using many of the same technques they'd developed for Toad. Between the first and second sites, a few things changed however. The two understood better how to organize a site, and developed a well organized flowchart.

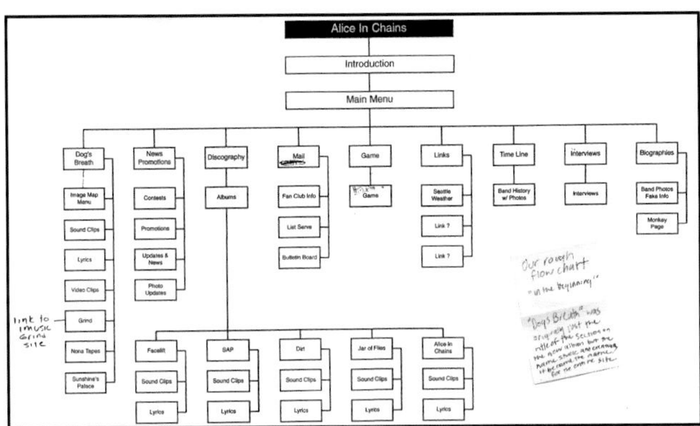

The flowchart for Alice in Chains. With the first site, Toad The Wet Sprocket, under their belts, Peter and Mary understood the importance of having a blueprint for the information flow.

On both sites, rather than copy what was already out there, Mary and Peter created something they could call their own. Mary used a lot of her personal photography for the Alice site, and worked with altering it using Photoshop techniques that are described in this chapter. Much of the imagery used within the Alice in Chains site was taken from vacation photographs Mary had shot in Seattle. She cut out pictures of her friends, and inserted pictures of the band, altered color images to black and white, and used collaging techniques inspired by David Hockney. Her creative process should serve as inspiration to many who think they have to use a stock picture library or clip art to come up with Web images.

With Mary's background as a print designer, working at 72 dpi for the Web was a big change. Because the Web is a "screen-based" medium, artwork should always be prepared at "screen resolution" of 72 dpi. Higher resolutions are reserved for print, because printers can produce artwork with more dots per inch than the screen can.

Mary chose to start with large artwork, as if creating for print, and then reduced her files down to small sizes as a final step. This working methodology came in handy when she was later asked to use graphics from the Web site for promotional print materials. It's easy to reduce graphics in size, but enlarging Web graphics to print resolution would not have worked, as the images would have become fuzzy and unacceptable in quality.

Artwork from the site ended up getting used in print campaigns, too. This sticker was created to promote the Alice in Chains site.

■ note

Photoshop Fun with Hi-Con

Over the course of designing the two sites with the black and white, gritty theme, Mary discovered that there were numerous ways to convert grayscale artwork to high-contrast images. Here are sample images that show some of the options Photoshop offers.

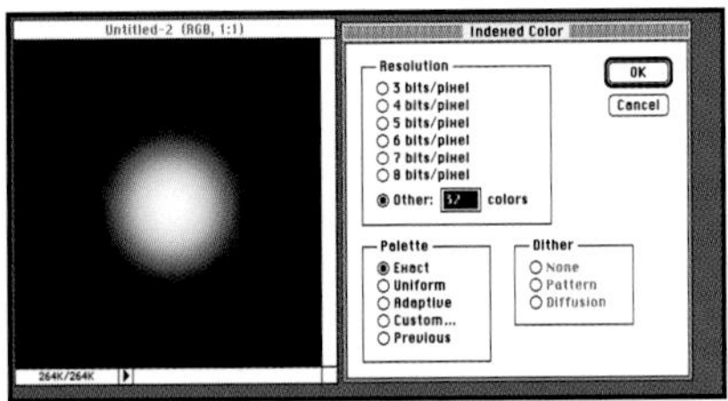

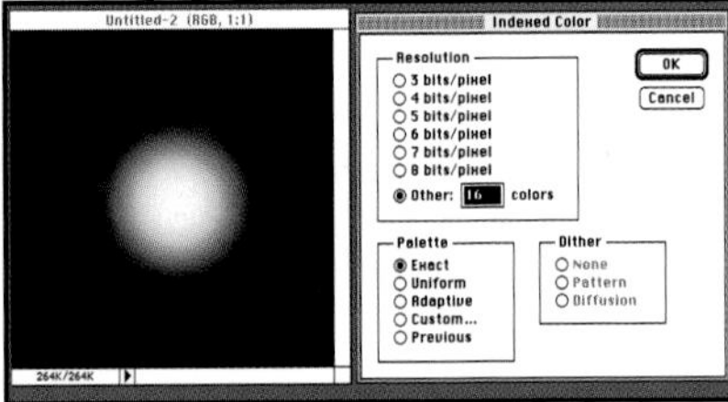

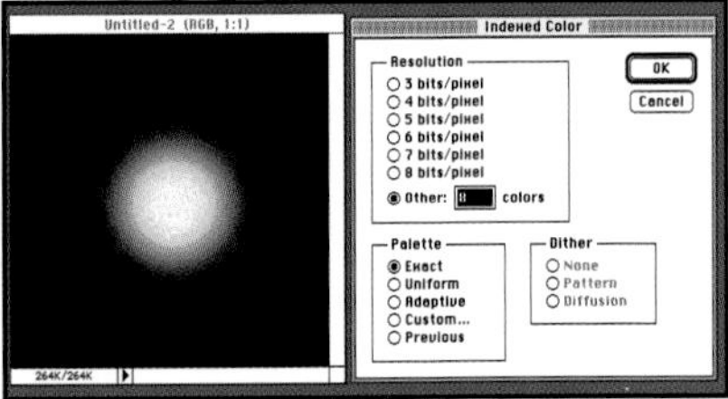

Artwork with glows or gradations converts to grayscale differently than line art, or artwork with a lot of solid areas. These images were converted by changing the mode from RGB to Indexed Color. This technique brings up the Index Color dialog box, where settings can be specified such as number of colors and whether the method uses dithering or not. These samples were made using 32, 16, and 8 colors. With diffusion dither checked, the edges of the glow become more and more gritty depending on how few levels are used.

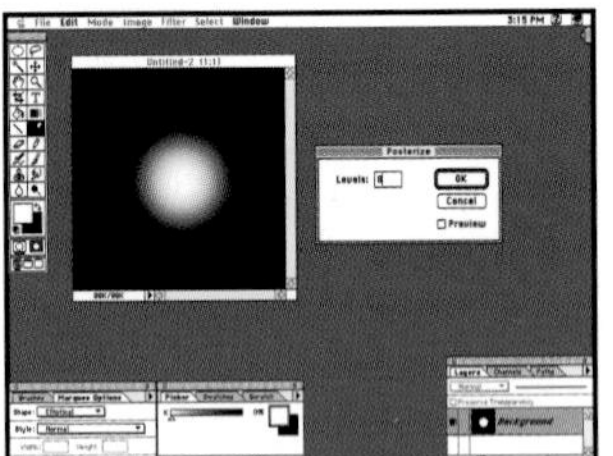

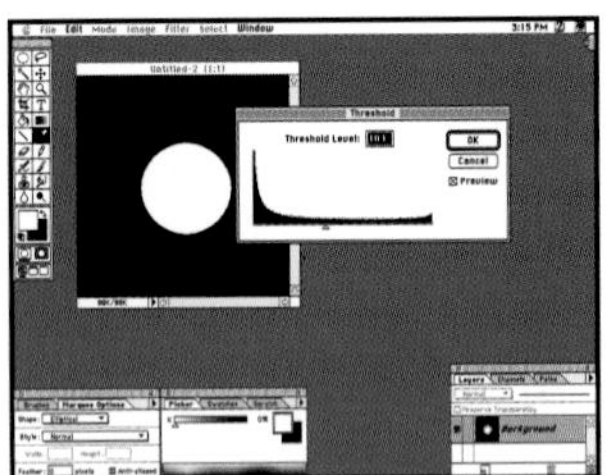

These images were made using the Adjust, Map menu command. The first is a Map, Posterize effect set to 8 levels and the second is a Map, Threshold effect. You can see that glows don't work when set to any level of Threshold.

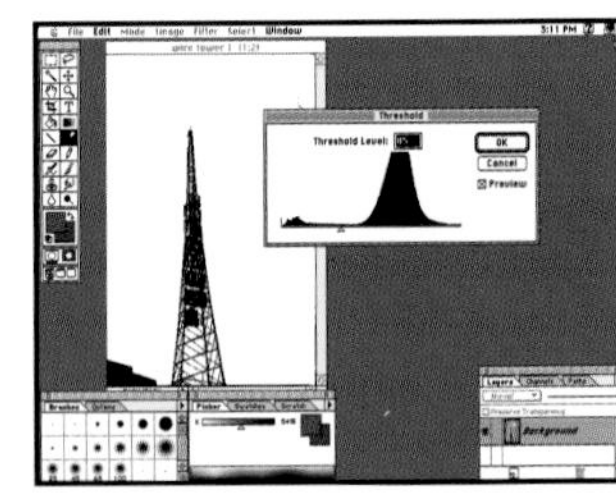

These examples show the results of using the Adjust, Map, Threshold menu command. The nice thing about this technique (which works very well on images that don't have glows or gradations) is you can adjust the slider before commiting to the effect.

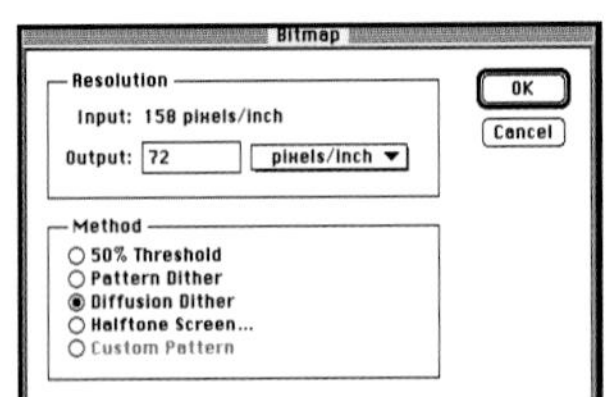

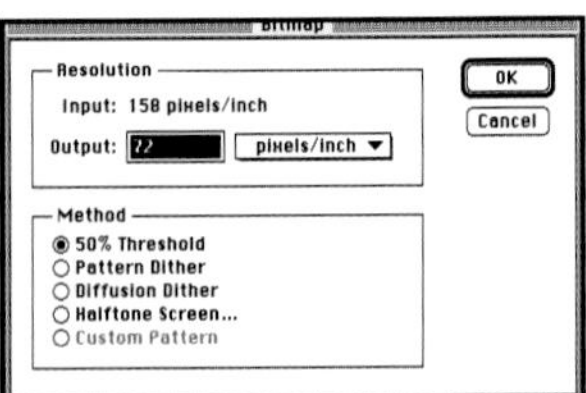

Another way to access threshold is to change Grayscale to Bitmap in the Mode menu. You are prompted to choose different settings. Mary alternated, depending on what she felt was appropriate, between diffusion dither and threshold methods. Keep in mind that when saving to GIF, anything with a "dither" or noise will compress more poorly than images with areas of flat color. The GIF compression scheme works most effectively on images with areas of flat color.

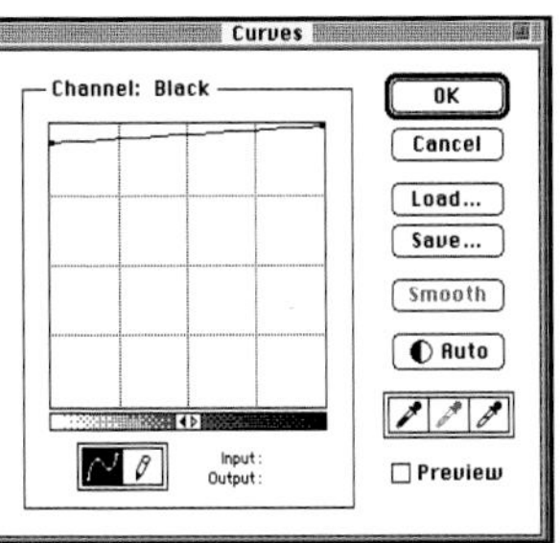

You can also choose Curves from the Adjust menu to affect black and white output. In this example, Mary took a photo of an old scrabble set, and converted it to custom typography for the site. Using the eyedroppers on the bottom right of the Curves dialog box will transform whatever you click on to either black, white, or middle gray. This is another way of controlling the level of high contrast within an image.

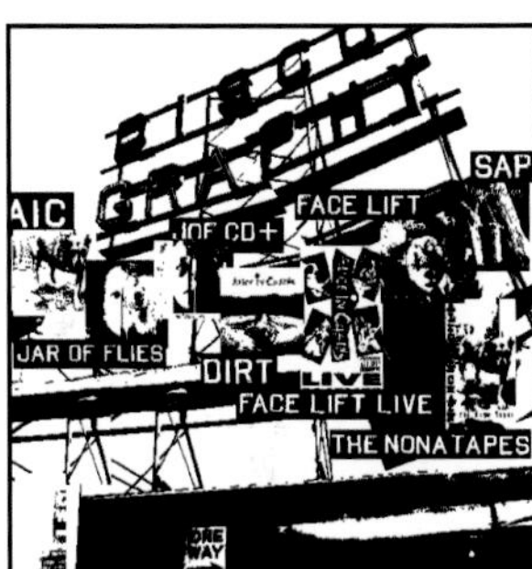

In this example, Mary took her vacation photos of Seattle's Pike Street Market, and assembled them in a David Hockney-like collage. She scanned and converted the results to high contrast images, and altered the signage using type she scanned from a children's letterforms set. After dropping in album art for some of Alice in Chains' titles, she took the entire finished collage into high contrast mode.

Here's another example of a vacation photo used on the site. The fresh fish sign was converted to high-contrast black and white using curves and the type "Bottom Feeder" was inserted.

For the ultimate in high-contrast fun, Mary inserted one of the Alice and Chains bandmembers inside a clip art illustration found in a book.

Animated GIFs using Hi-Con Artwork

Mary and Peter used the program GIFBuilder for their animated GIFs. You can read more about creating files using GIFBuilder (and GIF Construction Set for PC users) in Chapter 3, "Hollywood Records." This chapter concentrates more on the artistic content of these animated GIFs, and how the individual frames were designed.

Mary's goal was to create a "junkyard" of images, which would form the main page of the site. She approached Peter to "make it come alive." Even though it was a big graphic, Peter suggested the blinking signage idea, and they settled on a four-frame animation cycle to make the neon effect.

Mary and Peter created the animation artwork using a variety of images, most of which she shot herself. Using the hi-con techniques described earlier (adjusting Curves or Threshold or converting to Bitmap mode), they assembled a composite of black and white images with and without glows. Glows were then added on top of the black and white artwork using the Black Box Photoshop filter "Glow" from AlienSkin Software (■ http://www.alienskin.com/alien/). By alternating the glowing artwork with non-glowing artwork, she created a wonderful illusion of blinking neon signs.

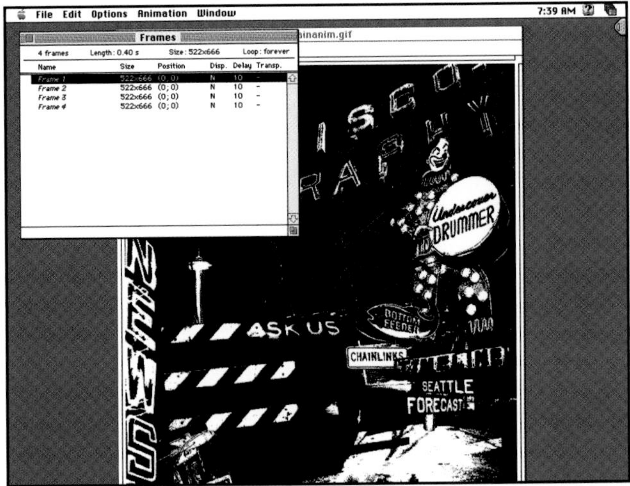

The main screen interface animation has four frames, set to 10 unit delays, with no transparency. The animated GIF was set to loop continuously. You can view this URL at: ■ http://www.music.sony.com/Music/ArtistInfo/AliceInChains/main.html

The four individual frames, if studied, show the different blinking signage, and how the artwork was designed to make blinking events occur in different locations with different timings on the screens. For example, look at how the sign "Undercover Drummer" glows in frame 3. Notice how the sign "Bottom Feeder" glows in frames 1 and 2. Mary and Peter experimented with turning glows on and off in this sequence to give the illusion of blinking neon. The Black Box Glow filter from Alien Skin (■ http://www.alienskin.com/alien/) and high contrast Photoshop techniques were used to create this artwork.

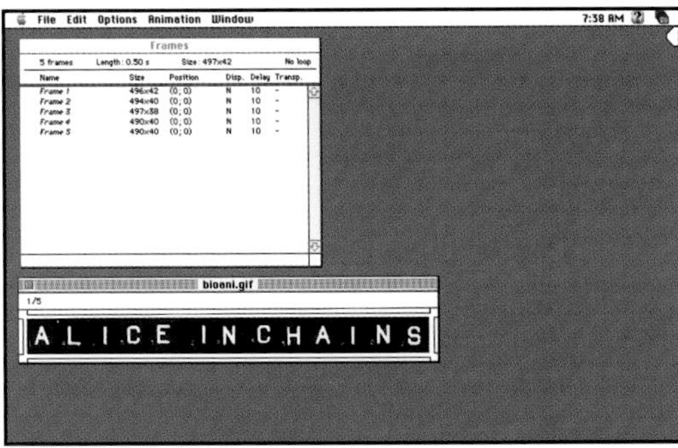

The Alice in Chains scrabble animation is composed of five frames, all with 10 unit delays. This animation was set to only play once. To see it play, check out the URL: ■ http://www.music.sony.com/Music/ArtistInfo/ AliceInChains/ bio.html

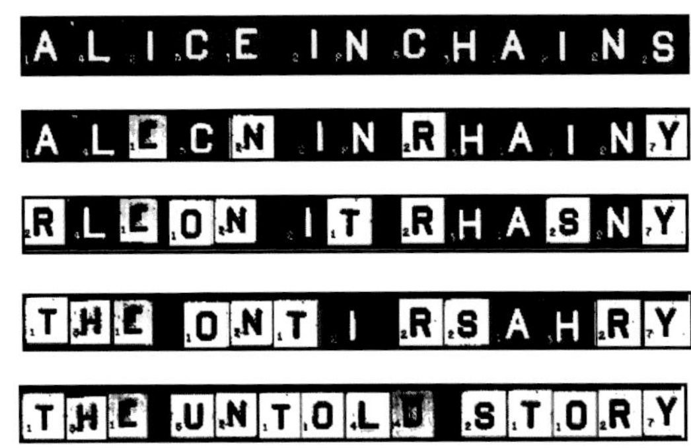

The five different screens. The placement of the letters causes them to look scrambled until they resolve into readiblity.

■ step-by-step

Creating a Neon Glow for GIF Animation

Step 1: Mary assembled letters from a children's toy set she collected and created a Photoshop document that spelled out the word NEWS, with the letters stacked vertically.

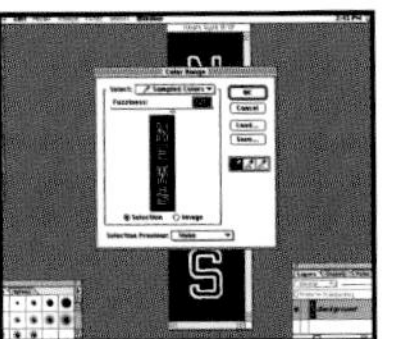

Step 2: Using the menu Select, Color Range, Mary was able to select the white areas of the inside of the letters.

Step 3: Mary dragged the letters into a separate document of a tower. By choosing the Image menu, Effect, Distort, she was able to change the shape of the letters to match the perspective of the tower.

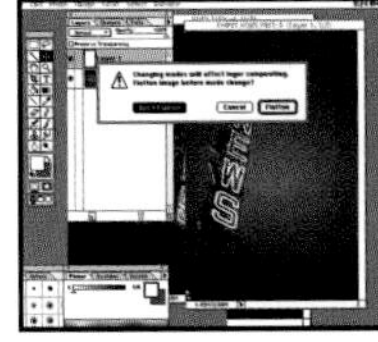

Step 4: Peter converted Mary's image to RGB in order to work with filters. It's not possible to apply filters in Indexed Color or Grayscale Mode. He chose to not flatten layers because she would be using the layers later for animation purposes.

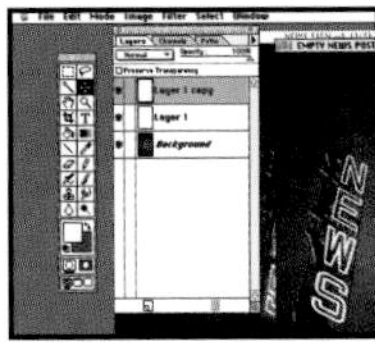

Step 5: Peter created another layer in order to apply a glow filter to one, and leave the other without a glow. This would enable him to create "blinking" artwork later.

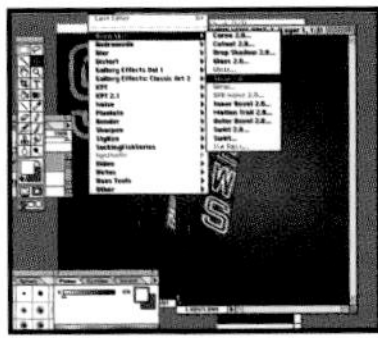

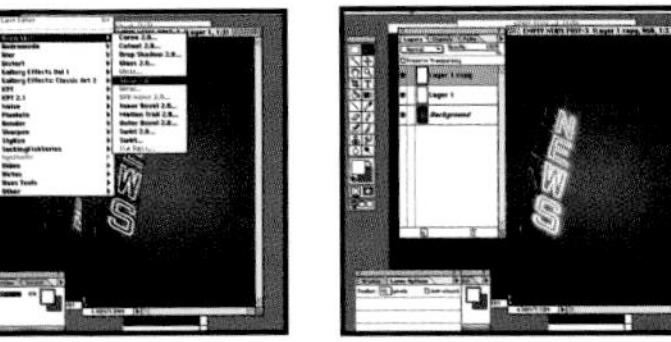

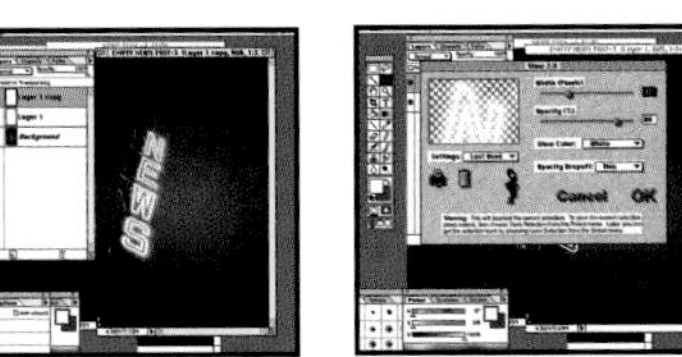

Step 6: Peter used the Black Box filter "Glow" by Alien Skin for the neon glow effect. By creating the glow on one layer, and having preserved a non-glowing layer in Step 5, he was able to save artwork in the two variations—one glowing and the other one not glowing. These two images were set to loop in the animated GIF settings, and created the blinking neon effect.

Two-Frame Animations: The LOWSRC Trick

Mary was anxious to introduce dynamic movement to her first Web site, for Toad The Wet Sprocket. When the site was developed though, animated GIFs (see Chapter 3, "Hollywood Records") were not yet around, and Server Push (see Chapter 8, "Discovery Channel Online") was too complicated to program. Peter came up with a wonderful workaround: using the LOWSRC tag for two frame animations.

What the LOWSRC tag does is load a preliminary image before loading a final image. It was originally a Netscape extension to HTML, designed to speed up the process of seeing images. The idea was to start with a lower quality image that loaded quickly, so the viewer could click elsewhere if they decided they didn't want to wait for the real graphic to download.

Mary and Peter refer to the LOWSRC screens as a "double-load," because they load twice. Instead of using the tag as Netscape intended however, Mary inserted two slighty different images. This created the illusion of a two-frame animation. The first image loads quickly, and the second loads from top to bottom, as if pouring paint over the first.

■ LOWSRC

■ IMG SRC

■ http://www.music.sony.com/Music/ArtistInfo/Toad/syrup.html

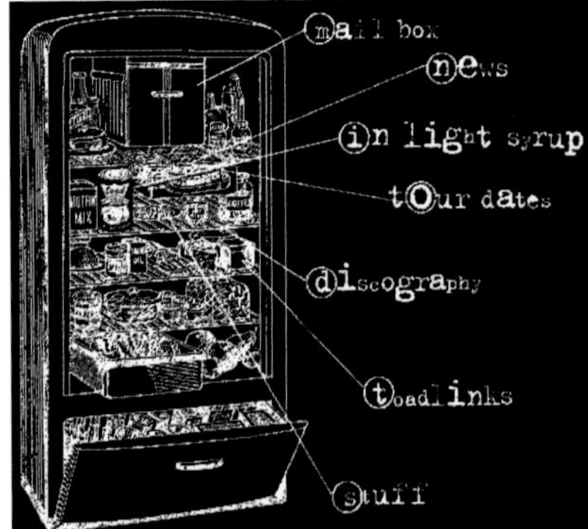

■ http://www.music.sony.com/Music/ArtistInfo/Toad/fridge.html

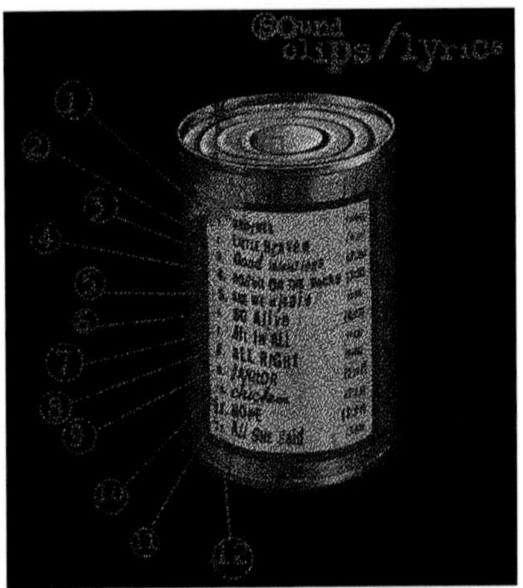

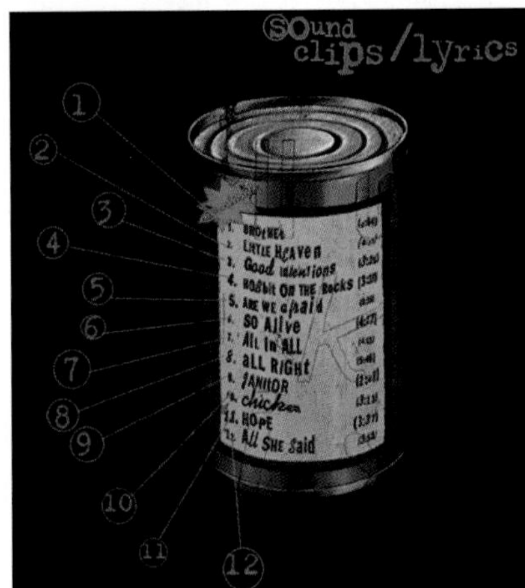

■ http://www.sony.com/Music/ArtistInfo/Toad/lyricclips.html

The LOWSRC is a great technique for limited, two-frame animations. It's imperative that the two images be exactly the same size for the animation illusion to work. The left-side images shown here load first, while the right-side images load second.

■ step-by-step

Setting up the LOWSRC Animation Artwork Trick in Photoshop

Here's an example of how to set up a LOWSRC file that's registered perfectly to the second loading image file.

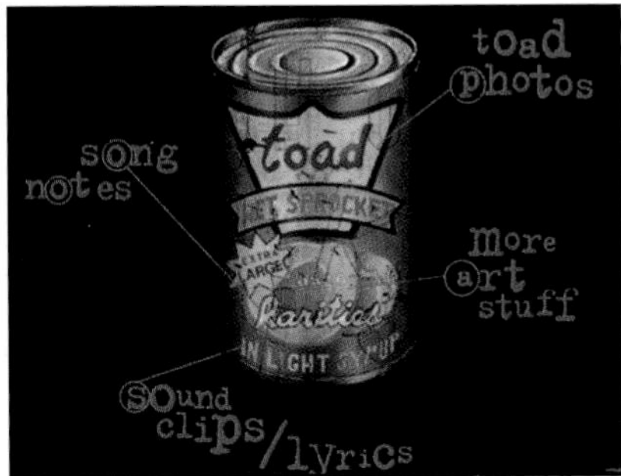

Step 1: Mary began with a color image of Bill Barminsky's album cover art for the In Light Syrup title, to which she added some catagories and lines using the same Trixie font used on other screens.

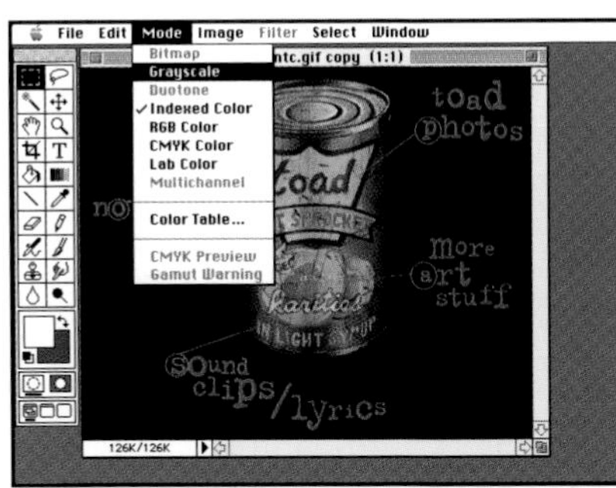

Step 2: Under the menu Mode, she selected Grayscale.

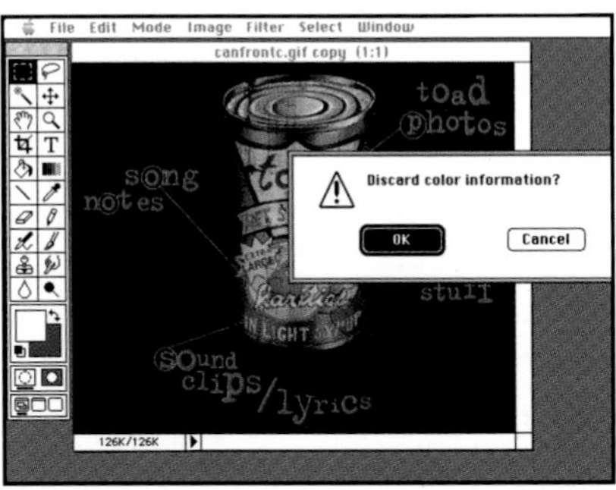

Step 3: When prompted to discard color information, she clicked yes.

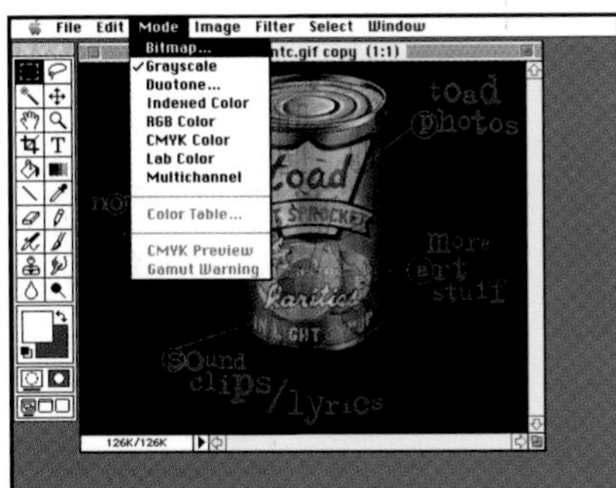

Step 4: Under the menu Mode, she selected Bitmap. Note that this option is not available from RGB. You must first switch to Grayscale before switching to Bitmap.

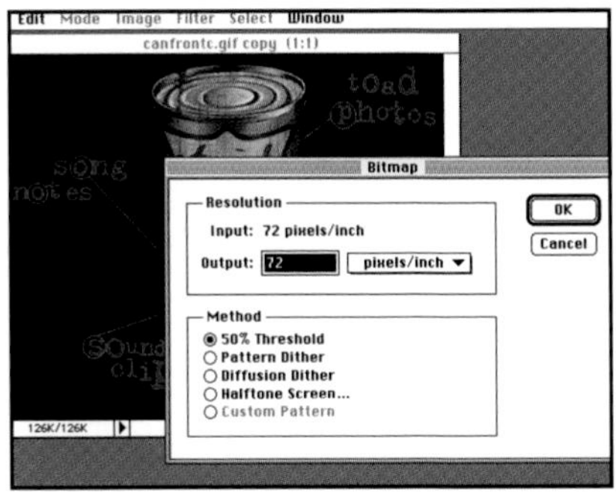

Step 5: Mary chose the 50% Threshold method.

Step 6: Here were the results. Too much information was lost, so she chose Undo.

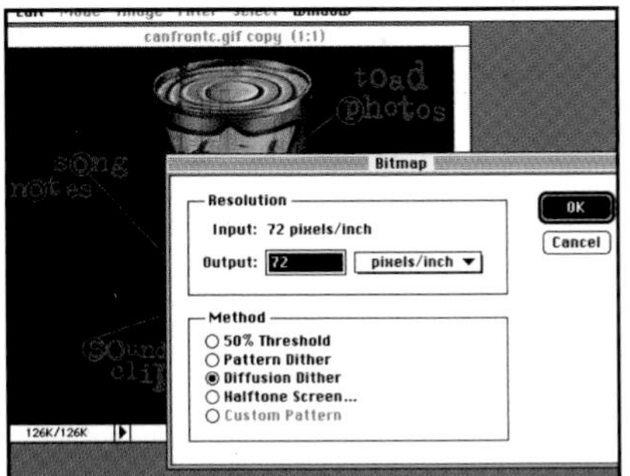

Step 7: She repeated Step 4. This time, she chose Diffusion Dither instead of 50% Threshold.

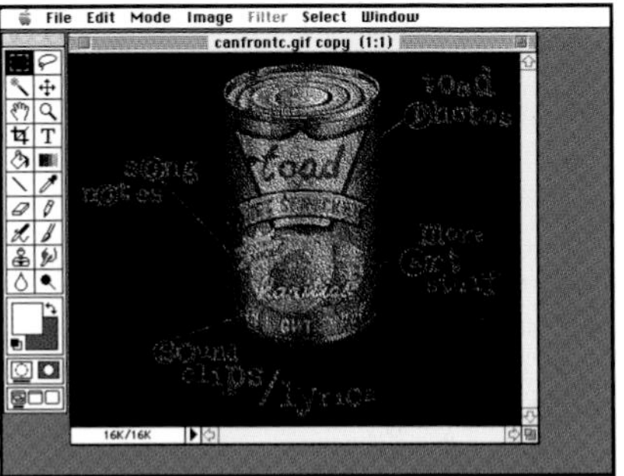

Step 8: Under Save as, Mary chose CompuServe GIF. Here's the finished result. It will match perfectly to the original color scan she began with because it was converted to gray from its original source image.

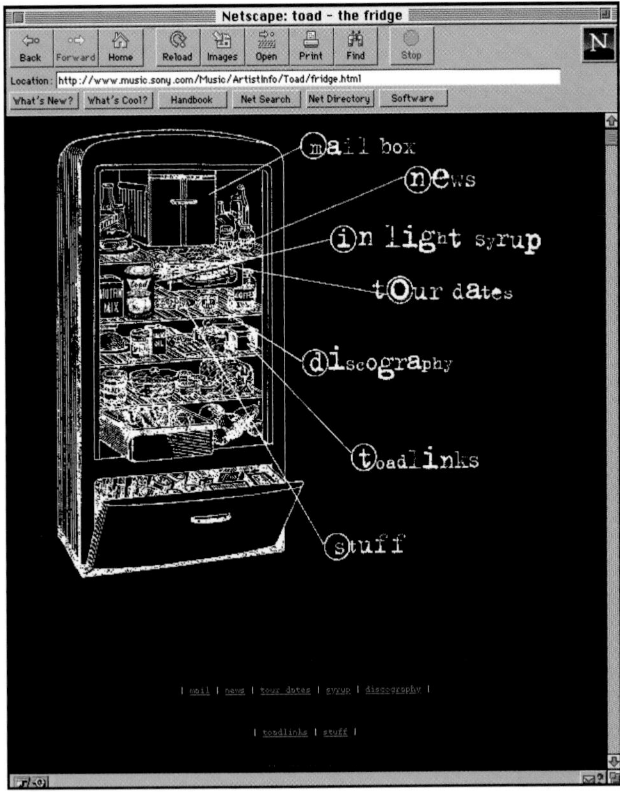

Here's an example of a screen that uses the LOWSRC tag to create a two frame animation. Check out: ■ http://www.sony.com/Music/ArtistInfo/Toad/fridge.html to view this online.

Here is the LOWSRC artwork "frclosed.gif." It loads first.

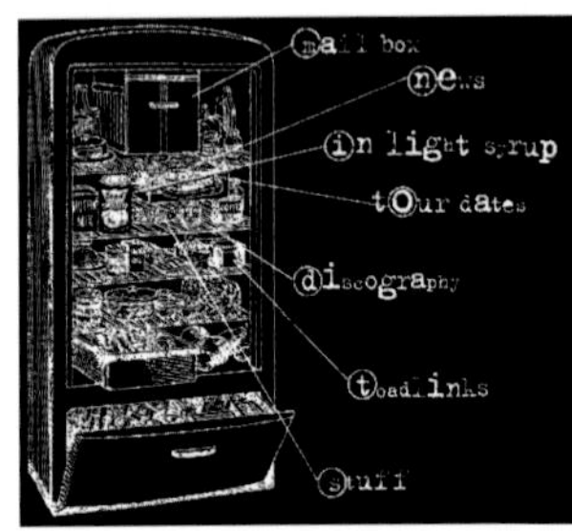

Here's the IMG SRC artwork "fropen.gif." It loads second.

LOWSRC HTML

```
   <BODY BGCOLOR = "#000000" TEXT = "#FFFFFF"
   LINK = "#FF0B00"
   ALINK = "#FFFEFE" VLINK = "#FFFEFF" >
   <title>toad - the fridge</title>
   <center>
   <a href="fropen.map">
1  <img  src="fropen.gif" lowsrc="frclosed.gif" ISMAP
   border=0></a>
   <p><br><br><br>
   <hr width=500>
   <br>
2  <tt><font size=2>
   ¦ <a href="mail.html">mail</a>
   ¦ <a href="news.html">news</a>
   ¦ <a href="usmap.html">tour dates</a>
   ¦ <a href="syrup.html">syrup</a>
   ¦ <a href="Discog.html">discography</a> ¦
   <p><br><br>
   ¦ <a href="links.html">toadlinks</a>
   ¦ <a href="stuff.html">stuff</a> ¦
   <p><br>
   <hr width=100>
   <br>
   ¦¦ <A HREF=stuff.html#credits>credits</A> ¦¦
   </center>
   </body>
   </HTML>
```

■ tags

LOWSRC Deconstruction

1 The <IMG SRC="fropen.gif"> is the second loaded image. The <LOWSRC="frclosed.gif"> loads first. The ISMAP indicates the use of an image map.

2 <tt> stands for "Typewriter Text." It is a container, and theclose tag </tt> is required. It specifies that the text within it should be rendered in a fixed-width font, if possible.

Programming Toad's JavaScript

Peter decided to add JavaScript to the welcome screen of Toad's site. Taking the text-based contents of Mary's graphic, he used JavaScript to create a scrolling message at the bottom of the screen.

JavaScript is similar to HTML in that it can be viewed in the source code of any given page. It makes it possible to try JavaScript techniques by copying and pasting someone else's code into your own HTML. The JavaScript deconstructed here would work on anybody's page. Just substitute the welcome screen's message with your own.

JavaScript has many other uses besides scrolling text. Some of the other purposes could be automatically setting up a specified size for a browser window, determining with which browser your end user is using to visit your site, and creating clocks and calenders. Here are a few resources for learning JavaScript:

- Netscape's tutorial for JavaScript: http://home.netscape.com/eng/mozilla/Gold/handbook/javascript/index.html
- Cool JavaScript Tip of the Week: http://www.gis.net/~carter/therest/tip_week.html
- JavaScript Usenet Group: news:comp.lang.javascript

■ note

Warning!

JavaScript is not supported by many browsers. At the time this chapter was written, it was only fully supported by Netscape 3.0 (which was still in beta). MSIE has plans to support it too.

■ note

Java versus JavaScript

Unlike HTML, where you can view the source within a browser or word processor, the source for regular Java cannot be viewed. This makes learning Java much more difficult than learning HTML, because many people teach themselves HTML by studying the source code on pages they like. Java is also much more difficult than HTML because it is a programming language, not a tagging system like HTML.

The reason why Java code can't be seen on HTML pages is because it has to be compiled before it can be viewed and executed by a browser. JavaScript, on the other hand, is interpreted by Netscape, rather than needing to first be compiled. That means that the code for JavaScript sits inside an HTML document and can be studied, just like HTML.

JavaScript is derived from simple scripting languages like HyperTalk and dBase. If you were new to programming, it would definitely be easier to learn JavaScript than Java. JavaScript is also more limited than Java, so serious programmers might choose in favor of using Java. JavaScript is somewhat of a Godsend for non-programmers, though!

Hint: You can copy and paste JavaScript just like HTML. If you go to a site and like their JavaScript, view their source and try it on your own page!

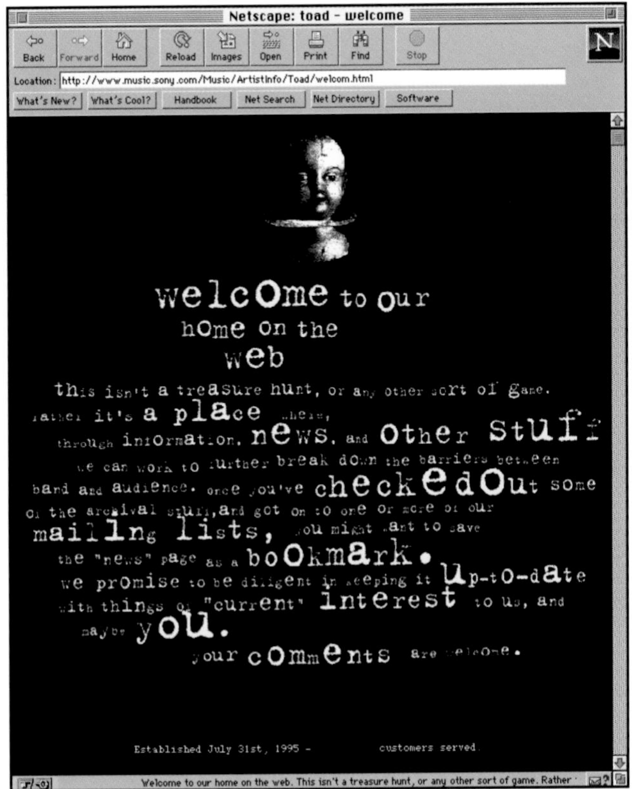

■ http://www.sony.com/Music/ArtistInfo/Toad/welcom.html

Welcome to our home on the web. This isn't a treasure hunt, or any other sort of game. Rather

A cropped-view of the bottom Netscape bar in which JavaScript causes the text to scroll.

JavaScript inside HTML

```
<!DOCTYPE HTML PUBLIC "-//IETF//DTD HTML 2.0//EN">
<HTML>
<HEAD>
<!--Begin of head-->
<!--
Author:            ANT
Created:     Friday, Wed 13, 1996
Time:        10:05 AM
-->
1 <SCRIPT LANGUAGE="JavaScript">
<!-- Beginning of JavaScript Applet --------
----------
2 /* ANT
   Credits  to DBA Websys, Inc.
*/
3 function scrollit_r2l(seed)
{
var m1  = "Welcome to our home on the web.";
var m2  = " This isn't a treasure hunt, or any other
sort of game.";
var m3  = " Rather it's a place where, through
information, news, and other stuff we can work to
further break down the barriers between band and
audience.";
var m4  = " Once you've checked out some of the
archival stuff, and got on to one or more of our
mailing lists, you might want to save the news page
as a bookmark. We promise to be diligent in keeping
it up-to-date with things of current interest to us,
and maybe you. Your comments are welcome.";
4 var msg=m1+m2+m3+m4;
var out = " ";
var c   = 1;
if (seed > 100) {
seed--;
var cmd="scrollit_r2l(" + seed + ")";
timerTwo=window.setTimeout(cmd,100);
}
else if (seed <= 100 && seed > 0) {
for (c=0 ; c < seed ; c++) {
out+=" ";
}
```

```
out+=msg;
seed--;
var cmd="scrollit_r2l(" + seed + ")";
    window.status=out;
timerTwo=window.setTimeout(cmd,100);
}
else if (seed <= 0) {
if (-seed < msg.length) {
out+=msg.substring(-seed,msg.length);
seed--;
var cmd="scrollit_r2l(" + seed + ")";
window.status=out;
timerTwo=window.setTimeout(cmd,100);
}
else {
window.status=" ";
timerTwo=window.setTimeout("scrollit_r2l(100)",75);
}
}
}
// -- End of JavaScript code -------------- -->
</SCRIPT>
<TITLE>toad - welcome</TITLE>
<!--End of head-->
</HEAD>
<BODY BGCOLOR = "#000000" TEXT = "#FFFFFF" LINK =
"#FF0B00" ALINK = "#FFFEFE" VLINK = "#FFFEFF"
onLoad="timerONE=window.setTimeout
('scrollit_r2l(100)',500);">
<!--Begin of body-->
<CENTER>
5 <A HREF="fridge.html"><IMG SRC="welcbab.gif"
lowsrc="welcbabbw.gif" border= 0 ALT="[please turn
on]"></A>
<br>
<A HREF="fridge.html"><IMG SRC="welc.gif"border= 0
ALT="[inline images...]"></A>
<br><br>
<tt> <font size=3><center>
<hr width=540>
<p>
Established July 31st, 1995 - <img src="/cgi-
bin/Toad-O-Meter" ALT="[counter]"> customers served.
<p>
<hr width=540>
<br>
In case you haven't already noticed this site is
optimized for
<br><br>
the
<A HREF ="http://www.netscape.com/comprod/mirror/
index.html">
Netscape 2.0</A> Navigator.
<br><br>
The House Of Toad is completely designed for this
browser.
<br><br>
You'll need it to see subtle animations and full-
effect graphics.
<br><br>
It's the best browser out there.
<br>
<br>
Oh yeah, please set options to auto-load
images......
</FONT><CENTER>
<br>
<hr width=100>
<br><br>
<center><tt><font size=2>
<a href="fridge.html"><IMG SRC="frigicon.gif"bor-
der=0></a>
<br><br>
|| <a href="fridge.html">the fridge</a> ||
</center>
</tt>
</font>
</body>
</HTML>
```

■ code & tags

JavaScript inside HTML Deconstruction

1 The <SCRIPT> tag is a container, so the close tag </SCRIPT> is required. It specifies that the code within it should be executed. The <SCRIPT> tag belongs inside the <HEAD> of an HTML document. (See below for JavaScript Deconstruction).

2 Comments in JavaScript follow the C convention of block-style comments between "/*" and "*/". Additionally, JavaScript supports C++ style comments where every- thing after "//" to the end of a line is considered a comment.

The first part of the source code is a comment that gives credit to DBA Websys, Inc. This code was originally written by Chris Skinner, founder of Websys, Inc. (and the creator of the animated meteor shower that Netscape Navigator displays when it's busy). He placed this code in the public domain with the requirement that an acknowledgment to Websys (and a link to their Web site, ■ http://websys.com/) is left in all copies of the source code.

It's worth noting here that an updated version of this script (available at ■ http://www.websys.com/javascript/) resolves a couple of the more annoying aspects of this, more ubiquitous, version. It automatically corrects the speed of the scrolling by adjusting for different platforms (e.g. Mac, Windows, or Unix), and (Hooray!) it temporarily removes itself when you pass your cursor over a link, so that you can see where the link goes.

3 The first part of the scrollit_r2l function is the initialization of the strings for scrolling. Here is where you would put the text that you want to scroll.

4 The rest of the function is the code that actually does the scrolling. This is a recursive function, so it actually invokes itself over and over.

The function works by either inserting spaces before the string (if the text is supposed to be scrolled over to the right), or chopping off the beginning of the text (if it's supposed to be scrolled off to the left). It determines how to do this by testing the value of the "seed" (which is simply a number that indicates how far along the scroll is).

5 In this example, the LOWSRC and IMG SRC are creating a two frame animation. The LOWSRC image loads first, and the IMG SRC file loads second.

LOWSRC "welcbabbw.gif"

IMG SRC"welcbab.gif"

Working with Type in Different Sizes

If you look at the Toad The Web Sprocket pages, most of the type was set in varying sizes to get a more organic, varied, and erratic look. This kind of typesetting is impossible to do within Photoshop, which has limited type handling capabilities. Photoshop allows you to set type in any font within your system, but doesn't offer size controls over individual letters.

Mary used QuarkXPress for laying out the typography for the Photoshop files. Because it's impossible to directly import a QuarkXPress file into Photoshop, Mary took screen captures (see Chapter 7, "Art Center," for an in-depth look at screen capture utilities) of those files. A screen capture takes a picture of anything that's on your screen, regardless of what program you're using, and creates a file that can be opened in Photoshop.

Mary also worked with Peter to see if he could program HTML text to simulate some of her QuarkXPress files. She was quite pleased with the results, which are deconstructed in the following section.

This image uses the same font (Trixie by Fonthaus. Fonthaus has a Web site: ■ http://home.cityqueue.com/CityQueue/business/fonthaus.html), but each letter is set in a different size. This was done in Quark, and was brought into Photoshop via screen capture software.

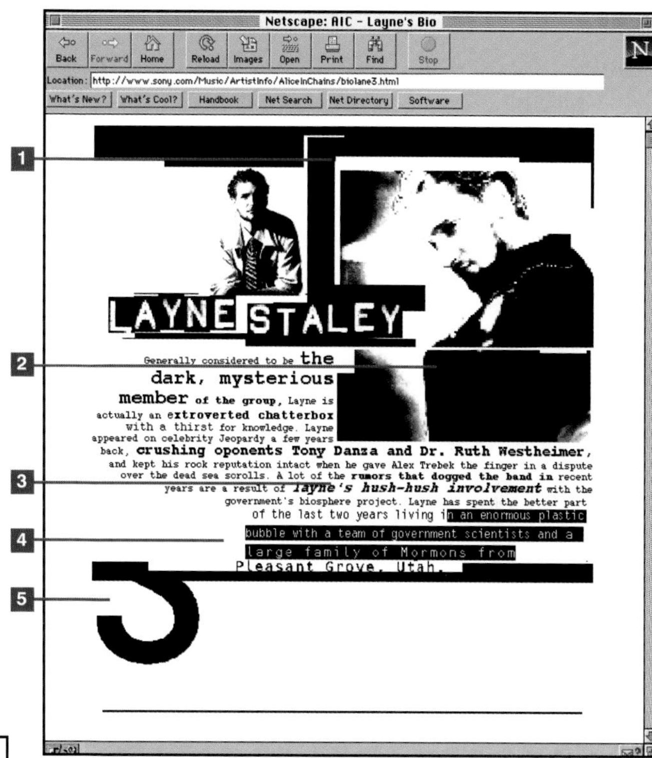

It's possible to mix sizes of HTML-based text too. This page can be viewed at ■ http://www.music.sony.com/Music/ArtistInfo/AliceInChains/biolane3.html.

Mixed Type Sizes HTML

```
<HTML>
<HEAD>
<TITLE>AIC - Layne's Bio</TITLE
</HEAD>
<body bgcolor="FFFFFF"  TEXT = "#000000" LINK =
"#000000" ALINK = "#E8F13A" VLINK = "#000000" >
<CENTER>
<TABLE BORDER=0 WIDTH=522 HEIGHT=200>
<TD NOWRAP WIDTH=522 HEIGHT=200 ALIGN="RIGHT">
1 <IMG SRC="biolaypg3hed2.gif"
LOWSRC="biolaypg3hed1.gif" WIDTH=520 HEIGHT=221>
2 <IMG SRC="biolaypg3hed3.gif" WIDTH=264 HEIGHT=93
ALIGN="RIGHT"><TT><FONT SIZE="3">
```

3
```
Generally considered to be <STRONG><FONT
SIZE="+3">the dark, mysterious member</FONT
SIZE="+3"> of the group,</Strong> Layne is actually
an <FONT SIZE="+1">e<STRONG>xtroverted
chatterbox</FONT SIZE="+1"> with a thirst</STRONG>
for knowledge. Layne appeared on celebrity Jeopardy
a few years back, <STRONG><FONT SIZE="+2">crushing
oponents Tony Danza and Dr. Ruth
Westheimer,</STRONG></FONT SIZE="+2"> and kept his
rock reputation intact when he gave Alex Trebek the
finger in a dispute over the dead sea scrolls.
A lot of the <STRONG>rumors that dogged the band
in</STRONG> recent years are a result of
<I><STRONG><FONT SIZE="+2">layne's hush-hush involve-
ment</I></STRONG></FONT SIZE="+2"> with the govern-
ment's biosphere project.  Layne has spent the bet
ter part
```
4
```
<IMG SRC="biolaypg3text.gif" ALIGN="CENTER">
```
5
```
<IMG SRC="biolaypg3bot.gif" WIDTH=522 HEIGHT=113
ALIGN="CENTER">
</TD>
</TABLE>
<P>
<BR>
<CENTER>
<HR NOSHADE WIDTH =500>
<P>
<BR>
<BR>
<TT>
<A HREF="biolane4.html">Next?</A>
<P>
<BR>
<BR>
¦¦ <A HREF="bio.html">Bios</A> ¦¦
</CENTER>
</BODY>
</HTML>
```

tags

Mixed Type Sizes HTML Deconstruction

1 Here's the LOWSRC trick again. The LOWSRC image loads before the SRC image.

The IMG SRC file "biolaypg3hed2.gif" loads second. It's the inverse of the LOWSRC file, causing the images to flash from black and white to white and black.

The IMG SRC file "biolaypg3text.gif."

2 The next IMG SRC is instructed to align to the right of the text, by using the ALIGN=RIGHT attribute. The <TT> tag indicates that mono-spaced type will follow, until it's closed container is specified.

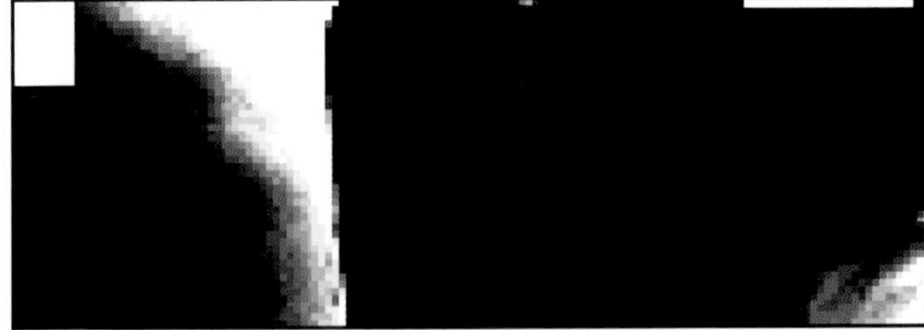

This IMG SRC file "biolaypg3hed3.gif" is instructed to align to the right of the text.

3 A number of different tags are present here that instruct the browser to display the type differently. <STRONG> creates bold text on most browsers. FONT SIZE indicates that the size of the text will be higher or lower than the default depending on whether the number is positive or negative. For a thorough listing of FONT SIZE values and their results, check out Chapter 3, "Hollywood Records."

4 The next image aligns center and butts up directly to the bottom of the preceding HTML text.

of the last two years living in an enormous plastic
bubble with a team of government scientists and a
large family of Mormons from

The LOWSRC image "biolaypgtext.gif" loads first.

5 This next image aligns CENTER and butts up directly to the bottom of the preceeding image.

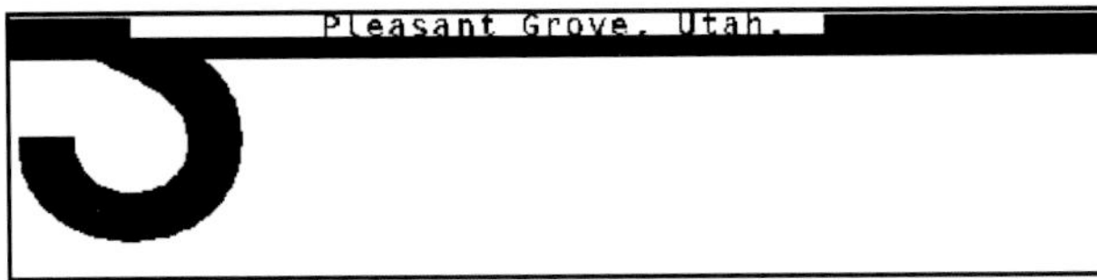

The IMG SRC file "biolaypg3bot.gif."

■ site summary

Sony Online

Mary Maurer and Peter Anton succeeded at creating a mood and environment that suited their subject matter, and understood the Web enough to respect its limitations. The LOWSRC animation trick is still useful, even though we have many other options today for dynamic Web presentation techniques such as Java, Shockwave, and animated GIFs. The use of black and white, high contrast artwork on this site gives it a custom signature, and makes everything load fast, too. Using Photoshop as a compositing tool made the images on this site look cohesive, even though they were pooled from many different sources, locations, and timeframes. The two sites, Toad The Wet Sprocket and Alice In Chains, scream with speed and originality.

■ Take your own photographs, and look to everyday objects and locations for inspiration, metaphors, and unusual ideas. Clip art is great, but nothing beats using your own photography and images for concepts that will give your site a more personal flavor.

■ The LOWSRC technique works well for two-frame animations, especially if you create the second image from the first image and have perfect registration between the two. Remember that the LOWSRC tag only works on Netscape.

■ One of the good things about JavaScript is that you can view it from within the source of HTML, and copy and paste source code from other pages to teach it to yourself.

■ If you're going to work on a design campaign that involves using artwork for both print and Web, be sure to save a copy of your work at a higher resolution than 72 dpi. If you try to print low resolution Web graphics for any kind of professional print project the results will look unacceptable.

■ www.music.sony.com/Music/ArtistInfo/Toad/
■ www.music.sony.com/Music/ArtistInfo/AliceInChains/

@tlas

tables and image maps

What this chapter covers:

- **Using Photoshop Layers and Modes**
- **How to Use Tables for Alignment**
- **Using HTML for Filtering Browsers**
- **Creating Client-Side Image Maps**
- **Supporting SGML and HTML Validators**

http://www.atlas.organic.com The fact that it's been difficult to make money directly from the Web has been a frustration to many, and a liberation to others. The non-commerical Web has created an idealized form of free communication—one where money is not the reward, but where freedom of expression is. The three founders of @tlas, Olivier Laude, Michael Macrone, and Amy Franchescini, were all attracted to the Web as an opportunity to publish their work without pleasing editors, advertisers, and clients. Their efforts and talents have created a site that is one of the best examples of visual design on the Web.

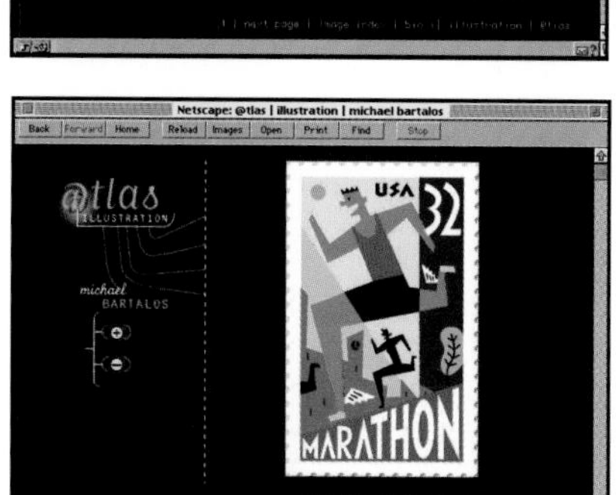

Web Design Firm: @tlas

URL: http://www.atlas.organic.com

Type of Site: Artist Portfolio/Web Design Experimentaion

Server: Intel 486

Operating System: Free BSD

Server Software: Apache

Content Aquisition: Oliviere Laude

Webmaster: Michael Macrone

Art Directors: Amy Francheschini, David Karam

Developement and Production Platform: Macintosh

Software: Photoshop, Illustrator, BBEdit, SiteMill

What is @tlas?

@tlas is an on-line magazine-based site for artists, housing the work of illustrators, designers, multimedia artists, photographers, and journalists. It has grown from residing on founder-Webmaster Michael Macrone's www.well. com account, to server space donated by www.organic.com. @tlas is presently searching for a permanent home that, as of writing this chapter, has yet to be established.

Typically when a site surpasses a certain level of popularity, it takes up too much "bandwidth" to maintain a "free" status. (Most popular on-line services have limits to how many hits a site can receive before the "free" status is withdrawn.) @tlas gets all the hits because it's one of the best examples of what the Web can be—it has original, compelling content that is graphically rich and innovative.

Original Content: Olivier Laude

Olivier Laude is a photojournalist with a great eye for talent and an even greater talent pool of friends. He had always wanted to start a magazine that would feature artists in a non-commercial, respectful way, and when the Web came along it seemed like the perfect vehicle. Without the need for outside funding or advertisers, he was able to do what he liked best; assemble a team of remarkably talented people and publish a portfolio of work for worldwide distribution.

Everyone works on @tlas for free—from the founders on down to the contributors. What's offered instead of money is freedom. Olivier can offer contributing artists something they'll be hard pressed to find elsewhere—the ability to show a large body of work exactly as they intended for it to be seen, without superfluous editing or fear of advertising censorship. Included in the mix is the ability to show that body of work to a worldwide audience. In looking through @tlas's logs, Olivier reports that there have been visitors from nearly every wired country in the world. If an artist wants an audience, there is no parallel to the global distribution the Web offers.

@tlas founder Olivier Laude's work is on the site. His portfolio deals with Guangzhou's horse racing track.

When Olivier gets a portfolio of work for submission into @tlas, the order that the photographer or designer wants them seen in is respected. If the photographer wants to write the captions for the work, that's fine, too. Otherwise Olivier will interview them and will write the captions himself. Olivier rarely changes anything about the work; his goal is to show the work as the author intended it to be seen.

The direction of @tlas is evolving. The first iteration of @tlas (art directed by Amy Francheschini) was in gallery format, where flat work was organized by each artist and viewed in sequence. The "Winter 96" and "Summer 96" versions of @tlas (art directed by David Karam) initiated a move towards more of a conceptual and editorial direction, where the content is better tailored to the medium of the Web. This means that GIF-animations, Java, and Shockwave are going to be more prevalent in the future than simple gallery-like exhibitions of work. A different editorial slant is already evident in the "Winter 96" version of the site (■ http:// www.atlas.organic.com/atlas/tocw.html), which contains witty stories, games, and corny ASCII art.

One of Olivier's roles in @tlas is to collect image submissions in the form of transparencies, Photo CDs, and flat art. He works on a Macintosh Centris 610 and scans with a Microtec UMAX flatbed scanner or a Nikon Super Cool slide scanner, depending on how the work is submitted. After he scans the images and numbers their order, they are e-mailed to Michael or Amy for further manipulation or file size reduction.

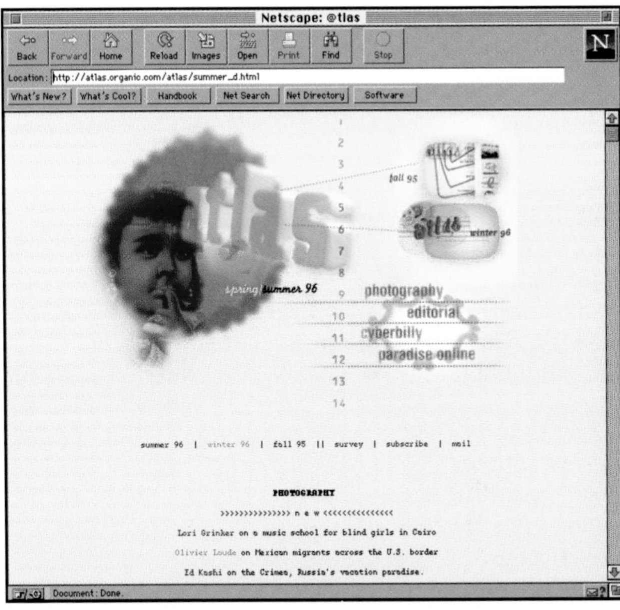

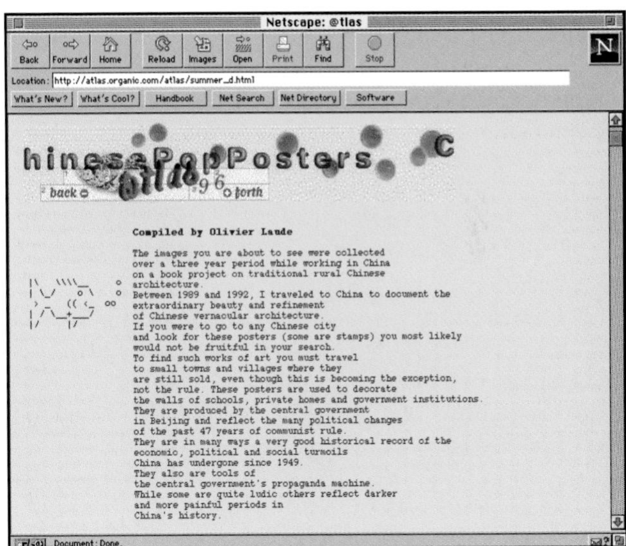

The art direction for @tlas evolves with each new issue. These are sample screens, designed by David Karam of Post Tools Design in San Francisco.

@tlas Art Director Amy Francheschini's Design Process

When Olivier asked Amy to design the interface for @tlas she had never designed a Web site before, or even seen one. Amy accepted the challenge with an open mind. There was no flowchart or formal plan for the site; she was simply given some scans of some of the featured artists' work and was left on her own to figure out the rest.

As an experienced digital designer in print and multimedia however, Amy did have strongly formed beliefs about interface design. She knew she didn't want the interface to be all spelled out with buttons everywhere; she wanted the site to be driven by text, graphics, and images.

Amy's aversion to buttons is strong. She likes using text instead of buttons and feels that people are moving too far away from text. Efforts to make "icons" and "graphics" for navigation bars are usually unsuccessful, in her opinion, because few know what the icons are supposed to stand for. Still, she is frustrated that you can't use very small typefaces for screen graphics like you can for print graphics, and often finds herself riding the line between making text small enough to her liking while keeping it readable.

Amy draws on personal sources of inspiration to arrive at graphical metaphors. She's always liked quirky things and unfolds and deconstructs common objects (like envelopes—the curved lines on the @tlas front page are derived from what a number 10 envelope looks like when it's unfolded) to find shapes and curves that she likes. She's more likely to find inspiration at a thrift store, sifting through old stationery or die-cut packaging, than by starting with a fixed idea. She laughed about how she's been known to often stare at things in an almost trance-like state, just thinking about their form or color.

Many people love the colors of the @tlas site, which are also drawn from Amy's personal aesthetic. She likes subtle and aged colors, like what you might find if you set a book outside or let a photograph discolor in the sun. Her favorite types of colors are those that no one could paint, but that are created by age and time.

Using Illustrator for Pre-Visualization and Templates

In designing for @tlas, Amy begins in Adobe Illustrator. Illustrator has certain features that Photoshop does not, like the capability to use rulers and guides, precise alignment tools, and superior text handling tools.

Amy first experimented with different grids for the page compositions, and then decided that each person who was featured in @tlas might be compared to having their own television show. She chose to put thumbnails of the work within shapes reminiscent of a television screen, with curved lines drawn to each catagory.

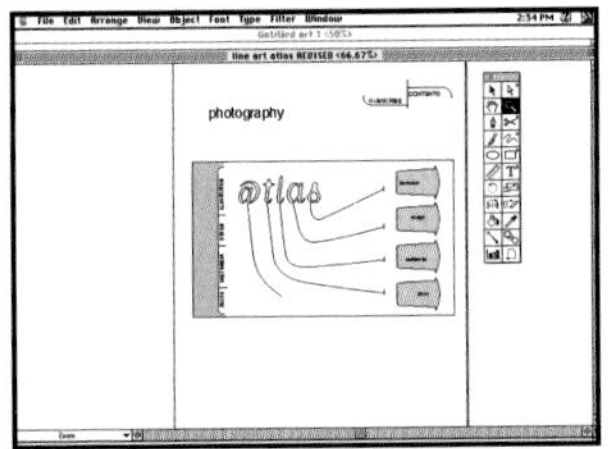

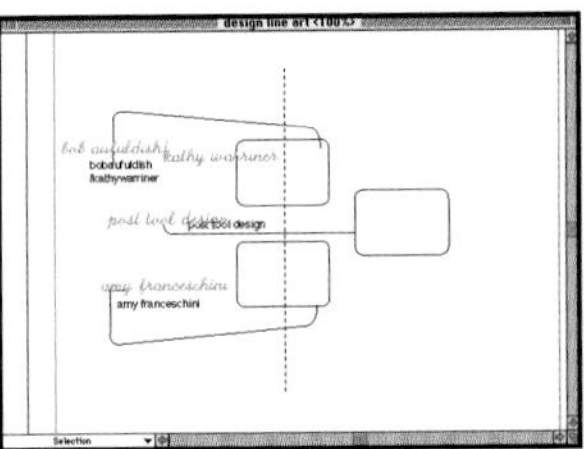

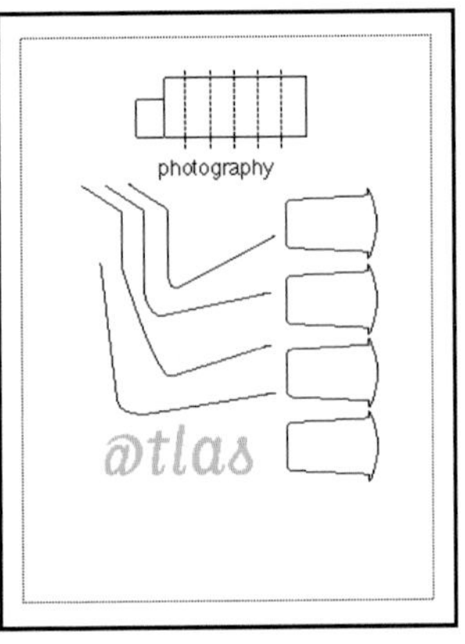

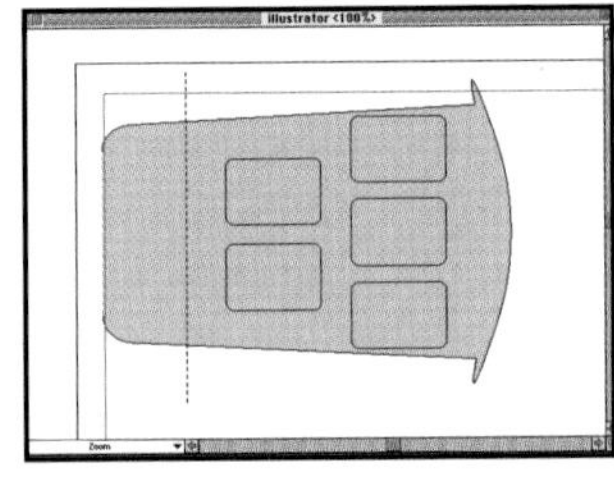

Amy used Illustrator to pre-visualize the grid for her page designs. She created the curved shapes, which were inspired by an envelope unfolding, using the Bezier Pen tool. The Illustrator files were copied and pasted into Photoshop, where they were "rasterized" and put on a separate layer. Rasterization is the process of converting vector-based line-art (as generated by Illustrator) to bitmap artwork (as generated by Photoshop). If you want to include artwork from Illustrator in a Photoshop document, it must be rasterized so it can be treated as a bitmap graphic. This process is described in detail in Chapter 2, "DreamWorks Interactive SKG."

Deconstructing Amy's Photoshop Layers

Most of Amy's Photoshop documents use lots of layers with compositing mode settings and varying opacities. This gives Amy's work a transluscent quality that possess a richly layered, almost magical feel. She uses the eye icon to turn layers on and off, and to try different ideas. Her Photoshop files are very complex, and are not terribly useful for making fast changes or edits.

The fact that Amy uses these personal and complex Photoshop techniques for image creation doesn't affect performance after the pages are loaded onto the Web. Michael Macrone does an excellent job of compressing Amy's images, and how they were made plays no role in their ultimate performance. This opening screen is 44k once converted to a JPEG, as opposed to a 1.4 MB Photoshop layered file.

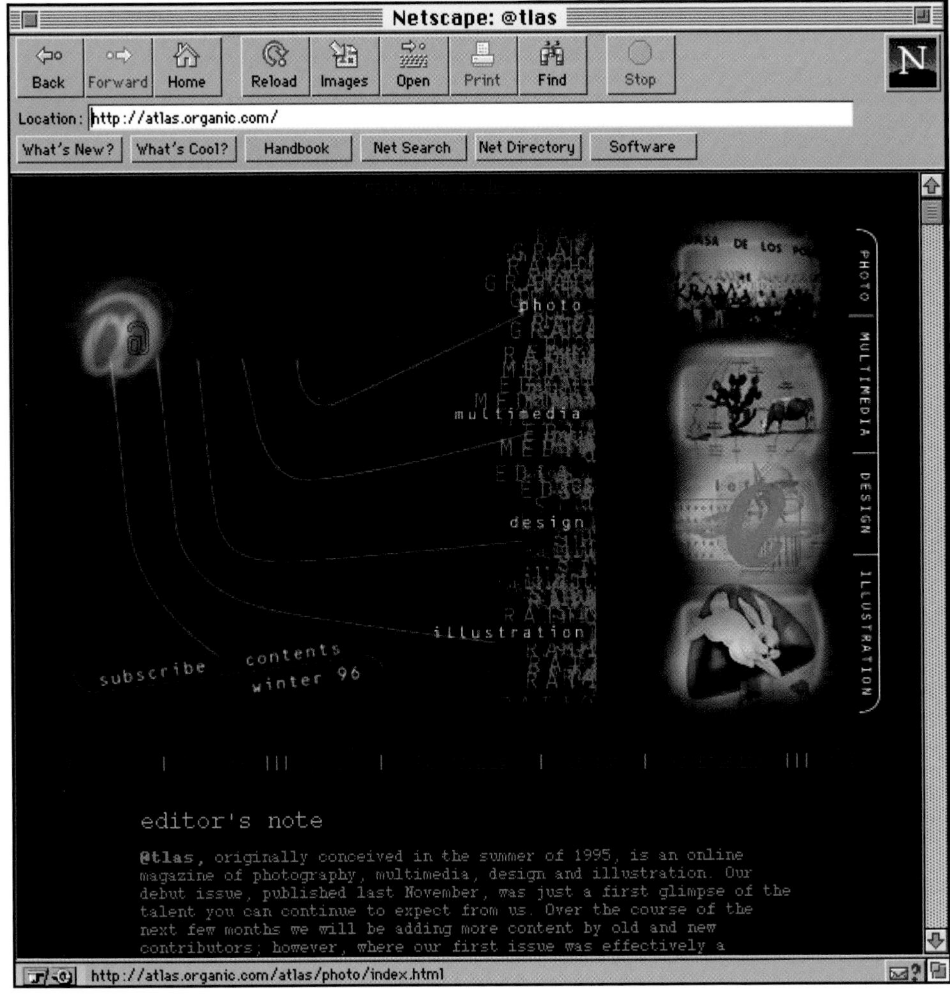

Here's a finished screen for the front page of @tlas as seen in Netscape. You can view this page at:
■ http://atlas.organic.com/atlas/fall.html.

Photoshop Layers Deconstruction

■ Composites

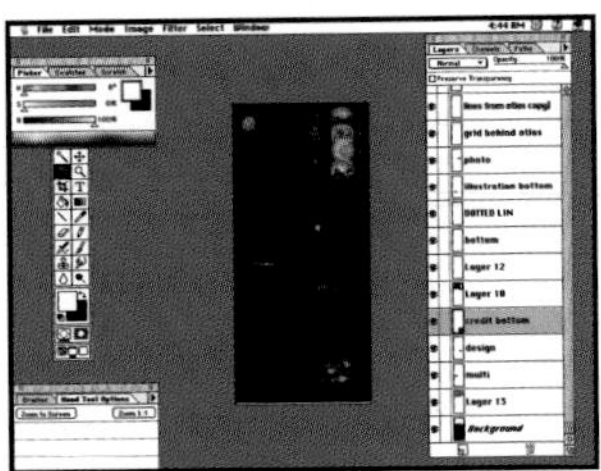

Amy's Photoshop document with all the layers turned on.

■ Individual Layers

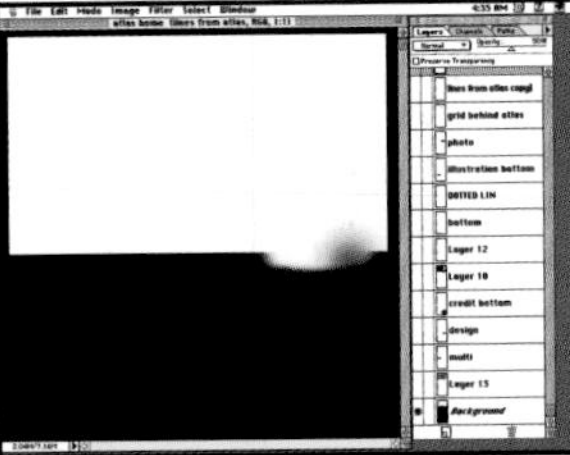

Layer 1 is set to a Normal Mode at 100% opacity.

■ Composites

Layer 2 is set to Multiply mode at 100% Opacity.

■ Individual Layers

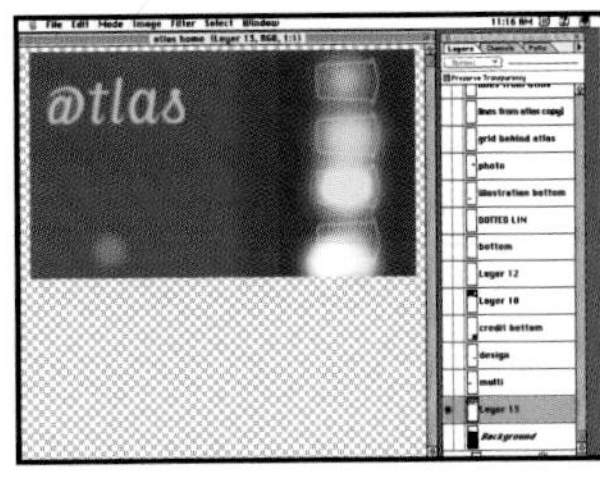

Layer 2 viewed in isolation.

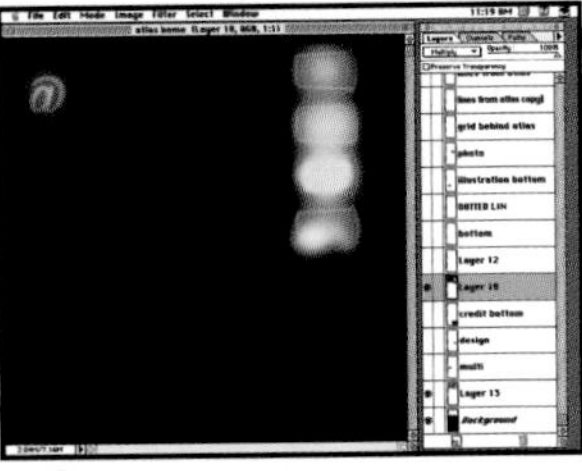

Layer 3 is set to Multiply mode at 100% opacity.

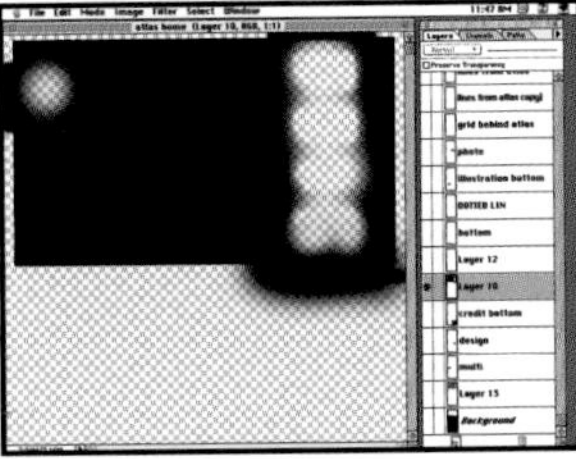

Layer 3 is serving to clip the underlying layer, because of the multiply mode setting. In multiply, the blacks are preserved, and lighter values drop out.

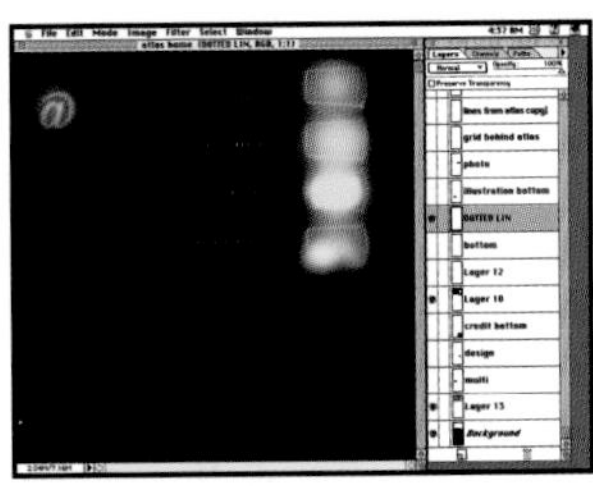

Layer 4 is set to Normal mode at 100% opacity.

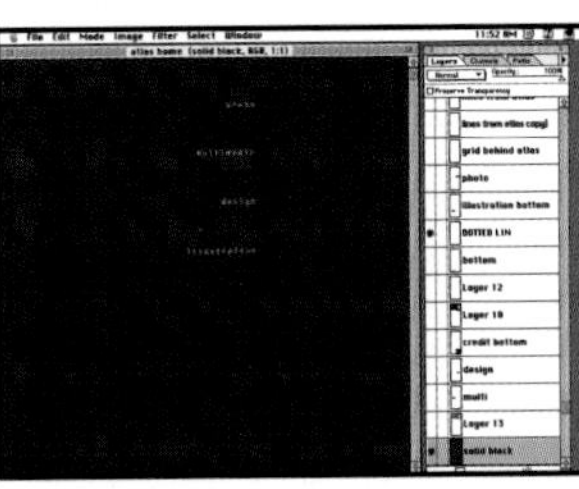

This layer is against gray because it's too light to otherwise see. The file is really on a transparent layer, so it will composite over the other layers.

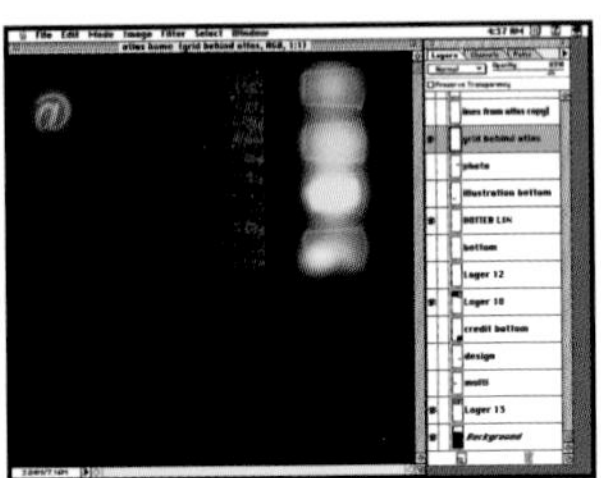

Layer 5 is set to Normal mode at 83% opacity.

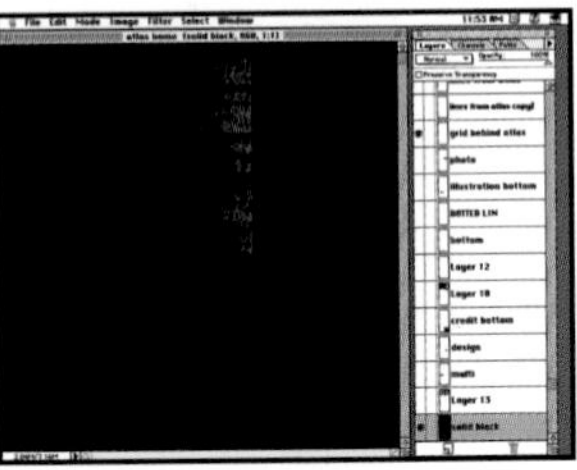

This layer is against black for display only. In actuality, the layer is against a transparent background. It's overlaying on top of the other layers at an 83% opacity.

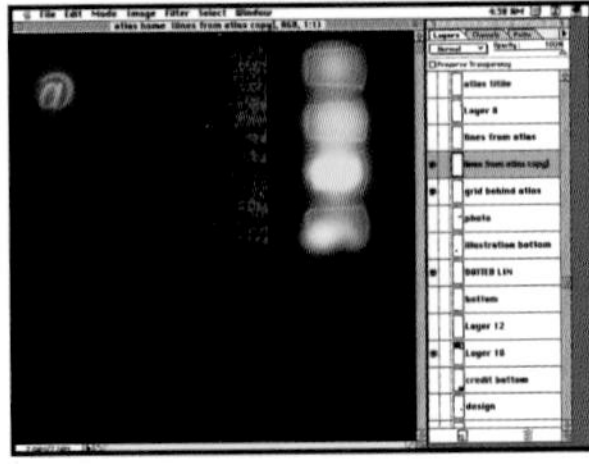

Layer 6 is set to Normal mode at 100% opacity.

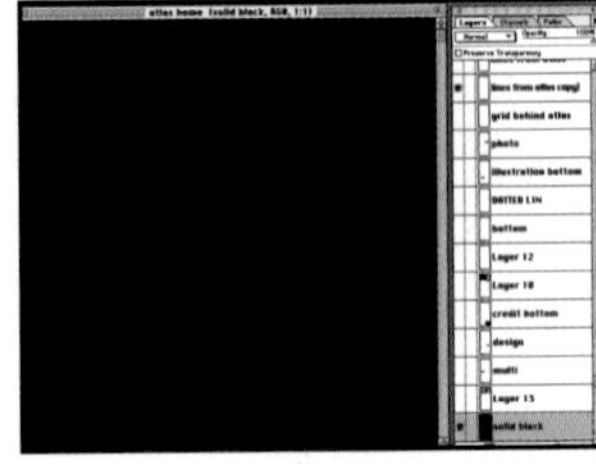

Again, this layer is really against a transparent cel, and layers on top of the other turned on layers.

■ Composites

■ Individual Layers

■ Composites

■ Individual Layers

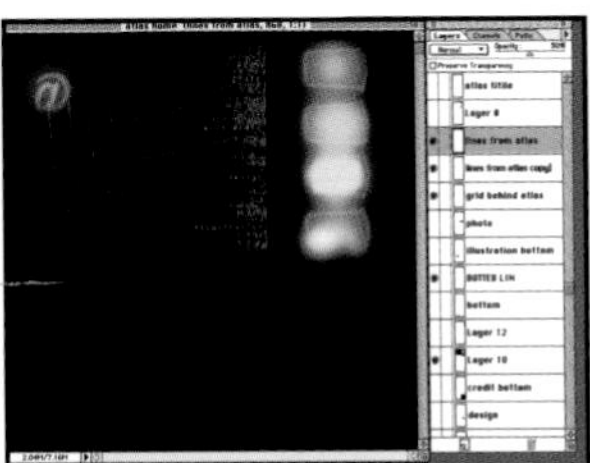

Layer 7 is set to Normal mode at 50% opacity.

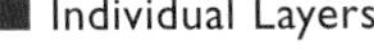

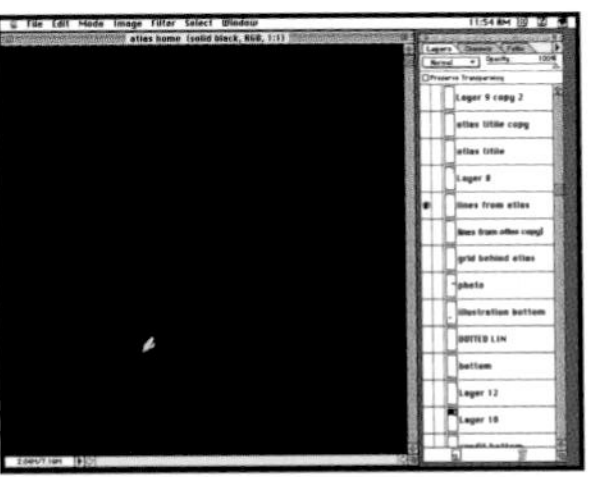

This layer provides a harder edged line weight that composites on top of Layer 6's more blurry, diffused line.

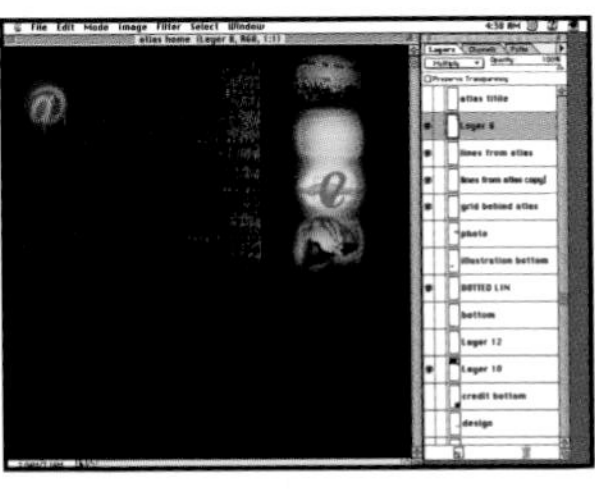

Layer 8 is set to Multiply mode at 100% opacity.

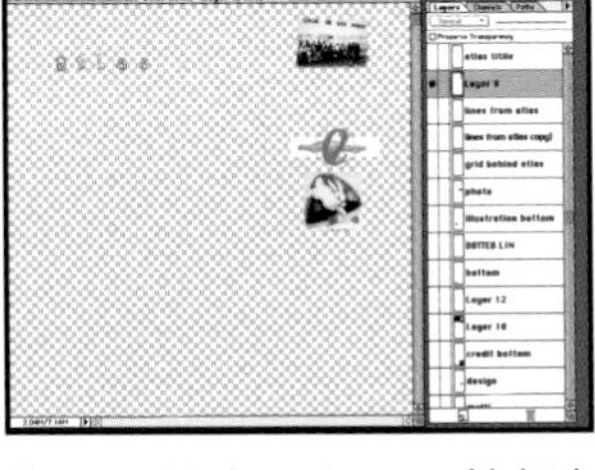

Because this layer is set to Multiply mode, the white hard edges drop out when they interact with the black images underneath.

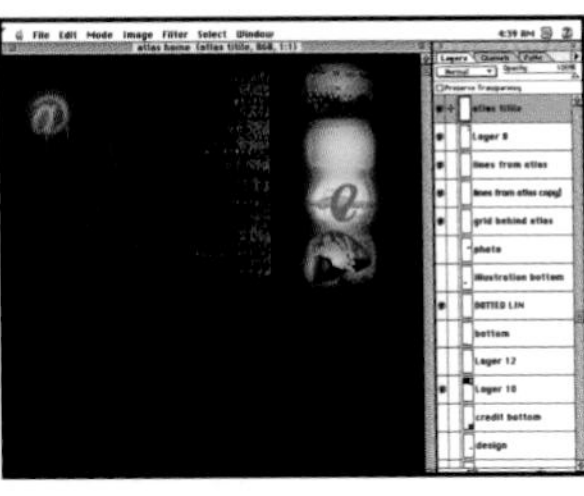

Layer 9 is set to Normal mode at 100% opacity.

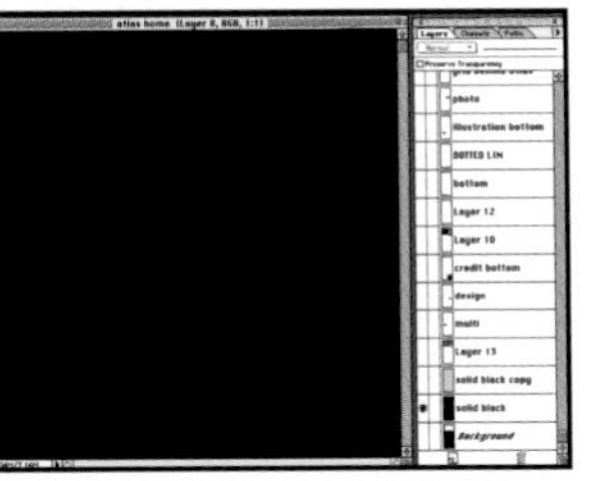

In reality, this layer is against a transparent background, and composites seamlessly onto the other layers.

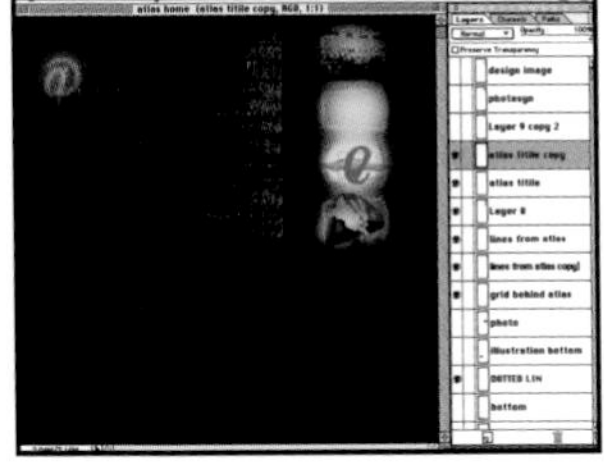

Layer 10 is set to Normal mode at 100% opacity.

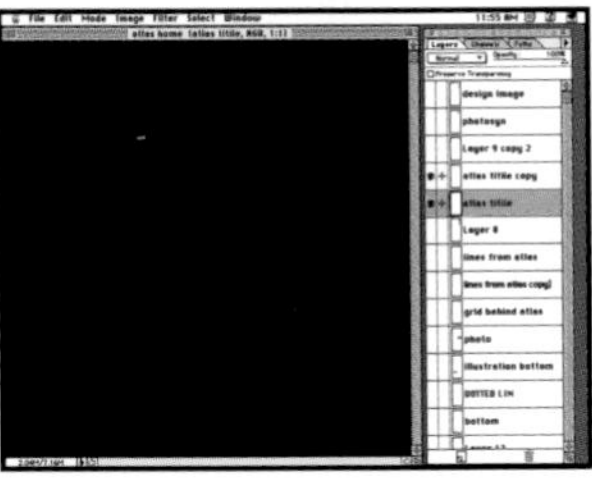

Layer 10 is identical to Layer 9, but when combined they both create a stronger (more opaque) image.

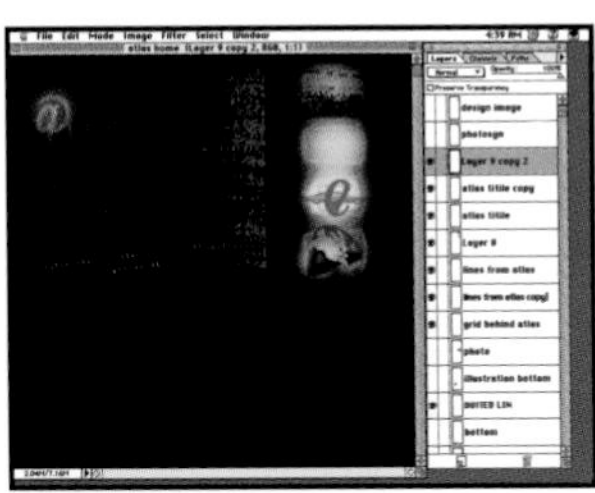

Layer 11 is set to Normal mode at 100% opacity.

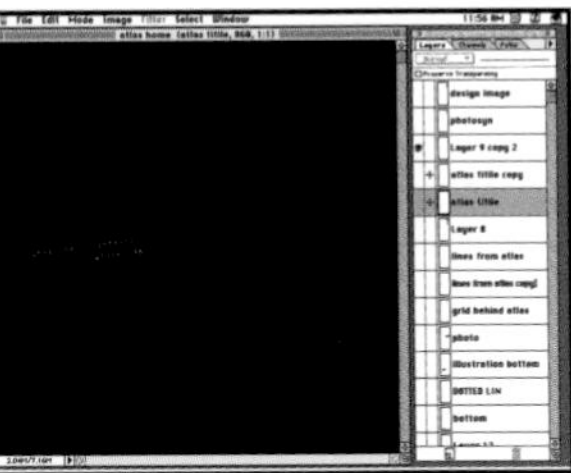

In reality, this layer is against a checkerboard, transparent background, and is shown here in black for visiblity.

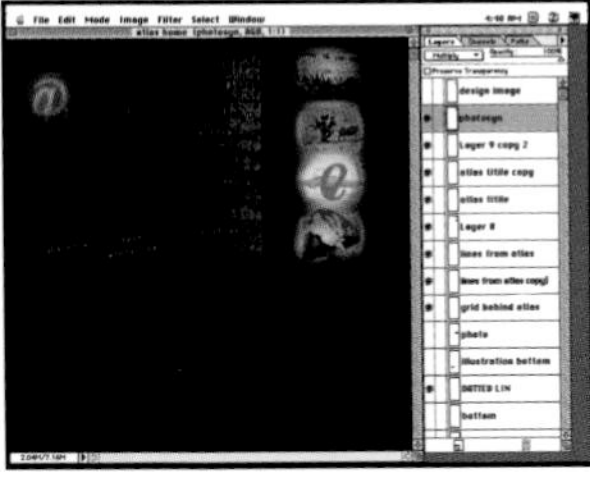

Layer 12 is set to Multiply mode at 100% opacity.

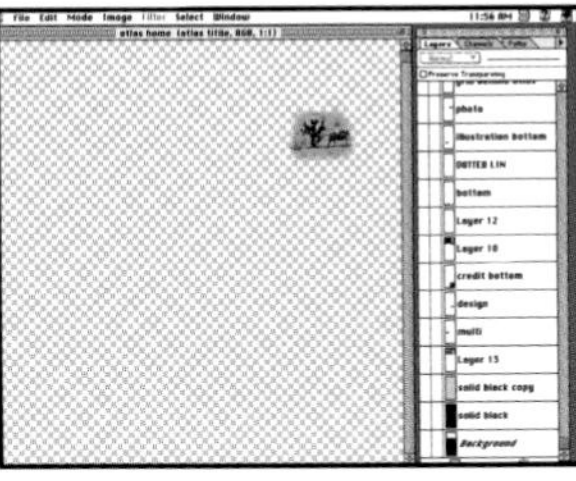

Because Multiply mode is in effect, the image composites softly over the rest of the layers.

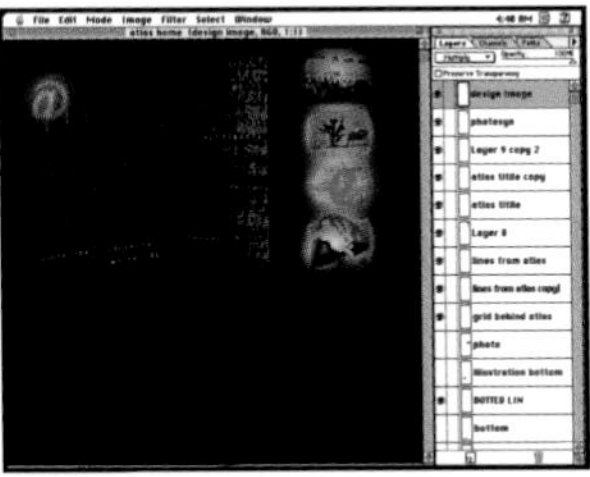

Layer 13 is set to Multiply mode at 100% opacity.

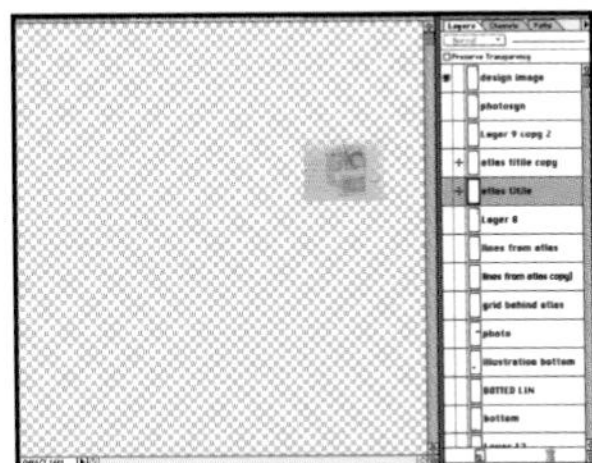

Again, Multiply mode is allowing this rectangular shape to be masked by the black layers beneath it.

Using HTML as a Layout Tool

When the first beta of the Mosaic Web browser was released almost two years ago, Michael Macrone was (and still is) a subscriber to San Francisco's reknowned online source, The Well (■ http://www.well.com). At that time, Well discussion groups were buzzing with excitement over the potential of the World Wide Web. In response, and as a free service to its subscribers, The Well offered Web space to anyone interested in using it. Michael downloaded a copy of MacWeb (a Mac-based shareware browser) and went to work on creating his first site.

Michael taught himself HTML by browsing the Web and viewing the source code of Web pages he liked. In the beginning, he spent a lot of time on NCSA's home page, studying Web page design tips and learning about HTML tags. It was easy to learn everything there was about HTML in those days because there were relatively few tags in existence. When Netscape was released, Michael instantly recognized the significance of Netscape-initiated alignment and table tags.

Michael remembers, "Tables were the answer to my alignment frustrations. They offered a grid paradigm, much like visual designers use on a printed page. Without grids, magazine design as we know it today would be impossible. Without grids, decent Web design was nearly impossible as well." Tables are used on virtually every page of @tlas, and they make it possible to align elements perfectly from one link to another. They are one of the reasons for @tlas's design continuity, and an indespensible tool to the site's success.

Programming Tables

Tables, which are used generously throughout the site, are challenging to program using HTML. Though they offer the "grid" that Michael is so grateful to have for alignment purposes, they are not intuitive to design. Michael often plots his tables out on paper first by drawing a grid, in order to pre-plan the pixel dimensions of the rows and columns. He also works with the outlines of the grids turned on until he's happy, and then re-programs the HTML to make them invisible on the final page design. See the deconstruction of tables that follows this section.

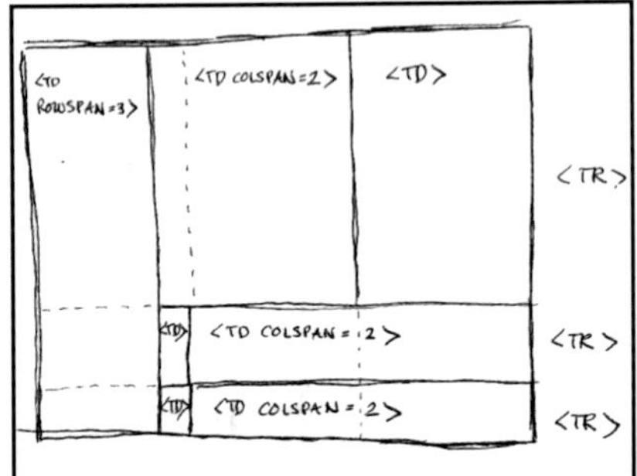

Michael usually sketches his tables first to plan the rows and columns before moving to program them in HTML. This is an example of one of his sketches. He's determined that he'll be using three rows (horizontal) and four columns (vertical) in this example.

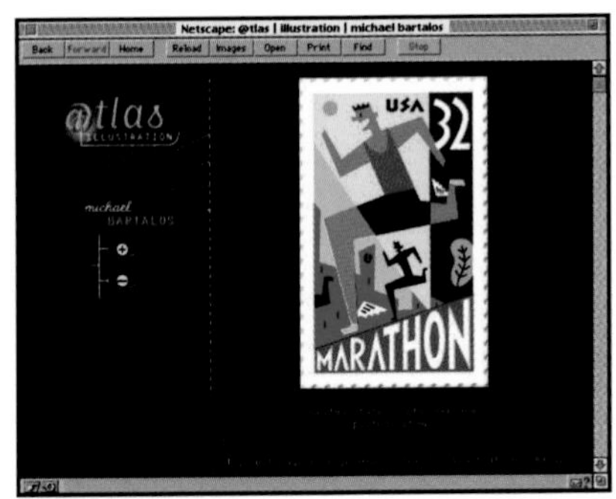

When he aligns the files he leaves the borders temporarilly turned on so he can see the table divisions to make sure they're what he wants. To turn on the borders in a table, he simply adds a border attribute to his <table> tag like this: <TABLE WIDTH=550 CELLSPACING=0 CELLPADDING=0 BORDER>.

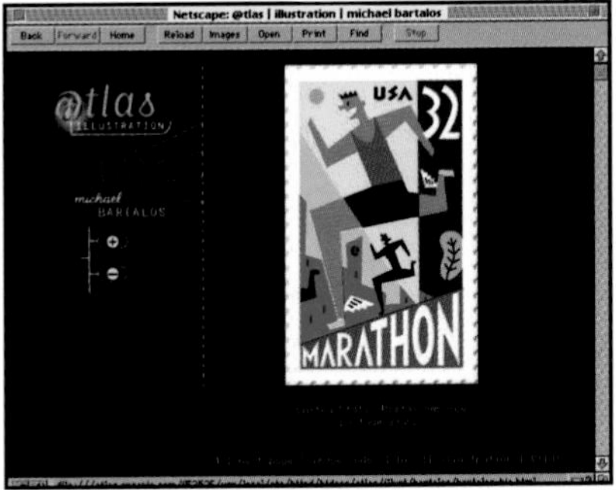

When he's satisfied with his table alignment, he removes the border attribute to turn the borders of the table off like this: <TABLE WIDTH=550 CELLSPACING=0 CELLPADDING=0>.

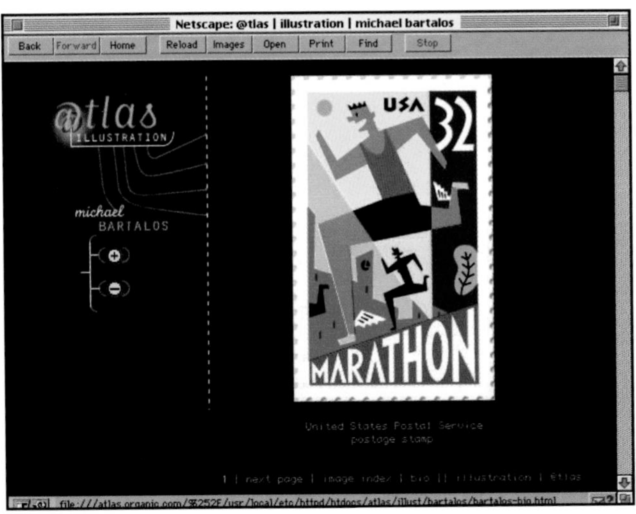

Micheal's HTML uses tables for alignment, and HTML alignment tags to align within the tables. You can view this at: ■ http://www.atlas.organic.com/atlas/illust/bartalos/index.html

HTML for Tables

```
1 <TABLE WIDTH=550 CELLSPACING=0 CELLPADDING=0>
2 <TR>
3 <TD WIDTH=184 ALIGN=left VALIGN=top>
  <A HREF="http://atlas.organic.com/cgi-
  bin/imagemap/atlas/illust/bartalos/bartalos_spb1.map">
  <IMG SRC="bartalos_nav.gif" WIDTH=182 HEIGHT=311
  ALT="michael bartalos" BORDER=0
  USEMAP="#bartalos_nav"
  ISMAP></A>
4 </TD>
  <TD WIDTH=340 ALIGN=center VALIGN=center>
  <IMG SRC="bartalos_spb1.jpg" WIDTH=190 HEIGHT=300
5 HSPACE=20 VSPACE=4 ALT="illustration" BORDER=0><P>
  <TT>United States Postal Service<BR>
  postage stamp</TT>
  </TD>
6 </TR>
  <TR>
7 <TD WIDTH=190></TD>
  <TD WIDTH=312 ALIGN=left>
  <PRE>
  <FONT COLOR="#f0bd00">1</FONT> ¦
  <A HREF="bartalos_spb2.html">next page</A> ¦
  <A HREF="bartalos_t/index.html">image index</A> ¦
  <A HREF="bartalos-
  bio.html">bio</A> ¦¦ <A HREF="../index.html">illus-
  tration</A> ¦
  <A HREF="../../index.html">@tlas</A></PRE></TD>
8 </TR></TABLE>
```

■ tags

HTML for Tables Deconstruction

1 The <table> tag marks the beginning of the table. It also includes information about the overall layout of the table.

The width=550 attribute defines the width of the table as 550 pixels; the cellspacing=0 attribute defines the space between the cells of the table as zero pixels; the cellpadding=0 attribute defines the space around the content of a cell as zero pixels. You can turn on the borders temporarily by adding the border attribute to the <table> tag.

2 The <tr> tag is used to define a table row. (Rows are horizontal.)

3 The <td> tag defines a column within a row. All the text and markup after the <td> tag is contained within the column. The width=184 attribute fixes the width of the column at 184 pixels. This is used to line up the graphics within the table.

The align=left attribute aligns the contents of the column flush-left. The valign=top attribute forces the contents to align at the top of the column.

4 The </td> tag ends a column. It is an optional endtag.

5 The HSPACE and VSPACE tags insert empty horizontal and vertical space. The values =20, or =3 refer to measurement in pixels.

6 The </tr> tag ends a row. It is an optional endtag.

7 This is an empty column set to a width of 190 pixels. This is done to force a specific width of space into the layout. Because it is in the same column as the column in #3 above (set to 184 pixels), it also forces that column to 190 pixels. All the cells in a given column in the table must be the same width, so they will gravitate to the width of the largest cell in that column.

8 The </table> endtag is the required endtag to mark the end of the table.

Adjusting File Size for @tlas Images

Michael doesn't subscribe to any standard in his Web graphics authoring methodology. He typically takes Amy's images through many iterations before he decides which best suits the page it's intended for. He'll start with a 4-bit (16 colors) setting, then go up to 5-bits (32 colors) all the way to 8-bits (256 colors). Additionally he'll make several JPEGs of the image, in Max, High, Med, and Low quality. In the end, Michael inserts all these different versions of files into his HTML document, and views them in Netscape. This allows him to try all the options, and confidently choose the best quality image with the smallest possible file size. What follows are a series of experiments where he can judge file size versus quality.

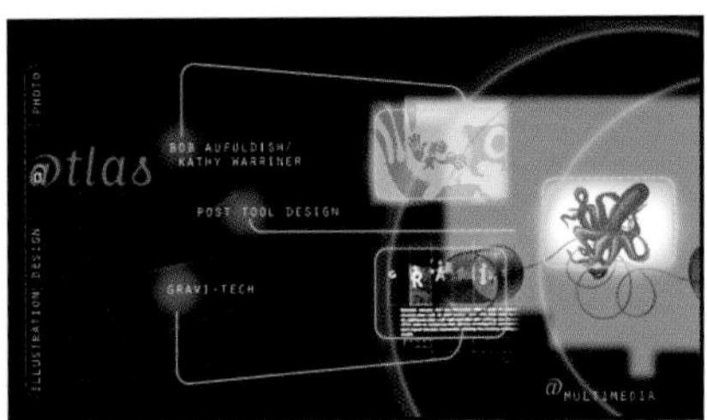

■ 713k orig.

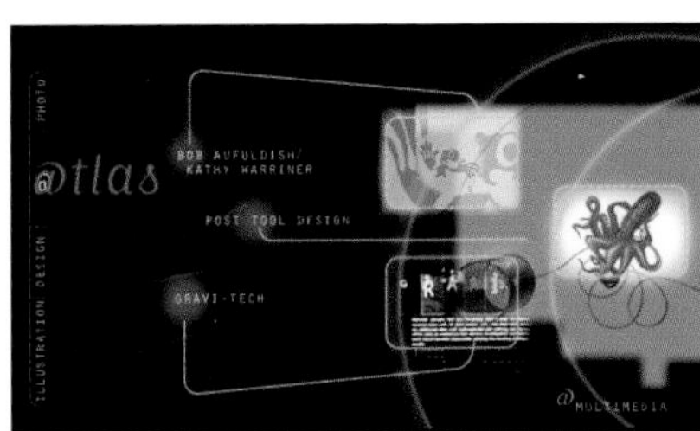

■ 61k JPEG max quality.

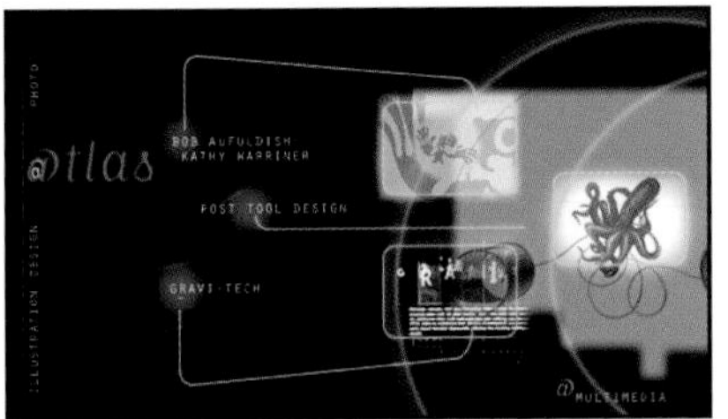

■ 42k JPEG high quality.

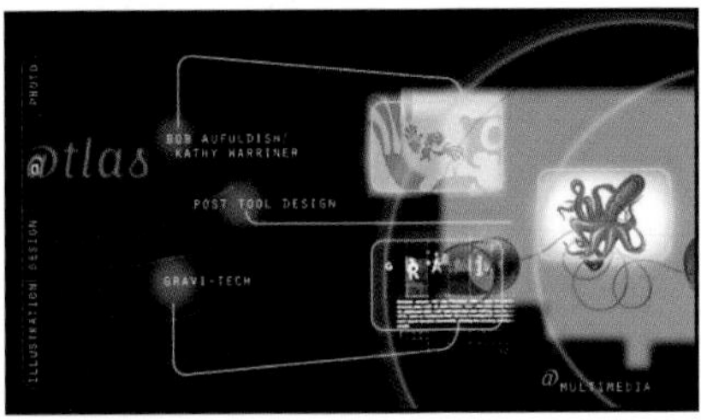

■ 29k JPEG medium quality.

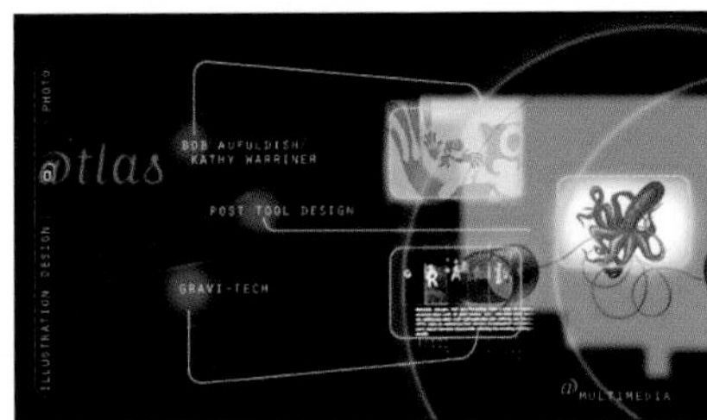

■ 25k JPEG low quality.

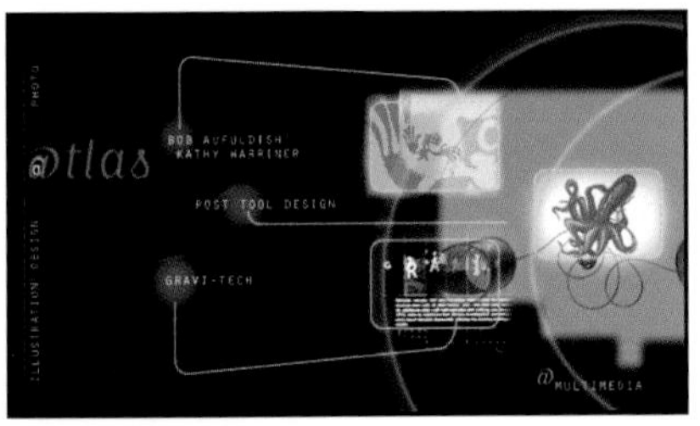

■ 86.6k 8-bit GIF 256 colors.

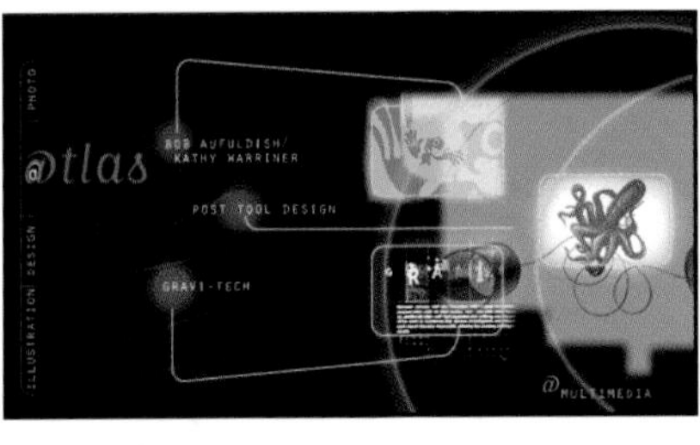

■49k 7-bit GIF 128 colors.

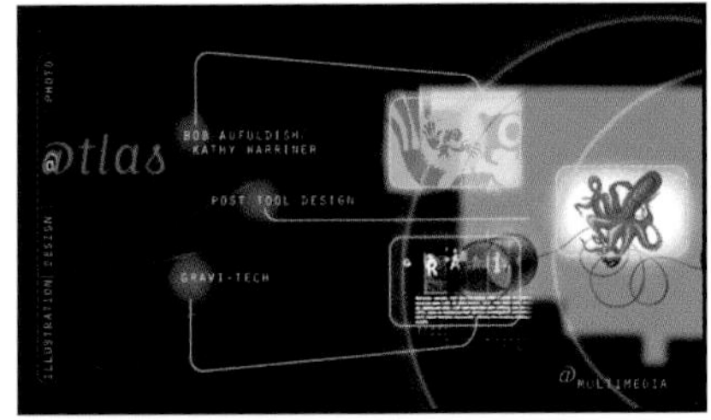

■ 42k 6-bit GIF 64 colors.

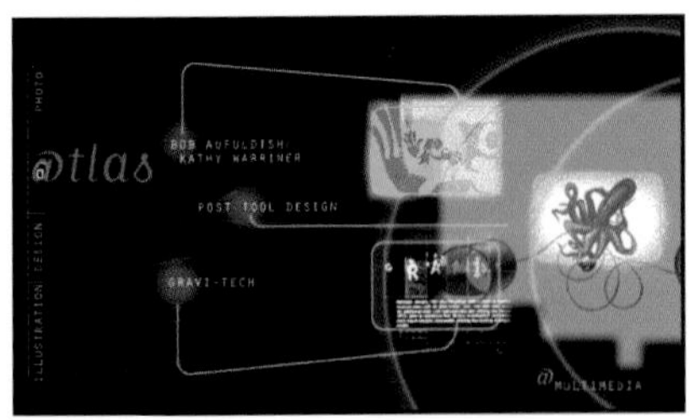

■ 36k 5-bit GIF 32 colors.

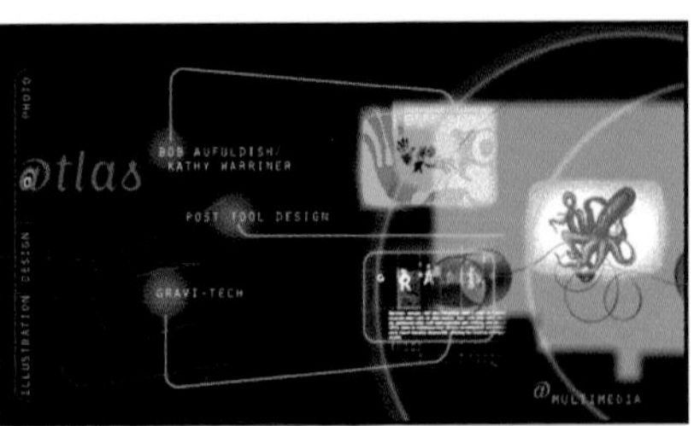

■ 29k 4-bit GIF 16 colors.

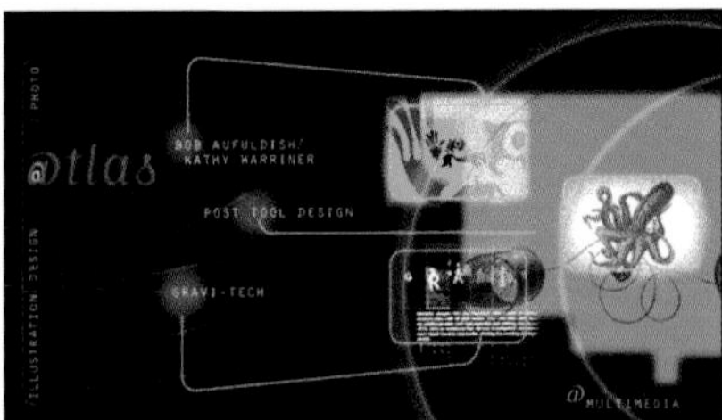

■ 25k 3-bit GIF 8 colors.

Michael experiments with compression to see how far he can push the image before it loses acceptable quality. Riding the line between file size and image quality is an extremely important job. Reducing file size can be done either by the Webmaster or the designer.

Background and Hexadecimal Color Methodology

Michael is not a huge fan of background tile patterns (which can easily clutter a page) or transparent images (which often load improperly). He usually chooses solid colored backgrounds (seeming to favor black and white as his predominant choices) and uses hexadecimal code to generate the background colors of pages, text, and links.

Hexadecimal numbers are used in Web design, because HTML requires that colors be defined by their RGB values, and that those values be converted to hex. For example, the color white, which is R:255, G:255, B:255, would convert to hexadecimal values as R:FF, G:FF, B:FF. The code within an HTML document required to indicate that you wanted white text would look like this:

```
<text="ffffff">
```

Working with hexadecimal numbers is a royal pain for anyone who isn't a mathematician or seasoned programmer, so many Web designers (including Michael), turn to helper applications and utilities that convert RGB color to hex automatically.

For hexadecimal color picking, Michael uses an Fkey shareware program, called "GetColor FKEY" (universal eyedropper tool), available from: ■ http://hyperarchive.lcs.mit.edu/HyperArchive/ Archive/gst/grf/get-color-124-fkey.hqx, which converts the eyedropper selection tool in Photoshop to its RGB values and stores them on the Clipboard.

■ step-by-step

Using HTML Color Picker

Michael uses "HTML Color Picker," which is a stand-alone Macintosh application available from: ■ http://hyperarchive.lcs.mit..edu/HyperArchive/Archive/text/html/ html-color-picker-203.hqx, to convert the RGB to hexidecimal code and places the resulting hex into his BBEdit HTML document.

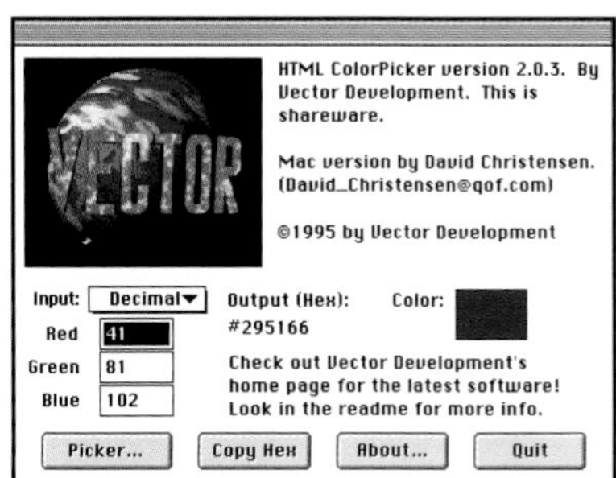

Step 1: Click on the color box.

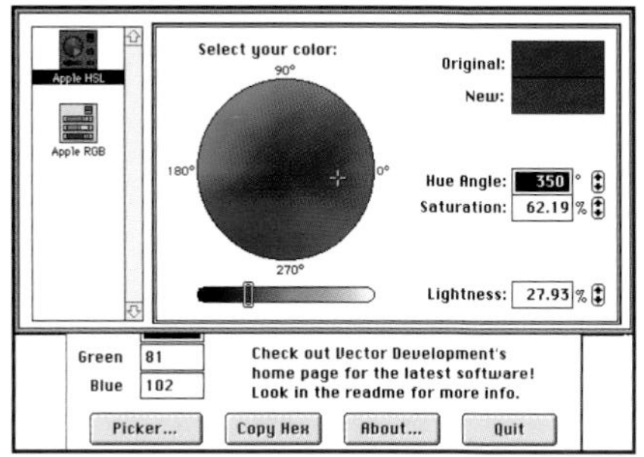

Step 2: The color picker opens. Select a color.

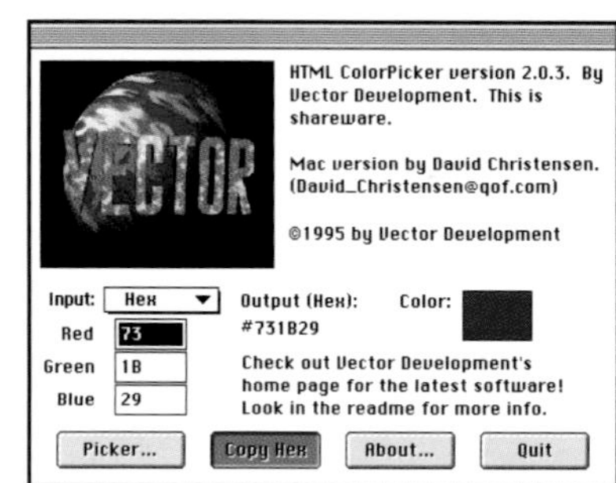

Step 3: The RGB is converted to hex and put into the clipboard for pasting into an HTML text document.

Making Image Maps

Michael uses WebMap available from: ■ http://www.city.net/cnx/software/webmap.html to generate his image map definition files. WebMap creates "server-side" image maps, meaning that these types of image maps require an additional CGI script, and need to reside on a server to work. Recently, Netscape introduced "client-side" image maps, which are programmed directly into the HTML, eliminating the need for the map definition file or CGI script. Michael uses the AppleScript droplet Map-Convert, available from: ■ http://hyperarchive.lcs.mit.edu/HyperArchive/Archive/text/html/map-convert-10-as.hqx to convert the map definition file to a client-side image map HTML document.

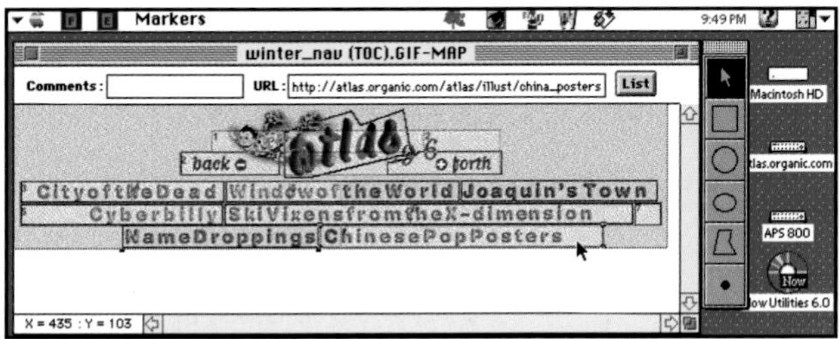

Here's an example of a WebMap file in action. The outlined regions are created with the rectangle and free polygon tool on the tool bar. As each region is highlighted, an URL can be typed in the URL data entry cell. When the regions are finished and URLs are defined, an image map definition file is automatically generated. The following HTML deconstruction is an example of what that map might look like.

Sever-Side Map Definition File

```
## atlas/winter_nav.map
# Format: NCSA
#
rect
http://atlas.organic.com/atlas/illust/china_posters/in-
dex.html 237,91
455,108
rect http://atlas.organic.com/atlas/droppings/index.html
61,91 236,107
rect http://www.well.com/user/macrone/index.html 479,74
501,91
rect
http://atlas.organic.com/atlas/multi/vixens/index.html
161,74 479,91
rect
http://atlas.organic.com/atlas/multi/cyberbilly/index.
html 5,74 161,91
rect
http://atlas.organic.com/atlas/photo/black_joaquin/index
.html 343,57
501,74
rect
http://atlas.organic.com/atlas/photo/laude_window/index.
html 161,57 342,74
rect
http://atlas.organic.com/atlas/photo/kashi_cairo/index.
html 5,57 161,74
rect http://atlas.organic.com/atlas/index.html 208,1
305,53
rect http://atlas.organic.com/atlas/index.html 306,36
376,54
rect http://atlas.organic.com/atlas/tocw.html#top 127,35
206,53
default http://atlas.organic.com/atlas/tocw.html
```

■ tags

Sever-Side Map Definition File Instructions

The following shows you how a server-side image map would need to be included into an HTML document:

1. The Map Definition file, is saved as a text-only document with the .MAP extension.

2. The .MAP file must be uploaded to a server to work.

3. You must have access to an image map CGI. In this example, it's assumed that the CGI is stored in a directory folder called cgi-bin.

4. The following code would be inserted into the HTML document. (Note the .GIF example here could also be a .JPG):

```
1 <a href="http://www.domain.nam/cgi-bin/filename.map">
2 <img src="imagename.gif"
3 border=0
4 ISMAP>
5 </a>
```

1 This establishes the anchor or destination of the links for the image map. Because the map definition file is included in the absolute path, the HTML will reference the image map coordinates and the cgi script.

2 This tag defines the name of the image to which the image map will be applied.

3 Whenever there's an <A HREF> tag, it automatically generates a default blue border around the graphic. The BORDER=0 tag will turn the border off.

4 The ISMAP command must be included at the end of a server-side image map tag.

5 The </A> is required to end the <A HREF> tag.

Client-Side Map HTML

The following shows you how a client-side image map is prepared. All the information from the map definition file (re-formatted for client-side include) resides exclusively within the HTML document, and does not require anything to be stored to the server in order to work:

```
1 <IMG SRC="imagename.gif"
2 BORDER=0
3 USEMAP="#winter_nav">
4 <MAP NAME="winter_nav">
5 <AREA SHAPE="RECT" COORDS="237,91,455,108"
  TARGET="_self"
6 HREF="illust/china_posters/index.html">
  <AREA SHAPE="RECT" COORDS="61,91,236,107"
  TARGET="_self"
  HREF="droppings/index.html">
  <AREA SHAPE="RECT" COORDS="479,74,501,91"
  TARGET="_self"
  HREF="http://www.well.com/user/macrone/index.html">
  <AREA SHAPE="RECT" COORDS="161,74,479,91"
  TARGET="_self"
  HREF="multi/vixens/index.html">
  <AREA SHAPE="RECT" COORDS="5,74,161,91"
  TARGET="_self"
  HREF="multi/cyberbilly/index.html">
  <AREA SHAPE="RECT" COORDS="343,57,501,74"
  TARGET="_self"
  HREF="photo/black_joaquin/index.html">
  <AREA SHAPE="RECT" COORDS="161,57,342,74"
  TARGET="_self"
  HREF="photo/laude_window/index.html">
  <AREA SHAPE="RECT" COORDS="5,57,161,74"
  TARGET="_self"
  HREF="photo/kashi_cairo/index.html">
  <AREA SHAPE="RECT" COORDS="208,1,305,53"
  TARGET="_self"
  HREF="index.html">
  <AREA SHAPE="RECT" COORDS="306,36,376,54"
  TARGET="_self"
  HREF="index.html">
  <AREA SHAPE="RECT" COORDS="127,35,206,53"
  TARGET="_self"
  HREF="#top">
7 </MAP>
```

■ tags

Client-Side Map Deconstruction

1 Unlike the server-side example, on a client-side example no <A HREF> tag is necessary. The image for the map is told to display via the <IMG SRC> tag.

2 Just like the server-side example, the border=0 tag turns the default blue border off. It's not necessary to turn the border off, but most designers (including those at @tlas) don't like it.

3 The USEMAP tag specifies the name of the client-side image map file to use. The # character must always precede the map name.

4 The map name is something that you define. It can be any name, but must match what is used in the USEMAP tag.

5 The TARGET="_self" tag indicates the links will display within the same window that the image map is currently in.

6 The HREF tag instructs the image map to load the referenced HTML.

7 The </MAP> tag is required to end the client-side image map.

■ note

Image Map Tags

Michael uses both the client-side and server-side image map tags within all the HTML for the @tlas site. This is a good practice, because not all browsers support client-side image maps.

■ note

Client-Side Image Map versus Server-Side Image Map

Netscape originated client-side image maps with version 2.0. An image map contains specific information, such as coordinates for regions within a single image that are hyperlinked to multiple URLs. A client-side image map means that all the information about the image map is stored within the HTML document.

A server-side image map requires that the information about the image map be saved within a "map definition file" that needs to be stored on a server and accessed by a CGI script. In general, a server-side image map is far more complicated to set up than a client-side image map. Server-side image maps work very differently on different systems—even different systems using the same brand of server!

Another difference is how the two types of image maps display data within the Netscape browser. A server-side image map shows the coordinates at the bottom of the screen, whereas a client-side image map shows the actual URL at the bottom of the screen, which is much nicer.

Here's an example of a server-side image map reading on the bottom navigation bar of Netscape. It shows the position coordinates.

Here's an example of a client-side image map reading on the bottom naviation bar of Netscape. It shows the URL! Much better.

Most people prefer client-side image maps over server-side image maps, but at the time of this writing, Netscape was the only browser to recognize the client-side tags. That's why most Webmasters include both types of image maps in their documents, otherwise the image map would only be visible to Netscape clients.

Site Management Error Checking

Michael lives by BBEdit's search and replace features that can batch process an unlimited number of HTML documents. (Batch processing means that multiple files can be changed at one time. If you changed the URL to a reference that was listed in 20 different pages, for example, they would all be changed at once.) Using Adobe's SiteMill, Michael runs all the HTML pages in his site (over 1,000!) through SiteMill's error checking feature. This takes a little over a minute (impressive, considering how large his site is) and results in an error report that finds and lists any broken links, structure problems, and missing images. Using the search and replace feature of BBEdit, he is then able to quickly resolve any errors and get the pages uploaded with the confidence that all the links and images are working properly.

File Management and Naming Conventions

Each page on @tlas contains its own navigation graphic that has an associated image map. Over 150 image maps are on the @tlas site, which poses a staggering file management challenge.

For this reason, Michael is also very precise and careful with his naming conventions. If an artist has 10 pages devoted to his or her section, the map file will be called by the artist's name, page number, and file type. This makes it very easy to work on large volumes of documents and keep track of everything.

For example, if you look at the directory structure of the following:

```
http://atlas.organic.com/atlas/photo/kashi_cairo/
```

■ you'll notice Michael's conventions. The directory is named after the photographer (Ed Kashi) and story subject (Cairo's City of the Dead). An abbreviated version of this name is used for the files in the directory:

```
kashi_c01.html
kashi_c01.JPG
kashi_c02.html
kashi_c02.JPG
...
```

■ Pages are numbered in sequence, so that if you're viewing kashi_c06.html, the previous page is kashi_c05.html, and the next page is kashi_c07.html. Every file has a corresponding image (for example, kashi_06.JPG) and server-side map file (kashi_nav06.map) with the same number.

All this numbering enables Michael to quickly assemble a story. Using the first page as a template, he chooses to "Save As" whatever the next page would be, then goes in and adds increments to all the relevant digits by one. (Save "kashi_06.html" as "kashi_07.html," then change all 5s to 6s, 6s to 7s, and so on.)

Another advantage to this way of naming files is if a link breaks, it's pretty easy to track down the HTML file and fix it. If every page had a descriptive name rather than a numerical name, Michael would have to keep trying to figure out where the page fell in the story sequence.

■ note

Keeping Current with HTML Specs

How does Michael keep current, given the ever-changing ways of the Web? Macrone subscribes to the following Usenet groups and mailing lists:

■ comp.sys.mac.com

■ comp.infosystems.www.authoring.html

■ ADV-HTML Mailing List
listserv@ualvm.ua.edu

■ Apple-Internet-Authoring Mailing List
listproc@solutions. apple.com

■ HTG-MAIN Mailing List
magjordomo@rpmdp.com

HTML Readability

Michael is an advocate of viewing the source of anything and everything that appeals to him. "I pay special attention to my own HTML code readiblity," Michael asserts. "If I were to die tomorrow, someone could pick up and carry on with @tlas pretty easily by studying my source code. I make sure it's neat, and will often use comment tags and underscored lines for separating text. I don't want to be the only one doing this job forever, so I'd rather not make myself indespensible and trap myself."

Deconstructing @tlas's HTML

The home page of @tlas uses frames in order to filter viewers from Netscape 2.0 and viewers from other platforms. This could also be done with CGI, but Michael decided to do it with HTML instead. He includes a "progressive JPEG" (see Progressive JPEG note) in the frames version, and a regular JPEG in the non-frames version.

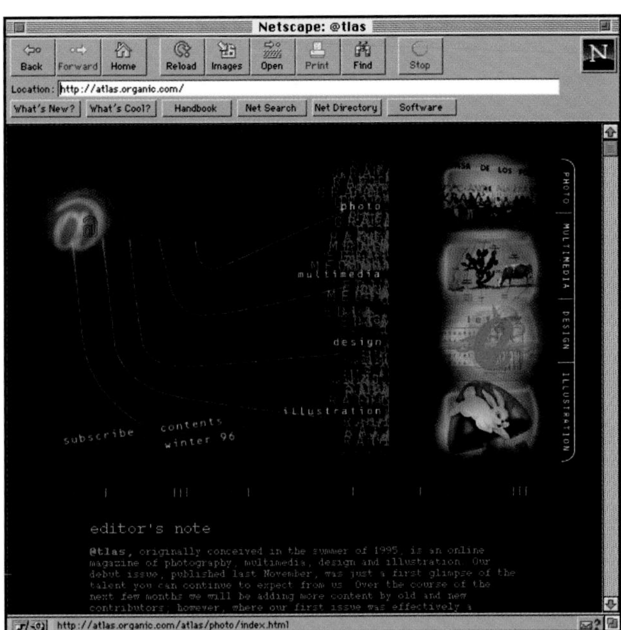

The home page for @tlas. It uses frames at 100% size of the window so they aren't visible to the end viewer, but serve as a filtering mechanism between those viewing the site from Netscape 2.0+, and other browsers. You can view this at: ■ http://www.atlas.organic.com/atlas/fall.html references.

@tlas's Home Page HTML

```
1 <!DOCTYPE HTML PUBLIC "-//Netscape Comm.  Corp.//DTD
  HTML//EN">
  <HTML><HEAD><TITLE>@tlas</TITLE>
2 <BASE TARGET="_top">
3 <META NAME="keywords" CONTENT="atlas, @tlas,
  \@tlas">
4 <META HTTP-EQUIV="reply-to"
  CONTENT="atlas@atlas.organic.com">
5 <LINK REL="owns"
  HREF="mailto:atlas@atlas.organic.com">
  <!-- Copyright (c) 1996 by @tlas productions --
  ></HEAD>
6 <FRAMESET ROWS="100%,*">
7 <FRAME SRC="index_pro.html" NAME="index" margin
  width=0
  marginheight=0 noresize>
  <FRAME SRC="icon/blank8.gif" HEIGHT=1
  WIDTH=1></FRAMESET>
8 <MAP NAME="main">
  <AREA SHAPE="POLYGON"
  COORDS="115,259,115,278,217,264,217,247,"
  TARGET="_top"
  HREF="atlas/tocf.html">
  <AREA SHAPE="POLYGON"
  COORDS="115,298,115,279,217,266,219,298,"
  TARGET="_top"
  HREF="atlas/tocw.html">
  <AREA SHAPE="POLYGON"
  COORDS="115,279,15,291,15,259,112,259," TARGET="_top"
  HREF="atlas/mail.html">
  <AREA SHAPE="RECT" COORDS="2,2,239,131"
  TARGET="_top"
  HREF="atlas/credits/index.html">
  <AREA SHAPE="RECT" COORDS="243,225,510,307"
  TARGET="_top"
  HREF="atlas/illust/index.html">
  <AREA SHAPE="RECT" COORDS="243,151,510,225"
  TARGET="_top"
  HREF="atlas/design/index.html">
  <AREA SHAPE="RECT" COORDS="243,82,511,150"
  TARGET="_top"
  HREF="atlas/multi/index.html">
  <AREA SHAPE="RECT" COORDS="243,1,510,81"
  TARGET="_top"
  HREF="atlas/photo/index.html">
  <AREA SHAPE="RECT" COORDS="512,209,535,307"
  TARGET="_top"
  HREF="atlas/illust/index.html">
  <AREA SHAPE="RECT" COORDS="512,147,536,207"
  TARGET="_top"
  HREF="atlas/design/index.html">
  <AREA SHAPE="RECT" COORDS="512,63,535,145"
```

```
TARGET="_top"
HREF="atlas/multi/index.html">
<AREA SHAPE="RECT" COORDS="512,1,535,60"
TARGET="_top"
HREF="atlas/photo/index.html">
9 </MAP>
<MAP NAME="main_nav">
<AREA SHAPE="RECT" COORDS="189,0,279,24"
TARGET="_top"
HREF="atlas/illust/index.html">
<AREA SHAPE="RECT" COORDS="131,0,186,24"
TARGET="_top"
HREF="atlas/design/index.html">
<AREA SHAPE="RECT" COORDS="53,0,129,23"
TARGET="_top"
HREF="atlas/multi/index.html">
<AREA SHAPE="RECT" COORDS="0,0,51,24"
TARGET="_top"
HREF="atlas/photo/index.html">
<AREA SHAPE="RECT" COORDS="0,0,51,24" TARGET="_top"
HREF="atlas/photo/index.html">
</MAP>
<MAP NAME="credits">
<AREA SHAPE="RECT" COORDS="24,39,107,49"
TARGET="_self"
HREF="atlas/design/index.html">
<AREA SHAPE="RECT" COORDS="2,72,136,95"
TARGET="_self"
HREF="http://www.well.com/user/macrone/">
<AREA SHAPE="RECT" COORDS="36,50,159,60"
TARGET="_self"
HREF="mailto:ame@atlas.organic.com">
<AREA SHAPE="RECT" COORDS="46,61,157,71"
TARGET="_self"
HREF="mailto:david@atlas.organic.com">
<AREA SHAPE="RECT" COORDS="8,13,153,37"
TARGET="_self"
HREF="mailto:olivier@atlas.organic.com">
</MAP>
10 <NOFRAMES>
<BODY BGCOLOR="#000000" TEXT="#b09a66" LINK="#285064"
VLINK="#285064" ALINK="#000000">
<CENTER>
11 <TT><A NAME="top" HREF="atlas/tocw.html">winter 96
is here
</A><TT>
</CENTER>
12 <TABLE CELLSPACING=0 CELLPADDING=0>
13 <TR>
14 <TD COLSPAN=3 ALIGN=CENTER>
15 <A HREF="http://atlas.organic.com/cgi-
bin/imagemap/atlas/main.map">
<IMG SRC="atlas/main.JPG" WIDTH=538 HEIGHT=311
ALT="imagemap"
16 BORDER=0 USEMAP="#main" ISMAP></A>
17 <PRE><A HREF="atlas/tocw.html">winter 96</A> |
<A HREF="atlas/tocf.html">fall 95</A> |||
<A HREF="atlas/photo/index.html">photo</A> |
<A HREF="atlas/illust/index.html">illustration</A> |
<A HREF="atlas/design/index.html">design</A> |
<A HREF="atlas/multi/index.html">multimedia</A> |||
<A HREF="atlas/mail.html">mail</A><P>
</PRE>
18 </TD></TR>
<TR>
<TD WIDTH=74 ALIGN=LEFT VALIGN=TOP>
19 <IMG SRC="icon/8.GIF" WIDTH=72 HEIGHT=8 ALT="">
</TD>
<TD ALIGN=LEFT>
20 <FONT COLOR="#ccccaa">
21 <H2>editor's note</H2></FONT>
22 <IMG SRC="icon/8.GIF" WIDTH=380 HEIGHT=4><BR>
23 <B>@tlas,</B> originally conceived in the summer of
1995, is an online magazine of photography,
multimedia, design and illustration. Our debut
issue, published last November, was just a first
glimpse of the talent you can continue to expect
from us. Over the course of the next few months we
will be adding more content by old and new
contributors; however, where our first issue was
effectively a showcase, future issues will be more
editorially driven--less like a portfolio and more
like a magazine. Our <B>
<A HREF="atlas/tocw.html">Winter 96</A></B>
issue, designed by <B>David Karam</B> of <B><A
HREF="atlas/multi/posttool/index.html">
Post Tool Design,</A></B> should give you an
idea of our future editorial
direction. <P></TD>
```

tags

@tlas's Home Page Deconstruction

1 This line uses SGML (Standard Generalized Markup Language) syntax that declares that this is an HTML document that is using Netscape HTML specs (see SGML note). This type of document header can also be read by HTML validators.

2 A BASE TARGET sets a default target type. A "top" setting will initiate a new page that does not use a FRAMESET. Michael wanted to clear the FRAMESET after this first page. He only wanted to use FRAMES as a filtering mechanism, and other functions within the rest of the site might have been jeapordized if they were viewed within Frames. "top" clears out the FRAMESET and uses the same window to display the new HTML page. This makes it so when you click on a link, it will go to the new window that you specify as a target.

3 Michael is using the META NAME to present "keywords" that tell indexers and robots (automated search detection programs that rove the Web to collect data about sites) that the CONTENT of this site is owned by @tlas. He has spelled @tlas three different ways, with and without the "@" symbol, and with a slash in front of the "@" symbol in order to ensure that the word @tlas is recognized. The "@" sign has special uses on the Internet, and the robots might not understand that it is part of the site's formal name.

4 In this case the "reply-to" within the META HTTP-EQUIV tag is also a service to robots and indexers to let them know what the mailing address is for the owner of this document.

5 The <LINK REL> tag has four possible attributes: owns, made, next, and previous. In this case its purpose is to identify individuals and their relationships to this document. The reply-to could refer to a Webmaster or third party, whereas an "owns" implies the proprieter of the document.

6 The <FRAMESET ROWS="100%,*"> defines two rows for the Frames—one that takes up 100% of the window and another that takes up whatever remains. Michael wrote it this way because he didn't want the Frames to be visible, hence the first frame will take up the entire screen. He is using Frames as a filtering device in order to show one page to Netscape 2.0+ viewers, and another page to viewers from other browsers.

7 The <FRAME SRC> tag identifies the content of the Frame to be the document "index_pro.html." The NAME "index" is assigned to that HTML document, so that in the future it can be referenced by the name "index" instead of "index_pro.html."

8 MAP tells Netscape 2.0 that everything between it and the "</map>" tag is a client-side image map. NAME="main" tells Netscape to search for an image that the programmer has named "main" with the USEMAP="#main"(see line #16). A client-side image map (see note) always begins with the tag MAP.

9 </MAP> closes the client-side image map. In this HTML document Michael didn't include a server-side image map because he has already filtered out the non-Netscape audience by putting the client-side map within the Frames part of his HTML.

10 <NOFRAMES> is followed by a duplicate version of the same HTML, but all tags relating to frames have been stripped. If a client lands on a page with a browser that doesn't support frames, all of the HTML after the <NOFRAMES> tag is loaded instead.

11 <TT> stands for typewriter text. This tag overrides any font that the user has specified, and forces the Netscape browser to instead load a monospaced font resembling a typewriter font. The only thing that can't be overridden using this or any other tag, unfortunately, is the user-defined size of the font.

12 By setting the CELLSPACING and the CELLPADDING to 0, the browser is instructed to eliminate the table border between each cell the distance between the contents of the cell and the edge of the table.

13 <TR> Table Row instructs the browser to start a row (rows go horizontally, columns go vertically).

14 <TD> means table data. The COLSPAN=3 tells the row to span three columns, and the ALIGN=CENTER tag specifies for it to be aligned center, relative to the rest of the table. Note: If Michael were to place <center> outside and before the <TABLE> tag it would make the entire table centered within the browser window.

15 In this case, Michael is anchoring an image to a map definition file. The image map definition file is called "main.map," and the cgi-bin is being referenced to call forth a server-side image map (see note).

16 Whenever a server-side image map is used, the ISMAP tag must follow the USEMAP instructions. Michael is also using the USEMAP command, which is calling forth the client-side image map that was defined and named earlier in this document. Why is he using both a server-side and client-side? See the note!

17 By using the <PRE> tag, the alignment of the text, as it was written in the HTML document is honored, as opposed to following regular HTML conventions. For example, without the <PRE> tag if you have 16 spaces down and seven to the right between two words in your HTML document, the browser will only read it as one space. With the <PRE> tag you actually get 16 spaces down and seven to the right separation between the two words. Warning: One important side effect of this tag is that it will not re-format to accommodate different window sizes as standard text will.

18 The </TD> ends the data cell within a table. The </TR> tag closes the row.

19 Michael is using an image "8.GIF" (which happens to be a transparent GIF 8×8 pixels in size) within this data cell. The next command (WIDTH=72 HEIGHT=8) stretches it so it is 72 pixels wide and eight pixels high. Using transparent images this way enables text to be aligned perfectly to whatever specifications Michael wants.

20 Using the <FONT COLOR> tag causes the text to change to a hexadecimal color, in this case, a cool white. Font color can be changed at any time using this tag, and must be closed with the </FONT> tag.

21 The words "editor's note" are changed to large, bold, "headline" text by using the <H2> tag. Note how <H2> text is somewhat smaller than the <H1> text. The </FONT> tag closes the tag for the cool white text and the rest of the document reverts back to the default text colors defined earlier in the HTML document.

22 Here's another example of the 8×8 transparent GIF being used right below the "editor's note" text. By entering WIDTH=380 HEIGHT=4>, a space of four pixels is inserted between "editor's note" and the following paragraph.

23 <B> causes the word "@tlas" to be bold, and is closed with the <B> tag.

■ note

Progressive JPEG versus a Standard JPEG

Progressive JPEG is a subset of the standard JPEG file format. Pro-JPEGs boast 30% more compression efficiency than regular JPEGs, and they have the added advantage of being "interlaced." An interlaced JPEG is similar to an interlaced GIF, in that it appears to "res-up," or come into focus as it's first being viewed.

So, Pro-JPEGs are a pretty neat thing, except that Netscape is the only browser (at present) to support them. So what, you might ask, doesn't @tlas use other tags and formats that are Netscape-specific? Sure, but here's the difference. The penalty for using a Pro-JPEG in a non-Netscape 2.0+ browser is a broken picture icon! In some cases, like with animated GIFs, if a browser doesn't support it, at least a single image still appears. Michael didn't want the front page of @tlas to not appear but he did want to use the advantages of a Pro-JPEG; hence, the use of frames and two sets of HTML documents to filter out the non-Netscape 2.0 visitors from the Netscape 2.0 crowd. A non-Netscape 2.0 viewer would see the page with the larger, regular JPEG formatted image.

■ note

SGML

SGML stands for Standard Generalized Markup Language, and is intended to ensure that documents are readable by different kinds of computers. SGML is a very specific structure for storing information, and includes tags, just like HTML. Unlike HTML though, different versions or different browser interpretations to SGML do not exist.

Every SGML document must include a legend or key that describes the mark-up used in that document. Each individual legend, or set of pre-defined SGML mark-up, is known as a Document Type Definition (DTD) or a Rules File.

If some of the mark-up used in SGML looks a lot like HTML, that's because HTML is SGML. HTML is actually one set of pre-defined SGML mark-up: it's a DTD. It simply happens to be such a widely accepted DTD that it is sometimes confused as a language itself.

The reason why Michael uses SGML syntax at the beginning of his HTML document is for future compatibility reasons. There's no telling what kind of browsers will exist in the future, and making an HTML document SGML savvy is insurance that the HTML might be translated accurately by browsers of the future.

For more information about SGML, go to SoftQuad's site at:

- http://www.sil.org/sgml/sgml.html

HTML Validators

HTML validators check the syntax and accuracy of tags within HTML documents. The idea is that validating an HTML document can ensure its portablity to existing and future browsers. The disadvantage to using an HTML validator is that it might hiccup on non-standard HTML code, such as certain Netscape-only or MSIE-only extensions. What Michael has done is to tell the validator that he is using non-standard HTML in the hopes that the validator will recognize why he is breaking tagging conventions.

If you're searching for an HTML validator, try:

- http:www.webtechs.com/html-val-svc/

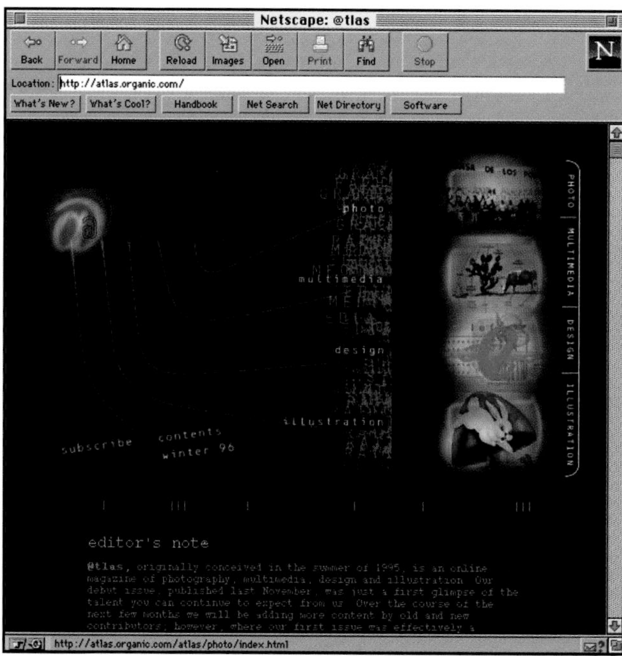

What follows is the HTML that the @tlas home page document references. Note that the background color of the page and text link colors are in this document, as opposed to the frames version. See the HTML decsonstruction for further explanation.

Nested Frames Document HTML

```
<!DOCTYPE HTML PUBLIC "-//Netscape Comm. Corp.//
DTD HTML//EN">
<HTML><HEAD><TITLE>@tlas</TITLE>
<BASE TARGET="_top">
<META NAME="keywords" CONTENT="atlas, @tlas, \@tlas">
<META HTTP-EQUIV="reply-to"
CONTENT="atlas@atlas.organic.com">
<LINK REL="owns"
HREF="mailto:atlas@atlas.organic.com">
<!-- Copyright (c) 1996 by @tlas productions --
></HEAD>
1 <BODY BGCOLOR="#000000" TEXT="#b09a66" LINK="#285064"
VLINK="#285064" ALINK="#000000">
<CENTER><TT><A NAME="top" HREF="atlas/tocw.html">
winter 96 is
here ...</A><BR>
<IMG SRC="icon/blank8.GIF" HEIGHT=2 WIDHT=2><TT>
</CENTER>
<TABLE CELLSPACING=0 CELLPADDING=0>
<TR>
<TD COLSPAN=3 ALIGN=CENTER>
<A HREF="http://atlas.organic.com/cgi-
bin/imagemap/atlas/main.map">
2 <IMG SRC="atlas/main_pro.JPG" WIDTH=538 HEIGHT=311
3 ALT="imagemap" BORDER=0 USEMAP="#main" ISMAP></A>
```

■ tags

Nested Frames Document Deconstruction

1 Very few differences exist between this document and the index.html document. The single major difference is found in this tag. Because this HTML was nested inside the first document's FRAMESET tag, it used the black background from this document and did not need to define its own.

2 Here's the whole reason for having the two documents—the fact that this PRO.JPG image is only visible to Netscape 2.0 browsers. Michael nested this PRO.JPG within his first HTML page by inserting the image inside this page instead of the first one.

3 Everything from this tag on down is identical to the first document. Michael actually only wrote the HTML one time, and then copied and pasted it into a new HTML file. He then added the PRO.JPG artwork, and left everything else in place. It was not necessary to duplicate all this information, it was simply convenient to do so.

■ site summary

@tlas

The @tlas site is a successful example of merging innvoative graphics, content, and HTML programming. The founders, who all work for free, are clearly dedicated and talented enough to stand well above the average Web design crowd. What makes the @tlas site so excellent? Original content, original graphics, original interface design, and outstanding HTML design.

■ An artist-based portfolio Web site is not only viable, but can outpace more commercial sites in terms of popularity and hits.

■ Art directors of Web sites don't necessarilly have to know anything about the Web, if they are teamed up with others who can do the programming and technical assistance. Good design skills are good design skills, on the Web or elsewhere.

■ Interface design doesn't have to take a sledgehammer approach. Innovation is welcome if it's well-thought out and well-implemented.

■ Experimenting with layers and modes in Photoshop can yield distinctive and flexible results.

■ When programming tables, it can help to keep the borders turned on when adjusting the regions until the desired effect is reached. It's then an easy matter to turn them off.

■ Tables are an excellent device to ensure consistent image alignment on a series of sequential pages.

■ Never make assumptions about image compression levels. When working with hybrid images that combine graphics and photographs, test to determine whether using GIFs or JPEGs is the best file format to achieve the smallest possible file sizes.

■ Though client-side image maps are great, don't assume everyone can view them. Be sure to include both a client-side and server-side map on your pages.

■ When working on a large site, arrive at naming conventions that will enable you to keep track of files and where they belong within the site's hierarchy.

■ Progressive JPEGs offer better compression than regular JPEGs, but are only currently supported by Netscape.

HotWired

using frames for interface navigation

What this chapter covers:

- **Designing for Frames**
- **Copy Editing for the Web**
- **Layered Photoshop Compositing**
- **Using Perl for CGI**
- **HTML for Frames**

http://www.hotwired.com/cocktail/ HotWired is one of the largest Web design ventures in the world—with 170 employees (and growing) who collectively work toward creating the coolest Web site they can. Because Web construction is relatively new to everyone, it's interesting to observe how HotWired deals with issues that plague all of us all who do this kind of work. One area that is constantly being questioned and challenged is "user interface" or "navigation" through Web pages. With version 2.0 release of Netscape, a new feature was introduced called "frames" that was poised to change the way Web page navigation worked. This chapter studies the Cocktail program of HotWired, and all the surrounding challenges their implementation of frames introduced.

Firm: HotWired

URL: http://www.hotwired.com/cocktail/

Server Hardware: SGI Challenge-S

Web Server: Apache 1.0

Operating System: Irix

Concept and Information Content: Laura Moorhead

Design Direction: Jonathan Louie

Design: Brady Clark

CGI/Database/HTML Programming: David Thau, Jill Atkinson, Chris Miller, Shaun Welch

Photo Editor: Marla Aufmuth

Cocktail Photography: Jon Lucich

Design Hardware: Macintosh

Programming Hardware: Macintosh

Design Software: Photoshop, WebMap, DeBabelizer

The Origins of HotWired's Cocktail Channel

When Laura Moorhead came up with the idea for Hot-Wired's Cocktail site, she was copy chief at HotWired. The concept behind Cocktail was to promote an irreverent, fun attitude—from lounge music, to vintage clothing, to campy furniture. The cocktail culture theme provided a great opportunity for Laura to generate stories related to the mystique of popular drink names such as the martini, aviation, and pegu. These stories would be humorous and tongue-in-cheek, yet based on fact.

The Decision to Use Frames

Jeff Veen, Interface Director, brought frames to Design Director Jonathoan Louie's attention when Netscape 2.0 was a couple of weeks old. Jonathan had just recently met with Laura Moorehead to discuss the Cocktail concept. He instantly recognized that frames could be put to good use as the interface for idea. Laura couldn't take a lot of time away from her job duties as copy chief to implement her idea, and the notion of using a template that involved frames seemed like it might save time.

Frames promised to be much less work than a free-form set of pages because the dimensions of each week's set of graphics could remain the same. Artwork assignments could be handed off to artists, Laura could handle the simple HTML, while Jill Atkinson, HotWired's program development coordinator, could handle the serious HTML coding. Staff engineers were assigned to create the Virtual Blender, a database of Cocktail's drink recipes. This set-up allowed everyone to work autonomously, while creating an end result that would later fall together like puzzle pieces.

What are Frames?

Frames are a newcomer to Web design vocabulary. They offer the capability to divide a Web page into regions, so that each region functions as its own Web page. This means parts of a page can change, while other regions of the page remain static. Frames are perfect for navigation bars that won't change from page to page, while other content can be set to change independently.

Frames sound great in theory, but there are some notewor-thy snags. Many site designers insert existing Web pages that were originally designed for full-screen browsers into cramped small frame regions. This forces the end-viewer to scroll through graphics and text inside smaller windows than the pages were originally designed for. Real estate on a Web page is already a precious commodity, and breaking apart a small screen into multiple small screens can do more dam-age to your presentation than good. It's recommended that you follow HotWired's lead, and use a maximum of three frame regions to a page, so your audience isn't frustrated by having to scroll through small windows.

HotWired chose to develop a site from the ground up that was tailored for the limits and benefits of frames, rather than putting existing sites awkwardly into a frames format. Studying HotWired's experiences serves as an excellent model from which to learn successful interface and naviga-tion design using frames.

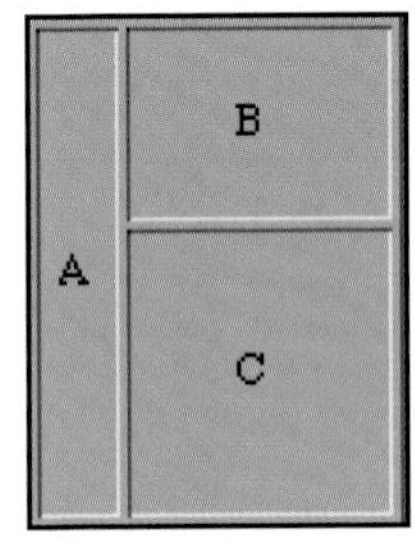

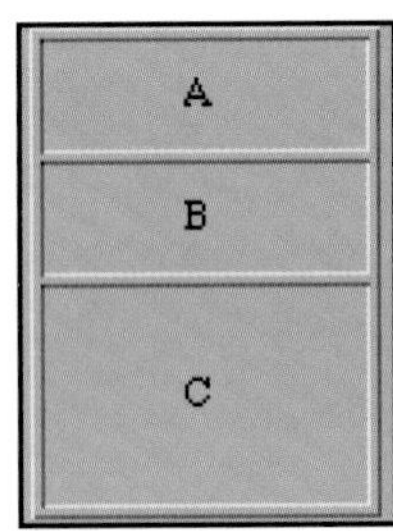

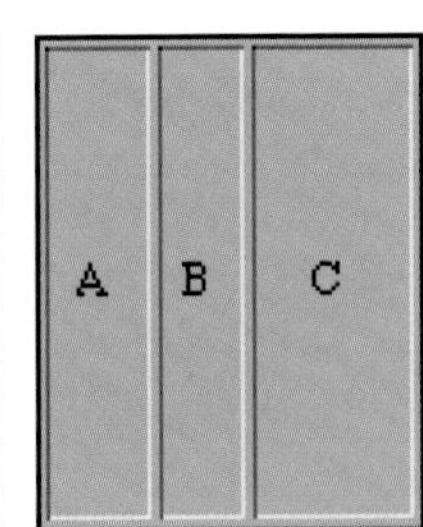

Examples of frame configuration screens, from an excellent tutorial-based site out of Japan: ■ http://ncdesign.kyushuid.ac.jp/html/Normal/frame.html

The Structure of Cocktail

Frames allow multiple pages to be nested within one HTML document. Cocktail has six main categories within their frame-version of the opening page. Here's an overview of what they look like:

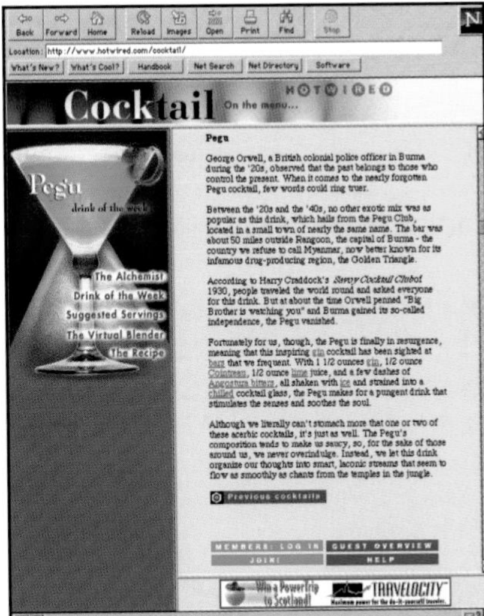

The site opens to the "Drink of the Week." Clicking the left Drink of the Week frame will send you to other areas.

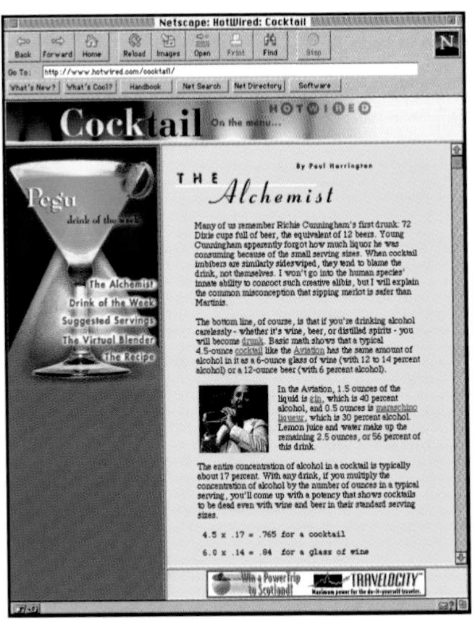

The Alchemist provides information that usually elaborates on some aspect of drinking or mixing.

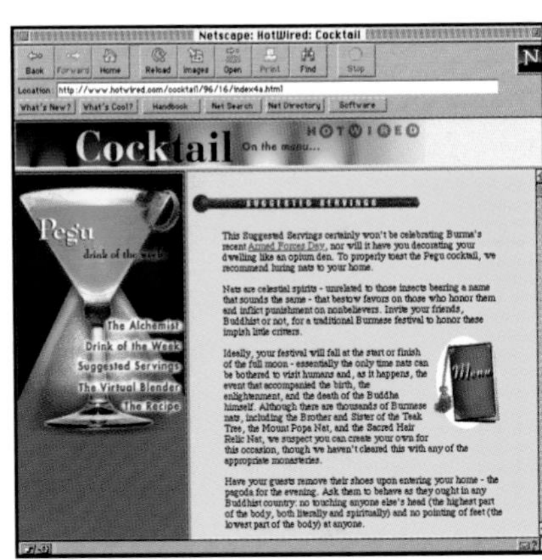

The Suggested Servings page provides mixing instructions for the drink of the week, and often goes off on other entertaining tangents.

The Virtual Blender page is where Cocktail visitors can do word searches for drinks by name or ingredients.

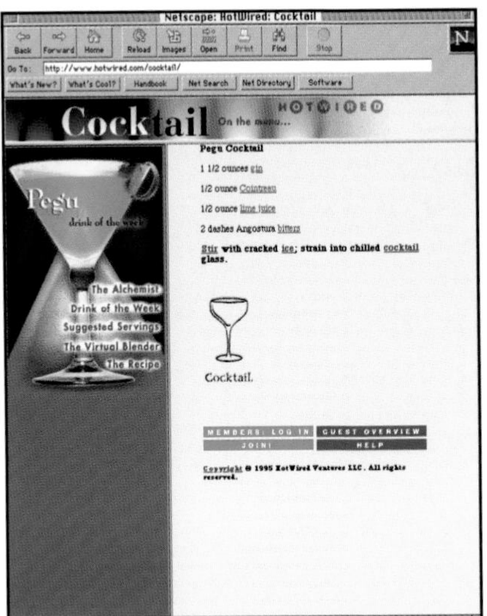

The Recipe page provides a list of ingredients and portion recommendations for the "Drink of the Week."

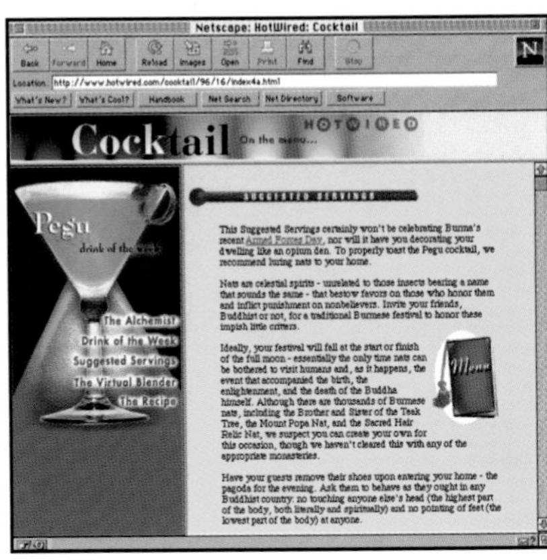

The Planning a Party? page is where visitors can enter information into a form and, based on their entries, are presented a list of recommended drink choices to serve.

Writing Content for Frames

People surfing the Web are a pretty fickle lot; if something is too slow they'll readily click elsewhere. Laura keeps this in mind when writing copy for Cocktail by using text-based hyperlinks whenever possible. If a story mentions a subject that is worthy of elaboration, she'll link to it, rather than expand on that subject within the main body of type. This makes for shorter amounts of text, but offers access to deeper information to people who are interested (while not boring people who are not).

Since Cocktail launched the first week of November 1995, Laura has been developing a library of stories that are relevant to a novice mixer, or anyone interested in trivia. If a visitor clicks on the hypertext link "shake vigorously" they might be treated to a QuickTime movie of Cocktail's resident alchemist Paul Harrington maniacally shaking a mixed drink at the camera. Clicking on the hypertext word "gin" might reveal that gin was first sold in the 17th century as a blooc cleanser, but was later preferred as a relaxant.

Laura's stories and links always fill the right frame within Cocktail's pages. The text fits perfectly withi this shape, because it is using default HTML text (see HTML deconstruction that follows later). If you use the <pre>, <no wrap>, or <table> tags, you text will not be as flexible as what's seen in Cocktail, and you'd have to measure in pixels how wide the frame would be to ensure the text would fit. By using default HTML text, the Drink of the Week page is flexible enough to fit correctly within any sized browser or frame.

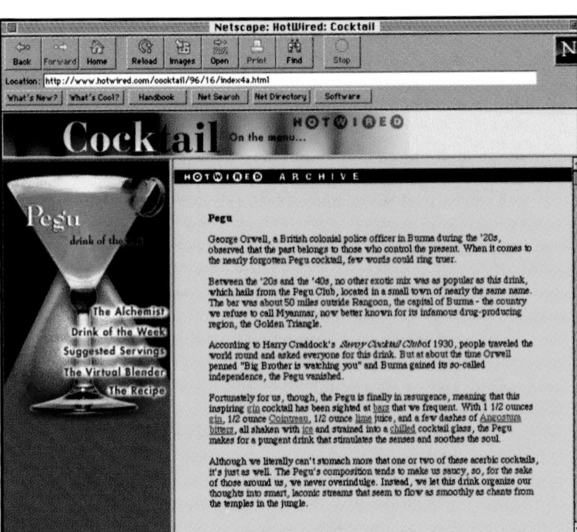

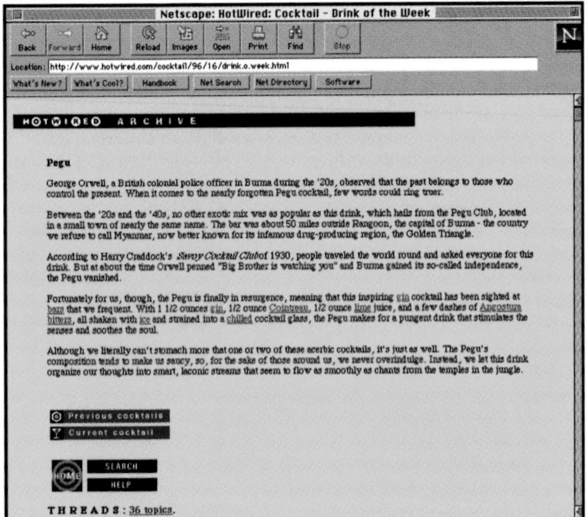

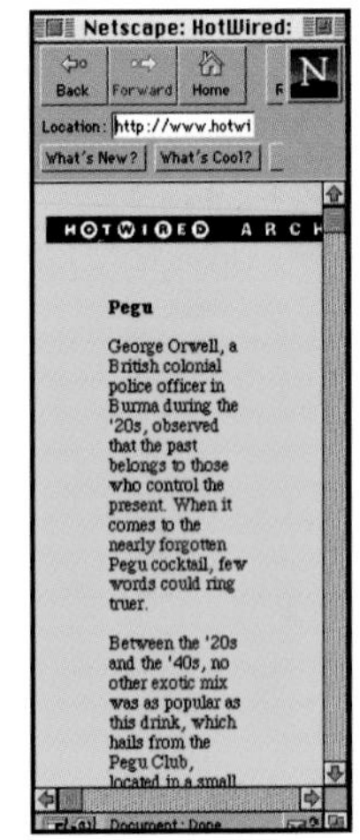

Regardless of how the text on this pages is viewed, whether within a frame, a full-screen browser, or a narrowly re-sized browser, the text always repositions itself properly. It uses the default text settings, without special tags like <pre> that would not resize in a flexible manner. This makes the type formatting look great within frames, without frustrating viewers by requiring that they scroll horizontally to view important information.

Art Direction for Frames

Design Director Jonathan Louie likes to refer to Cocktail's content as "not an ocean or a lake" but a "puddle." Frames, he warns, are perfect for navigating around a puddle, as if in a toy sailboat. Toy sailboats don't do well in deep oceans, and frames navigation can become easily swamped in high seas. If the site gets too deep, he warns, it would have to depend on unsightly scroll bars that would become a nightmare for navigation, and add unnecessary noise to an otherwise clean visual environment. Keeping Cocktail's pages rich and fun were his objectives, and he did not want confusing navigation to encumber those goals.

Early in the design process, the team defined their audience as non-technical, and entertaiment-oriented—college students, for example, who might own a pre-configured computer bought at a consumer-based retailer, with limited RAM, and screen size. Everything in Cocktail is designed to work well on a 480×360 or a standard 640×480 computer monitor screen.

The graphics within Cocktail were designed to function like a book dust jacket in order to provide a quick read that described the content and ambiance. Jonathan wanted the pages to be sensual, irreverent, and not serious, making Cocktail a place where people might want to come every Friday to check out what's new and let their hair down.

Jonathan created the original graphics for Cocktail in Photoshop on a Macintosh. His color choices were based on the lush and casual atmosphere of being in a bar, where there's lots of deep dark velvet, and cellophane colors on the lights and stage. Rich, dark, and smokey colors are his favorite, but sometimes, when a drink is very light in color, such as champagne, he will create colors that depart from this theme.

Within Cocktail, the top graphic never changes. The frame at the left of the screen that includes the "Drink of the Week" graphic functions as an imagemap. The image map has been programmed to link to multiple pages within Cocktail's pages. Jill Atkinson prepares the Cocktail image maps, and uses the program WebMap. For more information on using WebMap, and creating server and client-side image maps, see Chapter 5, "@tlas."

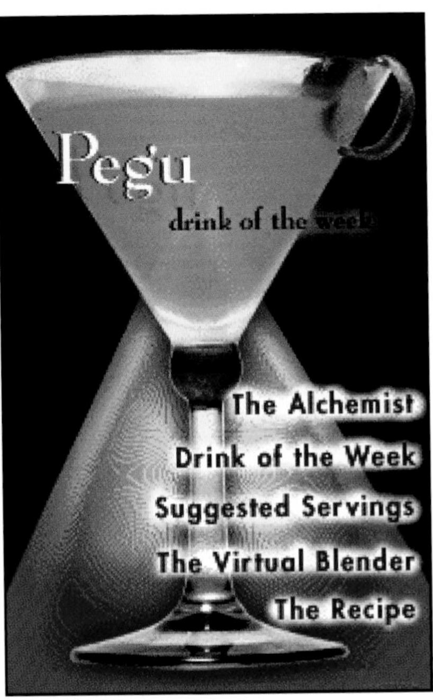

This graphic links to other pages through the use of an imagemap.

The Evolution of Cocktail's Imagemap Interface

Here's an overview of the evolution of Cocktail's frames. Notice how the image map area of the bottom left frame has changed over the months. It's a design challenge to figure out how to communicate that those lines of text are clickable image map regions. These different examples show highlighting the type, creating glows around the type, and putting the type into its own shape as graphic devices to imply the text should be clicked on.

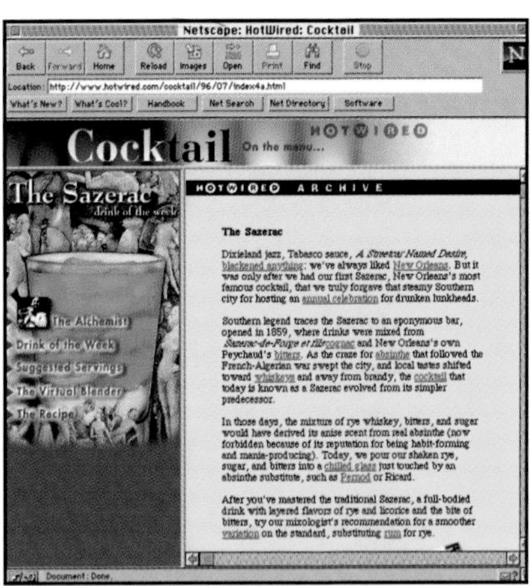

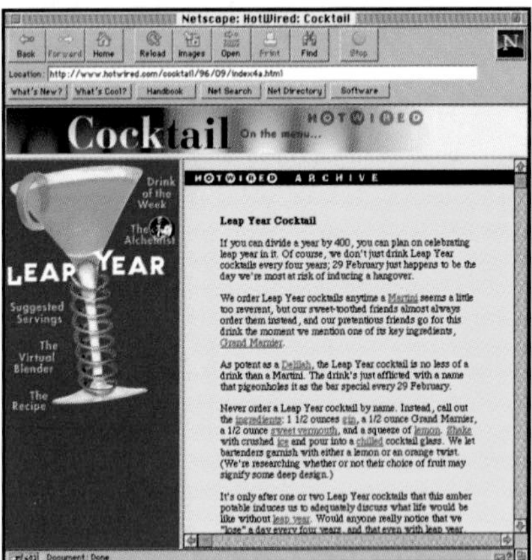

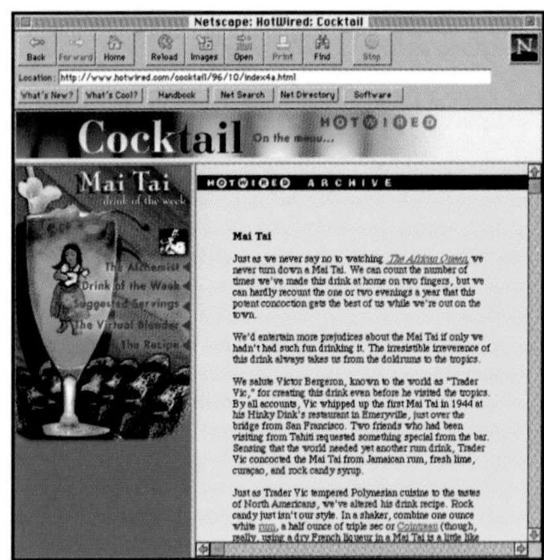

Six weeks worth of Cocktail's image map interface design.

Frames versus No Frames

Though a "no frames" version of the site is available, Jonathan noted that HotWired statistics show 70% of their users enter Cocktail using a frames-enabled Netscape or Microsoft Internet Explorer browser. The site's editorial direction was conceived from the ground up to be frames-specific, and he stands by this decision as an opportunity to advance interface design as much as the available tools allow.

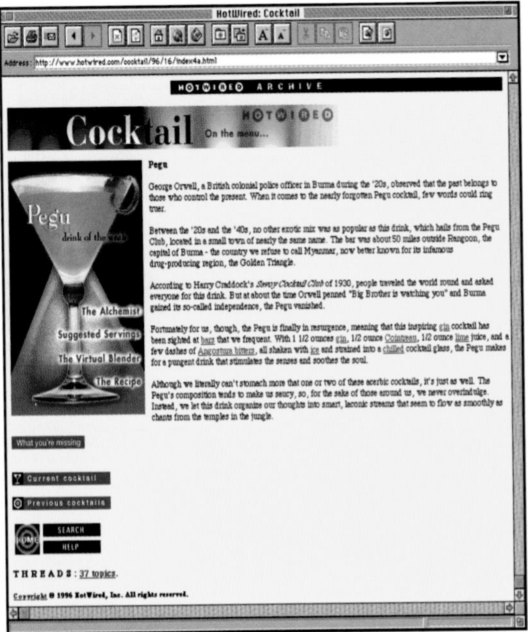

Those logging into ■ www.hotwired.com/cocktail/ with browsers that don't support frames will see this "no frames" version of the interface. To understand the HTML required to produce a frame version and no-frame version, read the HTML deconstruction that follows later in this chapter.

Art Production for Frames

After setting the look and feel, Jonathan turned Cocktail's graphic design over to junior designer Brady Clark. Once a week, Brady gets all the associated written copy from Laura Moorhead and illustrates the left-frame "Drink of the Week" graphic based on the history of the drink or his mental association with it. He works exclusively in Photoshop and creates photo montages using original photography of each week's cocktail that are shot by Jon Lucich. Most of the other sources for the layered imagery come from PhotoCDs, graphics found on the Internet that HotWired secures the rights to use, or custom photography by photographer Marla Aufmuth.

Original photograph by Jon Lucich, used as the source image for "The Drink of the Week" Photoshop composite.

■ Layers

Photoshop Layers Deconstruction

Brady places a photograph of the "Drink of the Week" within a Photoshop template that sometimes goes up to 30 layers deep. He has been sketching out newer ideas for the navigation bars, though he usually uses blue for the text as a cue that the text graphics contain links. As repeat readers are growing more sophisticated and familiar with the site, Brady might loosen some of these considerations.

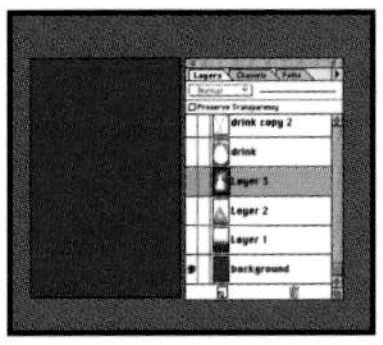

■ Background Layer

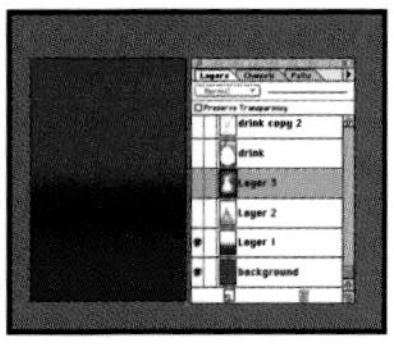

■ Background Layer & Layer 1

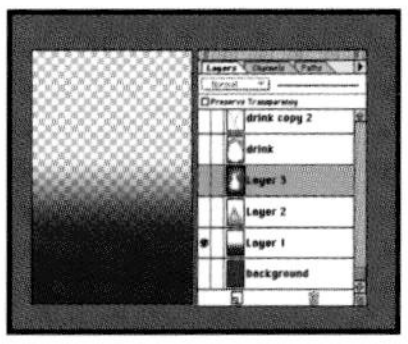

■ Layer 1 Alone

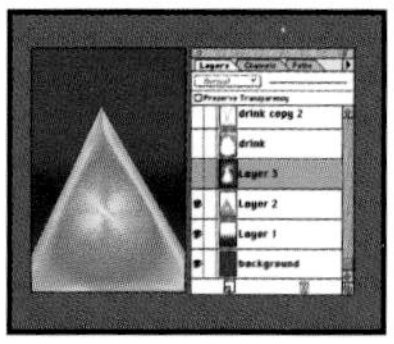

■ Composite with Layer 2

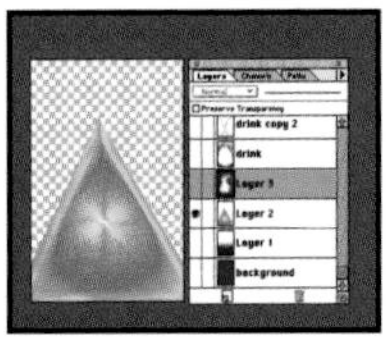

■ Layer 2 Alone

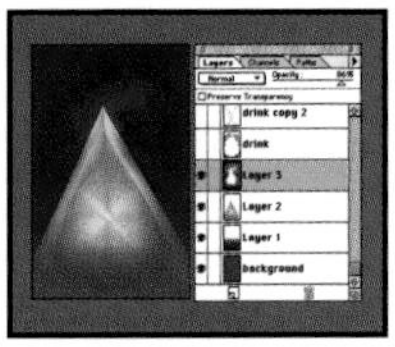

■ Composite with Layer 3

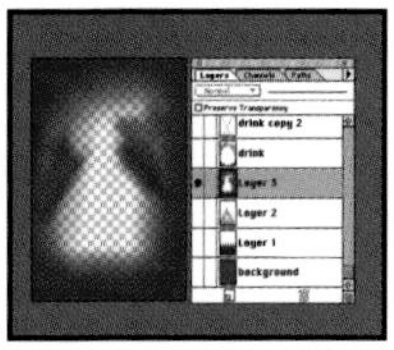

■ Layer 3 Alone

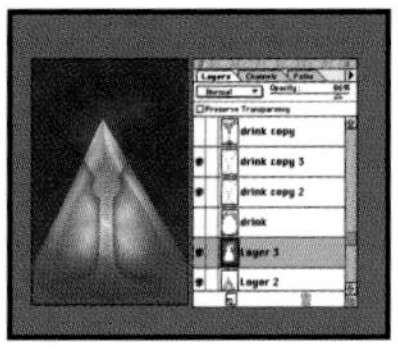

■ Composite with Layer 4

■ Layer 4 Alone

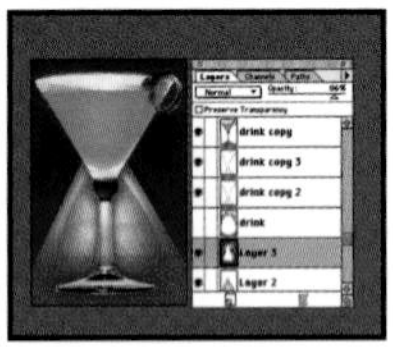

■ Composite with Layer 5

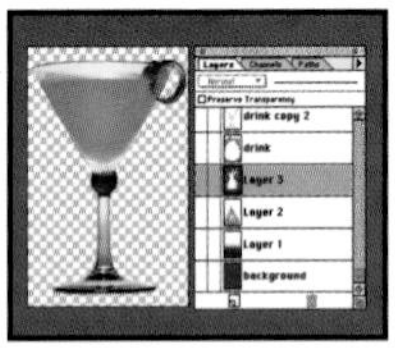

■ Layer 5 Alone

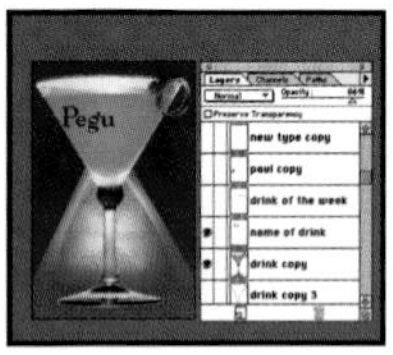

■ Composite with Layer 6

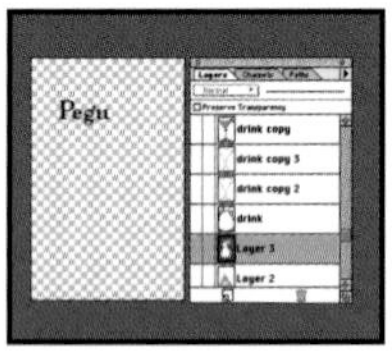

■ Layer 6 Alone

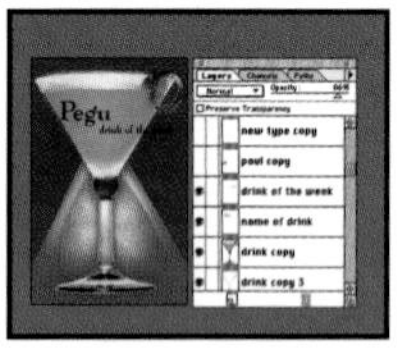

■ Composite with Layer 7

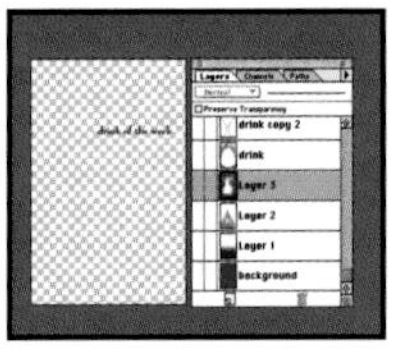

■ Layer 7 Alone

■ Composite with Layer 8

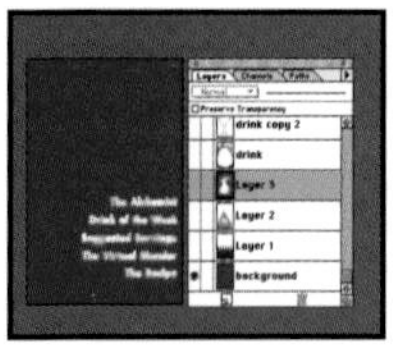

■ Layer 8 Alone

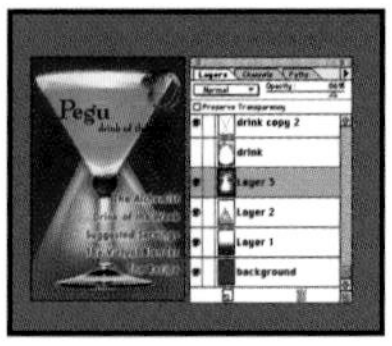

■ Composite with Layer 9

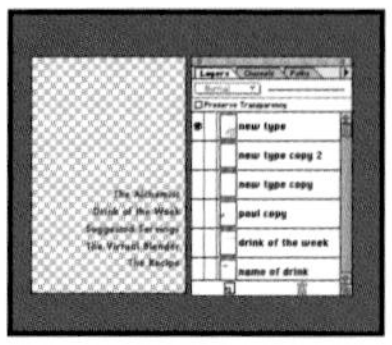

■ Layer 9 Alone

The Photoshop illustrations for Cocktail's "Drink of the Week" graphic are typically many layers deep. Brady Clark creates one photo-illustration per week for the site.

Preparing and Compressing Images for the Cocktail Site

After they are completed, Brady's layered Photoshop illustrations are flattened, which is a Photoshop process that merges all the individual layers into a single image document. This file is then converted by Jill Atkinson, who uses a program called DeBabelizer to change it to 256 colors and create a GIF file. Jill bases the 256 color palette on the image itself (this is called an adaptive palette) and leaves the image in 8-bit (256 colors) using the no dither method (see explanation that follows). She found that if she took the bit depth lower than 8-bit it might result in a smaller file, but the loss in quality was unacceptable. See the note about DeBabelizer versus Photoshop for more information on this subject. QuickTime movies are also included wherever possible on the site. Jill converts the video footage to a computer movie file using the Fusion digitizing system and AV card. She stores the movie at 160×120 pixels, 10–12 frames per second, using Cinepak compression. Movies within Cocktail are included in the HTML using an <img src> tag. The movie file must download fully to the hard drive before it can be viewed.

You do shake mixed drinks that have "complex" ingredients, such as bitters or simple syrup. When shaking a drink, pulverize the ice so there are flecks of it floating atop the bubbles. Shake [665Kbyte .mov] till it's so cold you can't hold on any longer. (Remember that although it's impossible to bruise a drink, you and those around you run the risk of injury.)

Movies are included as part of the Cocktail site. Note that the link "Shake" has the size of the movie next to it. This is a courtesy to readers, who are forewarned that the movie is 665k.

The Cocktail site's QuickTime movies are saved at 160×120 pixels, 10–12 fps (frames per second), and are compressed using Cinepak.

■ note

Internships at HotWired

At age 19, Brady Clark was the second design intern to be hired at HotWired. Brady, who was pursuing a BFA in Graphic Design at the University of Wisconsin Stout, became interested in working at HotWired after seeing a presentation by creative directors Barbara Kuhr and John Plunkett at the Walker Art Museum in neighboring Minneapolis.

At the presentation, Brady introduced himself and expressed interest in interning at HotWired. Told to "keep in touch," and that "there was nothing open at the moment," he took the initiative to send his portfolio anyway and kept in regular contact afterwards. Sure enough, the need arose, and he was honored many months later to get a phone call from Barbara Kuhr inviting him to San Francisco to intern under the direction of Jonathan Louie.

Things have gone well for Brady—his internship turned into a "real job" because he's been officially hired on as a junior designer at HotWired. He has also been put in charge of presenting future designers and design interns to Jonathan and Barbara—a job he takes seriously, considering the outcome of his own efforts. If you're interested in becoming an intern at HotWired, point your browser to:

- http://www.hotwired.com/hotjobs.

Dithering Methods Explained

When an image is converted from millions of color (24-bit) to 256 colors (8-bit) a loss in quality will always occur. This is because the computer has to figure out how to emulate the colors that have been removed. There are two different ways to do this: with dithering or without. Notice in the note below how the no dither methods are always smaller than their counterparts with dither. This is because GIF compression does a more efficient job when it encounters areas of flat color than when it encounters areas within an image that have a lot of noise.

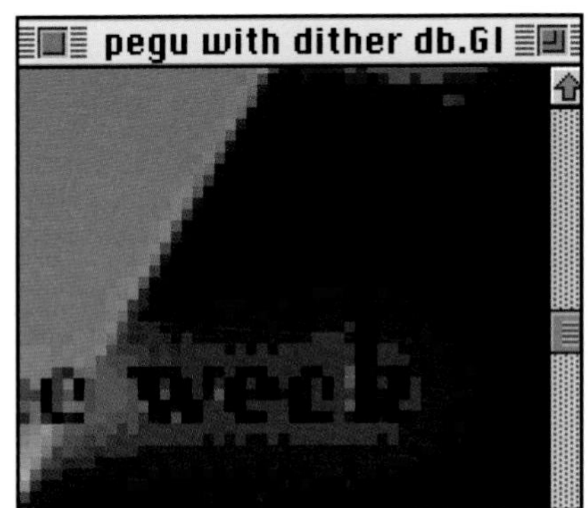

Here's a close-up of what dithering looks like. By using dithering in GIF conversions, the image often looks better, but takes up more disk space and takes longer to download.

The no dither method typically causes banding instead of the alternating dots found within the dither method. GIFs that use the no dither method are always smaller and faster to download. The trade-off is that they often don't look as good as GIFs that use the dither method. You have to try each method on a case-by-case basis to discover whether the trade-off in quality is worth the trade-off in size and download speed.

■ note

Photoshop versus DeBabelizer for Compression

Many Webmasters and artists use a Macintosh program called DeBabelizer to convert their images from Photoshop files to GIFs and JPEGs. DeBabelizer is a Mac-only program (the PC version is promised soon) that supports scriptable batch processing; the capability to repeat a series of scripted operations over multiple files. Some of the features DeBabelizer offers that can be scripted or batch processed are: changing bit-depth, creating custom palettes, file conversions, cropping, and scaling.

Jill Atkinson uses DeBabelizer to convert Brady Clark's Cocktail illustrations to the GIF format because it offers superior compression results. Here's an impressive comparison that supports her case.

38.6k Photoshop GIF
Adaptive Palette
No Dither

46.1k Photoshop GIF
Adaptive Palette
With Dither

32.0k DeBabelizer GIF
Adaptive Palette
No Dither

35.8k DeBabelizer GIF
Adaptive Palette
With Dither

Photography for Cocktail

HotWired, in general, has enough demand for original photography that they have a full-time in-house photo editor, Marla Aufmuth. Marla hired established food and product photographer Jon Lucich for the Cocktail site's "Drink of the Week" photo shoots. Jon has been hired every six months or so to photograph 24 new images of cocktail drinks within a single day's photo shoot.

A real bar is set up for the shoot, and resident Cocktail alchemist Paul Harrington, in full "cocktail attire" prepares the 24 drinks (one after the other) at breakneck speed. The shoot is also videotaped in order to make QuickTime movies from the footage.

Because it's understood that the images are the source material for further Photoshop manipulation and compositing, Jon's job is relatively straightforward. He shoots the bottom lit drinks against a white background, making sure that he captures plenty of detail. The lighting set-ups are simple, but he makes sure he's producing a clean separation between the background and any extra mint leaf, straw, or spoon that might extend beyond the shape of the glass.

HotWired is one of Jon's favorite clients, though it represents his first time "shooting for the Web." Jon admits that he prefers the look of print reproduction over the low resolution screen graphics of the Web. He's trained his entire career to do precise work that yields a high level of detail and fidelity, and the low resolution of the Web is something he's not used to.

Electronic Rights

Jon also raised concerns about the issue of electronic rights and usage. Photographers have traditionally earned their living through charging usage rights for their work. Reusing images, without permission, is a valid concern because files are so easy to copy. Jon expressed frustration that there are so many uninformed netizens who don't understand that images are not free for the taking.

Jon has a good point, and one that is often misunderstood: if you take someone's artwork off a Web site without permission, it is stealing and you can be prosecuted. HotWired, for example, always secures the rights to images before publishing them on their Web site. You will see copyright notices at the bottom of every page in HotWired that displays photography.

As photo editor Marla often tells first time Web photographers, reproducing low resolution images from the Web is not that practical or viable. Images from print sources could be scanned and appropriated at high resolution much more easily than images from the Web, which would not print well at 72 dpi. The real problem is not that people are stealing artwork off of Web sites for reproduction, but for their own use on their own Web site. If you want to use someone else's artwork or photography on your Web site, you must ask before you take.

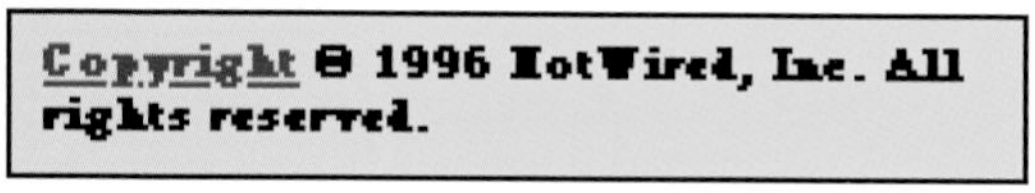

Copyright © 1996 HotWired, Inc. All rights reserved.

This copyright notice is at the bottom of every page on hotwired.com.

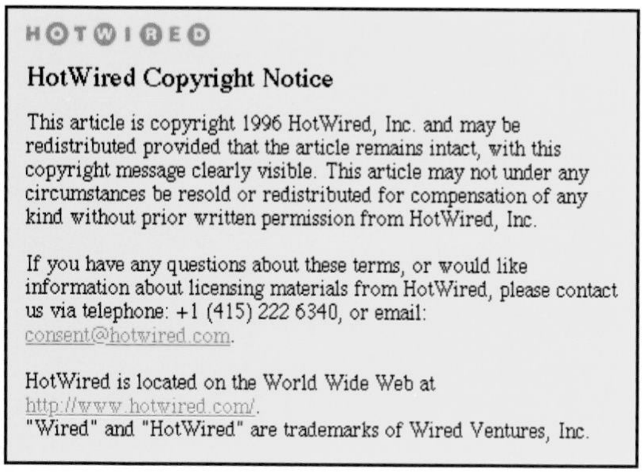

HOTWIRED

HotWired Copyright Notice

This article is copyright 1996 HotWired, Inc. and may be redistributed provided that the article remains intact, with this copyright message clearly visible. This article may not under any circumstances be resold or redistributed for compensation of any kind without prior written permission from HotWired, Inc.

If you have any questions about these terms, or would like information about licensing materials from HotWired, please contact us via telephone: +1 (415) 222 6340, or email: consent@hotwired.com.

HotWired is located on the World Wide Web at http://www.hotwired.com/.
"Wired" and "HotWired" are trademarks of Wired Ventures, Inc.

By clicking on the copyright notice, viewers are presented with this screen. Jon and all photographers are also credited for each of their photos.

Programming the HTML and CGI for Cocktail

As director of software engineering, David Thau tackled all sorts of new challenges working on the Cocktail site—from using frames for the first time, to implementing forms that relied on Sybase database programming, and making the Perl-based CGI scripting tie the whole thing together.

In version 2.0 of Netscape, the implementation of frames had a major flaw that is scheduled to change in the final version of Netscape 3.0. The Back button sent the end-user to the last page they visited, instead of the last frame they visited. The only way to visit the last frame was to bring up a hidden pop-up menu by holding the mouse down within a frame. Because many end-users are unaware of this work-around, the lack of an easy Back button understandably caused frustration among viewers of frame-based documents.

The design team decided to solve this problem by putting a graphic of a Back button into the Frames region that changed, so users would understand how to go backwards. The problem was, how would the Back button know where to go? For example, the page on gin could be reached from any number of the recipes that contained a link to it. The Back button would have to be smart enough to remember where a user had been. HotWired engineers Chris Miller and Sean Welch wrote a CGI that kept track of where the user had been, and generated new HTML on-the-fly to direct the Back button to trigger the proper frame.

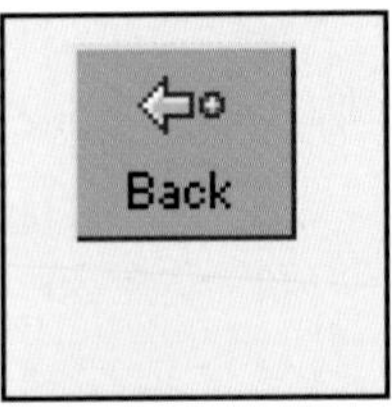

The standard Back button from the Netscape Navigator 2.0 browser navigation bar.

Back in Frame
Forward in Frame
Copy this Link Location

The Back in Frame pop-up menu, which allows you to return to the last frame visited. To find this pop-up menu, users have to hold down the mouse on a Mac, or click the right mouse button on a PC or Unix machine.

The design team created a custom graphic for a Back button, which was programmed using CGI to return to the last frame viewed instead of the last HTML page.

■ tip

David Thau's Recommendations for Learning CGI and Frames:

- *Programming Perl* by Larry Wall (who actually wrote Perl) and Randall L Schwartz [O'Reilly] ISBN:0-937175-64-1
- *Serving the Web* by Robert Jon Mudry [Coriolis Group Books] ISBN:1-883577-30-6
- http://www.stars.com/Zlib/ (a virtual library)
- http://www.gamelan.com/ (java)

Sybase Database Programming for Cocktail

Sybase is one of the United State's largest database companies. Its software products are used by companies for projects ranging from developing large payroll systems to designing the phone company's Yellow Pages. Sybase has added its own extensions to the standard database programming language, SQL. This makes it more powerful than other solutions, but it also incurs a steeper learning curve. It was a little easier than normal for David, who studied SQL (Structured Query Language) when he got his masters degree in Computer Science at the University of Michigan in Ann Arbor.

What does Sybase have to do with Web programming? The Virtual Blender uses "forms" that access a powerful database. When a user searches for drinks that can be made with gin or drinks that are served in certain types of glassware, a Perl script is triggered that accesses the Sybase database.

Some of the problems associated with the database programming for Cocktail were not so much technical, but structural. Originally, when the Virtual Blender was created, there were more categories than today's simple choices of either drink name, or mixer. One could also search by accent (such as lemon peel or mint leaf) or secondary liquors, like when a drink recipe includes a small portion of sweet vermouth and a primary portion of vodka. Through studying the behavior of Cocktail visitors, the HotWired design team decided they were offering too many choices and it was confusing to the end-user, so they settled on two choices instead.

A similar problem existed in the Party Planner section, where users were asked what kind of drink they wanted to serve. When Valentine's Day rolled around, it was discovered there were only two drinks listed under the category "romantic," and one of them was called Corpses Reviver! Dave advised programmers to be sure when you offer a category that you have content within that category. Seems obvious, in hindsight of course. And yes, if you search for romantic drinks now, more than two choices will appear!

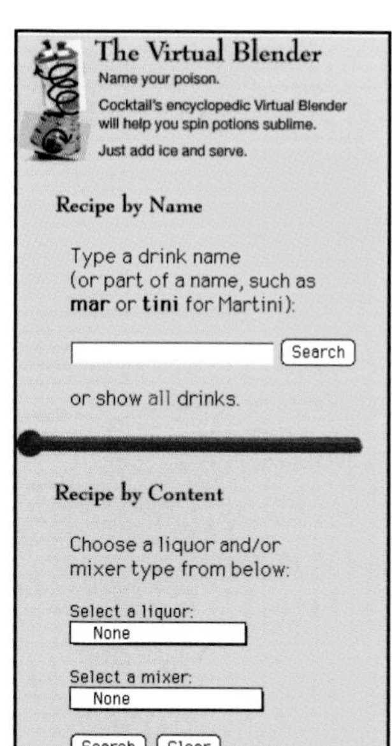

The Virtual Blender area of Cocktail where viewers can enter search parameters to find drink descriptions, history, trivia, and recipes.

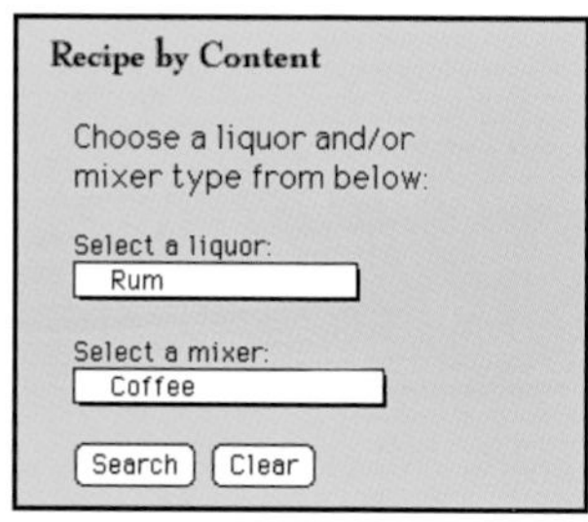

Within the Virtual Blender, it's possible to search by type of liquor and mixer.

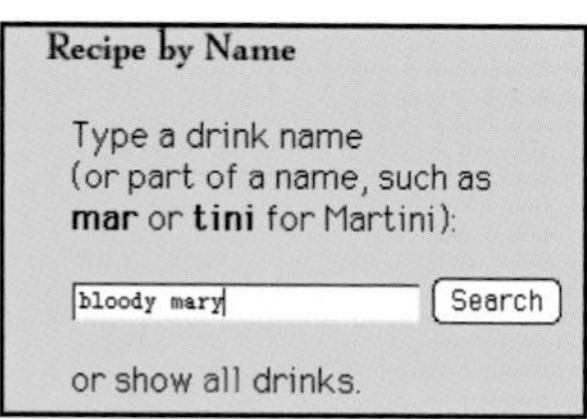

The recipe can also be retrieved by a name search.

Perl Programming

David chose Perl5 as the CGI scripting language because it didn't require compiling a time-consuming processing event that configures the code properly. Perl is much faster to develop with than C++ for this reason, but Perl creates programs that are not quite as efficient as C++, and are therefore slower to run on the server.

By using Perl, he was able to create libraries that would communicate with the Sybase database. Libraries are chunks of code that might get used over and over again for different purposes. David uses Perl 5.0, an object-oriented version of Perl, with a combination of HotWired's proprietary libraries and those found in public domain offerings. His favorite collection of libraries are called DBLib, a network interface for SQL databases.

Frames HTML

Starting with the HTML for frames, let's deconstruct the opening screen of the site. Frames are always more difficult to deconstruct than other types of HTML pages, because they include nested documents. One page, such as the opening screen, really includes three other HTML documents inside it, with potential links to hundreds of other documents.

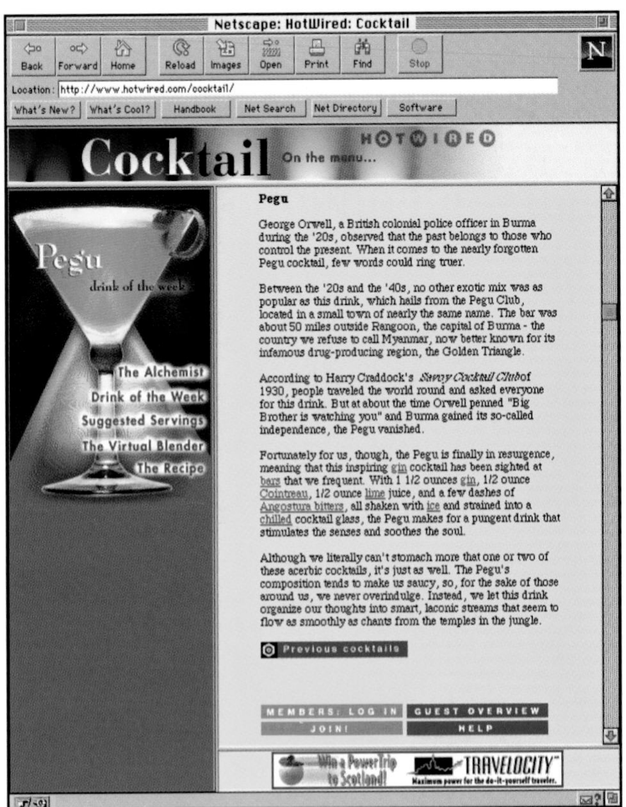

The opening screen actually includes three other screens nested within itself, called: cock.html, drink.main.html, and drink.o.week.frames.html. The opening screen can be viewed online at: ■ http://www.hotwired.com/cocktail/96/16/index4a.html

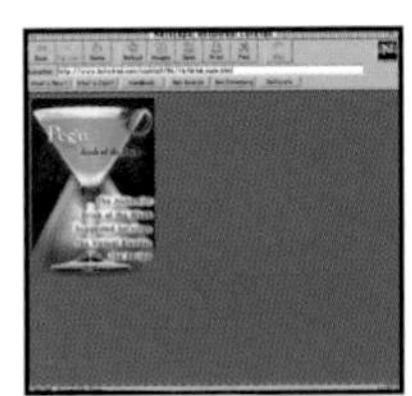

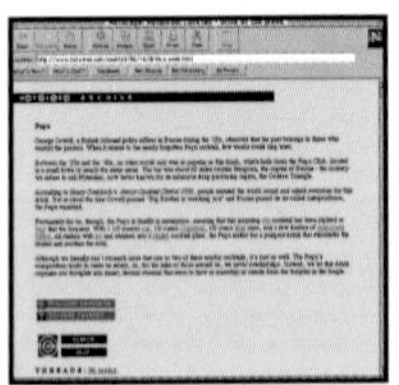

Here are thumbnail views of the three documents nested inside the Opening Screen HTML. They are named repsectively, cock.html, drink.main.html, and drink.o.week.frames.html. Deconstructions of the HTML within each screen are on the following pages.

Opening Screen HTML

```
<HTML><HEAD>
1 <!-- start local exec -->
2 <BASE HREF="http://www.hotwired.com/cocktail/96/
16/index4a.html">
<!-- end local exec -->
<title>HotWired: Cocktail</title>
</head>
3 <frameset rows="58,*">
4 <frame src="/cocktail/96/16/cock.html" marginwidth=0
marginheight=0
5 noresize scrolling="no"
6 name="header">
7 <frameset cols="205,*">
<frame marginwidth=0 marginheight=2 src="/cock-
tail/96/16/drink.main.html"
noresize scrolling="no"
name="main">
<frame marginwidth=0
src="/cocktail/96/16/drink.o.week.frames.html"
name="sidebar">
</frameset>
8 </frameset>
9 <noframes>
<body bgcolor=#ffffbf>
<h3 align=right>
<!-- start local exec -->
<a href="/advertising/blipverts/powertrip/index.cgi">
<img src="/advertising/blipverts/powertrip/banner
cock.gif" width=281 height=31 alt="-
Win a PowerTrip to Scotland  -"></a>
<!-- end local exec -->
</h3>
<p>
<a href="/help/cocktail/index.html">
10 <img border=0 width=480 height=50 src="/cock-
tail/96/16/stuff/cock.gif"
alt="[Cocktail: On the menu]"></a>
<pre></pre>
<a href="/cgi-bin/users/imagemap/cocktail/
96/16/stuff/pegu.10.map"><img align=left width=205
height=300 src="/cocktail/96/16/stuff/pegu.10.gif"
ismap border=0 alt="[Pegu, Drink of
the Week]"></a><p><b>Pegu</b>
<p>George Orwell,a British colonial police officer
in Burma during the '20s, observed that the past
belongs to those who control the present. When it
comes to the nearly forgotten Pegu cocktail, few
```

```
words could ring truer.
<p>Between the '20s and the '40s, no other exotic
mix was as popular as this drink, which hails from
the Pegu Club, located in a small town of nearly the
same name. The bar was about 50 miles outside
Rangoon, the capital of Burma - the country we
refuse to call Myanmar, now better known for its
infamous drug-producing region, the Golden Triangle.
<p>According to Harry Craddock's <cite>Savoy
Cocktail Club</cite> of 1930, people traveled the
world round and asked everyone for this drink. But
at about the time Orwell penned "Big Brother is
watching you" and Burma gained its so-called inde-
pendence, the Pegu vanished.
<p>Fortunately for us, though, the Pegu is finally
in resurgence, meaning that this inspiring
<a href="/cgi-
bin/back.cgi/cocktail/96/10/alchemist.html?/cock-
tail/96/16/index4a.html">gin</a>
cocktail has been sighted at <a href="/cgi-
bin/back.cgi/cocktail/links/nondivebar.html?/cock-
tail/96/16/index4a.html">bars</a> that we frequent.
With 1 1/2 ounces <a href="/cgi-
bin/back.cgi/cocktail/links/gin.html?/cock-
tail/96/16/index4a.html">gin</a>, 1/2 ounce
<a href="/cgi-
bin/back.cgi/cocktail/links/cointreau.html?/cock-
tail/96/16/index4a.html">Cointreau</a>,
1/2 ounce <a href="/cgi-
bin/back.cgi/cocktail/links/fruit.html?/cock-
tail/96/16/index4a.html">lime</a> juice, and a
few dashes of <a href="/cgi-
bin/back.cgi/cocktail/links/bitters.html?/cock-
tail/96/16/index4a.html">Angostura
bitters</a>, all shaken with <a href="/cgi-
bin/back.cgi/cocktail/links/ice.html?/cock-
tail/96/16/index4a.html">ice</a> and strained
into a <a href="/cgi-
bin/back.cgi/cocktail/links/chilling.html?/cock-
tail/96/16/index4a.html">chilled</a> cocktail
glass, the Pegu makes for a pungent drink that
stimulates the senses and soothes the soul.
<p>Although we literally can't stomach more that one
or two of these acerbic cocktails, it's just as
well. The Pegu's composition tends to make us saucy,
so, for the sake of those around us, we never
overindulge. Instead, we let this drink organize our
thoughts into smart, laconic streams that seem to
flow as smoothly as chants from the temples in
the jungle.
11 <pre> </pre>
<a href="/cgi-bin/back.cgi/cocktail/missing.html?/
cocktail/96/16/index4a.html"><img
border=0 src="/cocktail/images/missing.gif"
alt="[What you're missing]"></a>
<p><a href="/cgi-
bin/back.cgi/cocktail/archive/index.html?/cock-
tail/96/16/index4a.html"><img
src="/cocktail/images/archive.gif" alt="[What you
might have missed]" border=0 ></a>
<pre> </pre>
12 <dl><dd>
<!-- start local exec -->
<p>
13 <p>
14 <MAP NAME="mainbar_nonmembermap">
<AREA SHAPE=rect COORDS="0,23,137,36"
HREF="/reception/form.html" target="_top">
<AREA SHAPE=rect COORDS="142,6,280,20"
HREF="/login/overview.html" target="_top">
<AREA SHAPE=rect COORDS="142,23,280,36"
HREF="/help/cocktail/index.html" target="_top">
<AREA SHAPE=default
HREF="http://vip.hotwired.com/cocktail/"  target
="_top">
15 <AREA SHAPE=default HREF="http://vip.hotwired.com/
cocktail/index">
16 </MAP>
17 <a href="/cgi-bin/users/imap-url/cocktail/footer/
mainbar nonmember.map/IMURL/ http://vip.hotwired.
com/cocktail/index"><img src="/ cocktail/
footer/mainbar_nonmember.gif" border=0 alt="
[Login]"ISMAP USEMAP="#mainbar_nonmembermap">
</a><H4>T H R E A D S : <A HREF="/cgi-bin/interact
/threads?cocktail" targ et="_top">34 topics</A>.
</H4>
18 <h6><a href = "/full.copyright.html"
target="_top">Copyright</a> &#169; 1996 HotWired
Ventures LLC. All rights reserved.</h6>
<!-- end local exec -->
</dl>
</noframes>
</html>
```

■ tags

Opening Screen HTML Deconstruction

1 Anything in between the "<!--" and "-->" is a comment and is therefore not read by the browser. In this case the text, "start local exec" indicates that a CGI script has created the HTML on-the-fly, according to the specifications of the script. The HTML that's between the "start" and "end" of the local exec was inserted automatically by the CGI script.

---

2 A <BASE> tag sets the absolute URL base to be used for any relative URL links within this document. (An absolute URL has the entire string http://www. domain. com/etc/, whereas a relative URL would begin with a slash, such as /folder/filename.html.) In HotWired's case, the base tag was inside the <!-start local exec->, which means the HTML was generated on-the-fly by using a CGI script. This was used because HotWired is keeping track of whether users are members or not. A different set of documents are being served to members and non-members, and all the relative URLs within the rest of the HTML file are based on this first BASE tag.

---

3 <frameset> instructs Netscape to begin using Frames. rows="58,*" instructs Netscape to start two rows, one which is 58 pixels high, and one which takes up the remainder of the space. Rows determine how high the frame regions will be.

---

4 The <frame src> tag loads "cock.html" into the 58 pixel high row. The frames are loaded in the order in which they appear in the HTML file, which explains why the cock.html file goes into the first frame. The "margin width=0" and "marginheight=0" forces the contents of the frame so that it is flush with the border of the frame.

---

5 noresize means that the size of the frame cannot be changed. Without the "noresize" command the client would be able to drag the borders of the frames around and therefore change the size of each frame. A designer's nightmare! The comment scrolling="no" tells Netscape that if the contents of a frame go outside of the frame picture space, a scrollbar will not appear to let you "scroll" over to see the runoff. The default is "scrolling='auto'."

---

6 name="header" gives this frame (cock.html) the name "header" for targeting purposes. Later in the script, when an imagemap uses the target tag, it will refer to the frame called "header."

---

7 This frameset instructs Netscape to begin the next frame. cols="205, *" defines two columns; one 205 pixels wide and the other that takes up the remaining space (signified by the "*"). Cols determine how wide the frame regions will be.

---

8 </frameset> ends the matching "<frameset>" tag.

---

9 <noframes> defines the starting point for an alternate page that will be served to clients who visit with a browser that doesn't support frames.

---

10 <img...src"..."> tells the browser to load the image "cock.gif." If the browser does not support inline images, or the user has them turned off, the text in the alt= attribute ("[Cocktail: On the menu]") appears instead. border=0 turns off the outline that is otherwise drawn around the image when it is a hyperlink. Width=480 height=50 tells the browser exactly what the size of the image is. This speeds up the downloading process by allowing the browser to layout the page before it downloads the image.

---

11 The <pre> is normally used to fix text on a page to be exactly how it was typed, without any additional formatting. If one were to type letters with custom spacing or

alignment, the browser would honor the placement without HTML alignment, line break, or paragraph breaks. This tag also causes the text to display in a fixed-width font in most browsers. Note: When the <pre> tag is used, the text will not re-adjust itself to accommodate different window sizes as normal text will.

In this case, the <pre> tag is immediately followed by </pre>, which ends the effects of <pre>. This is because the HTML was generated by a CGI program that puts the tags in even when they are not used.

---

12 <dl> stands for "Definition List." This tag prompts the browser to start an indented list (without bullets) <dd>. Every new item on the list must start with "<dd>."

---

13 The <p> tag begins a paragraph. Note that because paragraphs are logical markup entities in HTML, using <p> followed immediately by another <p> does not create two paragraph breaks. If you want to add extra space, use the <br> tag instead.

---

14 MAP tells Netscape 2.0 that everything between it and the "</map>" tag is a client-side imagemap. NAME gives the imagemap a name to be used later by the "usemap='# mainbar_nonmembermap" attribute within the "<img src>" tag for that specific image.

---

15 <area shape=default href="..."> defines the default URL. If someone clicks on a part of the imagemap that has not otherwise been defined, it loads the default URL. The default URL is almost always the address for the same page where the imagemap resides.

Some believe that pointing "default" at the "same page where the imagemap resides" is a useless practice, because if you don't use "default" at all you can't click on undefined parts of the imagemap and the "finger" will only appear in the defined areas of the map.

In other words, not using "default" at all serves the same purpose more elegantly. "Default" is there for cases where you want a default action to take the user somewhere else.

---

16 </map> instructs the browser to end the client-side imagemap.

---

17 This is the beginning of a server-side imagemap. border=0 turns off the automatic border that normally appears on all hyperlinks. The use of the /cgi-bin/users /imap/ path and the ISMAP tag indicates that a server-side imagemap is in use. The usemap="#mainbar_non membermap" initiates the client-side imagemap that was named "mainbar_nonmembermap" back in line #17 as well.

This is an example of a client-side and server-side imagemap being used on one page. The purpose of using both types of imagemaps is to ensure that the imagemap is usable by browsers that do not support client-side imagemaps. See Chapter 5, "@tlas," for a more in-depth look at the differences between client and server-side imagemaps.

---

18 The <h6> tag instructs the browser to display the text in the "headline 6" size. Note how <h6> is much smaller than <h1>. The separate Web page "full.copyright.html" is set to load to its own full-screen window (eliminating frames) by using the TARGET="top" command. The HTML © instructs the browser to display the copyright symbol. HTML uses a logical character set, called ISO-8879-1, which is not limited to the 128 characters of the normal ASCII (American Standard Code for Information Interchange) character set that most personal computers use. This allows you to specify characters, like the copyright symbol, that are not normally found on a keyboard. The characters specified in this manner, such as © are called entities. An entity list appears in the appendix of this book.

The HTML for frames is often very difficult to deconstruct, because it, by nature, includes other "nested" HTML documents. The Cocktail opening screen page we looked at actually displays three other HTML documents. If you click on any of those page's links, it will connect to hundreds of other pages that could conceivably show up within the main page's frame regions. Let's examine the first three most obvious HTML documents.

■ The artwork within the top frame for the Cocktail site is an HTML document called cock.html.

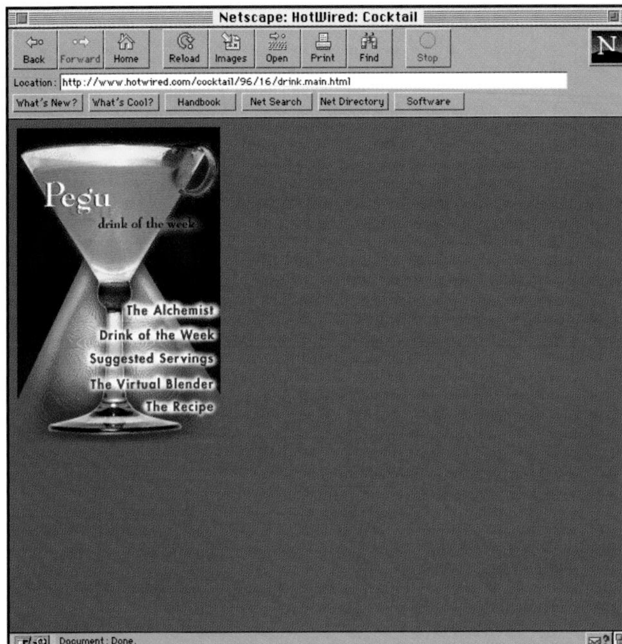

■ The left-hand side's frame "Drink of the Week" artwork is in its own HTML document called drink.main.html.

cock.html HTML

```
<html>
<head>
1 <META name="sybid" content="12615">
<title>HotWired: Cocktail</title>
</head> <body bgcolor=#edf1de>
<a href="/help/cocktail/index.html" target="side-
bar"><img border=0
src="/cocktail/images/cock.gif" alt="Cocktail" ></a>
</body>
</html>
```

■ tags

cock.html Deconstruction

1 The META creates specific HTTP header entry information. The name attribute gives the header entry a name, and the content is where a value can be stored. This tag was used for HotWired's purposes to give the client a unique ID number, generated on-the-fly by a CGI program, so that their actions could be monitored. This makes the Back button CGI possible.

drink.main.html HTML

```
<html>
<head>
<META name="sybid" content="12616">
title>HotWired: Cocktail</title>
</head>
<body bgcolor=#935400>
1 <base target="sidebar">
<map name="cocktail">
<area shape=rect coords="102,160,194,183"
href="/cocktail/96/16/alchemist.html">
<area shape=rect coords="74,185,194,205" href="/cock-
tail/96/16/drink.o.week.html">
<area shape=rect coords="62,207,196,227" href="/cock-
tail/96/16/ss.html">
<area shape=rect coords="61,230,193,248" href="/cock-
tail/blender/index.html">
<area shape=rect coords="118,249,193,273"
href="/cocktail/blender/recipes/pegu_cocktail.html">
<area shape=default
href="/cocktail/96/16/drink.o.week.html">
</map>
<a href="/cgi-bin/imagemap/cocktail/96/16/stuff/
```

```
pegu.map">
<img width=195 height=300
src="/cocktail/96/16/stuff/pegu.gif" usemap="#cock-
tail"
ismap border=0 alt="[Pegu, Drink of the Week]"></a>
</body>
</html>
```

tags

drink.main.html Deconstruction

1 The base target tag is being used to establish that everything within the following client-side imagemap will be displayed in the frame named "sidebar." The "sidebar" frame was defined in #9 cock.html.

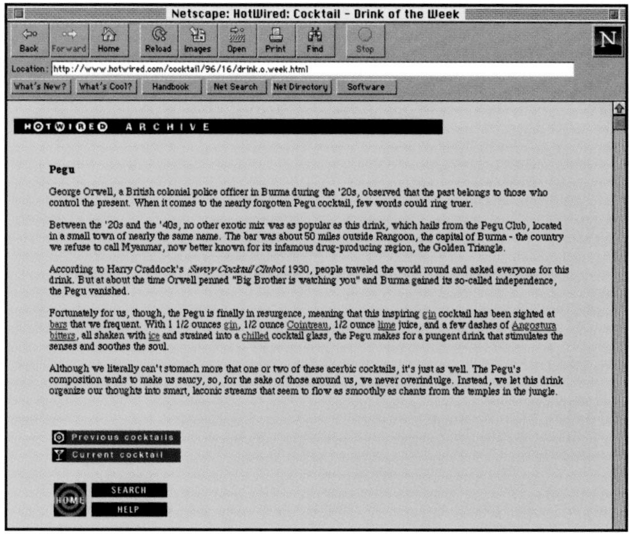

■ The text for the drink of the week has it's own HTML too, called: drink.o.week.frames.html.

drink.o.week.frames.html HTML

```
<html>
<head>
<title>HotWired: Cocktail - Drink of theWeek</title>
</head>
<body bgcolor=#fbd872>
<!--teaser: The Pegu of Burma, in Cocktail-->
<!--new: The Pegu, a drink as stirring as an ancient
temple chant-->
<!--flash:
The Pegu, as//
stirring as a//
temple chant,//
in *Cocktail*-->
1 <!-- start local exec -->
<!-- arvg[0] = /hot/www.tools/cgi-bin/header/
dynhead -->
<!-- sybid = 12618 -->
<!-- program = cocktail -->
<!-- type = deptidx -->
<!-- status = a -->
<!-- logo = 0 -->
<!-- In do_archive: -->
<!--  program = cocktail -->
<!--  type = deptidx -->
<!--  status = a -->
<!-- parsing archive tag, got -->
<!-- default: display text and archive -->
<!-- looking for /hot/www/cocktail/archive
/archive_top.gif -->
<!-- found it -->
<!-- looking for  /hot/www/cocktail/archive
/no_archive_top_text -->
<!-- found it, archive text disabled -->
<BR><img src="/cocktail/archive/archive_top.gif"
align=middle alt=" "><p>
<!-- end local exec -->
<pre>
</pre>
<blockquote>
<p><b>Pegu</b>
<p>George Orwell, a British colonial police officer
in Burma during the '20s, observed that the past
belongs to those who control the present. When it
comes to the nearly forgotten Pegu cocktail, few
words could ring truer.
<p>Between the '20s and the '40s, no other exotic
mix was as popular as this drink, which hails from
the Pegu Club, located in a small town of nearly the
same name. The bar was about 50 miles outside
Rangoon, the capital of Burma - the country we
refuse to call Myanmar, now better known for its
infamous drug-producing region, the Golden Triangle.
<p>According to Harry Craddock's <cite>Savoy Cocktail
Club</cite> of 1930, people traveled the world round
and asked everyone for this drink. But at about the
time Orwell penned "Big Brother is watching you" and
Burma gained its so-called independence, the Pegu
vanished.
<p>Fortunately for us, though, the Pegu is finally
in resurgence, meaning that this inspiring
<a href="/cgi-
bin/back.cgi/cocktail/96/10/alchemist.html?/cock-
tail/96/16/drink.o.week.html">gin</a>
cocktail has been sighted at <a href="/cgi-bin/back.
cgi/cocktail/links/nondivebar.html?/cocktail/96/16/
drink.o.week.html">bars</a> that we frequent. With 1
1/2 ounces <a href="/cgi-bin/back.cgi/cocktail/links
/gin.html?/cocktail/96/16/drink.o.week.html">gin</a>,
```

```
1/2 ounce <a href="/cgi-
bin/back.cgi/cocktail/links/cointreau.html?/cock
tail/96/16/drink.o.week.html">Cointreau
</a>, 1/2 ounce <a href="/cgi-
bin/back.cgi/cocktail/links/fruit.html?/cock
tail/96/16/drink.o.week.html">lime</a> juice,
and a few dashes of <a href="/cgi-
bin/back.cgi/cocktail/links/bitters.html?/cock
tail/96/16/drink.o.week.html">Angostura
bitters</a>, all shaken with <a href="/cgi-
bin/back.cgi/cocktail/links/ice.html?/cock
tail/96/16/drink.o.week.html">ice</a> and
strained into a <a href="/cgi-
bin/back.cgi/cocktail/links/chilling.html?/cock
tail/96/16/drink.o.week.html">chilled</a>
cocktail glass, the Pegu makes for a pungent drink
that stimulates the senses and soothes the soul.
<p>Although we literally can't stomach more that one
or two of these acerbic cocktails, it's just as
well. The Pegu's composition tends to make us saucy,
so, for the sake of those around us, we never
overindulge. Instead, we let this drink organize our
thoughts into smart, laconic streams that seem to
flow as smoothly as chants from the
temples in the jungle.
<pre> </pre>
2 <!-- start local exec -->
<!-- parsing archive tag, got -->
<!-- default: display text and archive -->
<!-- looking for /hot/www/cocktail/archive/
archive_bottom.gif -->
<!-- found it -->
<!-- looking for/hot/www/cocktail/archive/
no_archive_bottom_text -->
<!-- found it, archive text disabled -->
<!-- looking for /hot/www/cocktail/archive/index.html
--> <!-- found it -->
<p><a href="/cocktail/archive/index.html"
target="_top"><img
src="/cocktail/archive/archive_bottom.gif" align=mid-
dle alt=" " border=0></a><br>
<!-- channeldir not set -->
<!-- looking for /hot/www/cocktail/images/program
bar.gif --> <!-- didn't find it -->
<!-- programbar not found, tried/cocktail/images/pro-
grambar.gif -->
<p>
<p><!-- looking for /hot/www/cocktail/footer/main-
bar_nonmember.gif -->
<!-- found it -->
<!-- looking for /hot/www/cocktail/footer/
mainbar_nonmember-client.map -->
<!-- found it -->
<MAP NAME="mainbar_nonmembermap">
<AREA SHAPE=rect COORDS="0,23,137,36"
HREF="/reception/form.html" target="_top">
<AREA SHAPE=rect COORDS="142,6,280,20"
HREF="/login/overview.html" target="_top">
<AREA SHAPE=rect COORDS="142,23,280,36"
HREF="/help/cocktail/index.html" target="_top">
<AREA SHAPE=default
HREF="http://vip.hotwired.com/cocktail/"
target="_top">
<AREA SHAPE=default
HREF="http://vip.hotwired.com//
cocktail/96/16/drink.o.week.html">
</MAP>
<!-- looking for /hot/www/cocktail/footer/main-
bar_nonmember.map -->
<!-- found it -->
<a href="/cgi-bin/users/imap-
url/cocktail/footer/mainbar nonmember.map/IMURL/
http://vip.hotwired.com//cocktail/96
/16/drink.o.week.html"><img src="/cocktail/
footer/mainbar_nonmember.gif" border=0
alt="[Login]" ISMAP USEMAP="#mainbar_nonmem-
bermap"></a><H4>T H R E A D S :
<A HREF="/cgi-bin/interact/threads?cocktail" tar-
get="_top">34 topics</A>.
<!-- links disabled -->
</H4>
<h6><a href = "/full.copyright.html"target=
"_top">Copyright</a> &#169; 1996
HotWired Ventures LLC. All rights reserved.</h6>
<!-- end local exec -->
</blockquote>
</body>
</html>
```

tags

drink.o.week.frames.html Deconstruction

1 <!-- start local exec --> These HTML comments were generated by the CGI program that created the page. It is debugging information to allow the software engineers to see what was going on inside the program.

2 The second local exec is the same as the previous.

How to Create Your Own Frames Document

The HotWired site is rather complicated, as they are doing a lot of fancy CGI for record keeping and statistics gathering. This next deconstruction offers a more simplified example that demonstrates how to create a frameset similar to Cocktail's.

The first document in this example is named framed.html and displays three frame regions. The content of those frames are actually contained in three other HTML documents that this document references. The three other files are named header.html, menu.html, and info.html.

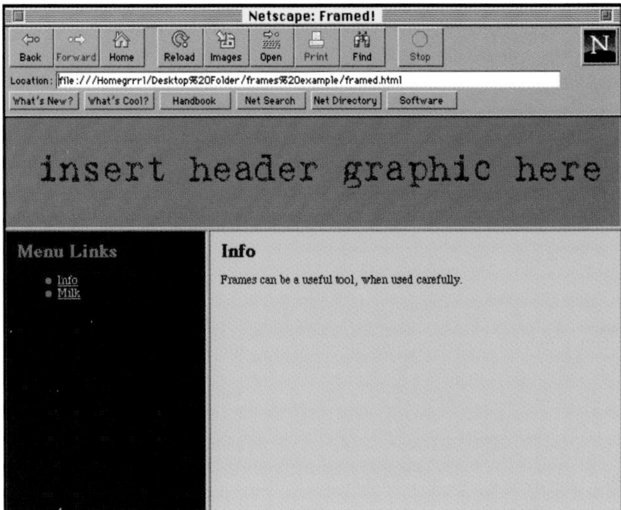

The opening page of the sample frameset, named framed.html. You can view this page at ■ http://www.lynda.com/decon/examples/framed.html/

framed.html HTML

```
  <html>
  <head>
  <title>Framed!</title>
  </head>
1 <frameset rows="108,*">
2 <frame src="header.html" marginwidth=0 margin-
  height=0
  noresize scrolling="no"
  name="header">
3 <frameset cols="200,*">
4 <frame marginwidth=10 marginheight=10
  src="menu.html" noresize scrolling="no" name="menu">
5 <frame marginwidth=10 marginheight=10
  src="info.html" name="info">
6 </frameset>
  </frameset>
7 <noframes>
8 <body>
  If you had frames, you'd be home by now.
  </body>
9 </noframes>
  </html>
```

■ tags

framed.html Deconstruction

1 <frameset> defines the parameters of the frames. This document has two nested framesets. The first defines two "rows." Rows are horizontal areas, one on top of the other. The top will be for the header, and the bottom row will have another <frameset> with two columns.

The first row is 108 pixels high. Netscape uses eight of those pixels for the frame itself, and the graphic is 100 pixels high. Frame sizes can also be defined in terms of percentages (25%) instead of pixels. When you are using a graphic with a known size, it is more useful to define the size of the frame in terms of pixels.

The second row is defined with a "*" which let's the browser use the rest of the space at its own discretion. It will take up whatever space is left after the 100 pixels of the first row are allocated.

---

2 The <frame> tag is used to specify the contents of an individual frame. The src= attribute specifies header.html as the initial content of the frame. Marginwidth and marginheight declare the margin sizes (zero in this case, to put an image right up to the borders), noresize tells the browser to disallow resizing by the user, scrolling="no" gets rid of any scrollbars, and name="header" names the frame for use by target tags later on.

---

3 The second row has another <frameset> tag instead of a <frame> tag. This is for splitting the row into columns. Two columns are defined, the first column will take up 200 pixels on the left side of the row. The second column will take the remaining lateral space in the row.

---

4 Each <frame> tag defines the next undefined frame specified in the immediately preceding <frameset> tag. This one is for the first column from the <frameset> in #3...

5 ...and this one is for the second column from the <frameset> in #3.

6 The <frameset> tag requires an ending </frameset> tag, to tell the browser that it is done defining frames.

7 Everything between <noframes> and </noframes> will be ignored by a frames-capable browser. The content within this section is what will be seen by people who's browsers cannot render frames.

8 The <body> tag is required in the <noframes> section. You can use it as you would in a normal HTML docu ment.

9 This ends the <noframes> section.

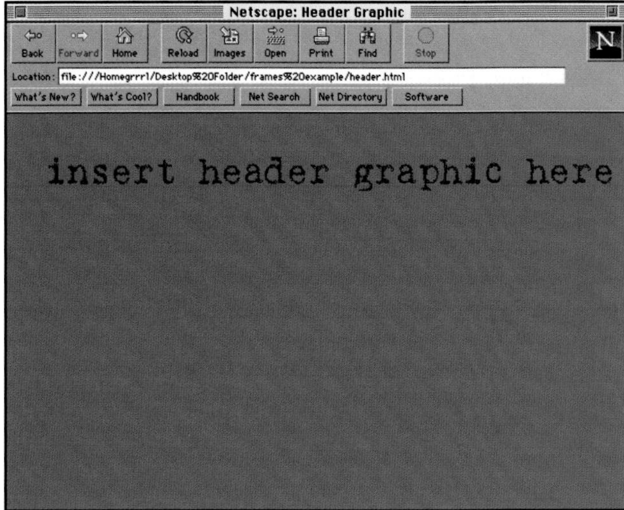

This is the document nested within the top frame of framed.html, it is called header.html.

header.html HTML

```
   <html>
1  <head><title>Hey! I thought I was in a frame!
   </title>
2  <body bgcolor=33cccc>
3  <img src=title.gif width=600 height=100>
   </body>
   </html>
```

■ tags

header.html Deconstruction

1 Because each HTML document could end up on someone's screen outside of a frame, it's a good idea to give it a title anyway.

2 When you give a framed document a background color, the background of the frame takes on the color. This document has a background color that is the same as the background of the title graphic. That way, if someone's screen is bigger than our graphic, it blends seamlessly.

3 The whole body of the document is just the image.

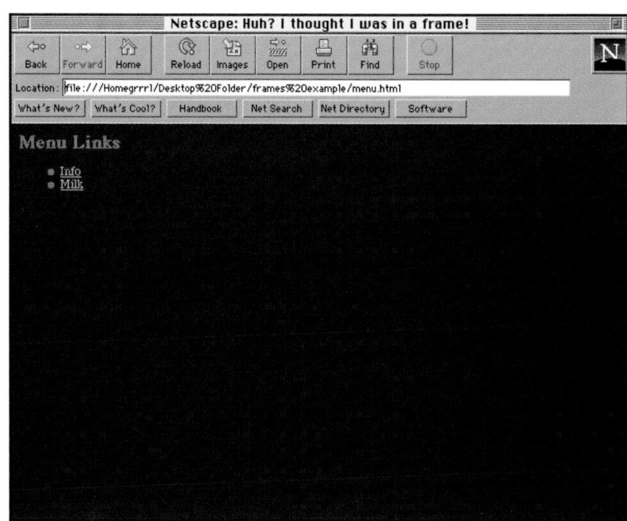

This is the document nested within the left frame of header.html, it is called menu.html.

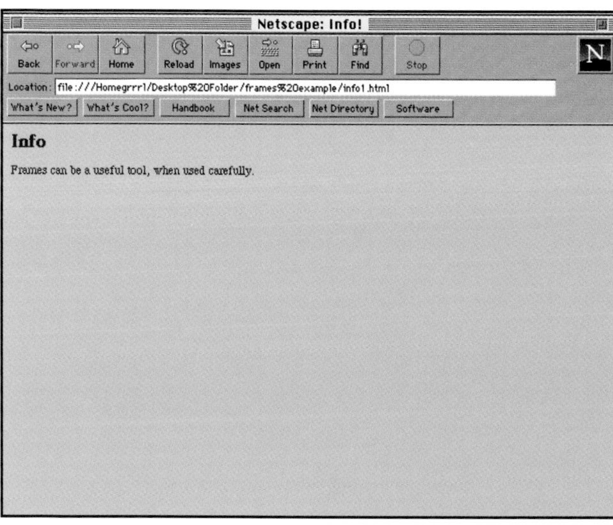

This is the document nested within the right frame of header.html, it is called info.html.

menu.html HTML

```
   <html>
   <head>
1  <base target=info>
   <title>Huh? I thought I was in a frame!</title>
   </head>
   <body bgcolor=000066 text=00ccff link=00ffcc
   vlink=00ffcc alink=00ccff>
   <h2>Menu</h2>
2  <menu>
   <li><a href=info.html>Info</a>
   <li><a href=milk.html>Milk</a>
   <li><a href=blue.html>Blue</a>
   <li><a href=light.html>Light</a>
   <li><a href=monster.html>Monsters!</a>
   </menu>
   </body>
   </html>
```

tags

menu.html Deconstruction

1 The <base> tag has a target attribute so that all the hyperlinks load in the frame named "info."

2 The <menu> tag is used to create a menu in the left-hand frame. Be sure to keep all your menu text as short as possible so that it fits in the frame.

Alternately, you could create a vertical imagemap designed to fit precisely in the frame.

info.html HTML

```
   <html>
   <head>
1  <title>Info!</title>
   <body bgcolor=cccc99>
2  <h2>Info</h2>
   <p>Frames can be a useful tool, when used carefully.
   </body>
   </html>
```

[Note: Each of the documents in the right-hand frame are structured as a normal HTML document. It's important to keep the amount of text to a minimum, so it fits nicely in the limited space of the frame.]

tags

info.html Deconstruction

1 The <title> tag describes the document, for people who might load it outside of a frame.

2 All the HTML in the document is designed just as you would a document that was not going in a frame.

■ site summary

HotWired

HotWired tackled a number of issues in the Cocktail site, such as how to enhance navigation with frames, adding Sybase database functionality using CGI, creating appropriate-sized artwork for Frames, and managing the vast information content of the site. Here are some lessons learned from HotWired's efforts:

■ When writing content for the Web, keep in mind that too much text can be overwhelming for your audience to absorb at once. Create smaller bytes of information and use hyperlinks to separate information on to different pages.

■ When creating artwork for use within frames, make sure that the images are conservatively sized. Frames take up a lot of screen "real estate." Making the content fit within the frames is a courtesy to your end-viewers and eliminates the need for them to scroll to see vital information.

■ Sites that use frames usually make a no-frames version as well. This increases the Web page author's work load on a frames-based site (because two sets of pages have to be generated) but it enables the pages to be seen by viewers who do not have access to a frames-capable browser.

■ If something doesn't work the way it should for a site, CGI programming can be used to enhance functionality. In HotWired's case, the way Netscape implemented the Back button in frames didn't work for their user interface. The HotWired engineers used custom CGI programs to solve the problem. If a Web site has the resources, working with CGI programmers can provide solutions to otherwise unsolvable problems.

■ Taking artwork off someone's Web site is illegal. If you're a photographer or graphic designer and discover that someone is using your artwork, you may take legal action against them. If you copy someone's artwork off their site without their permission, to print or use on your own site, you are breaking the law and stealing. Period.

■ QuickTime movies are also included wherever possible on the site. Jill converts the video footage to a computer movie file using the Fusion digitizing system and AV card. She stores the movie at movie 160x120 pixels, 10–12 frames per second, using Cinepak compression. Movies within Cocktail are included in the HTML using an <img src> tag. The movie file must download fully to the hard drive before it can be viewed.

Art Center College of Design

experimental design

What this chapter covers:

- **Creating Transitions between Pages**
- **QuarkXpress to HTML Conversions**
- **Invisible Objects for Table Alignment and Hyperlinks**
- **Treating Text as Images**

http://www.artcenter.edu Few visual designers appreciate the limitations HTML impose, such as lack of control over fonts, alignment, and layout. Art Center College of Design's Web site demonstrates an effort to reclaim a higher degree of design control over these limits. This effort met with success, as well as with its own set of compromises and trade-offs. The site was created as a joint project with Art Center's renowned design office and Gudrun Frommherz, a graduate student in Communication and New Media Design, who wrote her thesis based on issues presented within the design of the site itself.

Client: Art Center College of Design

Type of Site: College Catalog/Graduate Thesis

Server: SGI Challenge S, Macintosh Workgroup Server

Operating System: UNIX, MacOS

Server Software: Netscape Commerce, StarNine WebStar

Webmaster: Gudrun Frommherz

Webmaster and Production: Gudrun Frommherz, Darin Beaman

Art Direction: Darin Beaman

Associate Designer: Tiago Soromenho-Ramos

Photography: Steven A. Heller

Software: Photoshop, QuarkXPress, Illustrator, BBEdit, Netscape 1.12, Transparency, GIFConverter

The Goals of Art Center Site

The design office at Art Center is challenged every two years to create a new recruitment catalog. The goal of the catalog is to attract 18 to 23-year-olds with the school's educational philosophy, architecture, and showcase of student work. Over its 66-year history, the college has received widespread acclaim for the catalog's cutting edge graphic design and photography. Art Center's Web site, which is profiled in this chapter, represents the first on-line version of this printed catalog.

Graduate student Gudrun Frommherz's thesis, titled "Design for Networked Environments," focused on a need for synthesis and cooperation between design and technology. By creating Art Center's Web site, Gudrun was able to participate in a real-world project that related directly to her thesis research. She was given complete control over the conceptualization, structure, and programming of the site, and worked in collaboration with Darin Beaman of the Art Center Design Office who had been a lead designer on the most recent print version of the catalog.

Though Gudrun functioned as HTML designer and Darin as visual designer, as a premise of their collaboration, boundaries blurred, and the synthesis of their programming and design talents created a result that would not have been possible for either of them to achieve independently.

Changing Settings

The Art Center site is experimental in nature and took liberties that pushed beyond the Web's current limitations. It doesn't service all and isn't democratic, but is instead an attempt to experiment with design issues that concern visual designers, such as navigation, transitions, alignment, and using text as images.

When you first enter Art Center's Web site, a screen appears with a series of setting requirements. It suggests that the site is best viewed by changing fonts, turning underlining off, and resizing the browser window. Many viewers consider this an unacceptable interruption and are unwilling to make the settings changes. The penalty to ignoring the settings change request is that many of the innovative design features of the site will not be seen as intended. Herein lies one of the site's major controversies.

The decision to ask viewers to change their settings was carefully considered. The World Wide Web was not designed for designers or by designers. Gudrun and Darin take issue with the default settings of browsers, asserting that end users have been put at a disadvantage with design decisions that aren't optimum. Times Roman for example, the default font of most browsers, was designed for the printed page. Skinny serifs (The tapered ends at the end of letterforms such as T) don't translate well at screen resolution. Underlined text was developed for typewriters that didn't have settings for bold or italic typefaces. The font settings that the Art Center site requests are based on design considerations, not defaults.

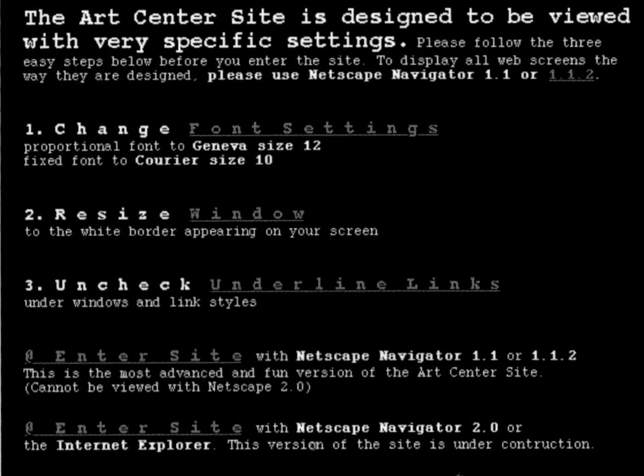

The settings window that requests the end-user to change underlined links, font settings, and window size.

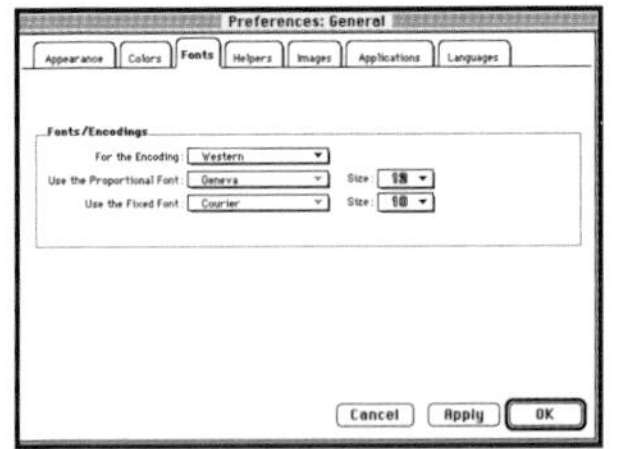

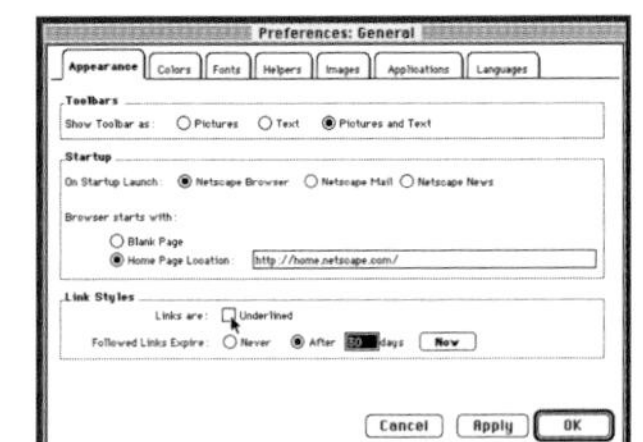

Within Netscape, these preference settings are located under the Options, General Preferences menu.

Alignment and Layout Issues

Another controversial decision was to use alignment and page layout techniques that could not work consistently across platforms. Even though the Web can be viewed from multiple platforms, what few realize is that pages do not display the same across platforms. Controlling the visual appearance of a Web page is exactly what most visual designers want to do. The choice between giving up design control or taking possession of design control is at the heart of this site's goals.

Cross Platform Warning

It's impossible to author screens that look identical in Mac and Windows browsers. Each platform has its own spacing and fonts, and different monitors have their own aspect ratio of rectangular or square pixels. Some of the pages on the Art Center site use exacting relationships between background images and foreground HTML text, and only look true to the intended design when viewed on a Mac platform.

Wanting precise visual control, Gudrun and Darin made a conscious choice to design the site for a specific audience. Studies showed that more designers use Macintoshes than any other computer platform. They, therefore, decided that most potential students interested in attending Art Center would be using Macintoshes and the Netscape browser. It follows that the font settings request for Geneva is a Mac-only typeface.

No one likes to be excluded or to exclude, and the fact that the Web is regarded as a democratic, information-for-all environment makes any effort that limits accessibility disturbing. From that perspective, the site can easily be criticized. It's important to keep in mind that Darin's and Gudrun's goals were to set a higher standard of visual integrity than the cross-platform Web currently offers. If you look at CD-ROMs and other interactive design mediums as examples, absolute design control is possible. Most CD-ROM developers make different versions of their products because it's impossible to use the same fonts and layouts between Macs and Windows.

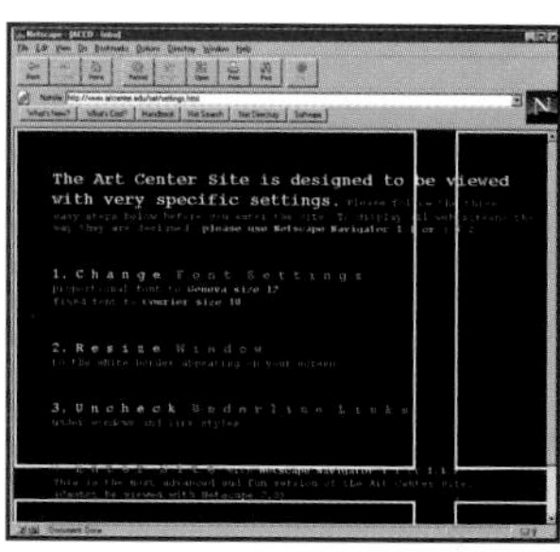

The images on the left show the proper alignment on a Macintosh. The images on the right show the identical screens viewed from a PC.

> **note**
>
> **Intranet versus Internet**
>
> These days, many firms are looking to create intranets as well as Internet-based Web sites. An intranet is a Web site that is self-contained and intentionally directed to a specific audience. A company, for example, might make an internal intranet to distribute information that's intended for employees only, or a sales force, or a select audience that has password-protected entry. The nature of an intranet is very different than a public Web site, and suits itself easily to a set of pages that are designed for specific hardware and software. HTML is a pain to learn, but hypertext and linked graphics are powerful tools, making a Web site a valuable communication medium whether it's available publicly or privately distributed. Many of the single-platform techniques in this chapter would work beautifully on a platform-specific intranet-based Web site.

Transition Screens

When you first enter the site, its text appears in total disarray—as if free-floating in "alphabet soup." Through clicking, the reader brings the letters to order. The intent of this sequence of screens is to make the end viewer an active participant in clarifying the information and in setting the pace of viewing the site. It establishes that the mood is very different here than on other sites. The goal was to define this site as a new design space, not just a forum in which to shuffle data around.

Gudrun decided that most information design revolves around reaching "landmarks." Less attention is usually paid to how one gets to and from landmark to landmark. The idea throughout much of the site was to create a sequence of screens that would transport the viewer from landmark to landmark, and make the process of getting there as engaging as seeing the final image. In Gudrun's words, "The Web as a fluid medium is as much about designing the transitions as it is about the information itself."

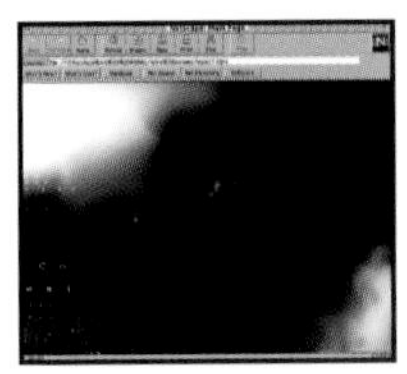
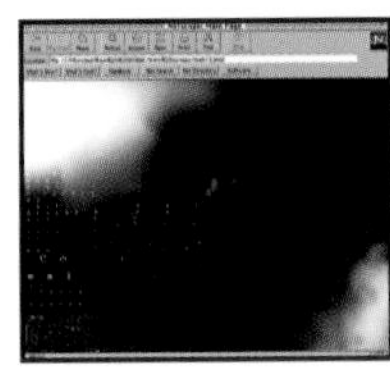
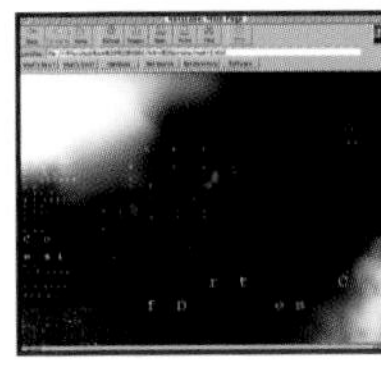
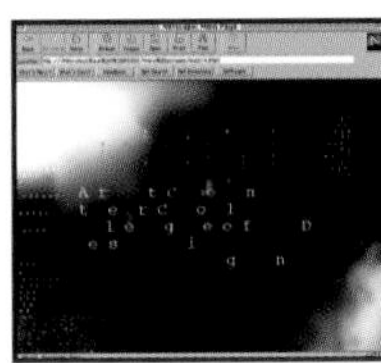
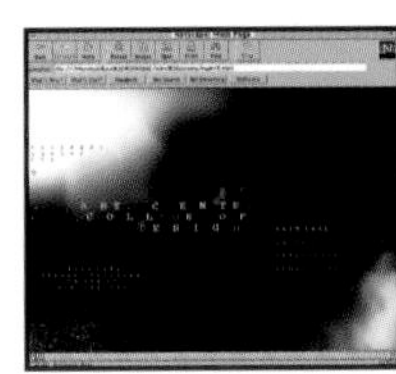

It takes five clicks to cause the scrambled words to build into legibility. This is an example of making the journey to the information as much of the experience as the final message.

Netscape 1.1 versus Netscape 2.0 and Above

When Art Center's Web site was designed, Netscape 1.1 was the browser in current circulation. Netscape 1.1 supported the capability to include multiple background images in one document, which enabled the backgrounds to load sequentially in order to create the illusion of limited frame animations.

Netscape 2.0 took away the capability to program multiple background images and also changed the order in which backgrounds loaded. It turned out that the multiple background feature was unintentional on Netscape's part, and was removed as soon as they released their next version. The Art Center site had been designed specifically to take advantage of those exact features found in the earlier version 1.1 in order to create transition effects between screens. It was heartbreaking to have put so much effort into screens that were no longer visible to those viewing the site from the newer version.

Gudrun has since programmed the HTML to work with either Netscape 1.1 or Netscape 2.0. The Netscape 1.1 version is much more engaging, however, because it has many dynamic screens and transitions that were lost in the newer version of the browser.

Even though the multiple background "feature" is no longer available, many designers, myself included, miss it and wish browser developers would put it back into the browser specs. Generally, when a new browser is released, you expect it to add new features, not take existing features away!

Dynamic Sequences and Transition Screens

Most of the screens within Art Center's Web site were created using two background images that loaded sequentially. The pages loaded like slide-shows, creating the illusion of limited animation. This was done by inserting multiple <body background> tags (see HTML deconstruction). Even though multiple backgrounds are no longer possible to insert via the <body background> tag, there are other methods for creating transition screens. Check out Chapter 4, "Sony Music Online," for the two frame animation technique of using a <low src> tag and animated GIFs, as well as Chapter 3, "Hollywood Records."

Within the multiple background screens, the theme of visually abstracted information transforming into information that was legible or vice versa again emerged. The action of seeing something illegible at first, then watching it transform into legibility, was intended to attract the viewer's interest and attention. Making information readable at first glance doesn't always have the same impact as creating "added drama" through involving the viewer in building the informational elements. Sadly, most of the screens that created these transition effects are only visible if the site is viewed with the older, outdated Netscape 1.1 browser.

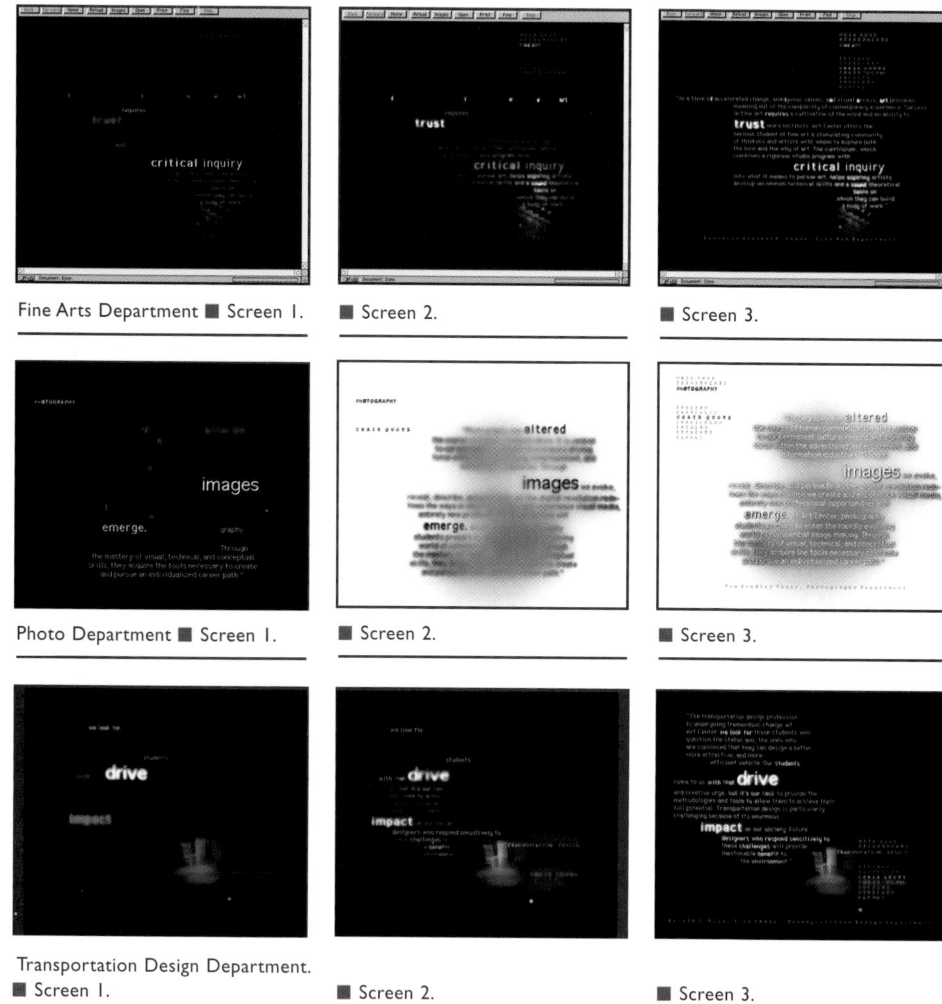

Fine Arts Department ■ Screen 1. ■ Screen 2. ■ Screen 3.

Photo Department ■ Screen 1. ■ Screen 2. ■ Screen 3.

Transportation Design Department. ■ Screen 1. ■ Screen 2. ■ Screen 3.

Art Center's Web site used the multiple background "feature" of Netscape 1.1 to build important screen information in stages. The visual device of building the information in three steps helped add more interest to hold the viewer's attention.

step-by-step

How the Art Center Dynamic Screen Sequences Were Built

Even though the multiple background "feature" is no longer available to Web designers, dynamic imagery—the capability to achieve movement through creating sequences of images—is still used all the time with animated GIFs (see Chapters 3 and 4), client pull and server-push (see Chapter 8), or Java and Shockwave (see Chapter 9). Designers use all kinds of techniques to create the source artwork for dynamic documents. In the case of Art Center's dynamic screens, QuarkXPress, Photoshop, and HTML text elements were used. Gudrun intentionally used methods that did not rely on outside plug-ins or complex programming to achieve dynamic effects.

Darin and Gudrun used a process of switching between HTML, QuarkXPress, and Photoshop to create some of the dynamic sequences.

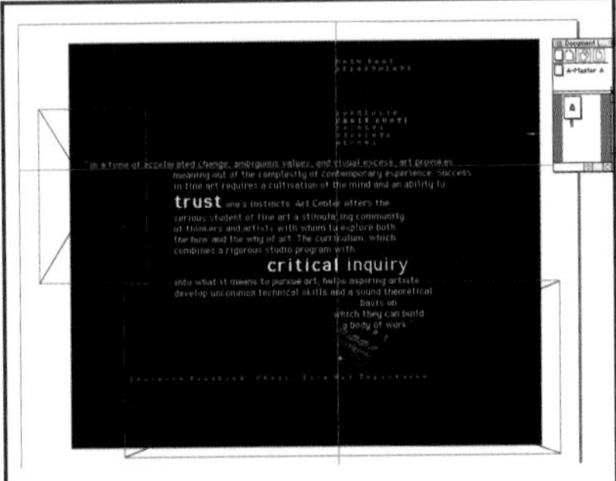

Step 1: Darin began the process in QuarkXPress by laying out a page for the Fine Art Department Chair Quote.

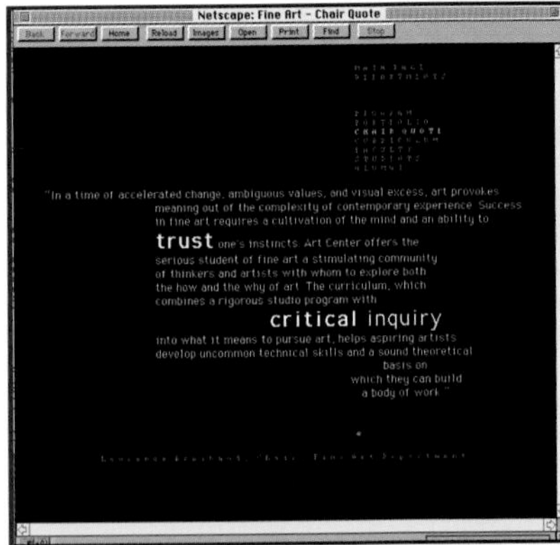

Step 2: Gudrun took Darin's layout and created an HTML document that would translate his design. The image to the left is the HTML code, and the image to the right is the result displayed in Netscape.

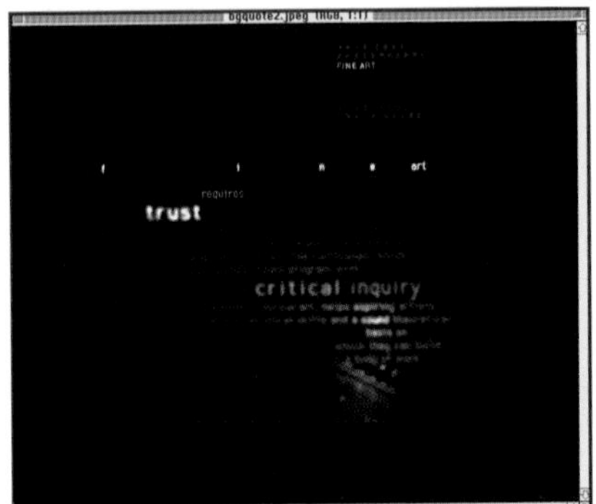

Step 3: A screen capture was taken of the HTML text and background image, which created a full-screen graphic of the Web screen. (Screen capture software takes a snapshot of a computer screen. For more information, see the note that appears on page 126). The screen capture was brought into Photoshop where it was blurred and image processed. This new image was saved as a JPEG and used as a background image behind the HTML text.

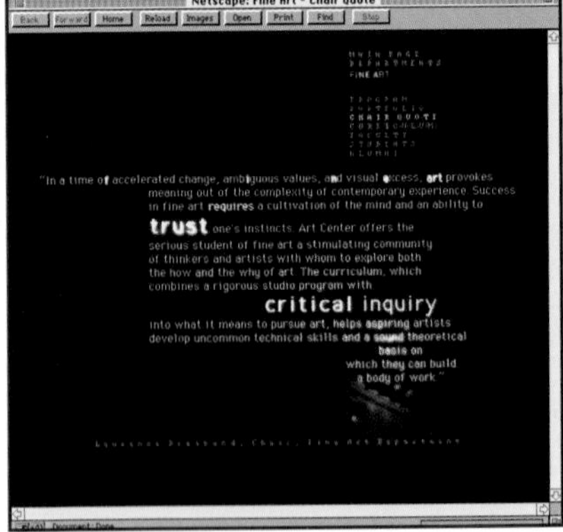

Step 4: The JPEG from Step 3 was used as a full-screen background tile, and the HTML text shown in Step 2 was placed on top of it again. The illusion of glowing text was accomplished through placing crisp HTML text over a blurry, Photoshop-generated background.

Text as Image/Text as Text

Throughout Art Center's Web site, Gudrun and Darin designed with the differences between "text as text" and "text as image." "Text as text" was defined as HTML-generated. The "text as image" artwork was created using Photoshop, Illustrator, and Quark-XPress, where custom typefaces were used along with image processing techniques to stylize their appearance.

Many consider HTML-based text on Web page screens as having more realism or truthfulness than images of text. Darin and Gudrun intentionally mixed the two in an effort to call attention to the tension between text as information and text as visual design. Throughout the site, you'll find text that's been blurred, distorted, and altered mixed on the same page with ASCII HTML text.

Text as Texture

Another technique used to enhance HTML text was to mix type sizes, fonts (Geneva and Courier), and styles, such as plain, bold, and italic. This effort ties in with treating the text as a visual element, as well as an informational element. The Art Center Web Site strived to point out that information and visualization are part of one and the same communication process.

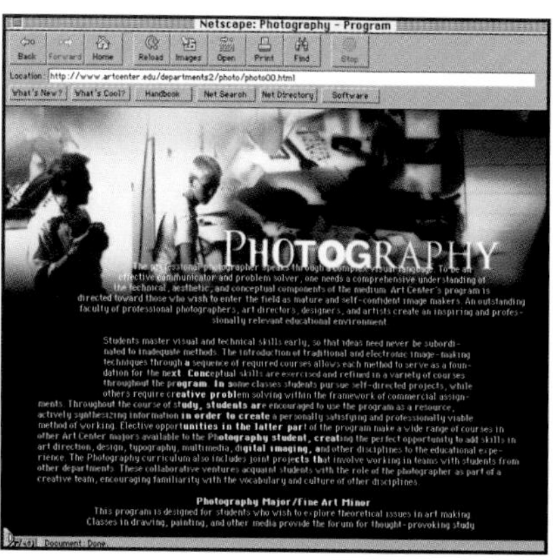

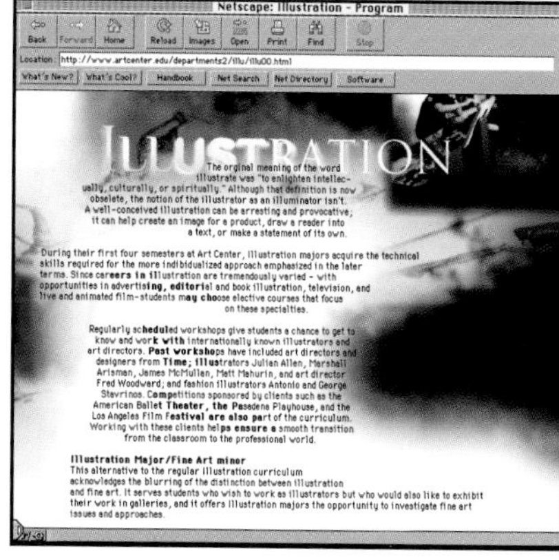

By using the <b> tag for making text bold, Gudrun was able to change the weights of the ASCII-based HTML typography through mixing bold and normal text characters. These shapes created abstract forms that please the eye, and invite the reader to study the content.

■ tip

Switching from Print to the Web

Art Center's Web site was Darin Beaman's first experience designing for the Web. This quote was taken from an interview with him, conducted by Geeta Sharma, for *Dot 2*, the Alumni Publication of Art Center College of Design.

■ "The Web makes typography and imagery kinetic. Text isn't passive here; it's alive. People view text on the Web as pure 'information'; there seems to be a consensus that the Web has finally emancipated the word from the designer's hand. But we think this notion of freedom is limited. It's limited by default type options and the Web's organization as a text-based medium. We've chosen to circumvent these limitations not out of 'designer conceit' or arrogance, but rather, to expand the visual language of the Web. In our site we have treated text as image to blur the notion that it is 'pure' information and to explore the richness of an information space beyond the purity of its surface." **-Darin Beaman**

Most agree that the appearance of HTML text is boring and bland. Gudrun's thesis argues that we are a visually rich culture that cannot be described by using ASCII text-based systems. Text as image has historical roots beginning with hieroglyphics all the way to the invention of the letterpress. The HTML-based ASCII Web is not nearly as rich a communication tool as what could be accomplished with image-based text.

■ code

Text as Texture Deconstruction

```
throughout the pr<b>ogram. In s</b>ome classes students pursue self-directed
```

■ Here's a sample line of HTML for making type bold with the <b> tag.

throughout the **program. In** some classes students pursue self-directed projects, while

■ Here's the finished result on the Web page.

```
<pre>
<font size="+4"><b>A r t C e n t e r</b></font>
<font size="+2">C</font>
<font size="+4">o   l   l   e   g   e   o   f</font>
<font size="+2"><b>D</b></font>
<font size="+3"><b>E    S    I    G</b></font>    <font size="+2"><b>N</b></font>
</pre>
```

■ Here's the HTML to create the words on the bottom. The <pre> tag forces the type to be represented in the Courier typeface. It also instructs the browser to honor the spacing between words and letters. The <font size> tag was used to change the size of individual letters.

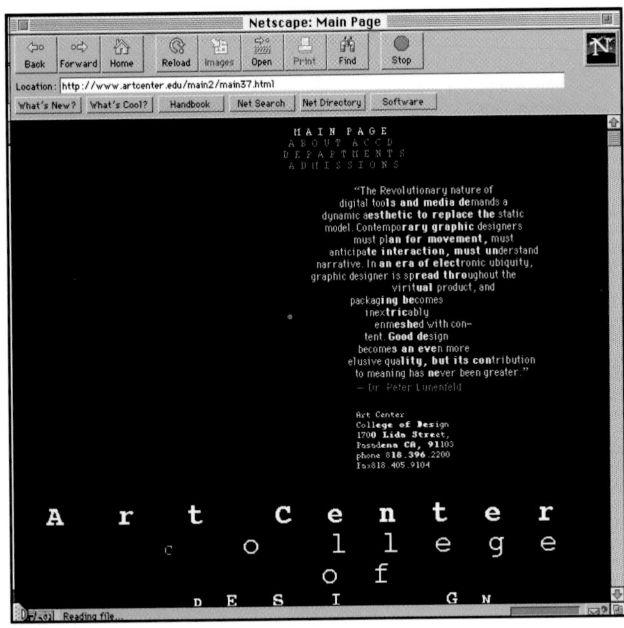

In this example, two typefaces—Geneva and Courier—are used, as well as setting different type sizes. This is accomplished by using the <pre> and <font> tags.

A close-up view of the lettering on the bottom of the screen that uses the <pre> and <font size> tags.

Header Tests (H[1-6])

This is a Header 1
This is a Header 2
This is a Header 3
This is a Header 4
This is a Header 5
This is a Header 6

Font Size (FONT SIZE=[1-7])

This is Font Size 1
This is Font Size 2
This is Font Size 3
This is Font Size 4
This is Font Size 5
This is Font Size 6
This is Font Size 7

Font Size (FONT SIZE=[-2-+4])

This is Font Size -2
This is Font Size -1
This is Font Size +0
This is Font Size +1
This is Font Size +2
This is Font Size +3
This is Font Size +4

This chart, created by Yoshinobo Takahas at Disney Online, illustrates how the font size tags work in Netscape. Feel free to use this chart as a guide for your own font size explorations.

Using QuarkXPress for Web Page Pre-visualization

All of the screens in the Art Center site were first built in QuarkXPress with the following guidelines, so the documents could be translated later to HTML:

- Limit the design to seven font sizes (the limit within HTML for the <font size> tag).
- Only use bold, italic, or regular styles.
- Keep the leading (the space between lines of type) to the default size of the font, because custom leading is not possible with HTML.
- Use monospace kerning. Monospace means that every text character takes up the same width. Kerning is the process of putting space between letters. The Web doesn't allow for custom kerning, like QuarkXPress does. If you want to add space between letterforms, each space has to equal the full space of a monospaced text character.

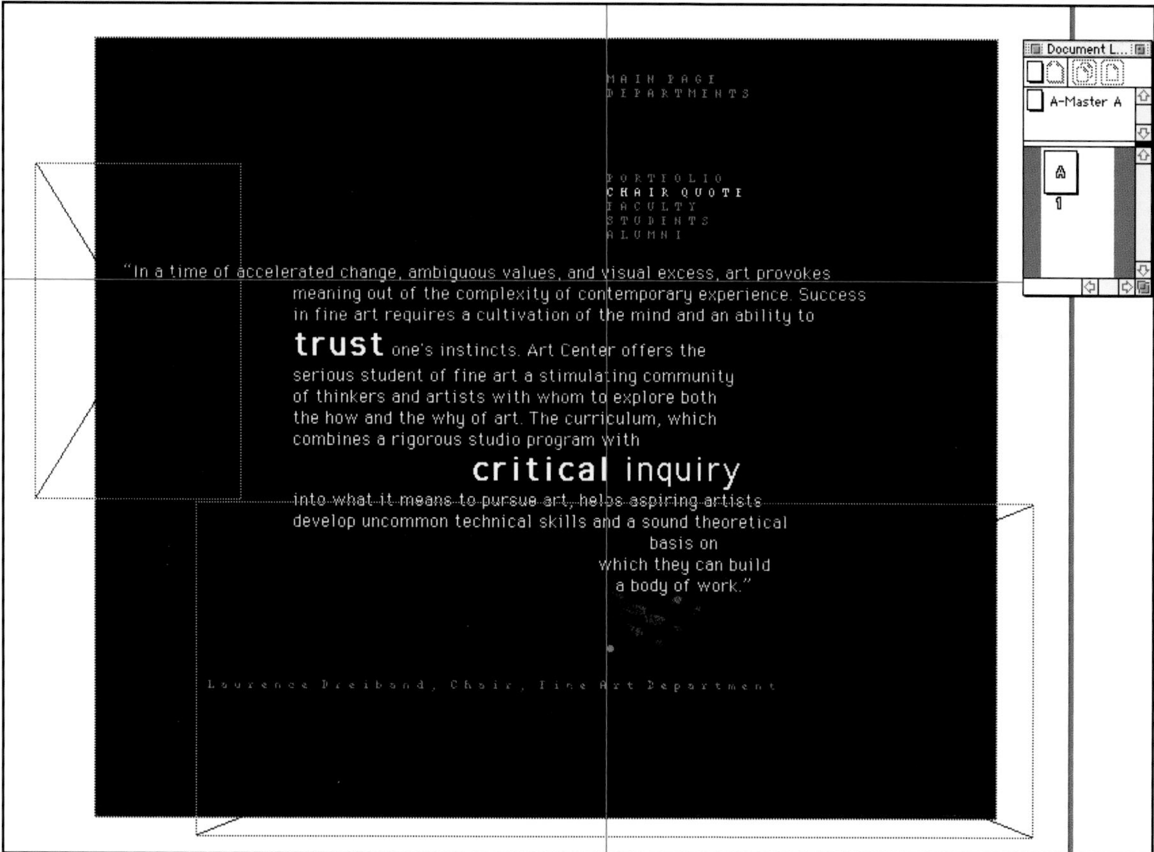

This QuarkXPress document, created by Darin, was used as one of many templates for Gudrun to translate into HTML. He placed a Photoshop document behind the QuarkXPress type, so he could align the foreground text with the background it would be against on the final Web screen.

■ note

Screen Capture Software

All computers are capable of taking a "screen capture," or a snapshot of any screen. On PCs, use the F13, or PrintSc key. This puts a copy of whatever screen has been captured into a buffer. Open any image processor and choose "paste" to see the results of the screen grab. On Macs use the keystrokes Command+Shift+3. This creates an image called PICTURE that is automatically stored on the hard drive.

Gudrun used a screen capture package called "Capture" for the Macintosh by Mainstay (■ http://www.mstay.com/). Gudrun's review of the utility follows: **"**Unlike the key-screen shot, one can select parts of the screen to be captured like the crop tool in Photoshop. One may specify the folder where the capture images will be saved and the image file format: Pict, Tiff 4, Tiff 5, MacPaint, clipboard, or scrapbook (which both are picts then). Another nice thingy: the keyboard command to trigger the 'shot' can be customized, images may be captured in different sizes (in percentages), with or without cursor, b/w, and they might be auto-named. All in all: small, handy, and nice.**"**

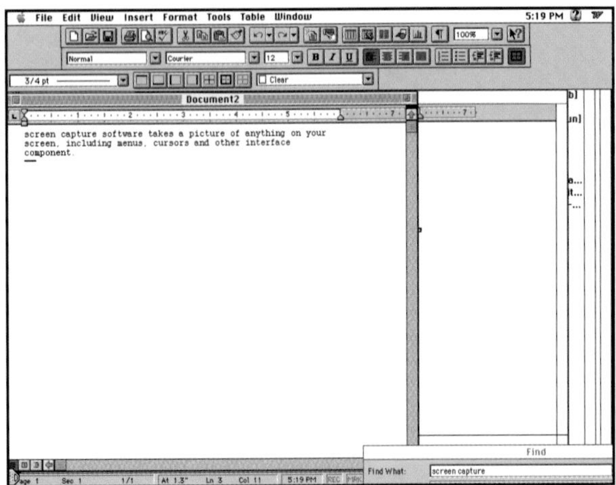

Screen capture software can take a picture of anything! Here's an example of a screen capture of a word processor.

There are many screen capture utilities available for Macs and PCs. These little programs are a lot more robust than the default screen capture capabilities and allow you to take pictures of dialog boxes and pull-down menus, and some even record movies of your movement on the screen. These utilities are generally inexpensive and can be found or purchased online.

Here's an incomplete list of URLs:

Mainstay—Capture
■ http://www.mstay.com/

AndroSoft—SuperClip 3.1
■ http://ourworld.compuserve.com/homepages/andromeda/

Bananas Software Inc—Image'n'Bits
■ http://www.ios.com/~banana/

C-Star Technology
■ http://www.c-star1.com/

TechSmith Corporation—SnagIt
■ http://www.techsmith.com/

Capture Professional for Win 95 & Win 3.1
■ http://www.csworx.com/

Beale Street Group, Inc.—
Screen Shot and Exposure Pro
■ http://www.beale.com/

SnapShot/32
■ http://198.207.242.3/authors/gregko/snap32.htm

MagicKey
■ http://emporium.turnpike.net/~jc/share.html

The HTML Translation of a QuarkXPress Document Template

One of the extraordinary accomplishments of this site was its success in aligning background images to HTML text. Remember, however, this type of precise alignment is only possible to do on a single platform site.

Gudrun used tables and invisible placeholder art to accurately simulate the placed text from Darin's QuarkXPress Template.

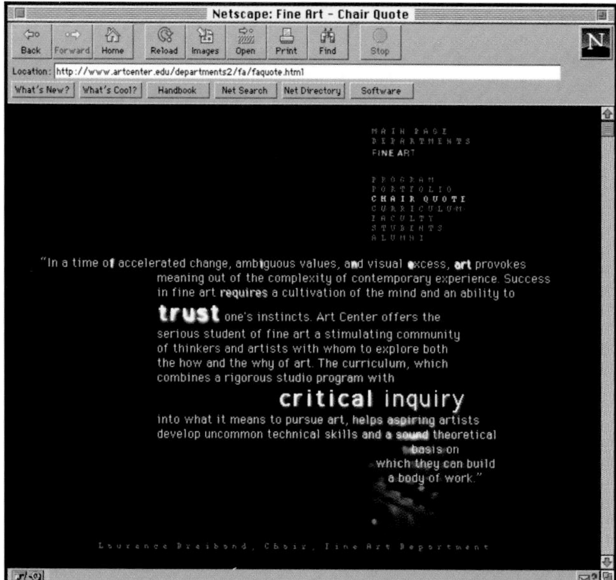

Fine Art Chair Quote screen, as seen in Netscape. The illusion of glowing text was accomplished by placing crisp HTML text over a blurry, Photoshop-generated background image.

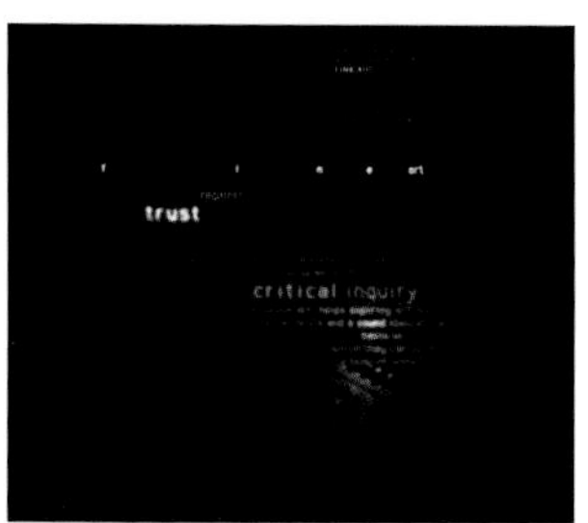

Here's the Photoshop image by itself, without the HTML text on top of it.

Here's the HTML text alone, without the Photoshop background. Combined, the effect appears to be glowing.

Fine Art Chair Quote Screen HTML

```
<html><head><title>Fine Art - Chair
Quote</title></head>
1 <body bgcolor="#000000" background="bgquote13.jpeg">
<body background="bgquote23.jpeg" text="#FFFFFF"
link="#B29000"
vlink="#B29000" alink="#FFFFFF">
2 <table width=600 border=0>
<tr>
<td width=20> </td>
<td width=180> </td>
<td valign=top>
3 <font size="-2">
4 <pre>
<a href="/main37.html">M A I N  P A G E</a>
<a href="/departments.html">D E P A R T
M E N T S</a>
<a href="fa00.html">P R O G R A M</a>
<a href="fa19.html">P O R T F O L I O</a>
C H A I R  Q U O T E
<a href="facurr1.html">C U R R I C U L U M</a>
<a href="fafac.html">F A C U L T Y</a>
<a href="/void.html">S T U D E N T S</a>
<a href="/void.html">A L U M N I</a>
</pre>
</font>
</td>
</tr>
<tr>
<td width=20> </td>
<td colspan=2>
5 &#179;In a time of accelerated change, ambiguous
values, and visual excess, art provokes<br>
6 <img align=left src="empty7.gif" width=120
height=220 border=0> meaning out of the complexity
of contemporary experience. Success <br> in fine
art requires a cultivation of the mind and an
ability to<br>
```

7

```
<font size=+3><b>trust</b></font> one's instincts.
Art Center offers the <br> serious student of fine
art a stimulating community <br> of thinkers and
artists with whom to explore both <br> the how and
the why of art. The curriculum, which <br> combines
a rigorous studio program with<br>
<img align=left src="empty7.gif" width=125 height=20
border=0>
<font size=+3><b>critical</b> inquiry</font><br>
into what it means to pursue art, helps aspiring
artists <br> develop uncommon technical skills and
a sound theoretical<br>
<img align=left src="empty7.gif" width=150 height=50
border=0>
<center>basis on<br>which they can build<br>a body
of work.&#178;</center>
</td>
</tr>
<tr>
<td width=20> </td>
<td width=180> </td>
<td><font size="-2">
<pre>
</pre>
<a href="http://www.artcenter.edu/map/
faQUOTEmap.html">&#128;</a>
</font>
</td></tr>
<tr><td align=center colspan=3>
<font size="-2">
<pre>
<a href="facbioD.html#ldreiban">L a u r e n c e
D r e i b a n d ,  C h a i r,
F i n e  A r t  D e p a r t m e n t</a>
</pre></font>
</td>
</tr>
</table>
</body>
</html>
```

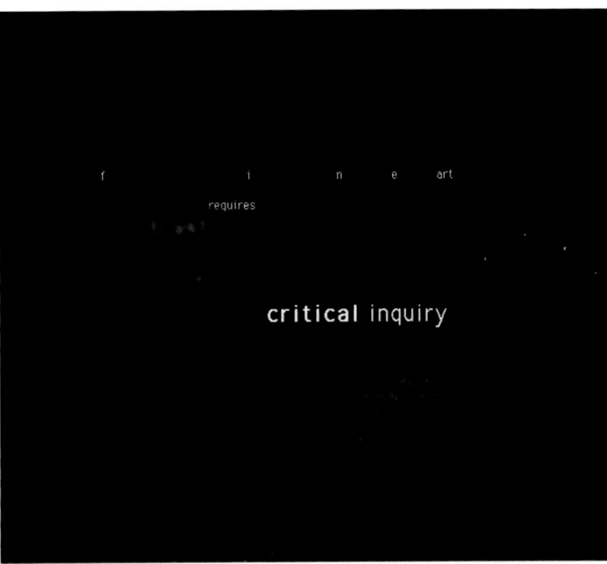

bgquote13.jpg is a full-screen image used as a background for the Web page. It is 12.4k and 680x550 pixels in dimension.

bgquote23.jpg loaded second as a full-screen background image. It is 12.6k and 680x550 pixels in dimension. The interplay between these two screens called attention to the words "trust" and "critical inquiry."

tags

Fine Art Chair Quote Screen Deconstruction

1 Under Netscape 1.1, it was possible to create two (or more) background images that would load sequentially. Looking at Gudrun's HTML, notice that there's a <body bgcolor> tag that sets the background color to black. Next, the background="bgquote13.jpeg" artwork is loaded and after that the <body background="bgquote 23.jpeg" is set to load last. In a final rendering pass, the active HTML text is loaded on top of the last background image.

---

2 A table width <table width=600 border=0> is being established that is a little smaller than the background image. This is being used to force all the HTML text into a precise layout. The <tr> tag defines a table row. A table row is horizontal. The <td width=20> </td> defines a column within a row. The width attribute fixes the width of the column to 20 pixels across. The second tag <td width=180> </td> defines a second column that will be 180 pixels wide. <td valign= top> is setting the vertical alignment of the contents of the column to align with the top of the column. The columns are being used for alignment purposes, in order to push the text contents to the upper right side of the screen.

---

3 The <font size="-2"> is establishing a smaller font, which is being used for the table of contents in the upper right hand part of the screen. The minus sign is used to set the font size relative to the size previously in use. "-2" will set it two sizes smaller.

---

4 The <pre> tag stands for pre-formatted, which means that custom letter spacing will be honored, such as typing spaced letters like M A I N P A G E where each letter has a space between it.

---

5 ³ is an entity, meaning it's a special character set for the left curly quote. A curly quote is not part of the ASCII definition, so it has to be programmed with entities within the HTML text. For a full-list of entities, see Chapter 3, "Hollywood Records."

---

6 The empty.gif is being used to create empty space for alignment purposes. It is a single color image that has been set to transparency. The width and height attributes are being used to stretch its shape for alignment purposes. It comes right before the word "meaning," which is where an indent is established for the rest of the document. Since such "empty gifs" do not hold any image data, their file size is minimal (1k).

---

7 The <font size="+3"> attribute is setting the word "trust" to be much larger than the other text in the paragraph. It's also been made bold, by using the <b> tag. The </font> tag closes the custom font size setting and returns the rest of the body of text to its previous state.

Using Full-Screen Backgrounds

A lot of the screens in the Art Center site use full-screen backgrounds. The <body background> HTML tag allows a single image to be inserted into the background of a Web screen. Most Web designers create small images that function as background tiles and fill the entire screen by repeating over and over again. See Chapter 2, "DreamWorks Interactive SKG," for an example of that type of background tiling.

Gudrun and Darin chose to create images with large dimensions that filled the entire screen instead of small background tiles. This technique offered them complete control over the image's content, something that would be impossible using HTML's limited layout and compositing capabilities. Much of the site's intrigue revolves around figuring out which parts are HTML generated and which parts are images made in Photoshop.

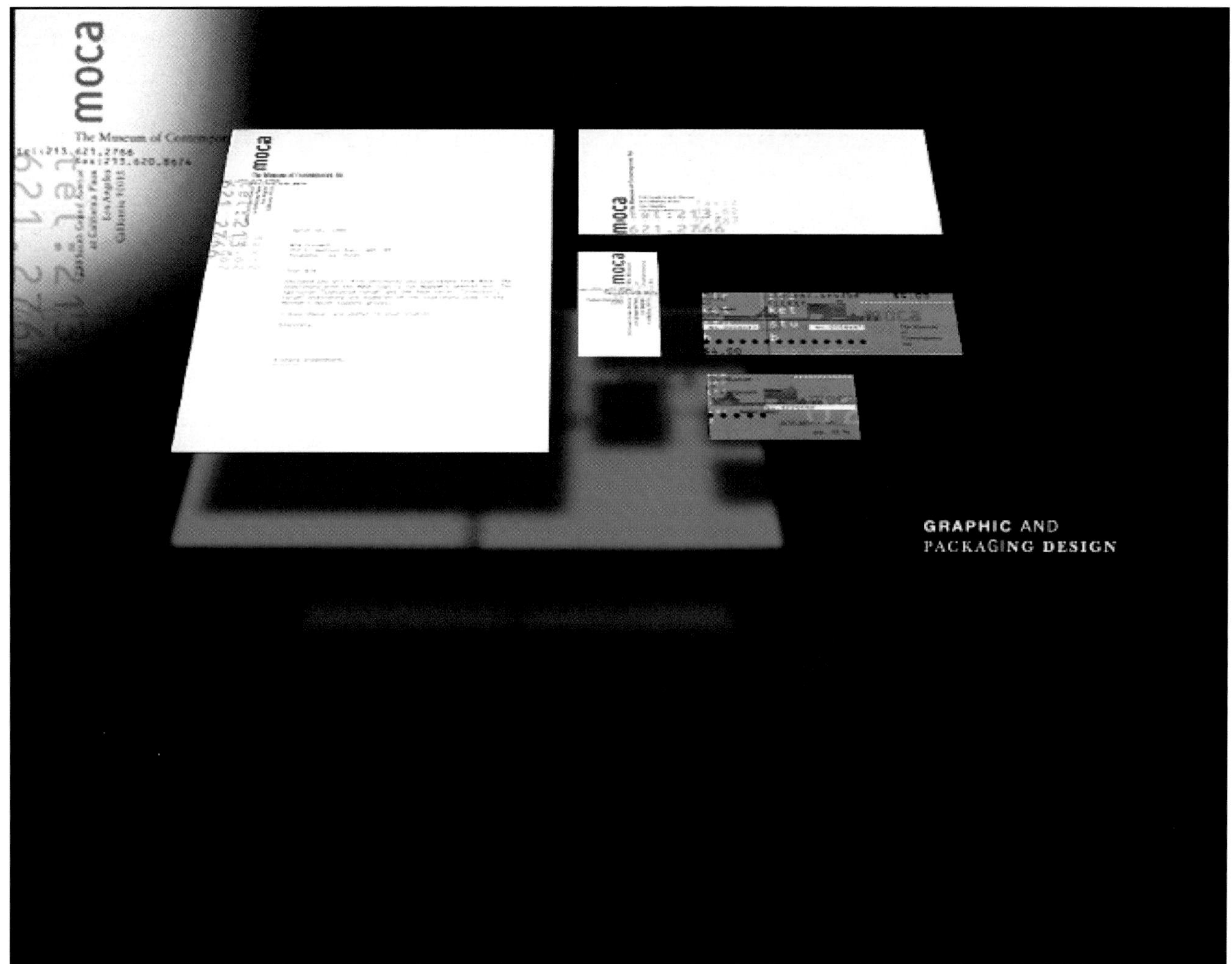

This 17.5k JPEG, which measures 680x550 pixels at 72 dpi was used as the background image for a student portfolio piece.

Using Invisible Buttons for Innovative Navigation

Art Center student Michael Abbink's graphic standards manual, being featured in this portfolio section of the Graphics and Packaging Department, included more than one page. Darin used Photoshop to create Web screens that showed off Abbink's work by skewing the images to appear in 3D space. Darin placed the sequence of samples so that the top image was in focus and the bottom samples were blurry. Gudrun created links that were placed over the blurry regions of the screens, which made it possible to trigger different views of Abbink's project.

The different screens were created as large full-screen background images. The problem with images placed into HTML using the <body background> tag is that they cannot contain any links. To get around this problem, Gudrun created transparent foreground images that functioned as invisible buttons, as links to other pages. Invisible graphics were created by making a solid color image and then turning that color off using the application Transparency, written by Aaron Giles and available from: ■ ftp:// ftp.uwtc.washington.edu/pub/Mac/Graphics/.

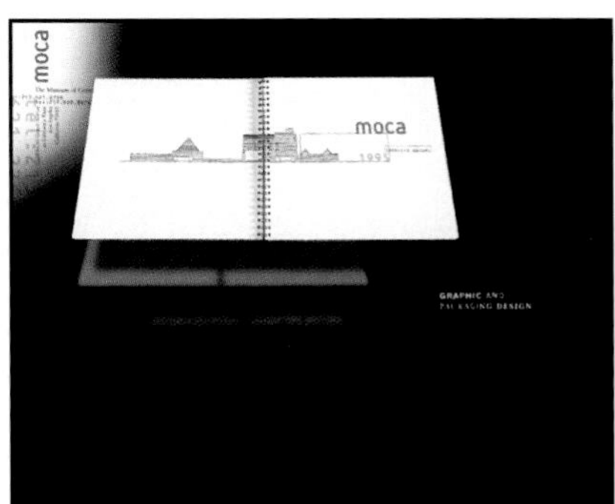

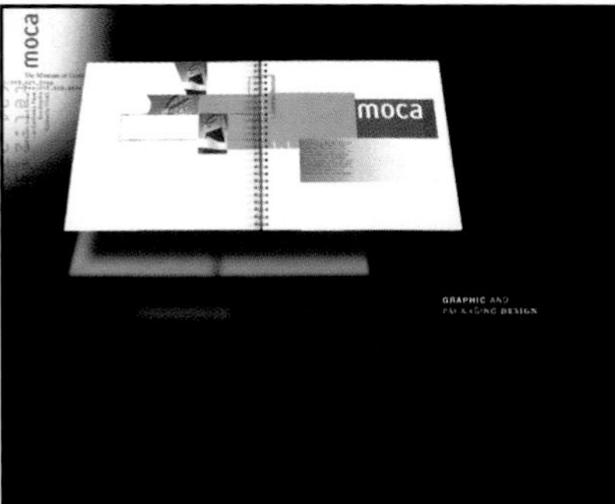

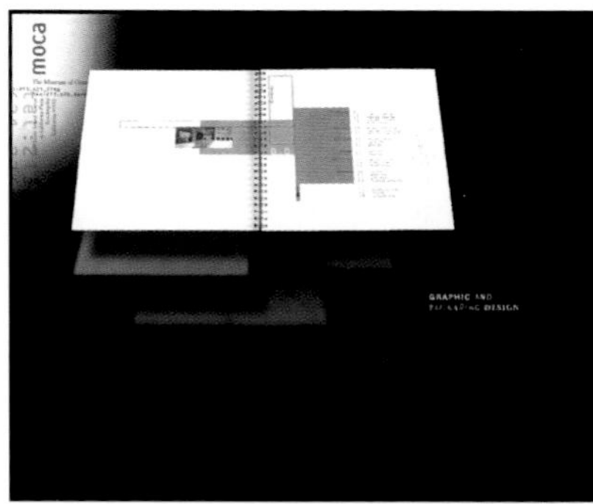

By clicking on the invisible buttons placed over the out-of-focus pages, different views of the student's project were presented. Here are the three different background images that are linked through the use of invisible buttons.

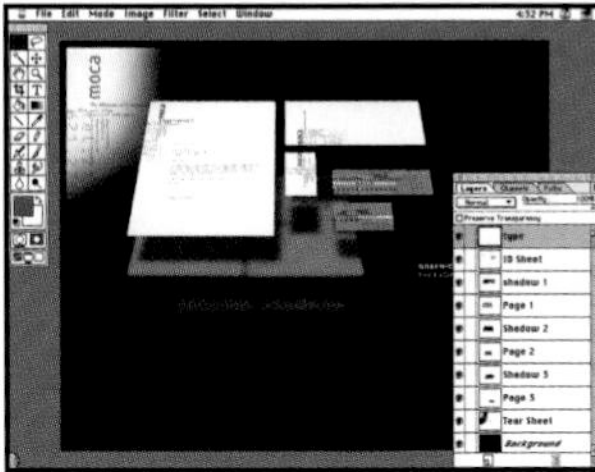

Darin began by creating the full-screen background image as a layered Photoshop file. All the shadows and blurred pages were created as separate layers.

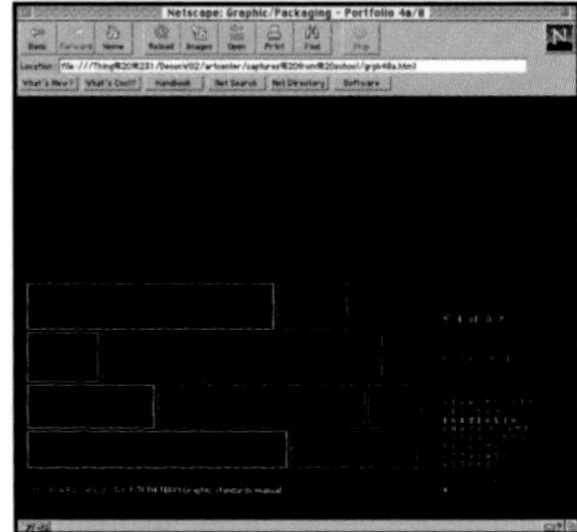

By removing the background image altogether, the borders of the table are more easily understood. The areas with yellow rectangles show where the transparent GIFs were placed. These invisible GIFs were programmed within HTML to link to other pages.

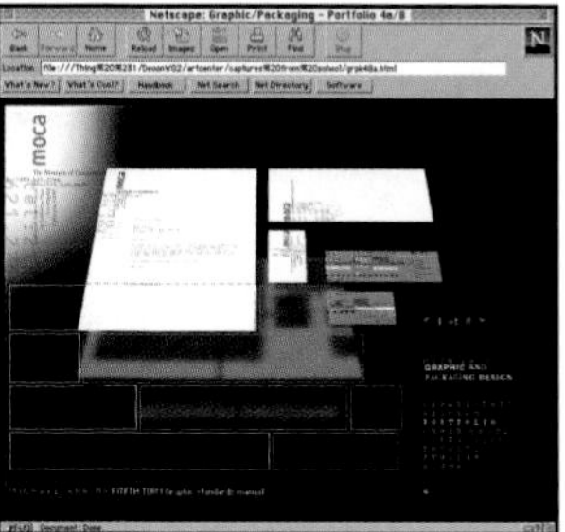

Darin's Photoshop image was converted to a JPEG and inserted into an HTML document as a full-screen background file. Gudrun used tables with borders turned off as a tool to position the invisible GIFs and align them to the background. By turning on the table borders temporarily, this figure illustrates where the tables were located within this screen's HTML.

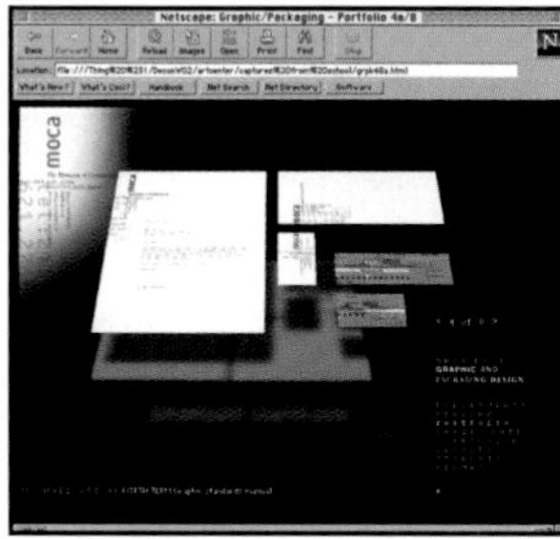

The finished page combines a full-screen background image, invisible GIFs inside tables with borders turned off, and HTML text. Visual clues hint at the active layers of the Web screen: the cursor icon changes into a hand symbol when moved over a "hot area."

■ step-by-step

Creating Invisible Objects with Transparency

Gudrun used transparent, invisible objects for alignment purposes throughout the Art Center site. This was easily accomplished by creating a graphic with a single color. Another advantage of this technique is that the same invisible image can be used multiple times throughout the Web site and gets cached so that it only needs to load once. Gudrun used the Macintosh program Transparency by Aaron Giles. Other transparency programs work well for her purposes, too. You can download "Transparency" from: ■ ftp://ftp.uwtc.washington.edu/pub/Mac/Graphics/

Step 1: Create a document with a single color. The size is important if you have a specific offset you want the transparent invisible object to create within your HTML. In Gudrun's case, she used the height and width attributes tags to stretch invisible objects when needed.

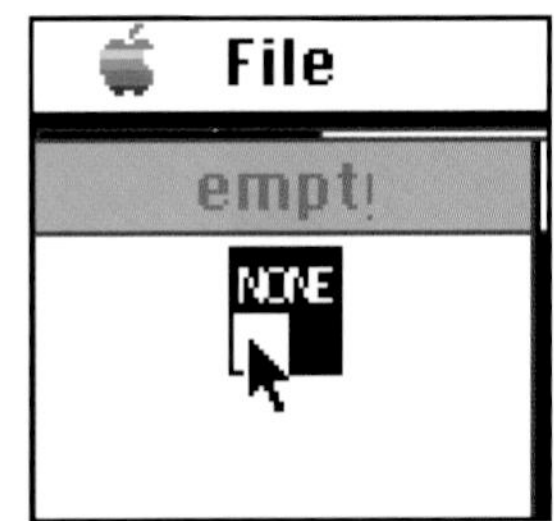

Step 2: Gudrun opened the white image in the program "Transparency." Holding the mouse down on the color white brought up the color palette. By selecting white from the palette, Gudrun instructed the program to make white the transparent color.

Step 3: She chose Save As GIF89a, which stored the transparency information along with the file so transparency was recognized when placed into an HTML document.

Invisible Buttons HTML

```
<html>
<head>
<title>Graphic/Packaging - Portfolio 4a/8</title>
</head>
1 <body bgcolor="#000000" background="bg48a.gif"
text="#FFFFFF"
link="#B29000" vlink="#B29000" alink="#FFFFFF">
2 <table width=600 border=0>
<tr>
<td height=194 colspan=2> </td>
</tr>
<tr>
<td width=480 align=left valign=top>
3 <img src="empty.gif" width=285 height=50 border=0>
4 <a href="grpk48b.html"><img src="empty.gif" width=80
height=50
border=0></a>
<br>
<img src="empty.gif" width=80 height=54 border=0>
5 <a href="grpk48b.html"><img src="empty.gif" width=325
height=54
border=0></a>
<br>
<img src="empty.gif" width=145 height=48 border=0>
6 <a href="grpk48c.html"><img src="empty.gif" width=240
height=48
border=0></a>
<a href="grpk48d.html"><img src="empty.gif" width=60
height=48
border=0></a>
<br>
<img src="empty.gif" width=300 height=40 border=0>
<a href="grpk48d.html"><img src="empty.gif" width=146
height=40
border=0></a>
<td valign=top>
<pre>
<font size="+2"><b>
<a href="grpk38a.html">&#60;</a></b></font> <font
size="+1">4 of 8</font> <font size="+2"><b>
<a href="grpk58.html">&#62;</a></b></font>
<font size="-2">
<a href="/main2/main37.html">M A I N  P A G E</a>
<a href="/departments2/departments.html">D E P
A R T M E N T S</a>
<a href="grpk00.html">P R O G R A M</a>
P O R T F O L I O
<a href="grpkquote.html">C H A I R  Q U O T E</a>
<a href="grpkcurr.html">C U R R I C U L U M</a>
<a href="grpkfac.html">F A C U L T Y</a>
<a href="/void2.html">S T U D E N T S</a>
```

```
<a href="/void2.html">A L U M N I</a>
</font>
</td>
</tr>
<tr>
<td valign=bottom width=480>
<font size="-2">
<a href="/void2.
html">M I C H A E L . A B B I N K</a> FITFTH TERM
Graphic standards manual
</font>
</td>
<td valign=bottom>
<font size="-2"><ahref="/map/grpkPFmap.html"
>&#128;</a></font></td>
</tr>
</table
</body>
</html>
```

tags

Invisible Buttons Deconstruction

1 The background image "bg48a.jpg" is defined as the background tile for this page.

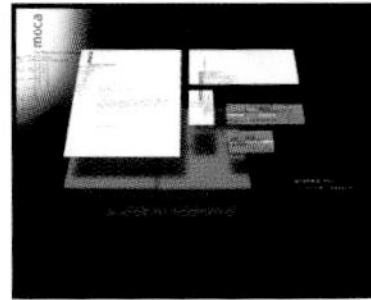

bg48a.jpg

2 The table for the page is creating a matrix that will hold the invisible GIF buttons. Notice the use of the COLSPAN attribute to create a column that spans the space of two columns.

3 The "empty.gif" image is the transparent image. It's being stretched to fit into the table by using the width and height tags.

empty.gif

4 The "empty.gif" image is set as a link to the page "grpk48b.html." The page that's being linked to contains a background called "grpk48b.jpg," which is a full-screen background image that contains a different view of Michael Abbink's student project.

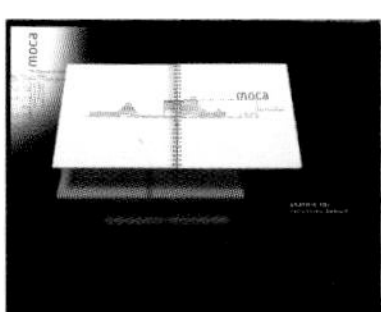

grpk48b.jpg

5 The "empty.gif" image is set as a link to the page "grpk48b.jpg." The page that's being linked to contains a background called "grpk48b.jpg," which is a full-screen background image that contains a different view of Michael Abbink's student project.

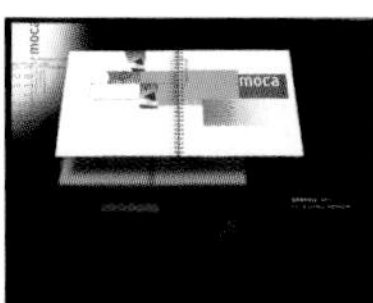

grpk48c.jpg

6 The "empty.gif" image is set as a link to the page "grpk48c.html." The page that's being linked to contains a background called "grpk48d.jpg," which is a full-screen background image that contains a different view of Michael Abbink's student project.

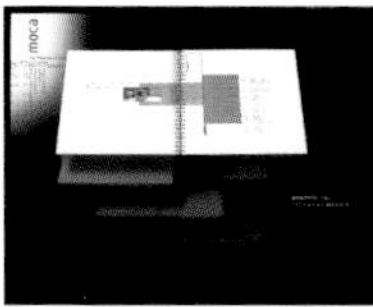

grpk48d.jpg

■ site summary

Art Center College of Desingn

The Art Center College of Design site represents an ambitious attempt to trick HTML at its own game. Through using clever Photoshop graphics, invisible buttons, tables, and alignment between foreground and background images, the site includes distinctive navigation and dynamic imagery.

Until HTML offers artists more control over page layout, alignment, and fonts, designers will scramble to find ways to trick the system into letting them have it anyway. This control can be at the expense of cross-platform accessibility. If you plan to try some of the techniques in this chapter, always define your audience first and decide whether the goals of your site will be compromised by creating a single-platform Web site.

■ Pay attention to the way screens transition to one another. It's possible to make the experience more compelling through the use of sequencing a progression of images that create the illusion of animation or dynamic changes.

■ It is not possible to accurately align a foreground and background image the same way on a Mac and PC. If you want to design a site that uses this type of alignment, you must make a choice between making your pages Mac, Unix, or PC-specific.

■ Background images cannot contain links. To get around this limitation, use GIF89a (transparent GIF) images that are invisible through transparency as linked graphics.

■ If you design screens in QuarkXpress that you intend to translate to HTML, be sure to use fonts and spacing that HTML can reproduce.

■ Control over layout and typography is hardly possible with HTML. Invisible images used as "spacers" aid in the arrangement of text and images on a Web screen.

Discovery Channel Online

server push and client pull

What this chapter covers:

- **Passive and Active Navigation Techniques**
- **Client Pull**
- **Server Push**
- **Getting Rights to Copyrighted Images**

http://www.discovery.com Discovery Channel is renowned for its progressive programming and excellent educational content. Introduced in 1995, its Web-based sister publication Discovery Channel Online follows in the same tradition of excellence. More than a site that re-purposes Discovery Channel content, Discovery Channel Online develops original material that is created specifically for Web delivery. The Muybridge pages are a wonderful example of what original research, non-linear storytelling, elegant visuals, dynamic media, and Web-savvy delivery techniques can bring to an online audience.

Web Design Firm and Client: Discovery Channel Online

URL: http://www.discovery.com/DCO/doc/1012/world/science/muybridge/muybrid/geopener.html

Type of Site: Educational

Server and Server Software: Netscape-Commerce/1.12
SGI Challenge S

Operating System: Irix 5.3

Producer: Peter Esmonde

Design Director: John Lyle Sanford

Art Director: Melissa Tardiff

Internet Architect: Jim Jones

Production Manager: Constance Miller

Media Editor: Sue Klemens

Design Manager: Lucy Kneebone

Designers: Irwin Chen, Anne Kim, Kathryn Poteet

Senior Programmer: Amnon Dekel

Programmers: Yair Sageev, Miriam Songster

Development and Production Platform: Macintosh

Software: BBEdit, VWPico HTML Editor, Photoshop, DeBabelizer

The Muybridge Site's Origins

Eadweard Muybridge's studies of human and animal motion have provided inspiration and invaluable reference material to the art and animation world since their publication in the late 1800s. His archetypal images of running horses and naked men, women, and children are burned into our collective consciousness without necessarily knowing who he was, where he came from, or what he accomplished in his lifetime. What few realize is that this man was a catalyst for the invention of moving pictures, as well as one of the first pioneers to bring artistic content to the early science of moviemaking.

Muybridge produced photographs that were taken in rapid succession, resulting in sequences of images that captured freeze-frame snapshots of motion over a series of still frames. As still images, they are incredibly powerful and offer the ability to analyze and dissect the mechanics of motion. Re-assembled as moving, animating images on the Web, these sequential still images recreate the same movements they originally captured.

Muybridge invented one of the first movie machines—a predecessor to the magic lantern and zoetrope—called a zoopraxiscope. He thrilled audiences by showing them his photographs as moving images. Discovery Channel Online, with their early adoption of Web-based animation techniques, has brought these images back to life for all to see.

There's a parallel here that the site's originators at Discovery Channel Online were keenly aware of. In essence, this site used a new medium to explore the emergence of a new medium from a past era. Studying the early days of moving imagery, with early tools like server push and client pull seemed ironic, if not downright appropriate.

Passive and Active Navigation Choices

Most Web sites are composed of navigation interfaces that require audiences to click from screen to screen in order to view content. The Muybridge site took a different approach—one that allowed viewers to either sit back passively and watch a slide-show of screens and animations with a single-click, or click through information screens at their discretion, using standard hyperlinked images and text.

When the site was developed in late 1995, it was one of the first examples of a Web interface that featured passive education as well as active information. Some of the technologies now are out-dated, but the idea of offering two different interface tracks is still an effective method for presenting information.

Viewers are offered the choice at the opening screen of two navigation paths: an animated intro or a story overview.

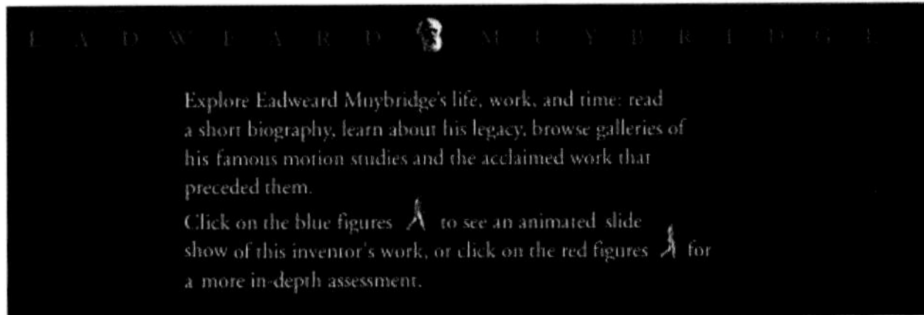

This screen explains the navigation interface. Blue figures trigger slide shows, while red figures offer more in-depth content.

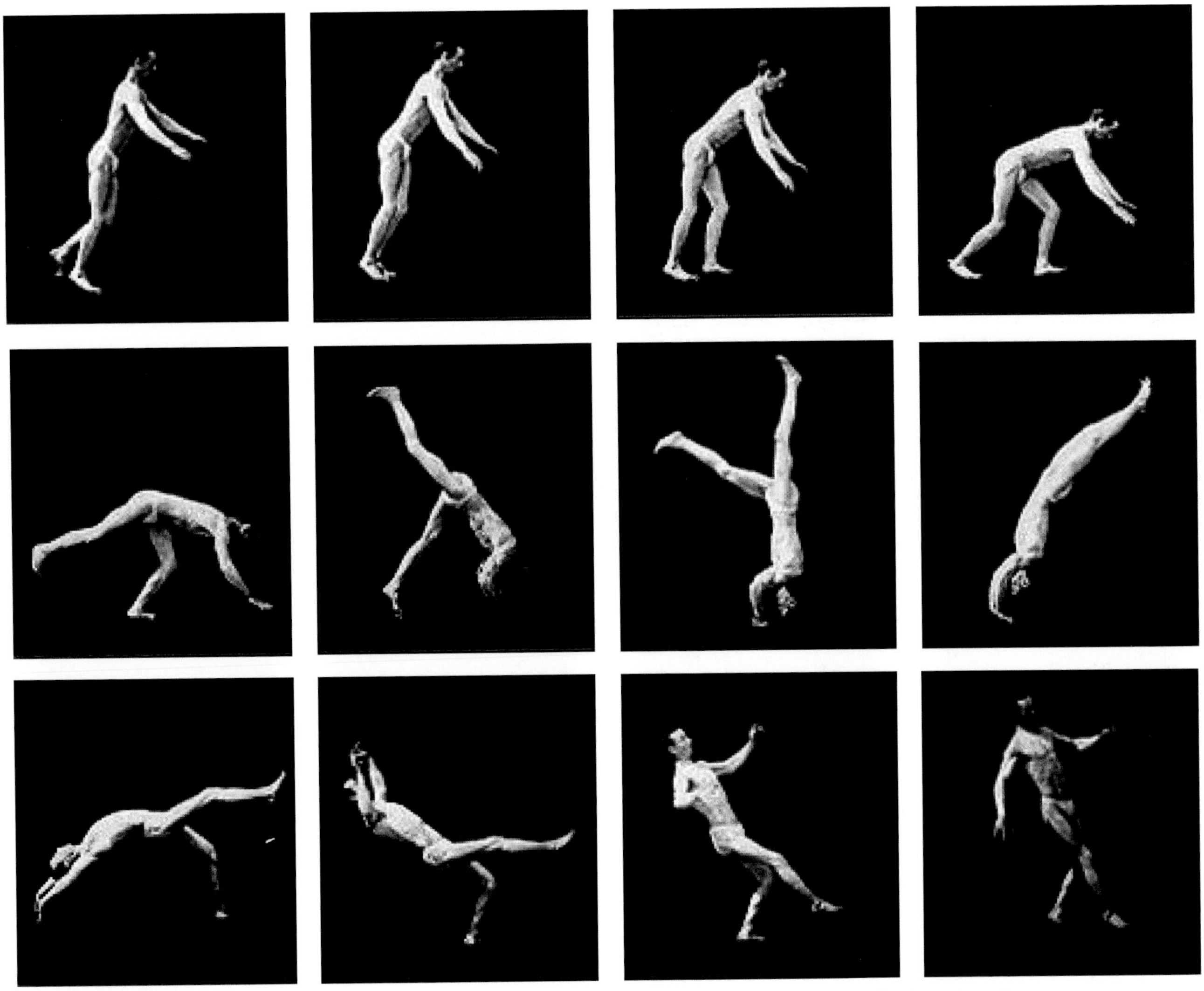

The animated intro displayed these images using a technique called server push (see deconstruction later in this chapter) to play a sequence of Muybridge's photographs.

The menu bar that recurs throughout the site. It's possible at any point to see a passive slideshow or choose to navigate through more in-depth, text-based coverage on your own.

Creating the Muybridge Site

If anyone ever suggests to you that planning a Web site is a simple thing, refer them to this page! Here's an evolutionary view of the Muybridge site planning. There are a lot of ways to visualize information flow, and you can follow the designer's thought processes through studying his or her notes and sketches.

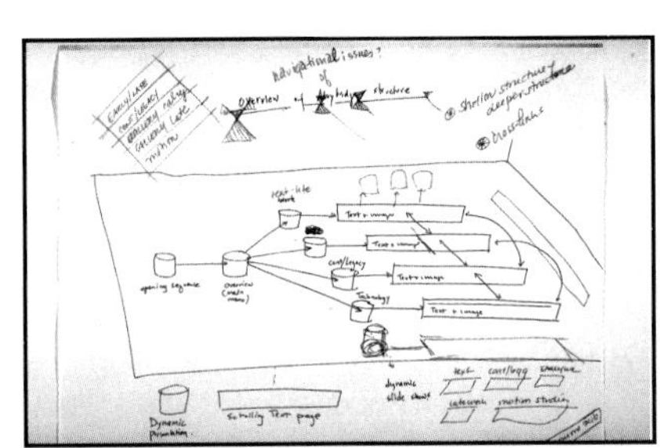

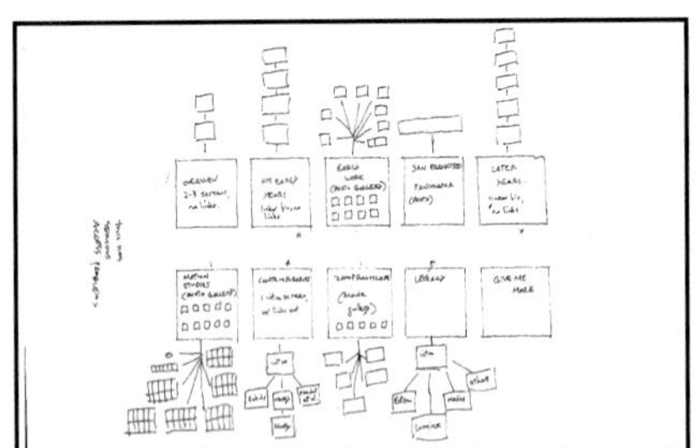

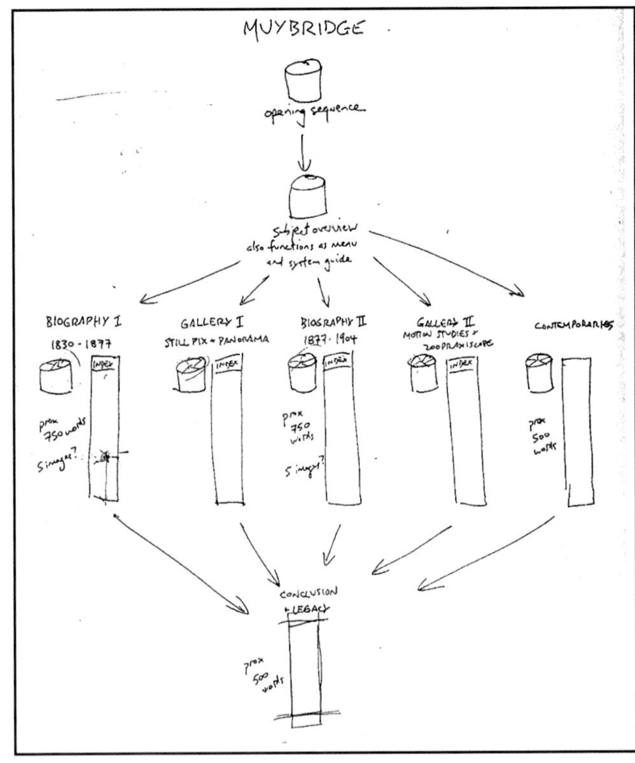

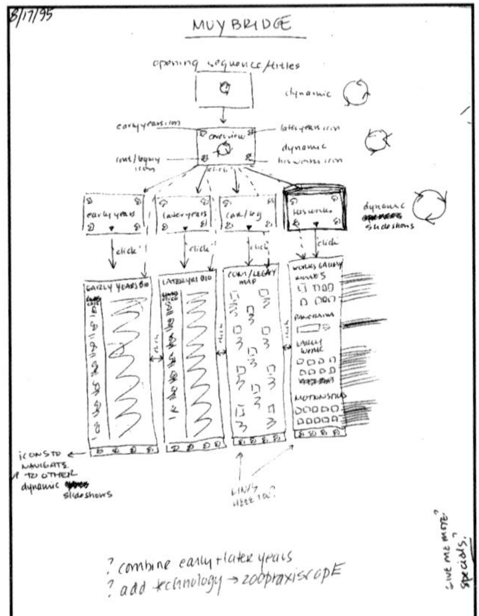

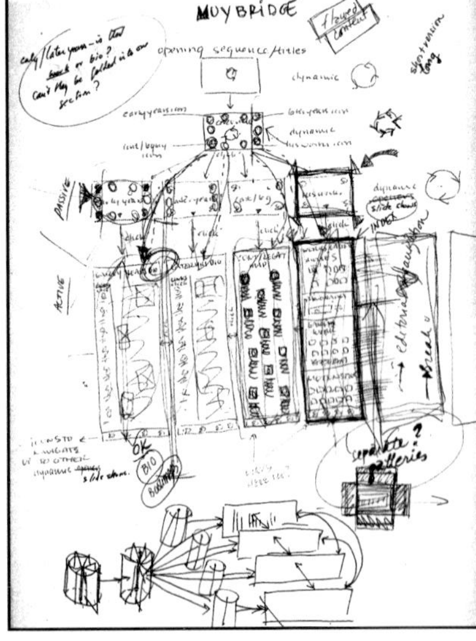

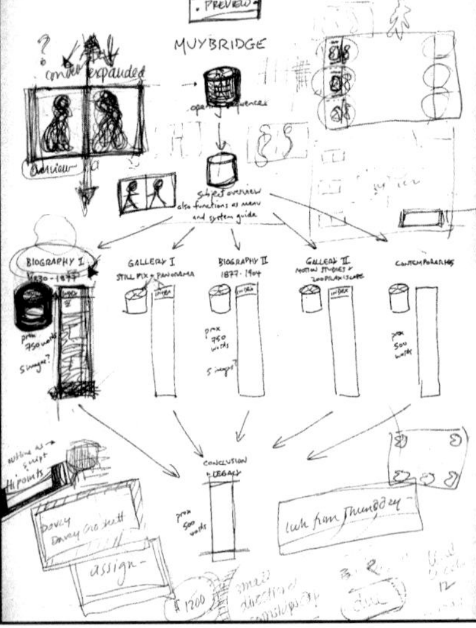

These are examples of the preliminary steps taken by the designers at Discovery Channel Online. Several notes, sketches, and flowcharts were created to organize the information delivery and plot the active versus passive navigation paths.

Client Pull for Slideshows

The passive, slideshow navigation component was achieved through a technique known as client-pull. Client pull relies on the client (your Web browser) to request (pull) the next page after a specified delay. This creates a slideshow effect. Because it is client-sided, client pull can be viewed locally from a hard drive or from within an Intranet, without the need to post the source images or HTML to a live Web server.

Client pull is relatively easy to author in HTML. It involves the META tag, which can be programmed to display a series of HTML pages with delays. A client pull can be rapid or slow, depending on the amount of refresh time specified.

The <META> tag has to structurally fall inside the <HEAD> tag of an HTML document, whereas most other tags need to be placed inside the <BODY> tag of a page.

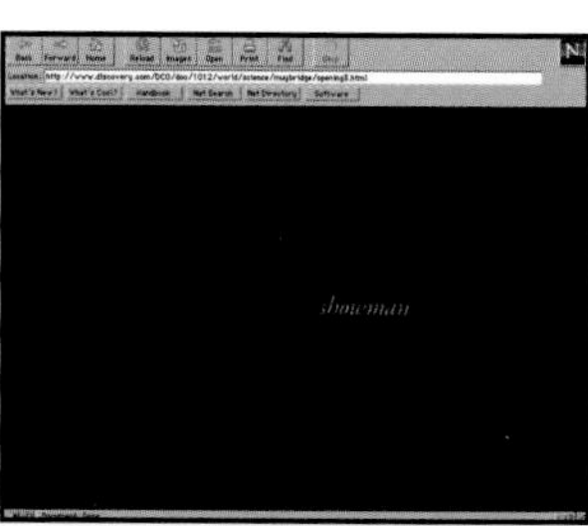

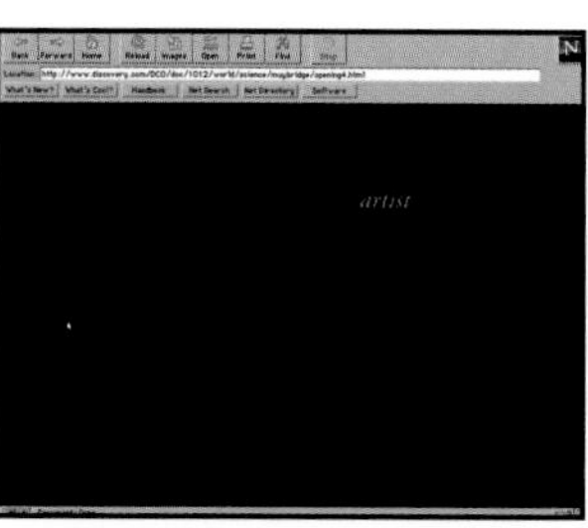

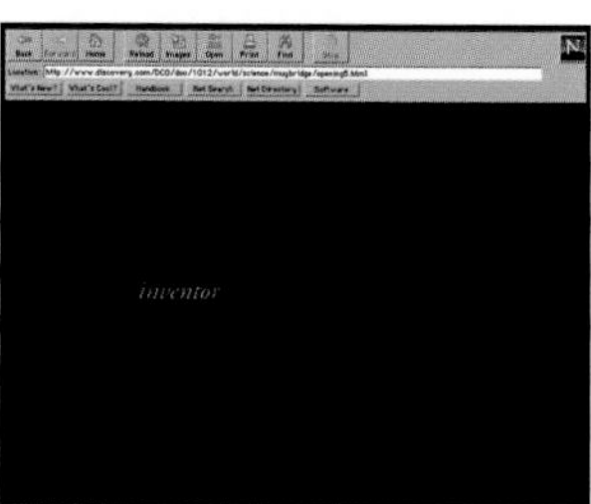

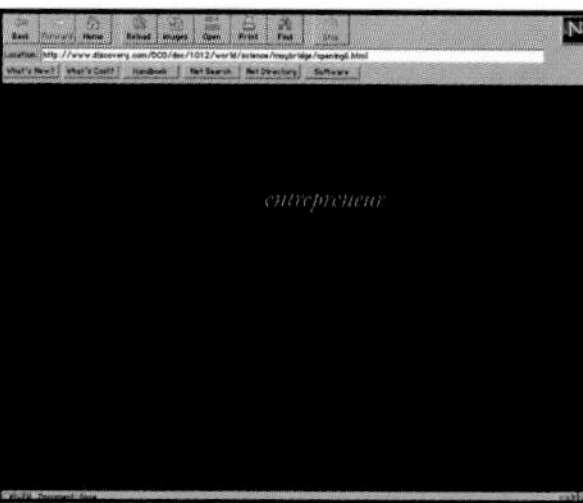

Each one of these sequential screens uses the META tag with a four-second refresh time, creating an automated slide-show effect otherwise known as a "client pull." This can be viewed at: ■ http://www.discovery.com/DCO/ doc/1012/world/science/muybridge/opening2.hml.

Client pull is still used by many Web sites, and has the advantage of presenting information in an automated fashion. The downside to using it is that sometimes the amount of refresh time is too short for slow connections and images won't load, or too long for fast connections and runs the risk of boring viewers. Because its timing is pre-determined within the HTML, it's impossible to have a client pull detect an end user's log on speed. Client pull also makes it frustrating when using the Back button, because the end user has to go back through every screen in the slideshow to find their starting screen.

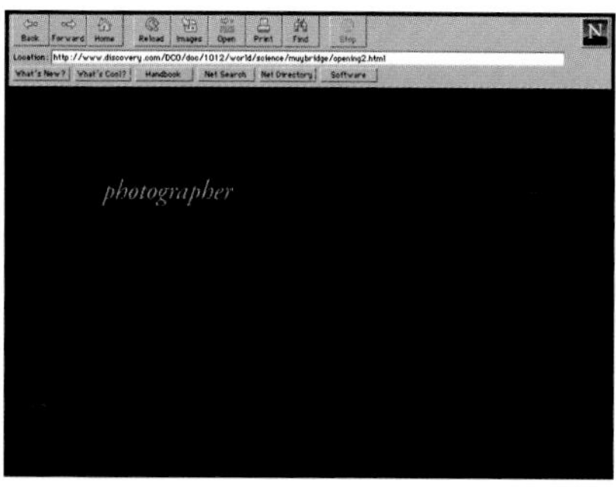

■ Opening 2 Screen: This is the first in a sequence of client pull screens, created using the META tag.

Client Pull Screen HTML

```
<HTML>
1 <META HTTP-EQUIV="REFRESH" CONTENT="4;
URL=/DCO/doc/1012/world/science/muybridge/
opening4.html"<TITLE>Eadweard Muybridge</TITLE>
<BODY BGCOLOR="#000000" TEXT="#666666">
<hr align=left width=600>
<TABLE BORDER=0 CELLSPACING=0 CELLPADDING=2>
<TR>
<TD WIDTH=602 VALIGN=bottom ALIGN=right HEIGHT=320>
<IMG BORDER=0 SRC="./gallery/opening3.jpg">
</TD>
</TR>
</TABLE>
<hr align=left width=600>
<TABLE BORDER=0 CELLPADDING=0 CELLSPACING=0><TR><TD
WIDTH=299><FONT SIZE=1>Copyright &copy 1995 Discovery
Communications, Inc</TD><TD ALIGN=RIGHT
WIDTH=298><FONT
SIZE=1></FONT></TD></TR></TABLE>
</BODY>
</HTML>
```

■ tags

Client Pull Screen Deconstruction

1 The META tag specifies a response back to the HTTP client or browser. It tells the browser to treat this content as if it were received as part of an HTTP response. Hence the name, HTTP-EQUIV for the first attribute. (The NAME attribute can be used interchangeably.) The "Refresh" argument tells the browser to refresh its display, or more literally, to request a new URL and display that new page in place of this old one. The CONTENT attribute gives the amount of time to pause (in seconds), and the URL to refresh with.

Server Push

Server push offers the capability to play a sequence of pages, images, or sounds that are programmed using a CGI script. It is called a server-side push because it relies on a live Web server in order to function. Because CGI is much more complicated to program than HTML, server push almost always requires a programmer's skills.

Jim Jones, Discovery Channel Online's CGI programmer for the Muybridge project, created a CGI for the server push that allowed non-programmers to create the content. Written in C, Jim's script allowed designers to assemble a list of images in a text file for server-push.

Jim set up the CGI so that it referred to a text document, such as leapmananim.sp. This script allowed non-programmers to create lists of image files. All they had to do was name the list with a .sp extension, and his CGI script would know which images to load.

■ code

leapmananim.sp Deconstruction

```
<set_pause 1>
<cd./gallery/earlyworksimgs/
someranim>
animation1.jpg
animation2.jpg
animation3.jpg
animation4.jpg
animation5.jpg
animation6.jpg
animation7.jpg
animation8.jpg
animation1.jpg
animation2.jpg
animation3.jpg
animation4.jpg
animation5.jpg
animation6.jpg
animation7.jpg
animation8.jpg
```

■ The script simply repeats numbers in order to make the animation loop.

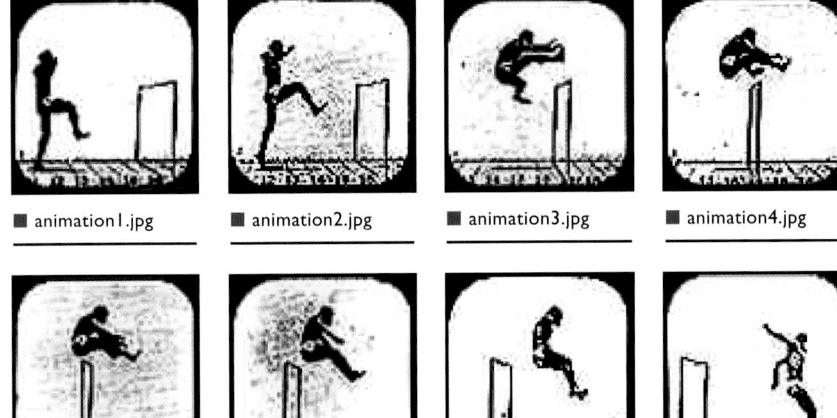

■ animation1.jpg ■ animation2.jpg ■ animation3.jpg ■ animation4.jpg

■ animation5.jpg ■ animation6.jpg ■ animation7.jpg ■ animation8.jpg

Theses are the image files the CGI script refers to.

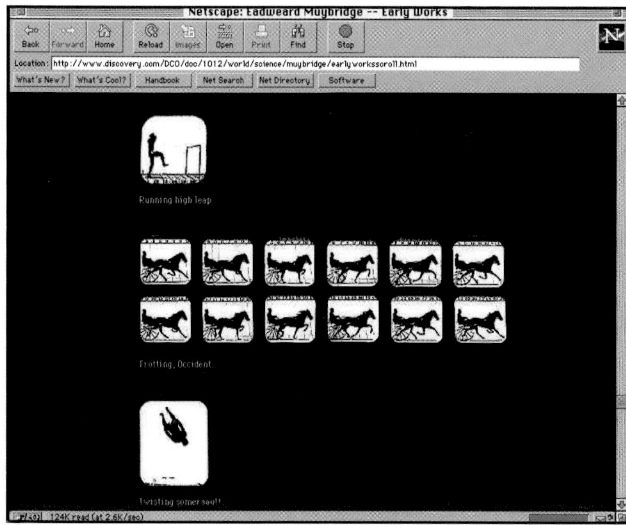

The finished page that used server push. This allowed the leaping man frames to play as a movie. You can view this URL at: ■ http://www.discovery.com/DCO/doc/1012/world/science/muybridge/earlyworksscroll.html.

■ tags

Server Push HTML Deconstruction

```
<IMG width=82 height=80 SRC="/cgi
bin/push?leapmananim.sp"><P>Running high
leap.<P><BR><P><BR><P>
```

■ Notice the SRC=/cgi-bin/push attribute. This is telling the browser to look for the "push" program in the cgi-bin folder. cgi-bin is a special folder in many Web servers. It's an alias used to keep CGI programs out of the Web document folders. Jim's server push program resides in this folder. The text, "?leapmananim.sp," is an argument that is passed to the CGI program that tells it to look for the sequence of images in a text file called leapmananim.sp. This directs the script to look to the text file leapmananim.sp, which contains the list of JPEGs.

■ code

Server Push CGI Script Deconstruction

■ The first part of a C program is almost always a series of #include directives for including header files for standard and locally-defined functions.

■ Notice how Jim uses comments to segregate different parts of the program. This is a good habit to get in to, as it makes it a lot easier for someone else to maintain your code.

```
/* ----------
* -- PUSH.C
*
* Copyright (c) 1995,1996 Discovery Communications, Inc
*/
#include <stdio.h>
#include <sys/types.h>
#include <syslog.h>
#include <errno.h>
#include <string.h>
#include <stdlib.h>
#include <unistd.h>
#include "../cgi-sub/cgi.h"
#include "../cgi-sub/doc_root.h"
#include "../gsub/log_err_msg.h"
```

■ This section defines text constants for talking to the server and the browser.

```
/* --
 * HTTP header constants
 */
#define F_MPART "Content-type: multipart/x-mixed-
replace"
#define F_SEP "+~+End-of-Frame-Delimiter+~+"
#define DEF_MIME_TYPE "text/html"
#define PROG "push"
```

■ The next set of constants are used internally to find commands in the .sp files, and to define buffer sizes. Keeping track of the size of buffers is especially important in C, because the language does not protect you from overwriting other data or code in memory.

```
/* --
 * Commands recognized in control files
 */
#define C_CHDIR "cd "
#define C_SETWAIT "set_pause "
#define C_WAIT "pause "
#define C_ABSDIR "abs_cd "
#define BSIZE 4096     /* I/O buffer for content being
served */
#define DEF_FRAME_WAIT 3    /* Default "between frames"
delay */
int fr_wait = DEF_FRAME_WAIT;
struct st_pair {
char *name, *mime;
};
```

■ This table is used to send the correct MIME-type for each file used in the server-push.

```
/* --
* Mapping of file extentions to mime types
*/
struct st_pair type_list[] = {
{"aiff", "audio/x-aiff"},
{"aiff", "audio/x-aiff"},
{"aifc", "audio/x-aiff"},
{"gif", "image/gif"},
{"jpeg", "image/jpeg"},
{"jpg", "image/jpeg"},
{"jpe", "image/jpeg"},
{"tiff", "image/tiff"},
{"tif", "image/tiff"},
{"html", "text/html"},
{"htm", "text/html"},
{"txt", "text/plain"},
{"qt", "video/quicktime"},
{"mov", "video/quicktime"},
{"avi", "video/x-msvideo"}
};
/* How the internal routines interact */
void send_frame_header( char *file);
int do_command( char *comm), send_frame( char *file);
/* --
*/
```

■ Every C program starts with a function called "main." This is used for the main entry point into the program. The parameters passed to main() are the arguments from the command line. The first parameter is the number of arguments, and the second is an array containing each argument. It is common to call these two parameters "argc" and "argv," but "narg" and "args" or any other names will work just as well. ("Would a rose, by any other name ...")

```
int main( narg, args)
int narg;
char ** args;
{  int rc, flushed = 1, nfile = 0, nskip = 0, ncomm =
0;
char fr_comm[ BSIZE], *st, *from, *dir;
FILE *parts;
```

■ This is the beginning of the actual code for the program. In C programs, it's not uncommon to have a lot of initialization code at the beginning. Because C doesn't do any of this for you, you must make sure that all the arguments are correct, that your memory is properly allocated, that the directories and files you're expecting are actually there, and that you can open and read or write the files that you need to. This level of detail is the price you pay for the extra power, speed, and flexibility that you get from writing in C.

```
/* We need to have a control file listing the parts, or
no go... */
if( narg < 2) log_err_msg( ERR_BAD_PARMS, PROG, "Called
with no arguments",
"", SYSLOG);
/* Call getenv() to fetch the referring page */
GET_ENV( SOURCE, from, st, PROG)
/* Figure out what our current directory should be by
dissecting the URL
*   and adding in the document root as needed.
*/
strcpy( fr_comm, DOC_ROOT);
if( strcmp( NOT_AVAIL, from))
{  for( ; *from && *from != '/'; from++) ;
for( ; *from && *from == '/'; from++) ;
get_string( &rc, from, "/", "", &dir, &st);
if( !rc) get_string( &rc, from, "DISCOVERY.COM", "",
&dir, &st);
if( rc)
{  for( st = dir + strlen( dir) - 1; st > dir && *st
!= '/'; st--) ;
if( *st == '/') *st = '\0';
if( strlen( dir)) strcat( fr_comm, dir);
}
}
/* Change the working directory so that relative refer-
ences to files
*   in the control file will work as intended.
*/
rc = chdir( fr_comm);
if( rc)
{
/* Hmmm...  Something ugly happened, make sure we can
at least find
*   the document root!
*/
log_err_msg( errno, PROG, "Can't set directory for list
```

```
file", fr_comm,
SYSLOG ¦ ERRNO ¦ RETURN);
rc = chdir( DOC_ROOT);
if( rc) log_err_msg( errno, PROG, "Can't set directory
to document root",
DOC_ROOT, SYSLOG);
}
/* The "root" for absolute pathnames for control files
is the document
*   root of the web server (just like URL's)
*/
if( *args[ 1] == '/' && strncmp( args[ 1], DOC_ROOT,
(sizeof DOC_ROOT) - 2))
{  strcpy( fr_comm, DOC_ROOT);
strcat( fr_comm, args[ 1] + 1);
}
else strcpy( fr_comm, args[ 1]);
/* Make sure it's a valid, readable file... */
parts = fopen( fr_comm, "r");
if( !parts) log_err_msg( errno, PROG, "Can't open frame
list file",
args[ 1], SYSLOG);
```

■ Next is the main "while" loop for the program. Notice that the loop uses the for(; rc;) construct instead of while-(rc). It's not uncommon for C programmers to do this. The code that comes out of the compiler is the same, but it allows the programmer a little more flexibility while writing and debugging.

```
/* Read each line of the file and do what is says. :)
*/
rc = (int) fgets( fr_comm, BSIZE, parts);
for( ; rc; )
{
/* Skip blank lines, comments, and leading whitespace
*/
for( st = fr_comm; *st && (*st == ' ' ¦¦ *st == '\t');
st++) ;
if( !*st ¦¦ *st == '\n' ¦¦ *st == '#') nskip++;
else
{
```

■ As Jim noted in his comments, not all servers work the same way. He noticed that he had to flush the output buffers with fflush(stdout) at the end of each block that he sends through the server to the browser. Otherwise, the animations may be jumpy or not display each frame completely. It's always a good idea to flush your buffers frequently when writing to streams in any communications environment. It will ensure that your data gets delivered in contiguous chunks, and not interspersed with data from another source.

```
/* Ah yes, if all web servers worked the same way...
Some servers
*   need a kick in the pants to send the data.
*/
if( !flushed)
{  fputc( '\n', stdout);
if( ferror( stdout)) log_err_msg( errno, PROG, "Write
failed", "",
SYSLOG);
fflush( stdout);
flushed = 1;
}
/* If it's a command, go interpret it */
if( *st == '<')
{  ncomm++;
rc = do_command( st);
}
/* Otherwise, it's a file to serve, send it... */
else
{
/* If this is the first segment, send the HTTP header
and
*   a segment delimiter string.  Otherwise, pause as
long
*   as necessary (as per the current global pause set-
ting).
*/
if( !nfile) printf( "%s;boundary=%s\n\n--%s\n", F_MPART,
F_SEP,
F_SEP);
else if( fr_wait > 0) sleep( fr_wait);
/* Send the indicated file */
nfile++;
rc = send_frame( st);
flushed = 0;
}
}
/* Get the next directive from the control file */
if( rc) rc = (int) fgets( fr_comm, BSIZE, parts);
}
```

■ At the end of the program, after the main loop has executed, it must close its files, handle any errors that may have happened, and make sure that the stream to the browser is properly completed.

```
/* If we ended due to error, save the error info for
debugging */
if( ferror( parts)) log_err_msg( errno, PROG,
"Read error on frame list file", args[ 1], SYSLOG);
/* Clean up and go home */
fclose( parts);
if( flushed) printf( "\n--%s--", F_SEP);    /* Bad, bad
user... */
else printf( "--");    /* Much better... */
fflush( stdout);
exit( 0);
}
```

■ From this point on, the rest of the program is utility functions for parsing the input file (parsing means to read the file and interpret its contents, distinguishing between commands and filenames, and so on), changing directories, and other similar details.

```
/* --
 * Routine to interpret directives from the control
file
 */
int do_command( comm)
char *comm;
{  int rc, val;
char *st, *req;
static char buff[ BSIZE];
/* Parse, parse, parse...  Find the beginning and end
of the command tag
*/
req = comm;
if( *req == '<') req++;
for( st = req; *st && *st != '>'; st++) ;
if( *st == '>') *st = '\0';
/* Is it an "immediate pause" request? */
if( !strncasecmp( req, C_WAIT, (sizeof C_WAIT) - 1))
{  rc = sscanf( req + (sizeof C_WAIT) - 1, "%d", &val);
if( rc == 1) sleep( val);
}
/* Is it a "set the global pause" request? */
else if( !strncasecmp( req, C_SETWAIT, (sizeof C_SET-
WAIT) - 1))
{  rc = sscanf( req + (sizeof C_SETWAIT) - 1, "%d",
&val);
if( rc == 1) fr_wait = val;
}
```

■ Directories (or folders) are hierarchical structures for keeping files segregated by purpose. The "Web document root" is the base of the directory tree that is used for serving Web documents.

```
/* Change working directory? */
else if( !strncasecmp( req, C_CHDIR, (sizeof C_CHDIR) -
1))
{  req += (sizeof C_CHDIR) - 1;
for( ; *req && (*req == ' ' || *req == '\t'); ) req++;
if( *req)
{  if( *req == '/' && strncmp( req, DOC_ROOT, (sizeof
DOC_ROOT) - 2))
{  strcpy( buff, DOC_ROOT);
strcat( buff, req + 1);
}
else strcpy( buff, req);
rc = chdir( buff);
if( rc) log_err_msg( errno, PROG, "Call to chdir()
failed", buff,
SYSLOG);
rc = 1;
}
else rc = 0;
}
/* Change to a directory without considering the web
document root? */
else if( !strncasecmp( req, C_ABSDIR, (sizeof C_ABSDIR)
- 1))
{  req += (sizeof C_ABSDIR) - 1;
for( ; *req && (*req == ' ' || *req == '\t'); ) req++;
if( *req)
{  rc = chdir( req);
if( rc) log_err_msg( errno, PROG, "Call to chdir()
failed", buff,
SYSLOG);
rc = 1;
}
else rc = 0;
}
/* Just ignore unknown commands */
else rc = 0;
return( rc);
}
```

■ This is where the actual images are sent to the Web browser. The specification for sending images as parts of a server push governs the way that these files must be sent. You can find a copy of that specification at: ■ http://www.netscape.com/assist/net_sites/pushpull.html

```
/* --
* Read/Write specified file
*/
int send_frame( file)
char *file;
{  int rc = NORMAL, nbyt;
char buff[ BSIZE], *st;
FILE *gf;
/* Skip leading junk in the filename */
for( st = file; *st && *st != ' ' && *st != '\n'; st++)
;
if( *st == ' ' || *st == '\n' ) *st = '\0';
/* Make sure we can read it... */
gf = fopen( file, "r");
if( !gf) log_err_msg( errno, PROG, "Open for file in
frame list failed",
file, SYSLOG);
/* Send the appropriate "Content-type" for this filename
*/
send_frame_header( file);
/* Lather, rinse, repeat... */
for( nbyt= fread( buff, 1, BSIZE, gf); nbyt > 0; )
{
/* Write out the buffer and bail if it fails (for
instance if the
*  user clicked through to some other page)
*/
rc = fwrite( buff, 1, nbyt, stdout);
if( rc < 1) log_err_msg( errno, PROG, "Write failed",
"", SYSLOG);
nbyt= fread( buff, 1, BSIZE, gf);
}
/* If something went wrong note it (so it can be fixed)
*/
```

```
if( ferror( gf)) log_err_msg( errno, PROG, "Read failed
for frame file",
file, SYSLOG);
/* Send out the end of frame delimiter to let the
browser do something
*   with the content we just sent
*/
printf( "\n—%s", F_SEP);
if( ferror( stdout)) log_err_msg( errno, PROG, "Write
failed", "", SYSLOG);
/* Push the data, close the input file and go back */
fflush( stdout);
fclose( gf);
return ( rc);
}
```

■ This is where the translation from file extension to MIME-type happens. It reads through the array to find the file extension, then takes the associated MIME-type from that entry.

```
/* --
* Figure out and send the appropriate "Content-type:"
header based on
*   the file extension.
*/
void send_frame_header( file)
char *file;
{  int wh, ntyp;
char *type = 0, *ext;
/* Find the file extension */
for( ext = file + strlen( file) - 1; ext >= file &&
*ext != '.'; ext--) ;
/* A face only a mother could love, but it works... */
if( *ext == '.')
{  ext++;
ntyp = (sizeof type_list) / (sizeof type_list[ 0]);
for( wh = 0; wh < ntyp && !type; wh++)
if( !strncasecmp( ext, type_list[ wh].name,
strlen( type_list[ wh].name))) type = type_list[
wh].mime;
}
/* Something has to be done if all else fails */
if( !type) type = DEF_MIME_TYPE;
/* done, print the results and go back */
printf( "Content-type: %s\n\n", type);
if( ferror( stdout)) log_err_msg( errno, PROG, "Write
failed", "", SYSLOG);
return;
}
```

■ note

Is Server Push Still Viable?

The Muybridge site was created in October 1995, before Java, Shockwave, or animated GIFs were available. Design Director John Lyle Sanford and Producer Peter Esmonde both commented that they would choose a different technology than server push if the site were being created today. For one thing, server push can cause server strain. A connection must occur as the images are being served. If many people are accessing a server push at the same time, it can actually tie up the entire server and make it impossible to serve other pages.

The Muybridge animations would have been better as animated GIFs, because they would have been less taxing on the server and no CGI programming would have been necessary. In spite of the disadvantages to server push, it is still used in some cases today. Unlike animated GIFs, server push can interact with data through scripts. It is a way for animation to be created on the fly. Possible candidates for server push might be an updating clock or calendar with custom artwork. This type of dynamic and interactive animation is also possible with Java, but server push is supported by more browsers and is less susceptible to crashing.

Getting Rights to Published Images

Most of the images on the Muybridge site were scanned from books. Discovery Channel Online made sure that they had obtained the proper usage rights to Muybridge's images by contracting the help of PhotoAssist, a Washington D.C.-based photo research company ■ info@photoassist.com.

Sasha Knop from PhotoAssist explained that the Muybridge project was very challenging. Even though the material was old enough to be considered public domain, most of the images came from books that were owned by museum collections or private publishers. The volume of images was immense, especially because the site designers used so much animation, which effectively required multiple images instead of single images.

PhotoAssist had been doing photo research and verification for Discovery Channel Online since July 1995, several months before the Muybridge story began. Even so, they had never tackled a project this large that was Web-based. Generally fees are paid to copyright owners based on usage. Typical usage might be a magazine ad, video sleeve, or book jacket cover image. Geography can also affect distribution, such as when an image is only being printed in North America, or for a regional audience. When an image is published on the Web it can potentially be viewed unlimited times, and be seen by a worldwide audience. Figuring what rate Discovery should pay for images that were Web-bound was tricky.

Sasha was pleased that most publishers and museums were cooperative and charged reasonable prices. (It averaged around $100 per image). Because pictures on the Web are low resolution (72 dpi), the owners of the Muybridge images were comfortable because they couldn't be printed out at high enough quality to reproduce elsewhere.

The amount of resources used on the Muybridge project was staggering. Photo credits included: Stanford University Libraries, Stanford University Museum of Art, Muybridge Collection, Library of Congress, Bancroft Library, University of California, Berkeley College de France, Hulton Deutsch, Addison Gallery of American Art, Kingston Museum and Heritage Service, Archive Photos, The Bettmann Archive, Philadelphia Museum of Art, and Woodfin Camp and Associates. Special thanks was given to film scholar Marta Braun and video clips were supplied by Second Line Search.

Original Photo Content

Since its inception in July 1995, Discovery Channel Online has posted over 600 stories to its Web site. Sue Klemens is their full-time Media Editor, and it's her job to edit, select images, and verify rights and pricing for the hundreds of stories and columns that change on a daily basis.

When she started, no standard prices had been set for commissioning original photographic content. Sue researched what photographers were paid for national magazines in order to arrive at a fair price to pay Discovery Channel Online contributors. There were many factors to consider that a magazine doesn't have to think about, such as the fact that pictures are often repeated on different pages, used as a running header for an entire Web site, or as a navigational button.

Sue and Design Director John Lyle Sanford arrived at the pricing structure of $125 per image, with a 50% increase if the same image were used more than once on the site. This price is not set in stone. As the medium matures and more images are commissioned, she expects the pricing structures to change as well.

Working on the Muybridge Site

Lots of time is spent at Discovery Channel Online refining stories and discussing how to take advantage of the Web as a unique delivery medium. Everyone I interviewed was passionate about their mission, and the quality of the site's content testifies to their dedication and hard work.

Evaluating the Muybridge site today, Design Director John Lyle Sanford commented that he would have probably added features to allow viewers to interact with the story. Most of Discovery Channel Online's current stories now offer e-mail-based discussion forums. Peter Esmonde, who spearheaded the Muybridge effort, added that they would probably add a site map as well, so that readers could see what the scope of the subject was, and be able to have a better sense of what was there to determine where to go.

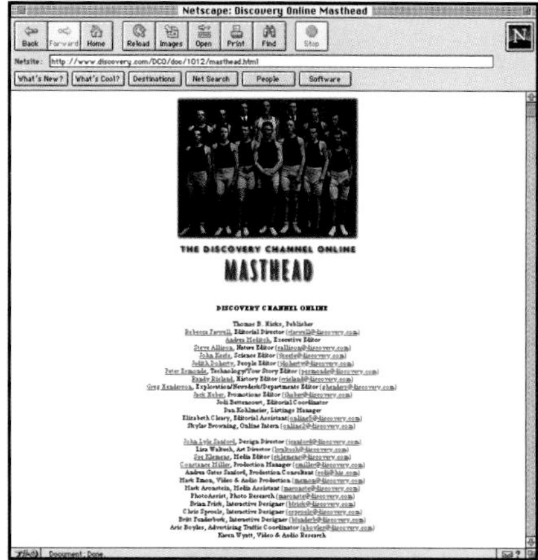

For a good time, read the bios of people who work at Discovery Channel Online at: ■ http://www.discovery.com/DCO/doc/012/masthead.html. It seems that everyone working at Discovery Channel Online must have talent as well as a healthy sense of humor.

This is indicative of how the Web is a different sort of publishing medium. With a magazine or book, when the job is finished one puts it to rest. On the Web, stories can stay alive and fluid, and it's a challenge to know when to stop working on them.

■ tip

Stock Agencies on the Web

Obviously, smaller Web firms and individuals might not be able to contract the help of a firm like PhotoAssist. Getting the rights to images is a time-consuming prospect however, and it might make more sense to use a stock photo agency instead. There are many such resources on the Web, including public domain sources such as NASA or the NIH.

Sue Klemens, Media Editor at Discovery Channel Online, recommended Publisher's Depot, which owns over 350,000 images. They have a Web-based catalog and online search engine.

Publisher's Depot is located at: ■ http://www.publishersdepot.com

Sue noted that many agencies will be turning to online selection, because shipping original photographs is costly and cumbersome. It's much easier to view and select images online than to accept physical shipment of them.

■ site summary

Discovery Channel Online

Discovery Channel Online is in the enviable position of working with some of the best editorial content in existence. The team's efforts toward choosing compelling ways to tell their stories through using appropriate and innovative technology sets this site's standards well above the rest. It's great to see a company like Discovery Channel putting so much of its resources into cultivating the Web as a new forum for communication. What we can learn from Discovery Channel Online's Muybridge site:

■ Consider different ways of telling the same story and offer your end viewer choices. Just because the Web is interactive doesn't mean you don't want to rule out more passive styles of entertainment such as animation and slideshows.

■ Server push is an older technology for adding animation and slideshows. There are newer, alternative methods for some of the same effects, such as animated GIFs, Shockwave, and Java, so be sure to weigh the options before deciding which technique to use.

■ Client pull is still an excellent methodology for presenting slideshows. It doesn't require any additional CGI scripting and is easy to program within HTML.

■ If you're going to use historical images on a site, don't assume that just because they're old they'll be copyright free. A photo research firm or online stock agency can be the answer.

typoGRAPHIC

tasteful use of java & shockwave

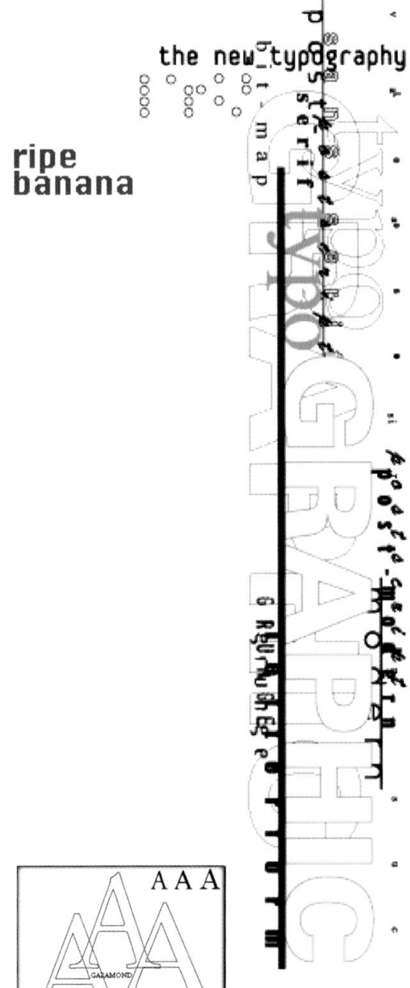

What this chapter covers:

- **Human Interface Design**
- **Using Java for Animation**
- **Using Director and Shockwave**
- **Creating Guest Books with CGI**

www.razorfish.com/bluedot/typo/ One hears a lot about Shockwave and Java these days, but finding examples of well thought-out designs that put these new tools to interesting use is still a challenge. The typoGRAPHIC site succeeds at offering compelling content that boasts technical originality, excellent design, and Web-respectful file sizes. Razorfish has been at the forefront of Web design since it first opened its doors in the fall of 1994. Founded by two friends (since nursery school!), Craig Kanarick and Jeffrey Dachis, the company is currently 23 employees strong. The typoGRAPHIC site within Razorfish was developed with no outside sponsorship, and has brought the company positive acclaim for its educational benefits, technical accomplishment, and innovative aesthetic.

Web Design Firm: Razorfish

URL: http://www.razorfish.com/bluedot/typo

Type of Site: Educational

Server: Sun Sparc 10

Operating System: Solaris 2.5

Server Software: Apache 1.0

Art Direction: Alex Smith and Craig Kanarick

Java Programming: Oz Lubling

Shockwave Programming: Stephen Turbek

Design and Programming: Craig Kanarick, Oz Lubling, and Steven Turbek

Software: Photoshop, Illustrator, Director, GIFBuilder

Platforms: Macintosh, Sun, PC

The Origins of typoGRAPHIC

Razorfish is aware that as a design firm, it's important to give its staff opportunities for creative expression and testing new ideas. The typoGRAPHIC site was inspired from off-hour discussions among Razorfish employees and evolved into a not-for-profit, educational project that was assigned full company support and resources.

The goal for creating typoGRAPHIC was twofold: To provide a showcase for Razorfish's talents, and to elevate design awareness of typography on the Web—an artform that is often ignored or poorly executed. The framework for creating a site around typography also provided a vehicle for experimenting with two new emerging Web technologies: Java and Shockwave.

Establishing typoGRAPHIC's Content

When you put a bunch of college students and graduates from Pratt Institute, MIT, and Brandeis University together who studied communication design, industrial design, computer science, and human interface design, there's bound to be a lot of strong opinions about a subject as challenging and personal as typographic expression.

After much group discussion, issues surrounding typography were defined and areas of personal interest became the blueprint for the table of contents. Subjects ranged from evolution of the typographic form, a historical timeline of typographic innovation, the anatomy of a typeface, and a gallery of typographic studies, to a guestbook for user feedback.

Each member of the creative team—Craig Kanarick, Oz Lubling, Alex Smith, and Stephen Turbek—brainstormed about what they thought the site should include, and took ownership of specific sections. This allowed for each individual to take a project of his or her own and build components that would join collaboratively at the end.

Art Direction for the typoGRAPHIC

Alex Smith, Razorfish's designer from Pratt Institute in New York, was the main catalyst for the creation of the typoGRAPHIC site. The project began as an effort to give Alex a non-commercial Web project with which he could flex his own aesthetic and creative muscles; and it eventually blossomed into a showcase for the entire company.

Alex art-directed the site (along with Craig Kanarick, a principal), as well as originated a lot of the content and copy for the various sections. The stark black and white look of the site was his mark, which was influenced by similar examples that he liked in print design. In Alex's opinion, visual design on the printed page is similar to visual design on the Web. It's all about communication, not technique.

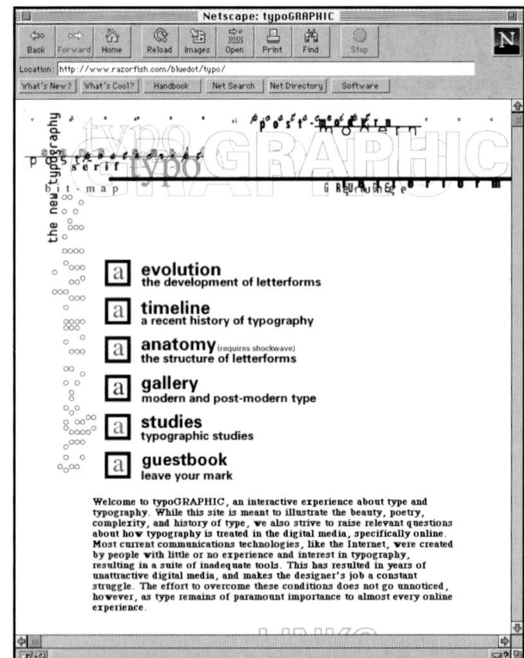

The first screen of typoGRAPHIC displays the menu for the site. The content was established primarily by a group of four people at Razorfish.

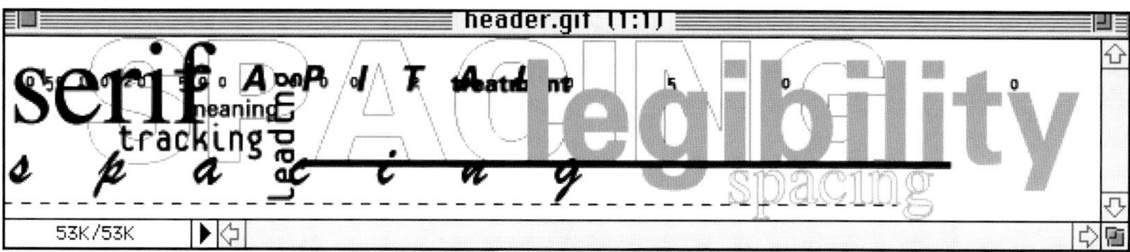

Notice how the word "legibility" inside this header graphic really stands out because of its color and size.

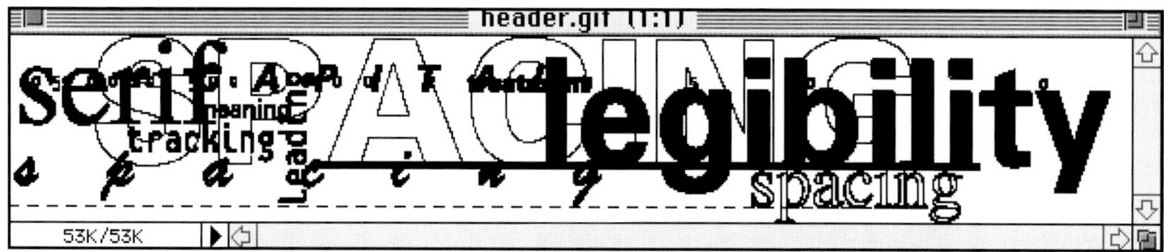

Here's the same example with everything changed to black. Notice how there's no hierarchy of information. Your eye doesn't know which text to read. Sparse color in a black and white environment is a powerful visual communication device.

Even though the site is mostly black and white, for navigation and interface reasons, Alex wanted to interject a sense of color coding, so that each section would be organized by color as well as content. He created all the "header" artwork on the site, using text set in black and white as textural elements, with earthtone color choices for the titles

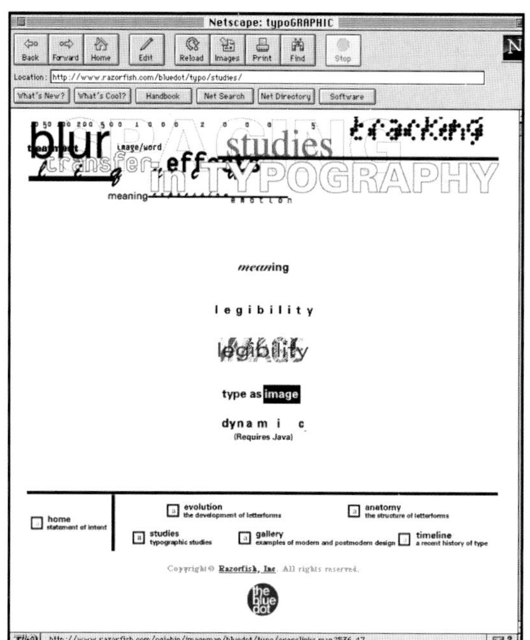

The Studies section examines how typography can impact meaning, legibility, and type as an image, as well as how typograpy is influenced by dynamic media, such as sound and animation.

Typogaphic Studies

One of the richest areas within the typoGRAPHIC site is called "Studies." Each section was created by a different artist or programmer at Razorfish, and utilized different design and production methodologies.

Typography placed over background images introduces legibility problems that have created a long-standing design challenge. Evidence of this problem is commonly found on the Web because Web page authors often place background images and tiles beneath text. Craig Kanarick based the "legibillity" section of typoGRAPHIC loosely on similar research conducted by David Small at MIT.

Each example within the legibility section was created with multiple layers within a Photoshop file. Here's the final document that shows how turning on different layers using the "eye" icon within Photoshop can generate multiple documents.

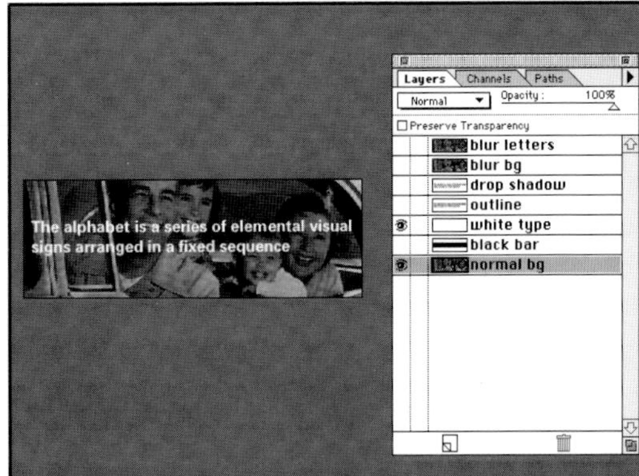

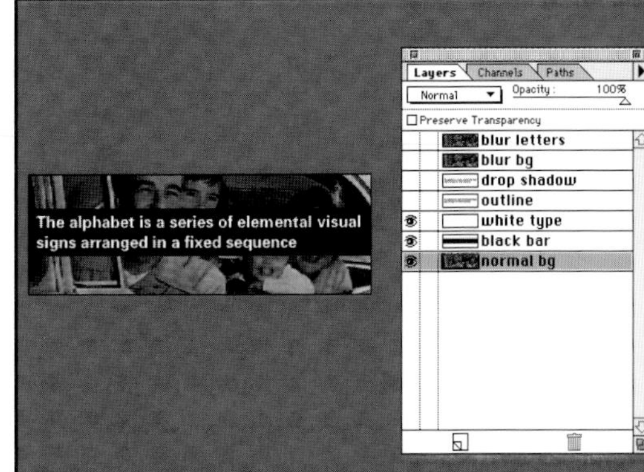

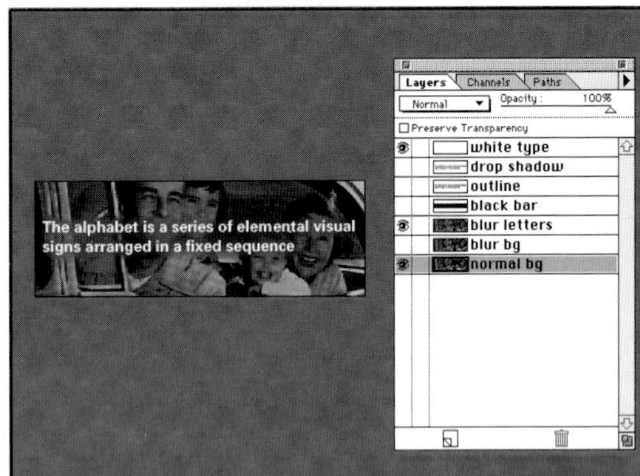

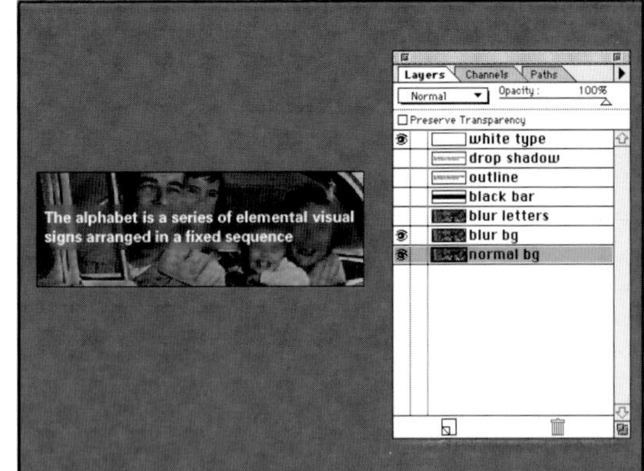

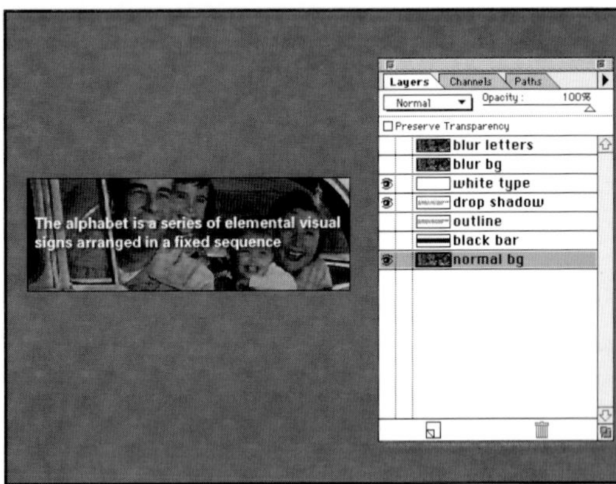

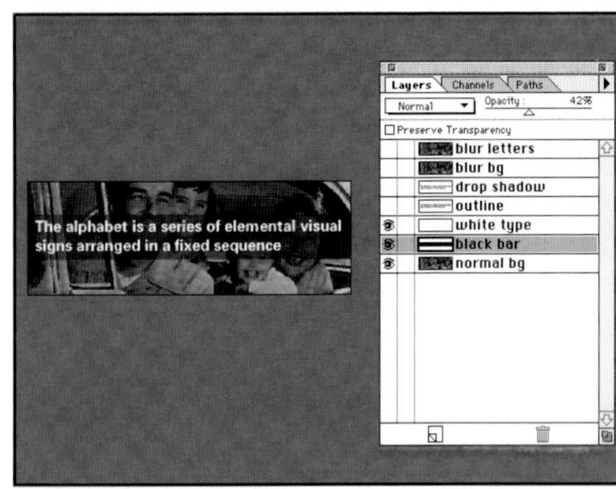

By turning on and off visible layers, a single layered Photoshop document can generate many hybrid documents. By using the Save a Copy command under the File menu, you can preserve the original layered documents and store different flattened variations based on them.

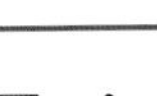

tip

Optimizing Grayscale Images

If an image is in Grayscale mode in Photoshop, it is already indexed to 256 colors or less. By switching modes from Grayscale to Indexed Color, you are not given the opportunity to change the numbers of colors or grays. By reducing the number of colors or grays within an image, the resulting GIF will be smaller. In order to do this with grayscale images, switch the mode first to RGB and then switch to Indexed Colors. This opens the Index Color dialog box, where it's possible to enter smaller values than the default 256. Converting an image to Indexed Color flattens the layers, so it's best to make your images first and then reduce them en masse.

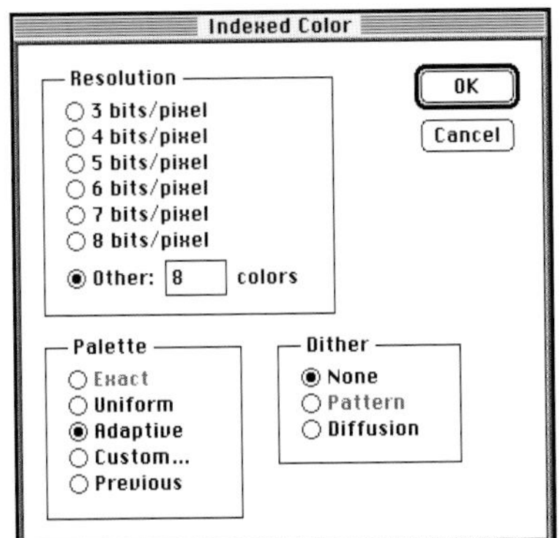

Through accessing this dialog box, it's possible to enter smaller numbers of colors (or grays) within a Photoshop document and greatly reduce file sizes.

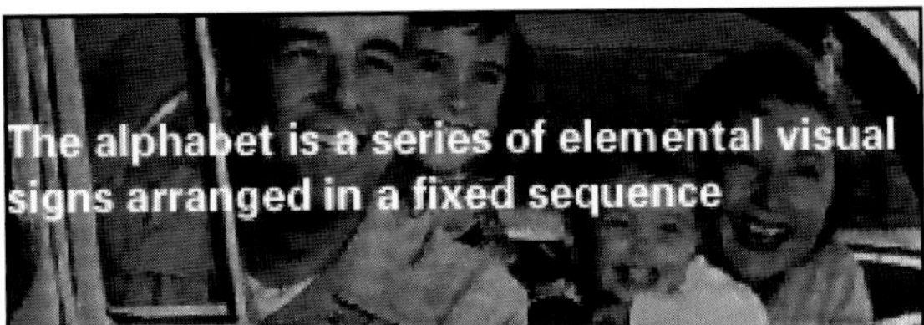

As a 16-color (gray) image, this GIF is 15k. As a 256-color (gray) GIF, it would have been 41k!

Dynamic Typography with Java

Java is used on the typoGRAPHIC site in the "dynamic typography" section. Java is a programming language that is used to produce applets, or mini-executable programs, that can be distributed over the Internet. Java was used on the typoGRAPHIC site to include movement and sound.

The Java animation example was used to demonstrate how dynamic media can influence the personna of typography. There are three examples: "bounce," "ripe banana," and "woo hoo."

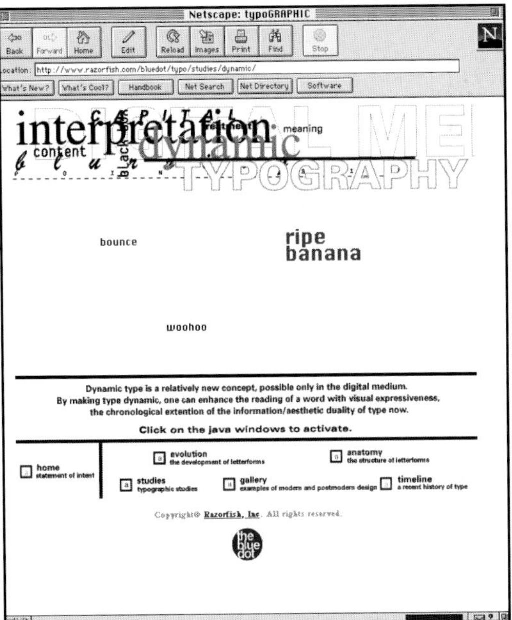

The opening screen for Dynamic Typography, which demonstrates how sound and movement can influence the impact of text through Java animations.

Oz Lubling, lead technologist for Razorfish, wrote the three Java applets that compose the dynamic typography section of typoGRAPHIC. He taught himself to write Java by reading minimal documentation available from the Sun site (www.javasoft.com). Today, one has many more options for learning Java (see Oz's resource list below). Because Oz was already an experienced programmer in C/ C++, Perl, Lisp, and TCL, learning Java was less of a stretch than it would be for a non-programmer!

Oz experimented with making sample applets to teach himself fundamental principles of Java. When it came time to write something relevant, he carefully planned out what he wanted to do. For example, with the "woo hoo" applet, he wanted the sound to sync with the animating point sizes of the text animation. He had to think about how that would happen in the most precise physical sense, such as does the sound play at the beginning, middle, or end of the animation. With the fading banana he had to think about how the palette shift would occur, exactly what colors would be employed during the ColorFade, and if this could be done with math instead of a pre-determined sequence of color values. These sorts of questions have nothing to do with Java per se, but are part of the programming design process as well.

After Oz settled on what he wanted to do, he set out to locate all the Java routines and methods that would make text and play sound, to see how they would fit into the algorithm he had defined. His last step was to translate the ideas to fit the methods available—and sometimes his design had to change to fit the tools. For example, within the current capabilities of Java, there are only a few fonts available and none are anti-aliased. This limited the design of what Oz might have initially planned, but he made do.

■ tip

How to Learn Java Programming

Oz advocates learning about Java by reading books (he recommends *Teach Yourself Java in 21 Days* by Laura Lemay/Sams.net), checking Java resource URLs, and participating on mailing lists. There is a big community of Java authors who share code and information. It's a drag to work on a program for months, only to discover that someone else already wrote something like it. These are a few resources he recommends:

- http://www.digitalfocus.com/digitalfocus/faq/howdoi.html
- http://weber.u.washington.edu/~jgurney/java/index.html
- http://www.javasoft.com
- http://www.javaworld.com
- http://www.gamelan.com
- http://www.jars.com
- http://comp.lang.java

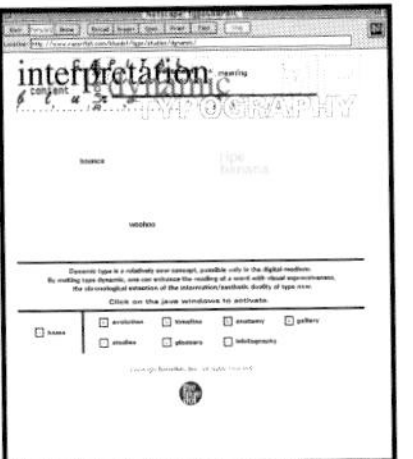

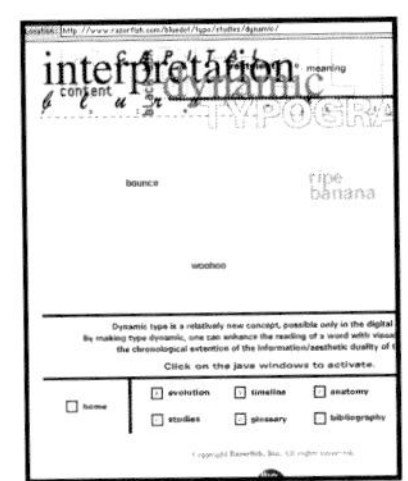

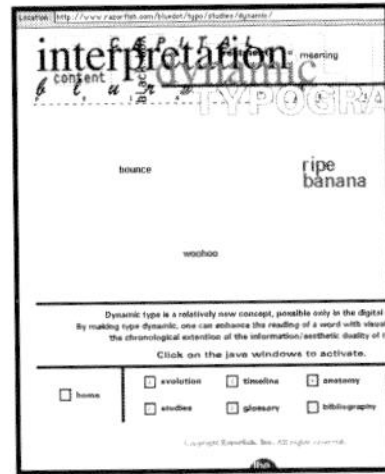

■ Five color transition frames (out of 50) of the ripe banana Java Applet. The text "ripe banana" changes colors as the banana ripens over time. Java is being used to demonstrate how our response to a word can be altered or enhanced by dynamic media.

■ tags

HTML Deconstruction

The HTML required to embed a Java Applet is simple. The <APPLET> tag tells a Java-enabled browser to load the code specified in the CODE attribute (for example, "ColorFade.class"). The WIDTH and HEIGHT attributes specify the dimensions of the applet on the browser's screen (WIDTH and HEIGHT are required by Netscape).

```
<applet code="Bounce.class" width=200 height=100>
+++
</applet>
<applet code="ColorFade.class" width=200 height=100>
+++
</applet>
<applet code="Word.class" width=300 height=100>
</applet>
```

■ Anything between the <APPLET> tag and the </APPLET> end-tag will be ignored by a Java-enabled browser, but will be displayed by a browser that does not recognize the <APPLET> tag. This allows you to put something else there that will tell a user that they are missing the Java content if their browser doesn't support Java.

■ code

Java Deconstruction

Here's the actual Java code that Oz wrote for the fading banana.

```
import java.applet.*;
import java.awt.Graphics;
import java.awt.Color;
import java.awt.Image;
import java.awt.Font;
import java.awt.*;
```

■ Java, like most object-oriented programming languages, is distributed with a number of class libraries that are used to build common objects. Classes are the heart of object-oriented programming; they are the definitions of classes of objects that can be reused to define new objects and new classes. The import statements here are invoking a few of these standard class libraries.

```
public class ColorFade extends Applet {
  Font f = new Font("Helvetica",Font.BOLD, 24);
  int STEPS = 100;
  Color colors[] = new Color[STEPS];
  Thread runThread;
public Graphics g;
  Color ozwhite = new Color(255,255,255);
  Color start_color
    =Color.getHSBColor(0.144f,0.98f,0.98f);

  // On Screen Buffer
  public Graphics onScreenBuffer;

  // Off Screen Buffer
  public Graphics offScreenBuffer;

  // Off Screen Image
  public Image offScreenImage;
```

■ Next, the ColorFade class is defined, along with its global variables and buffers. Variables are made global by declaring them with the public attribute. This makes them available to the rest of the program. Buffers are variables that have space in them for carrying blocks of data.

```
public void init() {

  onScreenBuffer = getGraphics();
  offScreenImage =  createImage(size().width,size()
    .height);
  offScreenBuffer = offScreenImage.getGraphics();
  offScreenBuffer.setColor(Color.white);
  offScreenBuffer.fillRect(0, 0, size().width, size
    ().height);

  setBackground(ozwhite);
  offScreenBuffer.setColor(start_color);
  offScreenBuffer.setFont(f);
  offScreenBuffer.drawString("ripe", 50, 50);
  offScreenBuffer.drawString("banana",50,70);
  repaint();

}
```

■ The init() function is called when the applet is first loaded. It is used to initialize the buffers and the initial conditions for the applet.

Oz uses the init() function here to create his various buffer spaces and initial graphics, including the text.

```
public void PaintColor() {

  //initialize the color array
  float h_start = 0.144f;
  float h_end = 0.111f;
  float hh = h_end - h_start;
  float h_inc = hh / (float)STEPS;

  float s_start = 0.98f;
  float s_end = 0.96f;
  float ss = s_end - s_start;
  float s_inc = ss / (float)STEPS;

  float b_start = 0.98f;
  float b_end = 0.48f;
  float bb = b_end - b_start;
  float b_inc = bb / (float)STEPS;

  float h = h_start;
  float s = s_start;
  float b = b_start;
  float c = 0;
  for (int i = 0; i <colors.length; i++) {
    colors[i] = Color.getHSBColor(h,s,b);

    c += .02;
    h += h_inc;
    s += s_inc;
    b += b_inc;
  }
```

■ The PaintColor() function creates the array of colors using the Hue/Saturation/Brightness model.

The HSB model specifies the color of objects in terms of their hue, saturation, and brightness instead of their red, green, and blue components. Java's internal Color class does the work of converting them back to the Red/Green/Blue values a computer monitor needs to display them.

```
//cycle through the colors
  int i = 0;
  for (int j = 0; j <colors.length; j++) {
    setForeground(colors[j]);
    offScreenBuffer.setColor(colors[j]);
    offScreenBuffer.drawString("ripe", 50, 50);
    offScreenBuffer.drawString("banana",50,70);
    paint(onScreenBuffer);
    i++;
    try { Thread.sleep(50); }
    catch (InterruptedException e) { }
    if (i == colors.length) i = 0;
  }
}
```

■ Oz is using HSB instead of RGB because it makes it easier to cycle through the range of colors he wants. This way, the computer will do all the math for him, and he can do the whole cycle in one loop.

The for() loop here cycles through the color table.

```
  public void paint (Graphics g) {

  g.drawImage(offScreenImage,0,0,this);
}

public void update (Graphics g) {
  paint(g);
}
public boolean mouseDown(Event e, int xx, int yy) {

  PaintColor();
  return true;
}
}
```

■ These functions are for controlling the flow of the applet so that the screen gets updated properly and the animation happens when the mouse is pressed over the applet.

Shockwave for typoGRAPHIC

Shockwave is the name of a technology that enables Director-based multimedia projects to be played on the Web. Multimedia can be described as anything that combines sound, animation, images, text, and interactivity. Macromedia Director is an authoring program for creating interactive multimedia for kiosks and CD-ROMs, and it has been around many years longer than the Web itself. The Shockwave file format boasts an impressive compression ratio of three to one, making the Director files a third of their usual size.

Afterburner is the free post-processing tool (available from ■ http://www.macromedia.com/Tools/Shockwave/Director/aftrbrnr.html) that offers authors who create Director multimedia projects the capability to convert them so they can be distributed over the Web. Once Afterburner has converted a Director project, it becomes a Shockwave file.

Designing the Interface for the Anatomy Shockwave Project

Stephen Turbek's background as an industrial designer brought a different perspective to the typoGRAPHIC design team. He's always been fascinated by how people interact with computer interfaces, and spent several weeks teaching himself Macromedia Director so he could program some of his own experiments with interface design. The Anatomy section within the typoGRAPHIC site gave him an opportunity to produce his first published Director project, where he was able to test some of his theories about human interface design.

Stephen's interface design succeeded by creating custom navigation controls that blended seamlessly with the overall aesthetic of the site.

Just like Oz and his pre-planning for the Java section, Stephen also had to spell out his ideas on paper before creating the graphics or the programming for the Shockwave piece. Storyboarding can mean many things to many people—from beautiful renderings to scribbles on index cards to words scrawled on paper. Regardless of how "polished" a storyboard looks, its function is to pre-plan and pre-visualize the scope of a project. For Stephen, carefully planning this project was key to creating the type of interactive experience he was aiming for. He calls his storyboarding style "verbal storyboarding," because he wrote his ideas with words rather than drawing them with pictures.

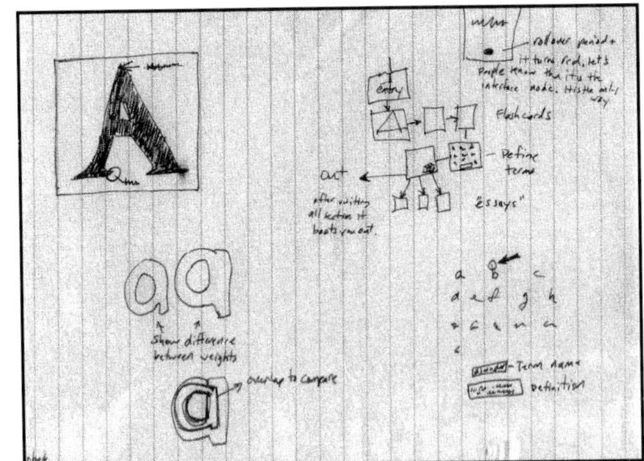

An example of Steven's verbal storyboarding method. The goal here is to work out ideas with words and concepts rather than to make pretty pictures.

A main concern to Stephen was understanding how to make a person learn a new interface. The "red dot" became a unifying design theme in his project. After the user learned that the dot changed to red and could be clicked to go to the next screen, the navigation for the piece was established.

A current trend in advanced multimedia and game design is to break away from obvious buttons with words on them. By using a simple red dot instead of a bulky button or conventional arrow icons, Stephen was able to keep the overall design of his Shockwave piece much more elegant and consistent with the established aesthetic of the typoGRAPHIC site. It's important to designers that interfaces integrate with the overall look and feel of an interactive experience. The days of predic-table beveled buttons with words have long worn out their welcome with most multimedia designers.

Stephen also strove to create an inviting interface that enabled users to explore and learn without cumbersome navigation graphics. He carried the rollover effect of objects changing from black to red throughout the piece. The next section of the project offered definitions for the anatomy of type, inviting the user to interact with red circles.

Another important component of Stephen's piece was to create maximum interactivity for the audience. Rather than a simple slide show, he chose to let the user move type around on screen themselves, to view the differences between serifs and typeface weights. This created a much more compelling example than simply showing visual examples of the differences.

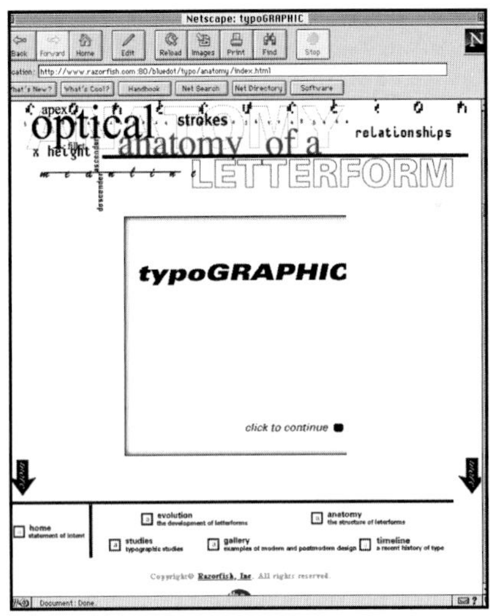

The centered window with the "click to continue" button is the embedded Shockwave document.

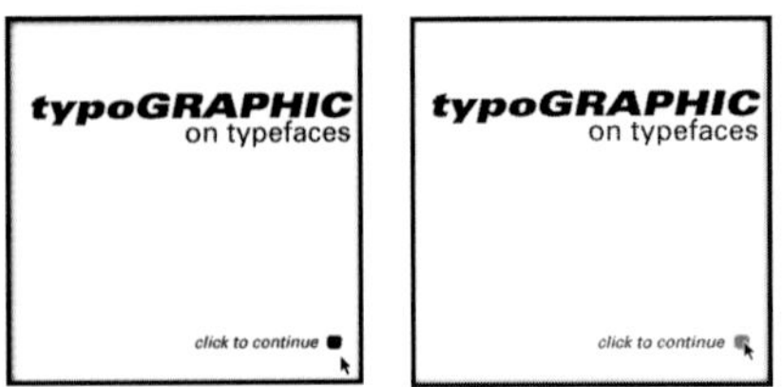

When the end user's cursor passes over the black rectangle, it turns red. This "rollover" effect signifies that the rectangle is a button that triggers interactive events.

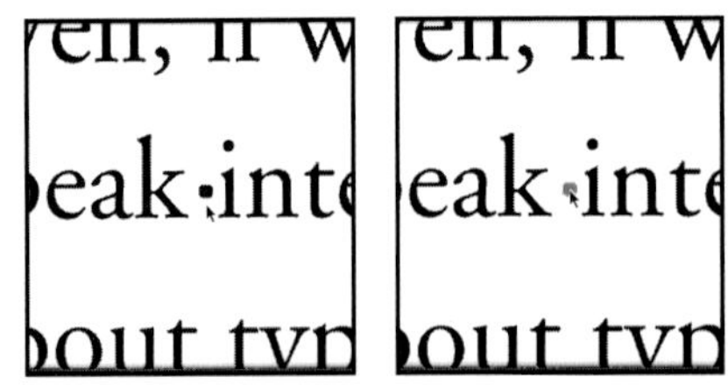

The red cursor metaphor is reinforced as a navigational cue in subsequent screens without the need to repeat the instructions "click to continue." The end user is being trained how to use the interface without further explanation.

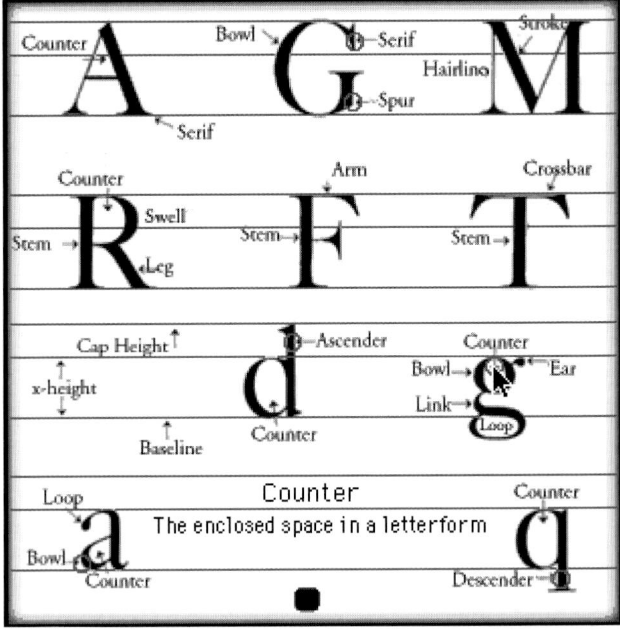

When a cursor travels over a red circle, the definition of the term is displayed at the bottom of the frame. The familiar black dot signifies that it can be clicked to advance to the next screen.

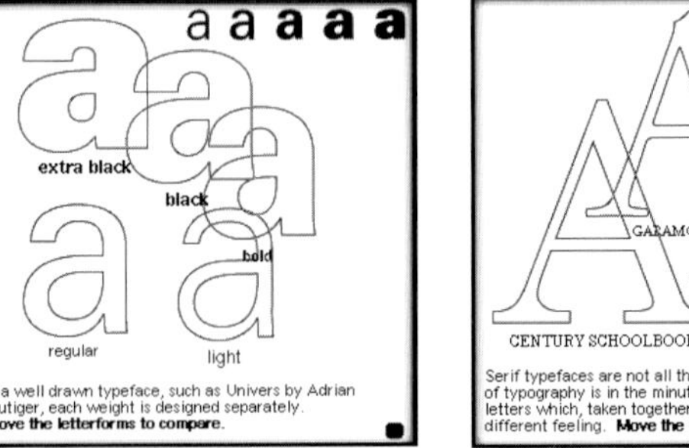

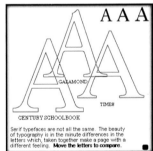

Stephen designed two screens that enable the user to move the letterforms into position. This level of interactivity is new to the Web, and requires using extra tools like Director and Shockwave.

Deconstructing the Lingo for Shockwave

Adding interactivity to Director projects is accomplished through using a proprietary programming language called Lingo. Lingo is touted as an easy programming language—though non-programmers might not necessarily agree with that analysis. Learning Lingo is possible by studying the manuals that are shipped with Macromedia Director, or through third-party books and Usenet groups.

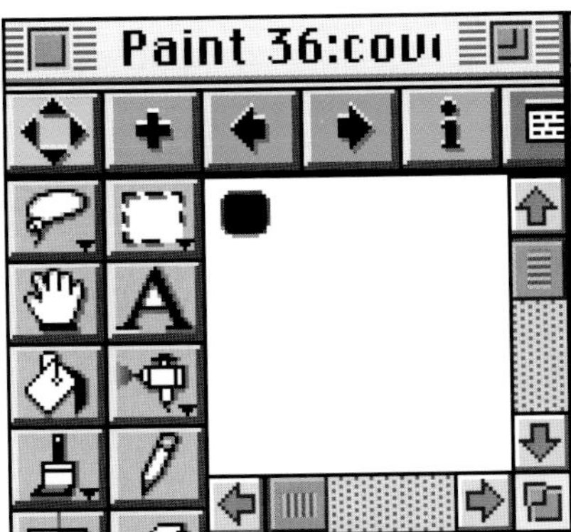

In order to color the black dot, it had to be a separate sprite (piece of artwork) within the Director project. This is the view of the artwork from within Director's Paint Window.

Inside the Director Score Window, the black dot is in the channel #3 position. Note in the Lingo script the follows how this artwork is referred to as "sprite 3", even though the artwork is named cover.pict, and is in the number 36 position in the Cast Window.

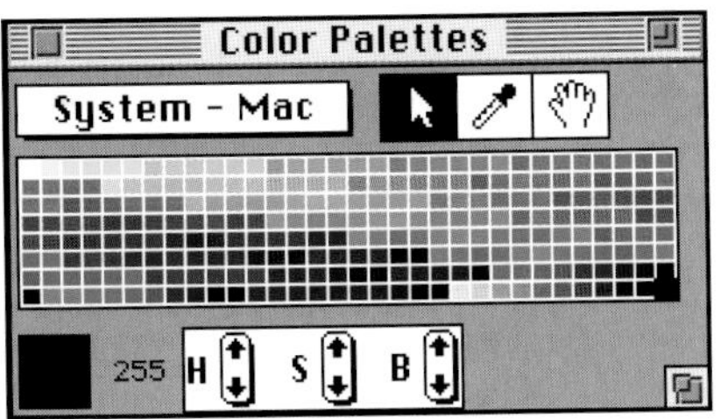

The Lingo is also specifying that the color black turn to red with the cursor rollover. Black is #255 within the project's Mac system palette.

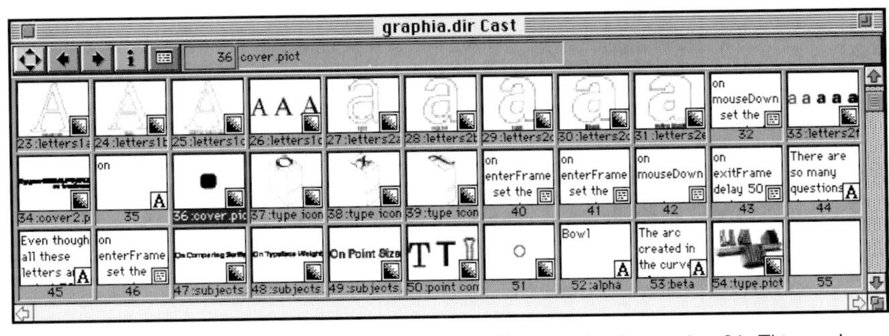

If you look at the channel #3 cel within the Score, you'll notice the tiny number 36. This number reflects the position of the sprite that has been assigned in the Cast Member Window.

Red is #217 within the project's system palette.

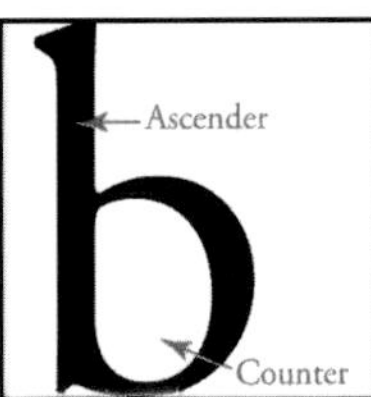

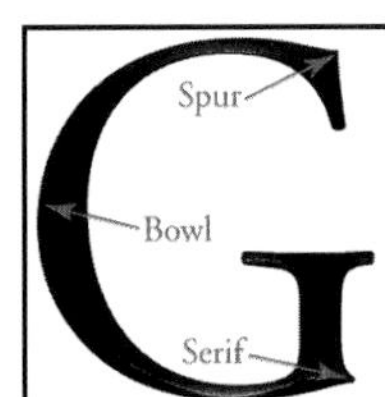

These three screens appear in succession, like a slide show. The slideshow effect was accomplished by assigning each frame to have a "delay" within the Lingo programming.

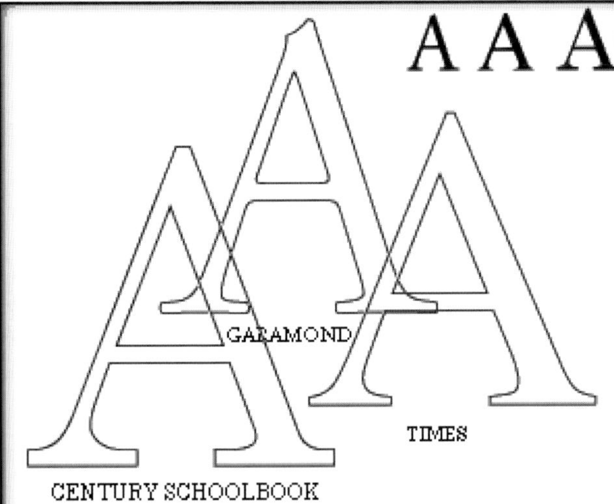

Allowing users to move images around on screen, such as the three letterforms here, is accomplished by assigning the object to be moveable.

■ code

Lingo Deconstruction

The Lingo for the red cursor rollover effect follows:

```
on enterFrame
  set the puppet of sprite 3 to TRUE
        if rollOver(3) = TRUE then
        set the forecolor of sprite 3 to 217
    else set the forecolor of sprite 3 to 255
  end if
end
```

■ The cursor turns red by instructing the color of the black (255) sprite to turn red (217). It's possible to set a custom palette within Director, but the Mac System palette is in use in this project.

The Lingo for the early slideshow effect follows:

```
On exitFrame
  go to the frame
end
```

■ To create the early slideshow effect, Stephen inserted "delay" times, which cause each frame of artwork to pause for a specified amount of time. Delays within Lingo are measured in "ticks." A second is 60 ticks, so each delay in this piece is a little less than a second.

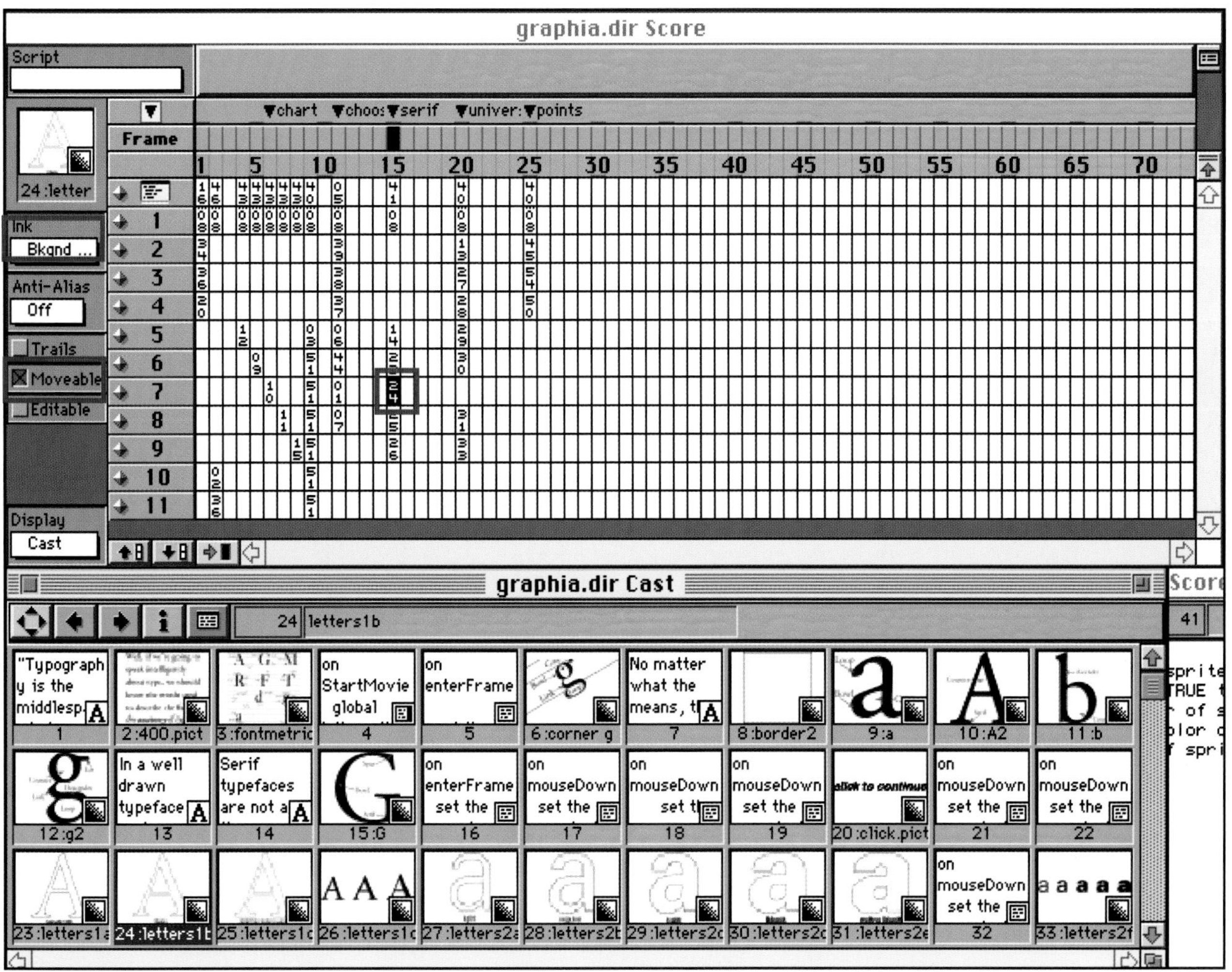

The Director score and cast windows with the "Moveable" box checked enable end users to move independent pieces of artwork.

■ Note how the number 24 is highlighted in the Director Score. To its far left is a check box called Moveable. By clicking this, the sprite is able to be moved by the end user. This piece of artwork is sprite number 24 in the Cast window. It also has been set to use Bkgnd Ink, which instructs the program to mask the background color of the graphic. In this case, the graphic's background color was white, so under the Bkgnd Ink setting the white was assigned to be transparent. Besides checking the Movable check box, another way to assign movability to an object is through Lingo. The advantage to using Lingo for this purpose is that the movable attribute can be turned on and off through the course of the project or be dependent on other actions. Clicking on the Movable checkbox is less flexible, because it's a global setting that lasts the entire duration of the Director project.

This is the Lingo to add movable functionality to a sprite:

```
set the movable of sprite x=true
```

■ **note**

New Director 5.0 Release

Director 5 has been released since Stephen made the Shockwave example on typoGRAPHIC. Some of the upgrade's improvements are support for anti-aliased text, and the capability to save directly in the Shockwave format without the use of Afterburner.

Shocking Director

The final step to preparing the Director document is to turn it into a Web-based Shockwave document. This is done with a free utility called Afterburner that can be downloaded from: ■ http://www.macromedia.com/Tools/Shockwave/Director/aftr-brnr.html

Afterburner is a post-processor for Director movies that compresses and prepares them for uploading to an HTTP server from which they will be available to Internet users. This can now be done in Director 5.0 directly, without using Afterburner. Uncompressed movies should be first saved in .DIR or .DXR format. Once compressed with Afterburner they will be in .DCR format. HTTP servers should set the MIME-Type for .DCR files to "application/x-director."

To include the Shockwave piece within the typoGRAPHIC site, the following HTML was used:

```
<EMBED SRC="images/graphia.dcr" width=304 height=300>
```

■ It's extremely important to include the dimensions of Shockwave documents in HTML code. The file will not function without it.

It is possible to code the HTML so an alternative image displays on browsers that do not support plug-ins by using the tag:

```
<NOEMBED ><img src="images/noshock.gif"></NOEMBED>
```

■ After the <NOEMBED> tag, an alternative graphic could be inserted that would only be visible to browsers that did not have the Shockwave plug-in installed, or support plug-ins.

■ note

Java versus Shockwave

Both Java and Shockwave offer solutions to deliver animation, sound, and interactivity to static Web pages. The question is, which one is better and why should you choose one over the other?

This often asked question is a little misleading, as Java and Shockwave are not the same thing; each with its own particular strengths and weaknesses. Java is a programming language and Shockwave is a file format for interactive presentations. Java presents information based on computational actions, whereby a script instructs an object to have certain behavior. Macromedia Director, which is used to create Shockwave files, is an authoring program that assigns attributes to objects that are pre-set, and then produces a finished pre-built presentation. Most programmers view Java as being much more flexible programming environment, but many like Director because it's an authoring tool instead of a programming language.

Shockwave is a plug-in while Java is incorporated directly in a Java-enabled browser. The Shockwave plug-in can be downloaded for free at:

- http://www.macromedia.com/Tools/Shockwave/Director/aftrbrnr.html

Both solutions, Java and Shockwave, have restricted visibility because not all browsers support either one. (At the time of this chapter, the only two browsers that support Java and Shockwave were Netscape 2.0 and above, and MSIE).

In the case of the Anatomy section of typoGRAPHIC, the time it took to develop the end product in the Director authoring tool was much faster than it would have been programming it from scratch within Java.

Macromedia Director boasts over 200,000 registered software owners, which means that the installed base of Director authors is much larger than the base of programmers who know Java. It could be said that Java produces content that is more compact and efficient, but Shockwave offers an easier-to-learn-and-use authoring environment. Unless, of course, you already know Java and have never learned Director!

An interesting side note is that theoretically you could bundle a Director animation inside a Java applet, and Director has future plans to support Java within its spec. In the future, Director and Java will most likely not be mutually exclusive of one another.

Guest Book CGI Programming

Razorfish includes "Guest Books" on all their sites as an effort to build community and interactivity with their audience. They only edit profanity and large images from the submissions they receive, and their CGI script creates the listings automatically.

Commonly, the part that creates the listings is built around an HTML forms interface, and the part that reads the guestbook is a common CGI program that is usually built in two parts with one listing implemented as a server-side include.

The CGI deconstructed in this chapter is similar in functionality to Razorfish's site, but was written and deconstructed by my brother, William Weinman, author of *The CGI Book* ISBN:1-56205-571-2/New Riders Publishing. This guestbook is in use at:

- http://www.lynda.com/guestbook/.

Check it out, and be sure to leave a note!

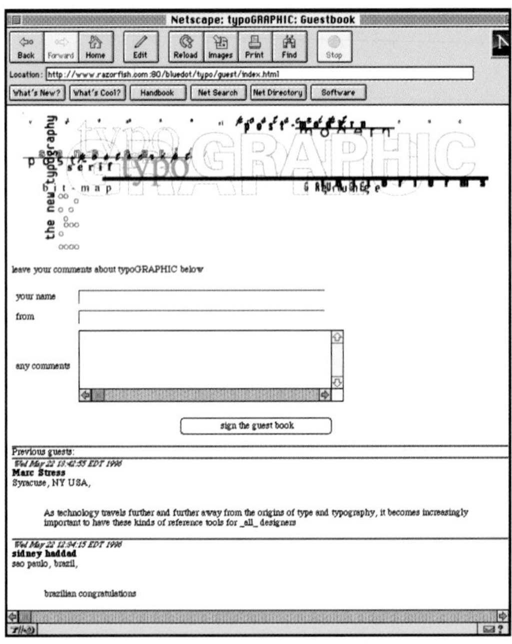

The guestbook at typoGRAPHIC allows for visitors to comment on the site, and hundreds have done so.

■ code

The Guestbook CGI Script

Here's the CGI for the Guestbook, written in Perl:

```
#!/usr/bin/perl
```

■ This line at the top of the program identifies the Perl interpreter as the program used to execute this file. It is a common way to run Perl scripts under Unix.

```
print "content-type: text/html\n\n";
```

■ This prints out a MIME "Content-Type" header to tell the Web browser that it will be receiving HTML. All CGI programs must start their output with a MIME header.

```
# convert any HTML to entities
foreach $q (keys %qs) {
  $qs{$q} =~ s/</&lt\;/g;
  $qs{$q} =~ s/>/&gt\;/g;
  $qs{$q} =~ s/"/&quot\;/g;
}
```

■ This section converts any HTML in the form data to entities that can be printed. This effectively prevents users from putting any HTML (for example, <img src=http://wwwhell.org/devil.jpg>) into their entries.

```
# create the record
open(MYDATA, ">$mydata");
print MYDATA <<RECORD;
<record>
Date: $today
Name: $name
From: $from
Comments: $comments
</record>
RECORD
```

■ Here we create the actual record in the guestbook database. The database is actually a textfile, with each record delimited by <record> and </record> in the file. This makes it easy for the reading program to find the beginning and ending of each record.

```
# put the new record at the top of the data file# by
reading the rest of the datafile into the
# end of the new datafile . . .
open(DATA, "<$datafile");
while(<DATA>) { print MYDATA; }
close(DATA);
close(MYDATA);

# then put the new datafile in the place of the
# old one.
rename($mydata, $datafile);
```

■ For the purpose of a guestbook, we want to make sure that each new record goes at the beginning of the file, rather than the end. This is the code that accomplishes that.

After writing the record to the MYDATA file, it opens the DATA file and reads it into MYDATA after the new record. Then it closes both files and renames MYDATA to overwrite the DATA file. This results in a new copy of DATA that contains the new record at the head instead of the tail.

```
$| = 1; # flush stdout on each write
```

■ The $| variable is a special variable in Perl that controls the behavior of the output buffer. If the variable is zero (the default condition), all output is buffered (that is, it can be held on to) by the operating system until it gets around to dealing with it. If it is non-zero, the output buffer is flushed (that is, the output is written immediately) as soon as the write action is finished.

It is important to set this to non-zero to make sure that the HTML that is sent to the output actually gets there in the order that you send it. Not setting this can lead to some very confusing results.

```
while(<DATA> && $i++ < 100) {
  loop if $_ ne "<record>";
  ($date) = <DATA> =~ /Date: (.*)/;
  ($name) = <DATA> =~ /Name: (.*)/;
  ($from) = <DATA> =~ /From: (.*)/;
  ($comments) = <DATA> =~ /Comments: (.*)/;
  $comments .= "\n";
  while(chomp($c = <DATA>) && ($c ne "</record>")) {
    $comments .= "$c\n";
  }
```

■ This is the code that deciphers the data file. It looks for lines that start with "Date:," "Name:," and so on, and stores their contents in variables. It also looks for "<record>" and "</record>" that marks the beginning and ending of each record.

```
  print "<hr noshade size=3>\n";
  print "$date\n";
  print "<br><strong>$name</strong>\n";
  print "<br><em>$from</em>\n";
  print
"<blockquote><pre>$comments</pre></blockquote>\n";
}
```

■ Notice that what we send here is HTML. It will be included right in the stream of HTML that is sent to the browser.

■ site summary

typoGRAPHIC

Razorfish earns high points for creating a great educational resource about typography, and showcasing their technical and design talents at the same time. Here's what we can learn from their site:

■ Good, strong content requires a lot of thought, discussion, and pre-planning. Don't discount the importance of these activities, thinking they take too much time. Many clients and employers overlook this important step and wonder why their content isn't compelling.

■ Color can play a huge role in visual communication. Follow Alex's lead, and look to print design for inspiration for color schemes and design themes on a Web site. Choosing a small number of colors can make a huge impact on the overall aesthetic of a site.

■ Using multimedia on a Web site can be a great tool, but make it fit the aesthetic of the site, and it will become a seamless experience. Try to develop interfaces that get away from bulky buttons and over-used clichés, and your site will stand above the rest.

■ Choosing between Java or Shockwave is a personal decision that relates partially to your resources. If you already know one or the other, development time might outweigh other considerations. Evaluate the scope of your project to decide whether programming from scratch is more sensible than using an existing authoring tool.

■ Join discussion groups, reference URLs, and read books about Shockwave and Java to help accelerate the long, time-consuming learning curves.

IUMA
including sound and video

What this chapter covers:

- **3D Effects on 2D Imagery**
- **Movie and Audio Web Formats**
- **Digital Audio and Video Terminology**
- **HTML for Audio and Video files**

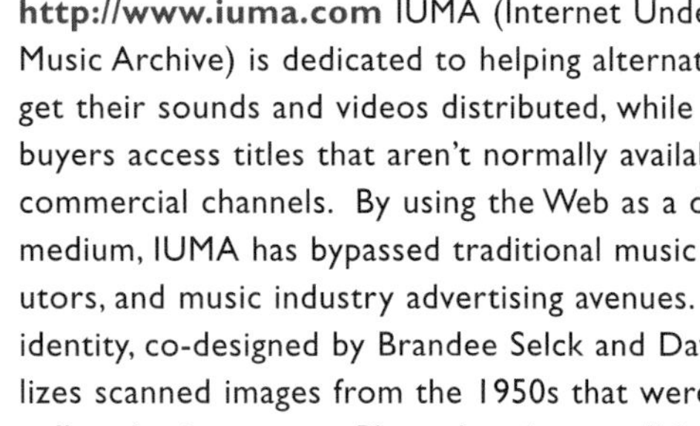

http://www.iuma.com IUMA (Internet Underground Music Archive) is dedicated to helping alternative musicians get their sounds and videos distributed, while helping music buyers access titles that aren't normally available through commercial channels. By using the Web as a distribution medium, IUMA has bypassed traditional music labels, distributors, and music industry advertising avenues. IUMA's visual identity, co-designed by Brandee Selck and David Beach, utilizes scanned images from the 1950s that were edited and collaged using custom Photoshop image editing techniques.

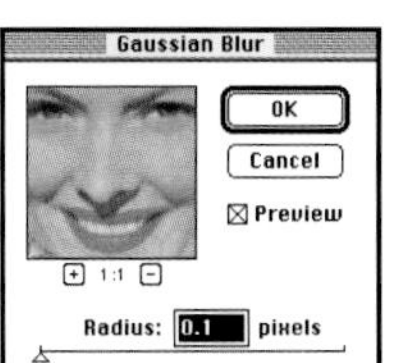

Client: IUMA

Type of Site: Music and Video

URL: http://www.iuma.com/

Server: SGI Challenge S

Operating System: IRIX 5.3

Server Software: Netscape Commerce

President and Technical Director: Jeff Patterson

Art Director: Brandee Selk

Assistant Art Director: David Beach

Multimedia Specialists: Ryan Melcher, Josh Salesin

VP of Projects: Danny Johnson

VP of Sales and Marketing: Todd Williams

Support Specialist: Adam Cantwell

Site Department Director: Evan Heidtmann

VP of Operations: Kevin Ratner

Software: Photoshop, Illustrator

What is IUMA?

IUMA was the brainchild of two University of California Santa Cruz college students, Rob Lord and Jeff Patterson. They believed that the Web would be the perfect vehicle for musicians to market their sounds and videos to audiences who couldn't get to them through any other means. In the process of creating IUMA, they developed a new publishing model for distributing music that has caught the attention of major record labels and national publications, such as *Time*, *Rolling Stone*, and *USA Today*.

The IUMA Web site houses over 800 underground bands' music recordings and videos. IUMA uses the Web to its best advantage as a global distribution medium, excellent retrieval/archive/database system, and interactive forum for audiences to interact with musicians.

This chapter looks at IUMA's Web site for its visual originality and its handling of sound and video files. It takes a lot of sophisticated programming and design skills to assemble a site that distributes mass volumes of different file formats and media files. Not to mention that it accomplishes all this and manages to look great too.

Establishing a Visual Identity for IUMA

The IUMA site has a 50s retro flavor, which was created using Photoshop layering and compositing techniques. IUMA was co-designed by Brandee Selck and David Beach, who had both tried their hand at designing smaller sites before tackling IUMA.

Brandee and David saw a direct correlation between the early days of TV and advertising in the 1950s and the early days of the Web. The obsession with technology as a future-techno paradise in the 50s seemed similar to the obsession with the Web in the 90s. The artwork was intended to be a tongue-in-cheek reflection and critique of pop culture.

Brandee found the source material for the 50s images from a variety of sources: old magazines, the University of California Santa Cruz library, thrift stores, parents' garages, and yard sales. Images were modified or collaged in almost every graphic for the site.

The opening graphic for the site sets the tone: irreverent, retro, and playful.

■ note

Image Usage Rights

It's important to make no assumptions when dealing with found images. Read Chapter 8, "Discovery Online" for tips about securing rights to existing images and working with stock picture agencies. You might also want to check out Internet and copyright law. Attorney Ivan Hoffman has posted extensive writings on this subject, found at:

- http://home.earthlink.net/~ivanlove.

Fun with Scanning

Everything for the IUMA site was scanned on a standard 600 dpi flatbed scanner. Because images from magazines contain dot patterns, when scanned, moirés were often a problem. (See Chapter 1, "Hot Hot Hot," for more information on techniques for getting rid of moirés.) Brandee and David found if they scanned at a large scale first and slightly blurred the images (using a .1 or .2 Gaussian Blur filter in Photoshop) that the moirés would disappear once the image was shrunk back down.

The Gaussian Blur filter in Photoshop enables you to type or use a slider to try different radius amounts. This easy process is one technique to eliminate moirés.

Sometimes objects were even placed directly on the flatbed scanner, such as the tray and the napkin on the Cool Extras page. One wouldn't expect that the results would be so true to the original subjects, but this technique is a great and fast method for getting images into the computer when you can't afford the time to photograph something first.

The napkin used on the Cool Extras page was scanned directly on a flatbed scanner. The tray was created from a piece of scanned metal which was used as a texture.

A Pyrex container with apple juice and ice was set directly on the scanner as source material for this graphic. The buttons were made from bottle caps of various liquors that were also laid on top the scanner and composited later into the image using Photoshop.

3D Effects on 2D Images

Even though the graphics for IUMA are clearly taken from older sources, they have an updated, contemporary appearance. One of the reasons for this is the frequent use of subtle drop shadows and embossing effects that give the images a slight three-dimensional appearance. It is one thing to scan old images and put them on the Web, but great care was taken with all the IUMA screens to customize the images and make them look like a uniform family.

Brandee used alpha channels for these 3D effects, often combining scans from many sources. Alpha channel operations take a long time to master (see Chapter 2, "DreamWorks Interactive SKG," for more information on alpha channels). The basic principle behind alpha channel use is that the channel offers permanent storage for selection regions. By being stored in a channel, these regions can be called up at any time and will select the image for different manipulations. The selections can be filled with color, as in the case of a drop shadow, or used to cut things out, as in the case of the mask seen below in the shape of the tray.

This image was created using layers to combine images from different sources The tray and many of the drop shadow elements were created with alpha channels.

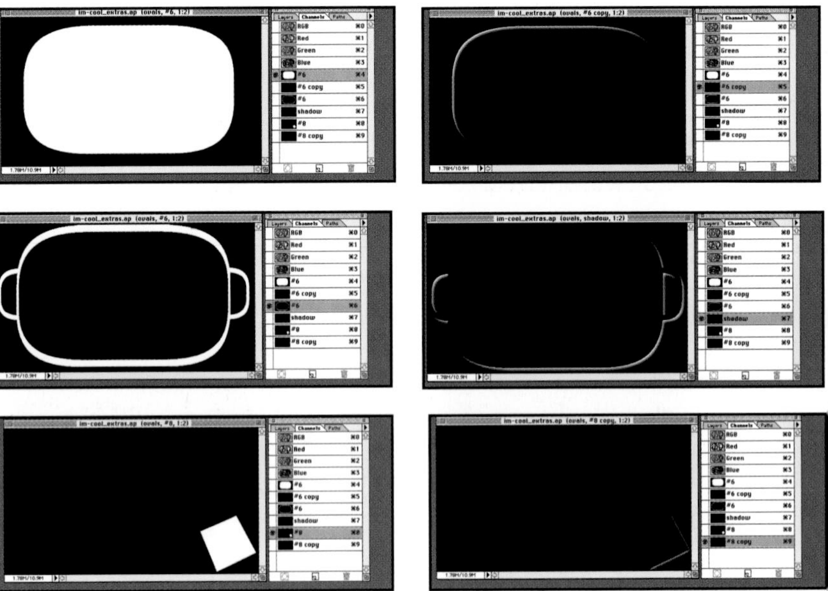

Here's an assortment of alpha channels that were stored with the Cool Extras layered Photoshop file. Brandee and David used these channel selections to create drop shadows and cut out specific shapes. By studying the final image, it's possible to see where these alpha channels were used, and what types of effects were created by loading them.

Embossing Effects

There's a great filter set available for both Mac and Windows platforms called The Black Box by Alien Skin (■ http://www.alienskin.com). This software is one answer to Photoshop users' prayers in that it eliminates the need for complex alpha channel editing, and achieves the same, if not better, results. With the use of a preview window, it can accomplish what takes many steps using other techniques in Photoshop, and shows the results interactively using sliders that can be adjusted easily. Note that Brandee and David did not use this method; they used a more complex technique that involved working with alpha channels.

Before using the Black Box filters, a selection must be active. In this example, the selection is in the shape of type, which was accomplished by using the text tool in Photoshop with the typeface "Suburban" by Emigre (■ www.emigre.com/) loaded.

The Black Box filters offer precise control over 3D effects, such as allowing the light source to be changed, or increasing/decreasing shadow and highlight information.

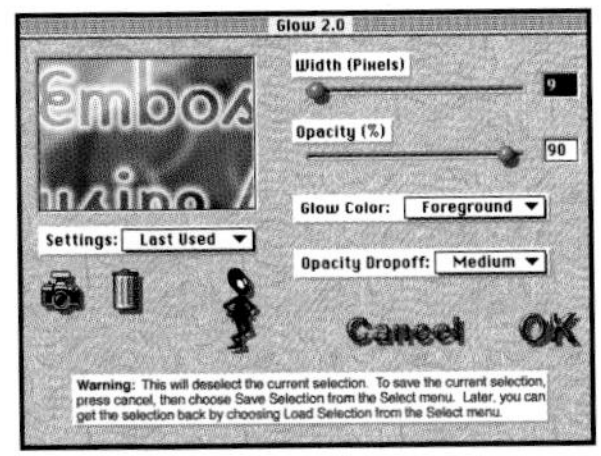

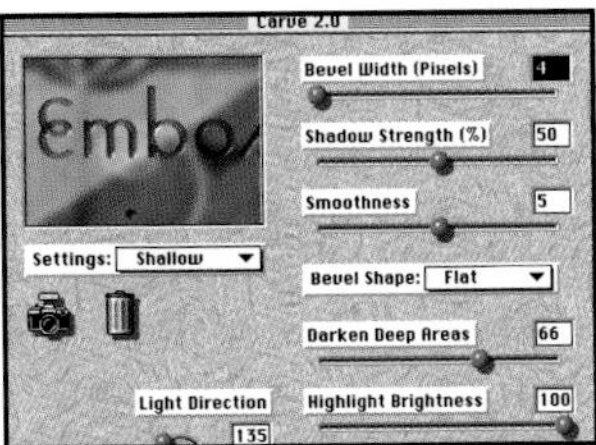

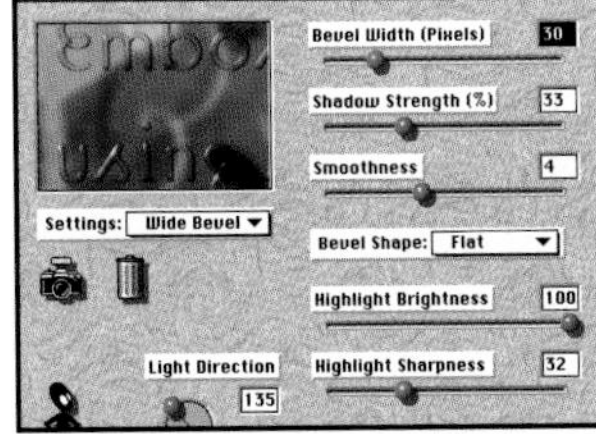

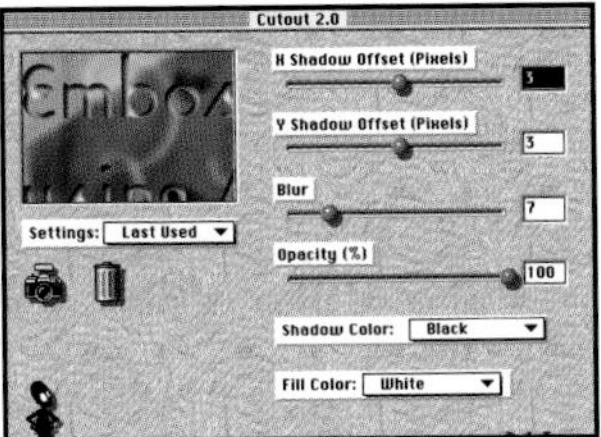

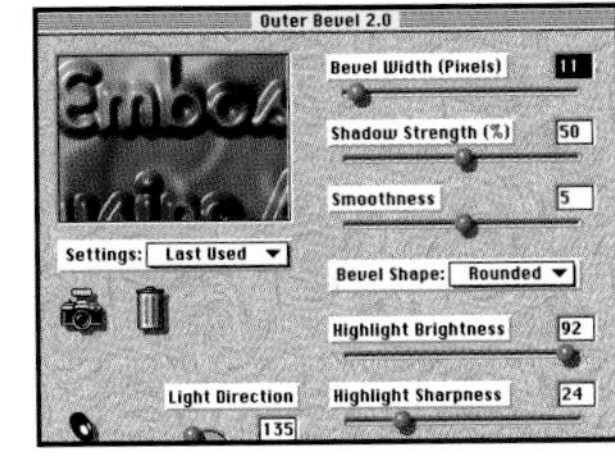

Here's a sampling of other 3D-type effects offered by the Black Box filter collection by Alien Skin Software.

■ note

Getting Photoshop Skills

Brandee had only studied Photoshop for two weeks while majoring in Fine Arts at University of California Santa Cruz. She taught herself the skills necessary to do the IUMA site through trying things, playing around, and practicing. For a good Photoshop reference Brandee recommended *The Photoshop WOW Book*, by Linnea Dayton and Jack Davis/Peachpit Press. She also learned a lot from Kai Krause's Macintosh-based Photoshop Tips pages found at ■ http://www.metatools.com/kptips/mactips.html. For Windows-based Photoshop users, try ■ http://www.metatools.com/kptips/wintips.html.

IUMA Navigation Overview

One of the great challenges to the site's designers was how to organize the information, both physically and visually. Brandee and David came up with a system of navigational elements that looked consistent, and helped viewers choose options based on various criteria.

IUMA paid a lot of attention to organizing the site so viewers could find their material by band name, genre, or location. The effort to structure the information was shared by the visual designers and the HTML/CGI programmers. Through collaboration, they arrived at a system that worked well with a clear-cut navigational interface.

This graphic is an image map, which offers viewers an alternative navigational device with which to find the bands, sounds, and video files. (See Chapter 5, "@tlas," for image map deconstruction.)

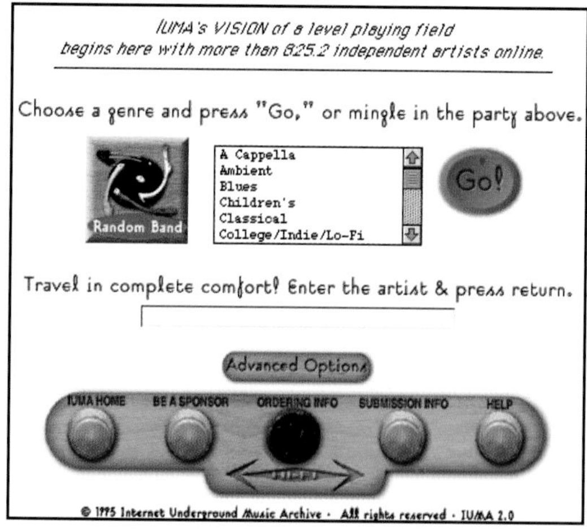

This screen demonstrates how forms were used to create the organizational structure used to search for bands, sounds, and image files. Forms are used heavily on the site. (See Chapter 1, "Hot Hot Hot," for forms processing deconstruction.)

Clicking the Random Band button will retrieve an unknown artist. This graphic is linked to a CGI script that generates a page to a random band.

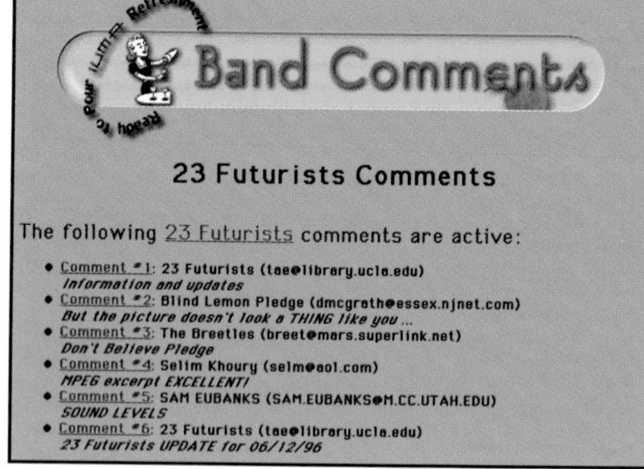

Being able to comment on each band's content is something unique to Web-based publishing. IUMA encourages viewer feedback, something that has never been available before as a marketing tool in other publishing mediums.

Putting Media on a Web Site

Supplying audio and video is key to IUMA's purpose. Unfortunately, including and preparing audio and video for a Web site can be a complex matter. First of all, the technology for displaying and embedding media on the Web is in flux, and the number of authoring options and file formats to chose from can be daunting.

One of the newest developments in this area is the advent of "streaming" technologies. Streaming means that the audio or video can be viewed or heard while the file is downloading. This is an obvious advantage to the way audio and video files are handled now, which requires them to be downloaded first, and then played.

IUMA intends to adopt streaming technologies on their site in the near future, but was still using older, more established delivery methods when this chapter was written. While IUMA likes to be cutting-edge, they are not interested in becoming bleeding-edge. They have taken a cautious approach to adopting streaming because of the tendency for new technologies to lack reliable performance. IUMA is more interested in making sure their audience gets to see and hear their files than experimenting with uncertain new approaches.

By the time you read this chapter, IUMA's site should include RealAudio—the first audio streaming technology to be widely adopted on the Web. It requires that the listener have a RealAudio player installed, and that the host has paid RealAudio a server licensing fee. It's necessary to use a proprietary encoder (software to encode, or record the data digitally) supplied by RealAudio in order to author these files. RealAudio's Web site with more information is located at: ■ http://www.realaudio.com.

MIME Types and Browser Configurations

IUMA has tackled the issue of audio and video on more levels than simply including these files on their site. First there's the issue of helping viewers out with instruction on how to configure different browsers so they can play IUMA's files. They've devoted a lot of Web space to this effort, and have some of the best documentation found on the Web for Mac, PC, and UNIX-based browser configurations.

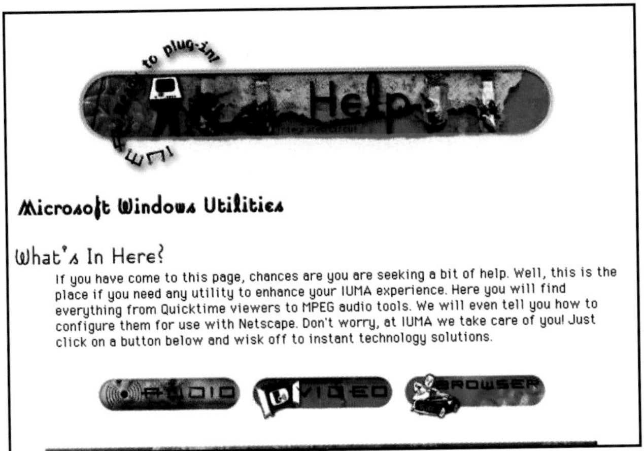

IUMA provides lots of help screens for visitors so they understand how to configure their browsers to view the various audio and video file formats IUMA offers. Their help pages are found at: ■ http://www.iuma.com/IUMA-2.0/help/

MIME stands for Multipurpose Internet Mail Extensions, which is an Internet standard method of indicating a specific format for transferring non-text data, such as sound and video. A centralized list of official MIMEtypes is maintained by the Internet Assigned Numbers Authority (IANA), available at: ■ http://www.iana.org/. It's necessary to configure a Web browser so it uses a specific MIMEtype for a specific task. For example, when the browser encounters an MPEG movie file (MIMEtype "audio /x-mpeg"), it must be instructed to know which program to launch on your computer in order to play the file.

If you don't have the given MIME type configured correctly on your machine, not only will the IUMA help pages offer suggestions, but they also supply links to the various players for easy downloading.

If you get this dialog box when trying to play a sound or video off the IUMA site, you need to download and specify the correct MIME player.

■ note

Digital Audio Terminology

■ **Sample rates:** Sample rates are measured in kilohertz (KHz). Sound editing software is where the initial sample rate settings are established. Standard sample rates range from 11.025 KHz, 22.050 KHz, 44.10 KHz, to 48 KHz. The higher the sample rate, the better the quality. The sample rate affects the "range" of digitized sound, which describes its highs and lows.

■ **Bit-depth or Sampling Resolution:** Sampling resolution affects quality, just like dpi resolution affects the quality of images. Standard sampling resolutions are 8-bit mono, 8-bit stereo, 16-bit mono, and 16-bit stereo.

■ **µ-law:** µ-law used to be the only file format you'd find on the Web, as it is generated by Unix platforms. Now that Macs and PCs are the predominant platform of the Web, µ-law files are not seen as much. The sound quality is generally much lower than other sound formats, but the files are much smaller too. µ-law files always have the filename extension .AU.

■ **AIFC:** AIFC is a new spec for the older Audio Interchange File Format (AIFF). Both AIFF and AIFFC files can be read by this format. AIFF and AIFC files are commonly used on SGI and Macintosh computers. Only 16-bit sound data can be recorded using this format.

■ **MPEG:** MPEG audio is well-respected as a high-quality, excellent audio compression file format. MPEG audio has the advantage of a good compression scheme that doesn't sacrifice too much fidelity for the amount of bandwidth it saves. MPEG files tend to be small, and sound good. On the IUMA site, there are two sizes of MPEG files: stereo and mono. MPEG audio layer 2 files always have the filename extensions .MPG or .MP2. MPEG Audio layer 3 files have an .MP3 extension.

■ note

Digital Video Terminology

■ **FPS:** FPS stands for frames per second. A movie contains a certain number of frames, and the fewer frames, the more jerky the motion and the smaller the file size.

■ **Codec:** A codec is the type of compression and decompression standard used to make the movie file smaller for Web delivery.

■ **QuickTime:** QuickTime is a movie file format, just like GIF or JPEG is an image file format. QuickTime movies can either have a .MOV or a .QT filename extension.

■ **Data Rate:** Data rate relates to how fast the movie data was captured.

■ **Cinepak:** Cinepak is a very high form of movie compression. The compression type is called "lossy" because it causes a visible loss in quality. It is to video what µ-law is to audio.

Audio and Video Formats

Just like images, compression is critical to make audio and video files Web-savvy. IUMA supports a wide choice of file formats and compression-types, in both its audio and video areas.

IUMA accepts audio in any format, including cassette, CD, Dat, and vinyl. Evan Heitman, IUMA's site director, is responsible for converting the band's original analog submissions to digital files. An SGI Indy is used for the conversions, using onboard sound digitizing hardware and sound editing software.

The audio files are initially created as raw sound files saved in the AIFC format at the highest sampling rate and bit-depth (see audio and video terminology note). From there, they are converted to 8-bit/11.5 KHz µ-law files, and 44.1 KHz mono and stereo MPEG files. Xing's MPEG conversion software (■ http://www.xingtech.com/) is then applied. Each artist's page includes four possible selections for sounds: a short AU or MPEG excerpt, and a mono and stereo version of the entire song saved in MPEG.

Movies are digitized on a Macintosh 8100, using a video digitizing board. They are recorded at 160×120, 15 fps, using Cinepak compression and saved as QuickTime movies. Evan uses Premiere for simple editing features, like creating fades and dissolves in order to make shorter, smaller final movies.

One of the nice things about the IUMA site is the fact that file sizes are noted on their Web pages. This helps a potential listener know how long they must wait before downloading a file. See HTML deconstruction to learn how to set this up.

Movie and Audio File Tips from the Experts

If you're considering including audio or video on your Web site, here are some useful tips:

■ Remember that audio and video files will be downloaded, so keep file names short so your Windows 3.1 audience won't be excluded. Follow the eight-dot-three convention with your naming procedures, meaning your files should be named with titles no longer than eight characters, separated by a dot, and include a three (or two) letter extension. Here are some examples: sound.au, sound.mpg, video.mov.

■ QuickTime movies must be "flattened" before they can be viewed from the Web. This changes the resource fork so that the file can be read by all platforms, and not just Macintosh. There are many flattening utilities that can be downloaded from the Web. If you don't own one, try ■ ftp://ftp.utexas.edu/pub/mac/graphics/flattenmoov.hqx and download the program FlattenMoov. Premiere has a flattening feature found under the File, Export menu.

■ Make your movies small—small in pixels (160×120 is a standard size) and small in file size. Generally, most Web sites use Cinepak or Indeo codecs because they offer the most compression. Low fps rates help too—try 10–15 fps.

■ Always work from a high-quality original. Never recompress an already compressed movie or sound file. It will add ugly artifacts or unwanted noise.

■ Be sure to warn your audience about the file size, type, and player requirements for sound and video in advance of downloading.

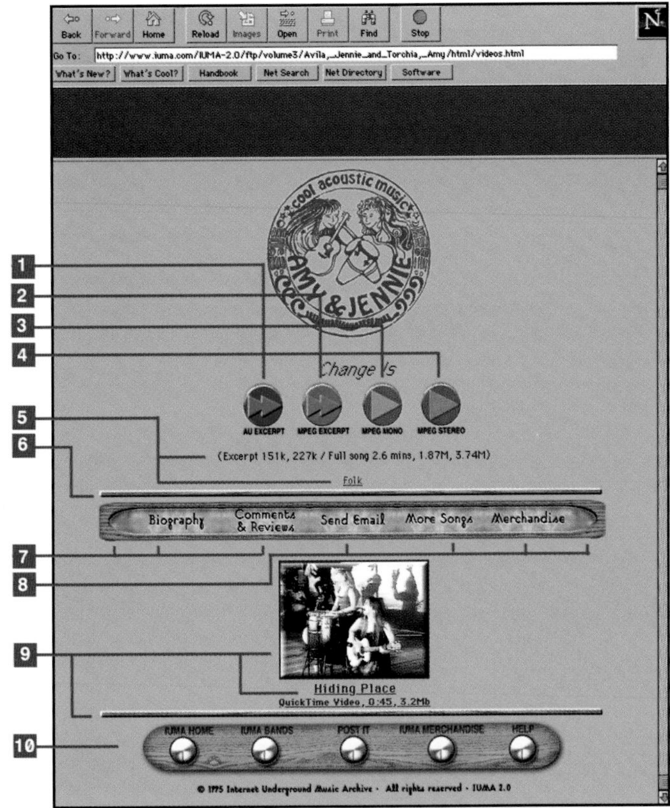

■ http://www.iuma.com/IUMA-2.0/ftp/volume3/Avila,_Jennie_and_Torchia,_Amy/html/videos.html. In this example, note the four types of audio files: AU Excerpt, MPEG Excerpt, or the full song in MPEG mono or MPEG stereo. The respective file sizes for both the audio and video files are also listed as a courtesy to viewers so they'll know how big the files are before deciding to download.

Embedding Media HTML

```
<!-- BEGIN SOURCE -->
<!-- TITLE Avila,_Jennie_and_Torchia,_Amy /TITLE -->
<BODY BGCOLOR="#c6c6c6">
<BASE TARGET="_top"
HREF="http://www.iuma.com/IUMA/Bands/Avila,_
Jennie_and_Torchia,_
Amy/html/">
<!-- AD INSERT -->
<!-- END -->
<CENTER>
<H1>
<IMG
ALT="Avila, Jennie and Torchia, Amy" SRC="/IUMA-
2.0/ftp/volume3/Avila,_Jennie_and_Torchia,_
Amy/sm-logo-Avila,_Jennie_and_Torchia,_Amy.gif">
</H1>
</CENTER>
<CENTER>
<I><FONT SIZE=5>Change Is</FONT></I><BR>
1 <A HREF="/IUMA-
2.0/ftp/volume3/Avila,_Jennie_and_Torchia,_
Amy/mono-excerpt-
Change_Is.au"><IMG ALIGN=MIDDLE BORDER=0
ALT="[AU Excerpt]"
SRC="/IUMA-2.0/imgs/olas/bandage/bdg-butt-
au-excerpt.gif"></A>
2 <A HREF="/IUMA-
2.0/ftp/volume3/Avila,_Jennie_and_Torchia,_
Amy/mono-excerpt-
Change_Is.mp2"><IMG
ALIGN=MIDDLE
BORDER=0
ALT="[MPEG Mono Excerpt]"
SRC="/IUMA-2.0/imgs/olas/bandage/bdg-butt-
mpeg-excerpt.gif"></A>
3 <A HREF="/IUMA-
2.0/ftp/volume3/Avila,_Jennie_and_Torchia,_
Amy/mono-
Change_Is.mp2"><IMG
ALIGN=MIDDLE BORDER=0
ALT="[MPEG Mono]"
SRC="/IUMA-2.0/imgs/olas/bandage/bdg-butt-mpeg-
mono.gif"></A
4 <A HREF="/IUMA-
2.0/ftp/volume3/Avila,_Jennie_and_Torchia,_
Amy/stereo-Change_Is.mp2"><IMG
ALIGN=MIDDLE BORDER=0
ALT="[MPEG Stereo]"
SRC="/IUMA-2.0/imgs/olas/bandage/bdg-butt-mpeg-
stereo.gif"></A>
<P>
5 <FONT SIZE=2>(Excerpt 151k, 227k / Full song 2.6
mins, 1.87M,
3.74M)</FONT></P>
</CENTER>
<CENTER>
<FONT SIZE=2>
<A HREF="/IUMA-
2.0/olas/genre/FO_001.html#Avila,_Jennie_and_
Torchia,_Amy">Folk</A>
</FONT>
</FONT>
</CENTER>
<CENTER>
```

6
```
<IMG ALT="---------------------------------------------------------------"
WIDTH=547 HEIGHT=11
SRC="/IUMA-2.0/imgs/olas/bandage/bdg-hr.gif">
<CENTER>
```
7
```
<IMG
ALT="[ "
WIDTH=36 HEIGHT=40
SRC="/IUMA-2.0/imgs/olas/bandage/bdg-butt-
lft_end.gif"> <A  HREF="/IUMA-
2.0/ftp/volume3/Avila,_Jennie_and_Torchia,_
Amy/index.html"><IMG
ALT="Biography"
BORDER=0
WIDTH=95 HEIGHT=40
SRC="/IUMA-2.0/imgs/olas/bandage/bdg-butt-
bio.gif"></A><A
HREF="http://www.iuma.com/iuma-bin/view-ola-
comment.pl?Avila,_Jennie_and_Torchia,_Amy">
<IMG  ALT="¦¦ Comments & Reviews"BORDER=0
WIDTH=95 HEIGHT=40
SRC="/IUMA-2.0/imgs/olas/bandage/bdg-butt-
comments.gif"></A>
```
8
```
A  HREF="mailto:jenamy1@aol.com"><IMG
ALT="¦¦ Email" BORDER=0
WIDTH=95 HEIGHT=40
SRC="/IUMA-2.0/imgs/olas/bandage/bdg-butt-
email.gif"></A>
<A  HREF="/IUMA-
2.0/ftp/volume3/Avila,_Jennie_and_Torchia,_Amy/html/
songs.html">
<IMG
ALT="¦¦ More Songs"
BORDER=0
WIDTH=95 HEIGHT=40
SRC="/IUMA-2.0/imgs/olas/bandage/bdg-butt-
mr_songs.gif"></A><A
HREF="/iuma-bin/buy.pl?init=Avila,_Jennie_and_
Torchia,_Amy"><IMG
ALT="¦¦ Ordering Info"
BORDER=0 WIDTH=95 HEIGHT=40
SRC="/IUMA-2.0/imgs/olas/bandage/bdg-butt-
order.gif"></A><IMG
ALT=" ]"
WIDTH=36 HEIGHT=40
SRC="/IUMA-2.0/imgs/olas/bandage/bdg-butt-
rt_end.gif">
<BR>
</CENTER>
</CENTER>
<BR>
<CENTER>
```
9
```
<AHREF="/IUMA/Bands/Avila,_
Jennie_and_Torchia,_Amy/Hiding_Place
.MOV" >
<IMG
WIDTH=160 HEIGHT=120
VSPACE=3
ALIGN=CENTER
SRC="/IUMA/Bands/Avila,_Jennie_and_
Torchia,_Amy/Hiding_Place-
bt.gif"><BR>
<B>Hiding Place<BR>
<FONT SIZE=1>QuickTime Video, 0:45,
3.2Mb</FONT></B><BR></A>
</CENTER>
<CENTER>
<IMG ALT="======="
WIDTH=547 HEIGHT=11
SRC="/IUMA-2.0/imgs/olas/bandage/bdg-hr.gif">
<BR>
```
10
```
<A HREF="/iuma-bin/nimagemap/IUMA-2.0
/imaps/bandage-
toolbar.map">
<IMG ALT="[Fine Oak Finished Toolbar]"
WIDTH=460 HEIGHT=59 BORDER=0
SRC="/IUMA-2.0/imgs/olas/bandage/bdg-tb.gif" ISMAP
USEMAP="#bandage-toolbar"></A>
<BR>
<MAP NAME="bandage-toolbar">
<AREA HREF="http://www.iuma.com/IUMA-
2.0/pages/home_page/homepage.html" SHAPE="rect"
COORDS="1,1,95,67">
<AREA HREF="http://www.iuma.com/IUMA-2.0/olas/"
SHAPE="rect"
COORDS="97,0,191,63">
<AREA HREF="http://www.iuma.com
/IUMA-2.0/olas/postit/" SHAPE="rect"
COORDS="194,1,271,69">
<AREA HREF="http://www.iuma.com/IUMA-
2.0/olas/extras/merch/"
SHAPE="rect" COORDS="273,1,387,65">
<AREA HREF="http://www.iuma.com/IUMA-2.0/help/"
SHAPE="rect"
COORDS="391,1,463,67">
</MAP>
<IMG ALT="Copyright (C) 1995 Internet Underground
Music Archive"
WIDTH=365 HEIGHT=16
SRC="/IUMA-2.0/imgs/copyright.gif">
</CENTER>
```

tags

Embedding Media Deconstruction

1 The anchor tag <A HREF> links to the .AU excerpt sound file. The image tag <IMG> links to the au-excerpt.gif, which is an arrow icon.

2 The anchor tag <A HREF> links to the .MPG excerpt sound file. The image tag <IMG> links to the mpeg-excerpt.gif, which is an arrow icon.

3 The anchor tag <A HREF> links to the mono .MPG sound file. The image tag <IMG> links to the mpeg-mono.gif, which is an arrow icon.

4 The anchor tag <A HREF> links to the stereo .MPG sound file. The image tag <IMG> links to the mpeg-stereo.gif, which is an arrow icon.

5 This is where the file size warnings are located.

6 A custom horizontal rule was used here. The ALT tag, used for text-only browsers so they know what this document contained without seeing the graphic, is suggesting a rule with the long underline, while the <IMG SRC> is specifying the artwork bdg-hr.gif.

7 The <IMG SRC> tag is used to specify the artwork butt-lft_end.gif. The entire bar that says Biography, Comments & Reviews, Send Email, More Songs, and Merchandise is made up of individual linked images that rest next to each other. This is an alternative method to using image maps.

8 The mailto tag is being used within the anchor tag to specify the e-mail address of this band. It is linked to the <IMG SRC> butt-email.gif.

9 The anchor tag <A HREF> is linked to the QuickTime movie file, AmyHiding_Place.MOV. The actual movie does not appear as an inline image within an HTML page. Instead, a GIF is used to represent a frame from the movie. The image tag <IMG> links to the Hiding_Place-bt.gif file.

10 The bottom toolbar, unlike the middle one, is an image map, rather than a series of linked images. It's both a client-side and server-side map. You can always tell a client-side map by the use of the USEMAP and MAP NAME tags. You can always tell a server-side map is in use when the ISMAP tag is present. For more information on client-side and server-side image maps, read Chapter 5, "@tlas."

IUMA's Use of CGI Programming

IUMA uses proprietary CGI programming for many of the features on their site. One script reads the http header of each visitor to the site and displays a different page with or without a frame depending on which incoming browser is detected. Another script collects statistical data, giving the 800+ band members who use IUMA's services details on how many hits their pages are getting and which of their songs or videos are most popular.

STATISTICAL REPORT:

```
Statistical report for: Avila,_Jennie_and_Torchia,_
Amy Date range: /extra/log/phrase-2/96-04-01 thru
/extra/log/phrase-2/96-06-30

  Biography: 658
  Small images: 5505
  Other images: 1794

  These_Small_Things
    Stereo: 15
    Mono: 8
    Excerpt: 11

  Change_Is
    Stereo: 117
    Mono: 46
    Excerpt: 253

  Song access breakdown for location
    US Commercial (COM): 158
    Network (NET): 109
    Unknown (UNKNOWN): 66
    US Educational (EDU): 52
    Japan (JP): 22
    Canada (CA): 6
    Sweden (SE): 5
    Australia (AU): 5
    France (FR): 4
    Malaysia (MY): 3
    US Government (GOV): 3
    Belgium (BE): 2
    Germany (DE): 2
    Non-Profit (ORG): 2
    Mexico (MX): 2
    New Zealand (NZ): 2
    Norway (NO): 1
    Uruguay (UY): 1
    Netherlands (NL): 1
    Spain (ES): 1
    Denmark (DK): 1
    Israel (IL): 1
    Finland (FI): 1
```

Here's an example of a statistical report for one of IUMA's clients. It breaks down each hit, which files were accessed, and country of origin.

IUMA recently introduced rotating advertising banners that appear at the top of every page. A script is used to change the banner every 30 seconds, which gives each sponsor equal time on any given page within the site. The IUMA CGI scripts were programmed by Jeff Patterson, Technical Director and President of IUMA, who uses everything from sh, Perl, and TCL to C Shell.

Jeff learned programming when he took classes at Berkeley in C and C++. Learning Perl and some of the other languages he writes scripts in was much easier after having one programming language under his belt. Though Jeff is excited about many of the new Web technologies like Java, Shockwave, and VRML, he has adopted a cautious approach toward using technology for technology's sake. It's important that the technology have enough added value to warrant the potential loss of accessibility to those IUMA visitors coming to the site with older browsers.

Here are Jeff's recommendations for learning CGI and Java:

- *Programming Perl* by O'Reilly and Associates
- *Java in a Nutshell* by O'Reilly and Associates
- http://www.cuiwww.unige.ch/eao/www/TclTkMan/
- http://www.java.sun.com/products/JDK/CurrentRelease/apil

The biggest challenge for Jeff was creating the advertising banner campaign, which creates statistics reports for both internal use, and for the advertisers. His program is able to even tell advertisers how many times their ad was viewed, and by what location and country.

IUMA introduced advertising banners as an effort to minimize the costs to independent musicians who want to use IUMA's services. The response to the banners has been overwhelmingly positive, even though advertising on the Internet is usually a fairly controversial issue. Most IUMA visitors and members are appreciative of what the site offers, and are grateful that costs to subscribers are kept low through advertising subsidies.

■ site summary

IUMA

IUMA has designed a business that offers a service to its viewers and members that couldn't be achieved through any other medium than the Web. It demonstrates how important it is to have a clear mission and goal, and how skillful and practical use of technology and design can help reach those objectives.

■ A visual identity system needs to make a statement and stick to it with consistency. The IUMA screens work on both an aesthetic and functional level to establish navigation and viewer confidence.

■ Having a thorough command of advanced Photoshop techniques can make the difference between standard images or exceptional graphics.

■ Scanning doesn't have to only include flat artwork. 3-D objects can be set on a flatbed scanner and produce remarkable effects.

■ When embedding movie and sound files, be sure to let your audience know how big they are and what file formats to expect.

Construct

designing for vrml

What this chapter covers:

- **What is VRML?**
- **VRML Deconstruction**
- **VRML Browsers**
- **VRML Authoring Tools**

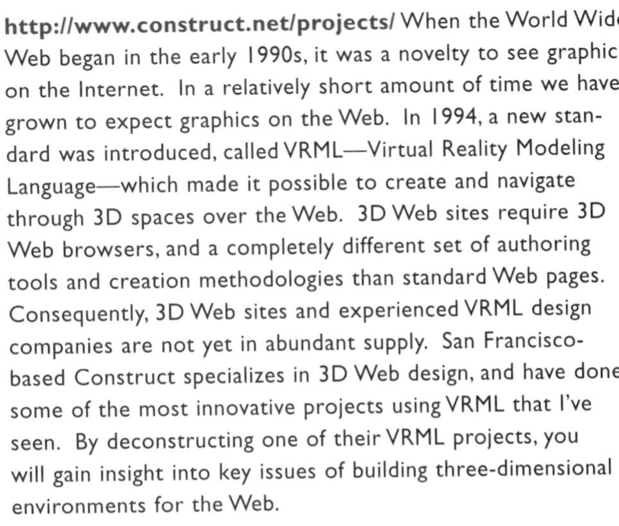

http://www.construct.net/projects/ When the World Wide Web began in the early 1990s, it was a novelty to see graphics on the Internet. In a relatively short amount of time we have grown to expect graphics on the Web. In 1994, a new standard was introduced, called VRML—Virtual Reality Modeling Language—which made it possible to create and navigate through 3D spaces over the Web. 3D Web sites require 3D Web browsers, and a completely different set of authoring tools and creation methodologies than standard Web pages. Consequently, 3D Web sites and experienced VRML design companies are not yet in abundant supply. San Francisco-based Construct specializes in 3D Web design, and have done some of the most innovative projects using VRML that I've seen. By deconstructing one of their VRML projects, you will gain insight into key issues of building three-dimensional environments for the Web.

Client: Fourth Foresight Conference on Molecular Nanotechnology

URL: http://www.construct.net/projects/

Type of Site: VRML

Server: Sun Netra

Operating System: Solaris 2.4

Server Software: Netsite Communication Server

Project Manager: Todd Goldenbaum

Webmistress: Annette Loudon

Lead Designer: Mark Meadows

3D Architect: Michael Gough

Software: 3D Studio Max, 3Design, FormZ, Web Space Author

Construct: A 3D Web Design Firm

Construct was formed in 1995 by a team of volunteers who got to know each other while working at the 1994 Interactive Media Festival, which was held at the Variety Arts Center in Los Angeles. The group developed one of the first VRML sites: a 3D online version of the festival's gallery, called ARC (■ http://spark.com/). Based on the success of that project, they became convinced of the need for an Internet design firm that specialized in the creation of 3D online experiences, and formed Construct.

Construct has built and designed many noteworthy VRML sites. Some of their most advanced work has included VRML spaces for multi-users, a 3D gallery space that anyone can post images to, and a 3D Virtual Trade Show kiosk. If you are interested in seeing more of their work than what this chapter covers, pay their site a visit at: ■ http://www.construct.net.

I chose their work for The Fourth Foresight Conference on Molecular Nanotechnology as the project to profile in this chapter because of its simplicity. Though Construct has created many VRML projects far more complex and cutting-edge than this one, I am assuming that most of the readers of this book are new to 3D and VRML, so this project seemed appropriate.

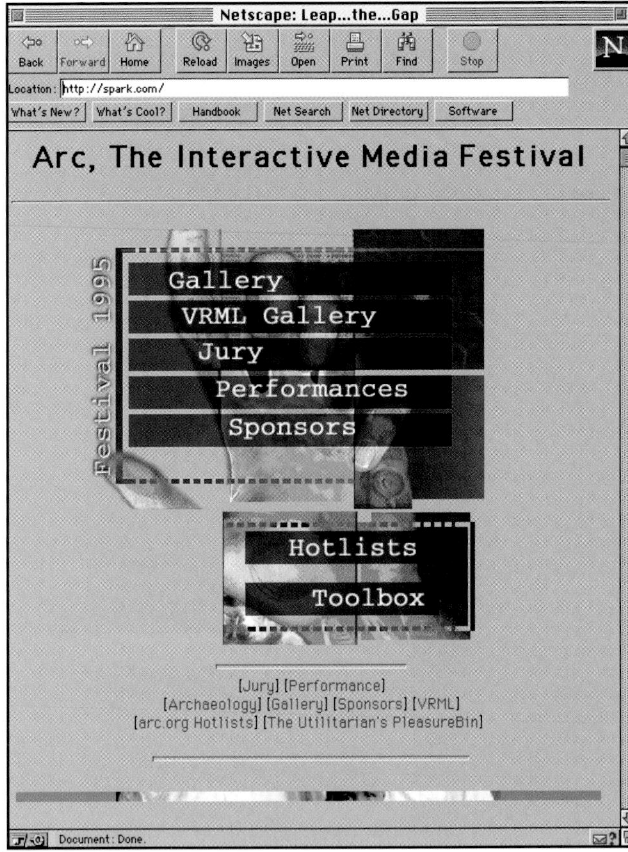

Visit ARC (■ http://spark.com/) to see one of the first implementations of a VRML-authored site. Construct was formed from the same group who worked on the Interactive Media Festival's project.

What is VRML?

VRML (Virtual Reality Modeling Language) is a protocol for distributing and viewing 3D models over the Internet. HTML has become the industry standard for authoring 2D Web pages, and VRML is its 3D equivalent. VRML enables authors to build models and assign colors, lighting, texture, and behavior attributes and publish them on the Web for distribution. VRML-enabled browsers provide the capability to display 3-dimensional objects, adjust lighting, and navigate freely around them. Most importantly, VRML enables 3D objects and groups of objects, or worlds, to link to other objects, text, images, sounds, and other worlds.

How VRML Works in Simplified Terms

Creating a VRML site involves building 3D models; assigning physical attributes such as color, lighting, and texture; and saving the data in the .wrl or .wrl.gz format so a VRML-enabled browser can display the results (to find a VRML-enabled browser, refer to the list at the end of this chapter). The 3D models are generally created in an authoring tool, such as a 3D modeling and animation program. This is contrary to HTML, which is generally written from scratch using a text editor. VRML data is automatically generated from a VRML authoring tool or translator, though it can also be easily modified in a text editor.

Many 3D programs write files in the .wrl format, which is what VRML browsers require (similar to the way the .html or .htm extensions work for HTML files). If you are used to working with a 3D software application, and find that it doesn't support the .wrl format, there are many "translator" programs (see the list that appears at the end of this section) that will convert common 3D data (such as .DXF files) to VRML data.

After the .wrl file is transferred to a live Web server, VRML worlds need to be viewed from a VRML-enabled browser (see the list at the end of this section). Most browsers allow users to navigate around 3D space and models, change lights, and access hyperlinks.

The principle behind VRML is that the data gets rendered on the client's machine. That means that when you access a VRML site, you are only downloading a small model with a small script. The browser interprets the script, displays the model, and renders an image with lighting, color, and texture on your machine. Everything happens much more quickly than if fully rendered models were being transferred.

Many VRML files are much smaller than standard 2D Web pages. When texture maps are in use, they need to be downloaded as well. Typically the model geometry with assigned attributes is quite small, whereas texture map files are larger and take the most time to download.

■ note

Short Glossary of VRML and 3D Terms

Like any new computer language or protocol, VRML has its own terminology that is foreign and intimidating at first. This chapter is intended to demystify some of the issues present when authoring, viewing, or navigating VRML worlds. Here's an abbreviated glossary of VRML and 3D terminology:

■ **Attributes:** Defined appearances or behaviors of 3D objects. For example, a lighting attribute would affect the colors and lights of an object. A texture attribute would affect the surface texture of an object.

■ **Lighting:** 3D artwork responds to lighting in a realistic manner, so lighting will affect overall appearance and color.

■ **Materials:** Material attributes affect the appearance of models, such as how shiny or transparent they appear.

■ **Model:** A 3D model is constructed with X, Y, and Z (width, height, and depth, respectively) coordinates. 2D artwork only has X and Y coordinates (width and height). 3D models are generally constructed with back, front, side, bottom, and top views, so that they can be viewed from any angle.

■ **Modeling:** The process of creating a model.

■ **Modeler:** A person who builds models.

■ **Object:** The word "model" and "object" are sometimes used interchangeably. A model could be built from many objects. Sometimes the individual components within a model are called objects.

■ **Object Resolution:** Relates to how many polygons form a shape. High resolution objects include many polygons, look the best, and take the longest to render. Low resolution objects have fewer polygons and render more quickly.

■ **Polygon:** VRML data is constructed from polygons. The dictionary definition of a polygon is: a closed plane figure bounded by straight lines. Triangles, squares, geodesic domes, hexagons, and cubes are all created with polygons. Spheres, when created from polygons, are formed with many straight lines. If the amount of polygons within a sphere is low, the sphere will have a lot of "steps" and won't look smooth. Most polygons are triangular; some are quadrangular.

■ **3D Render:** The computer process of calculating 3D data and displaying the results on the computer screen.

■ **Texture Map:** 2D artwork that is applied to the surface of a 3D shape.

■ note

3D VRML Terminology

■ **Behaviors:** In VRML 2.0, behavioral information can be embedded into any object. A common type of "behavior" is animation. A simple example could be a 3D model of an electric fan, and the fan blades could be assigned a fixed "behavior" to rotate.

■ **Group:** Grouping allows collections of objects to be treated as single objects. The group is a container for all the objects, so that nodes can be applied to multiple objects. If an object has two colors, chances are it has two groups.

■ **Inlining:** The process of embedding one VRML file into another.

■ **LOD (Level Of Detail):** The process of including more detailed models with higher polygon counts that are accessed based on the distance of the viewer. A low resolution object can appear at a faraway distance, and be replaced with a more detailed model at close-up distances.

■ **Node:** Theoretically, VRML objects can contain anything from 3D geometry to MIDI files or JPEG images. What the object contains is called a "node." VRML defines three different categories of nodes: shape, property, and group nodes.

■ **Worlds:** Instead of Web "pages" or "screens," VRML sites are called "worlds."

The Nanotechnology VRML Project

For the Fourth Foresight Conference on Molecular Nanotechnology, Construct modeled visualizations of sleeves, bearings, nanomechanical computers, and assemblers in an attempt to create a more useful visualization of what nanotechnology might look like. The models were all based on the diagrams shown in K. Eric Drexler's book, *Nanosystems.*

Designing for 3D Space

Lead designer Mark Meadows chose to make the Nanotechnolgy models look dark and mysterious, using deep saturated colors for the lighting and surface colors, even though, in reality, the models would theoretically be made from flat, black carbon, and be too small

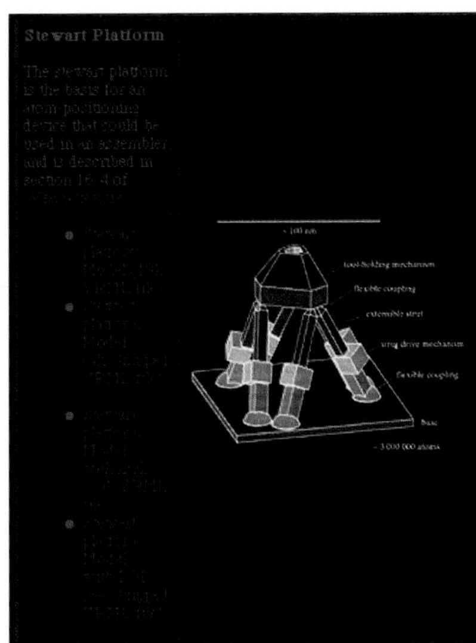

Here's an example of an original diagram for the Stewart Platform Device from K. Eric Drexler's book, *Nanosystems*, from which the VRML models were based: (■ http://www.construct.net/projects/).

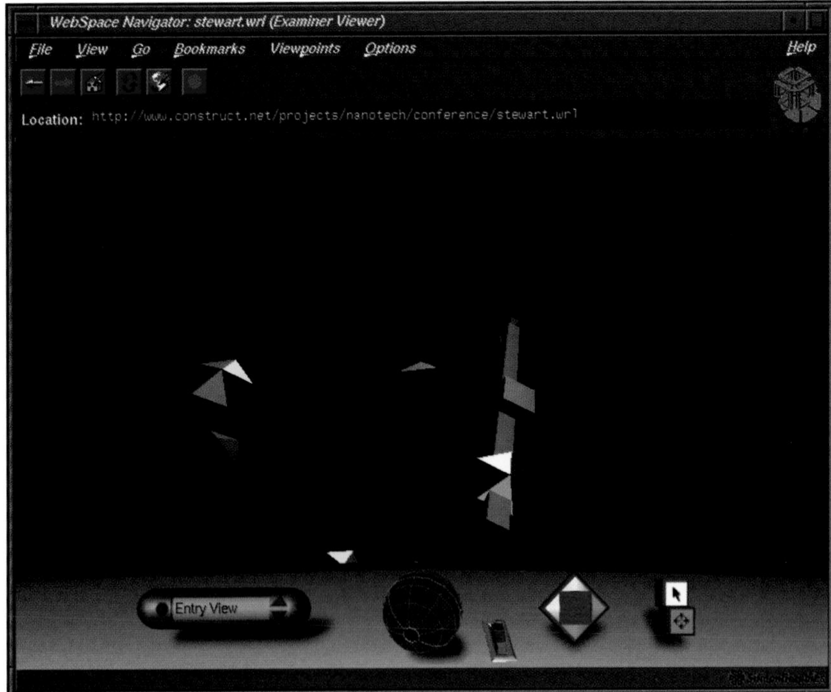

Here's an example of the Stewart Platform computer model built, lit, and colored by Construct, as seen within a VRML browser. A VRML-enabled browser would let you view this model from any distance or angle.

to see—they'd be the size of a molecule! Mark took artistic liberties to add color and lighting to make the models more compelling and attractive.

Mark talked about his three key objectives when designing 3D sites: interface, architecture, and compatibility:

Interface is a somewhat theoretical pursuit. The Nanotechology site did not pose a difficult interface challenge. The viewer was expected to view one model at a time; each within its own context. But in other projects, where one is dealing with complex, multi-tiered environments, arriving at solid interface metaphors is critical. Mark referred to the early days at Xerox Parc, where engineers first created GUIs (Graphical User Interfaces). Back then, no one had thought of embedding a window within a window, and even though the interface was graphical, it still relied heavily on scrolling text. Mark thinks the early days of VRML are equivalent, in that the emphasis so far has been on getting through the technical hurdles of establishing a 3D protocol. The next big thrust, in his opinion, will be making navigation and interface more cohesive and meaningful.

Architecture is a term rarely used in 3D graphics, but Construct believes that 3D spaces involve many of the same issues as building physical spaces in the non-virtual world—complete with rooms, floorplans, and ergonomics considerations. It's no surprise that they've hired Michael Gough, a trained architect, to design some of their 3D spaces. Another architect, Mark Lawton, shares the load.

Compatibility relates to paying close attention to which VRML features are supported within which browser. Just like in HTML, decisions have to be made in terms of which browsers support certain tags. It's possible to include or omit a feature that makes a VRML site platform- or browser-specific, so Mark and team keep a close watch on new browser beta releases. Working with as few polygons as possible is also of paramount importance. Mark compared the notion of defining a shape with minimal detail to Japanese gesture drawing. Working with fewer polygons makes it more challenging to the designer; but Mark and team seem to thrive on overcoming limitations and using economy of design to their best interest.

note

VRML 2.0

When VRML 1.0 was released, its creators, Mark Pesce and Tony Parisi, knew it would be missing some key features. The idea was to agree quickly upon a standard so development could begin, with the understanding that more features would be offered later. The Nanotechnology project, profiled in this chapter, for example, was authored in VRML 1.0.

The most significant new feature added to version 2.0 is the capability to embed "behaviors" into 3D scenes. This means that objects can now include animation properties, or pre-set capabilities. You could, for example, include an oil rig in a VRML scene and show it pumping while the viewer could navigate around it and look at any view while it was still moving.

■ tip

3D Design Process

"Three dimensional Internet design is a largely unexplored landscape. The technology is embryonic, the issues are tangled, and the applications are distant, but that's what makes it fun. It's unknown. It's raw imagination; architecture, sculpture, stage sets, illustration, light engineering, and a million other disciplines all fall under the too-broad heading of "3D Design." The sheer number of the implications is a swarm that confuses people that are approaching the field, distracting them from the most important issues of this branch of digital design: information and interactivity.

■ Here are three very general, though useful, approaches to follow as you build worlds:

The first is the ability to abstract—the ability to compress an idea or image. Abstraction takes the parts of the idea and distills those ideas down to their most important components, stripping obvious, or understood, elements and leaving a calcified kernel that is then rehydrated with the imagination of the viewer.

You only have a limited budget of information to work within—use it well. As you consider what polygons to use where, suggest form more than you represent it. Sketch more than sculpt. For example, if you only have 20 boxes that you can use to describe the human form then be sure to use them wisely, showing the most important information first. Ask yourself what you look at most when you see a human form—the fingers or the eyes? The ears or the hair? The lips or the feet? Where is the critical information? Once you've answered that question, you know what to model and what to strip.

The second is the ability to improvise. Improvisation is a survival skill where there are few resources, and VRML is certainly sparse terrain. Improvise your use of line, your suggestion of space, and your overall composition and content. Ask yourself what VRML can do that no other protocol can do, and use those answers to guide your improvisation. Explore the grammar for the sake of the poetry. Push the protocol to its limit. Unless you do otherwise, you're developing for another medium. This ain't TeeVee and it ain't a magazine.

The third approach is the ability to optimize. Optimize everything. Virtual reality is more about interactivity than it is about geometry, so make sure things move fast and that the user is able to both orient themselves and navigate the space so that their disbelief is suspended and they feel free to go where they will. Make sure the files you are building can be interactively rendered at above 10 frames per second on a Pentium 90 MHz. Dont build VRML for the SGIs and high-end workstations. Let those guys build their own. Build rich worlds that anyone can look at on a simple machine. And "rich" doesn't necessarily mean complicated, either. Sometimes it means just the opposite. Interactivity is what makes the file interesting beyond its graphical representation—it's the single element that offers freedom to the user. And aside from freedom interactivity adds a whole level of design that needs to be carefully considered—kinematics.

VRML design is not about replicating reality, but about articulating imagination. Cyberspace is a different environment from the one we live in. If you want the real world, don't look for it in the computer. Go outside."

-Mark Meadows, Lead Designer at Construct

Modeling Tools for VRML

Learning to work in 3D space is very different from creating graphics in a 2D environment. Most of us don't think in terms of X, Y, Z coordinates, building objects with polygons, or creating artwork with techniques that involve lathing, drilling, and extruding.

Learning a modeling program is a complex undertaking because there are very few similarities from program to program. Learning one modeling program does not necessarily make it easier to learn the next one. The result is that most people like to stick with whichever modeling program they know well, and it's hard to want to change because the learning curve can be so high. Some of Construct's modelers use Macs, some Windows, and some SGIs. The point here is that almost everyone in the company has a different preference for specific modeling software. Consequently, the Nanotechnology site's models were created on FormZ for the Mac, 3D Studio MAX for Windows, and Webspace Author for SGI.

Because efficient Web delivery depends on downloading speed, VRML modelers must learn to create objects with the fewest number of polygons possible. The fewer the polygons, the faster the rendering speed. The file size is not always the problem, it's also the speed of rendering on the end user's CPU.

Just like print designers who are used to working on 100 MB files, professional modelers pride themselves on making high resolution models with plenty of detail and definition. The mindset of the VRML modeler must think in terms of economy of design and polygons.

Most 3D programs offer "primitives," or stock objects like cones, cubes, and spheres as building blocks for models. This approach to modeling is perfect for VRML because using simple shapes with low polygon counts is critical to the success of each project. Many VRML modeling programs additionally offer a feature called "decimation," which is a mathematical process of reducing the polygon count through a filtering process.

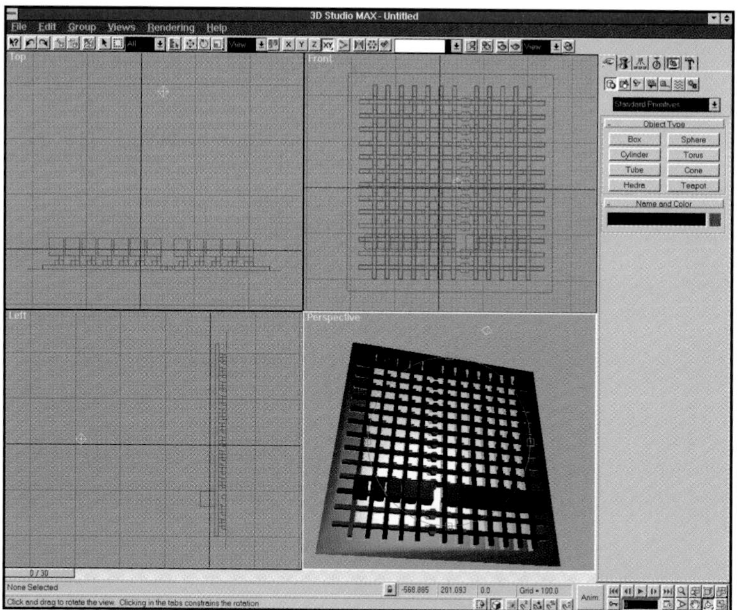

The nanochip model was created in 3D Studio MAX. Note the four views: top, side, front, and preview perspective. This enables a modeler to accurately position and assign lights and colors to the object while still being able to freely edit the shapes.

In 3D Studio MAX, it's possible to interactively pull on a shape, such as the burgundy chip in the lower preview perspective view, and see the results in all the windows. This process is called "extruding."

LOD Nodes

A popular technique in VRML is to create LOD nodes, or Level Of Detail models. This is the process of creating two or more models; one in low detail and the other in high detail. The browser knows when to show which model. If the range is long (that is, if the object is far away) the low-poly model is shown. If the range is short, then the high-poly model is shown. This saves rendering time, which translates into speedier browser and viewing performance.

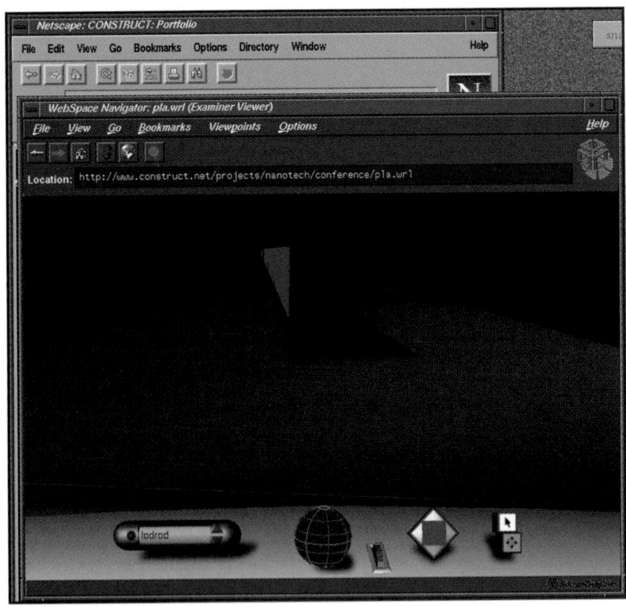

Here's an example of LOD in action. This model looks simple from far away.

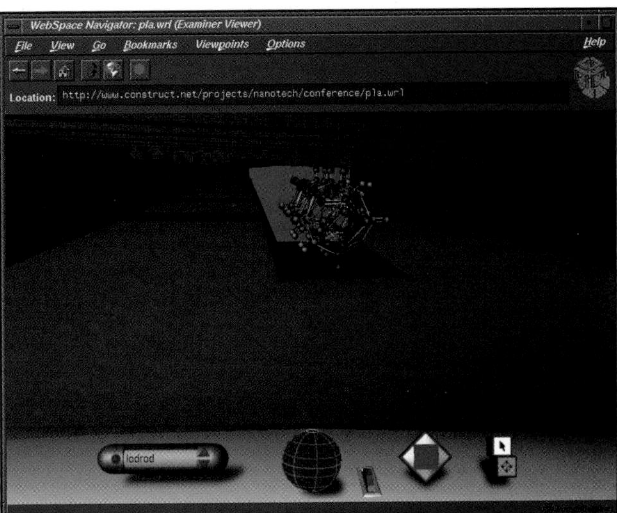

When you zoom into the object, a higher detail model appears. This is called LOD, or Level Of Detail.

Lighting and other Surface Attributes

Lighting and surface attributes are typically set up in the modeling/authoring program, which stores the information in a resulting .wrl file. The .wrl file contains the data about the object, its position in a 3D environment, its position relative to other objects, and its lighting and surface attributes.

If you examine the code in the VRML deconstruction, you'll find settings for options such as transparency, specularity, emissive light, and diffusion. Here are some visual examples that explain what these terms mean:

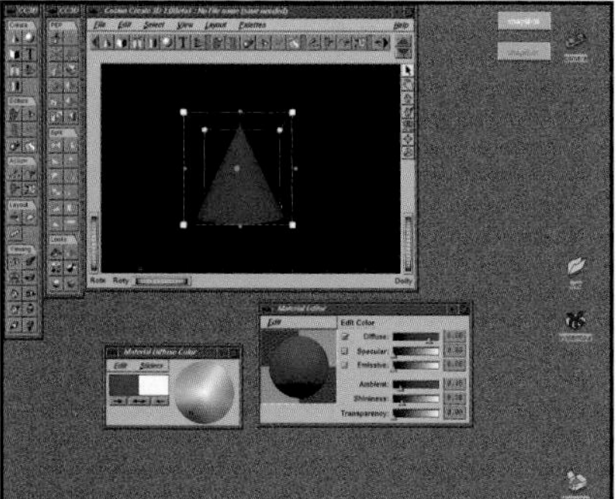

Adjusting the "diffuse" attribute affects a model's color.

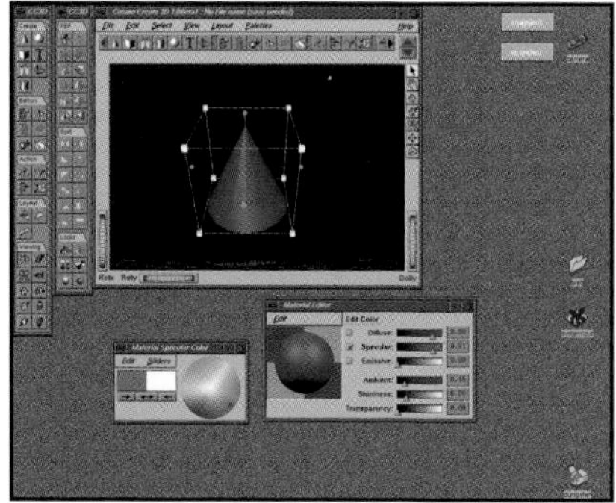

Setting the attribute for "specular" lighting. The specular light is pink, and its specular value affects how reflective the cone is.

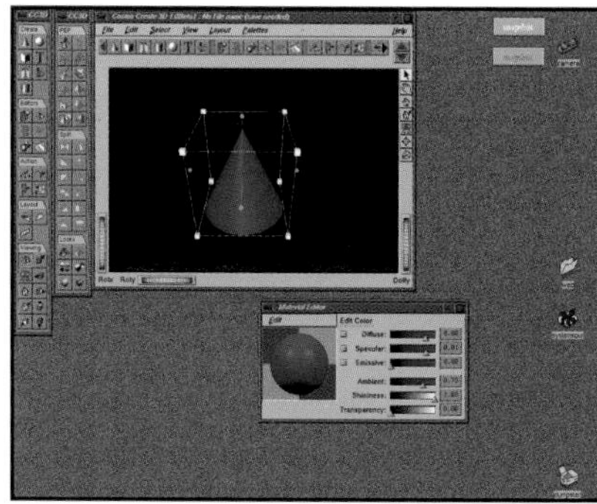

Here's an example of "shininess" turned all the way up.

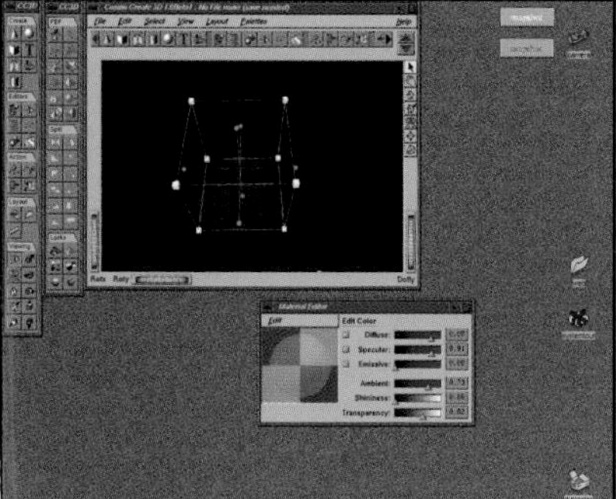

Previewing what the object looks like with transparent settings.

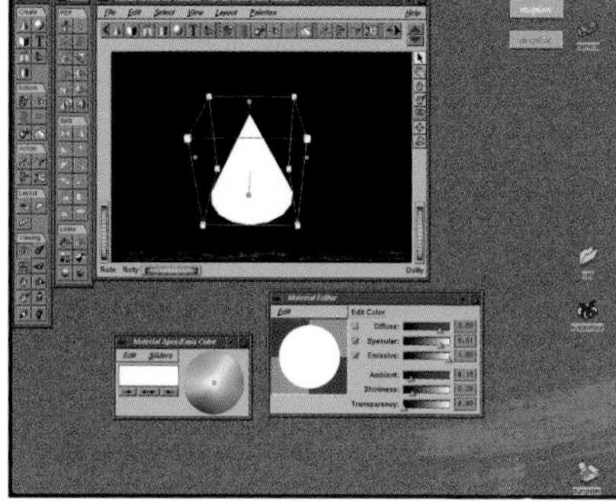

Emissive light can overpower other types of lighting. It is intended to simulate the appearance of light from within an object.

VRML Deconstruction

Unlike HTML, VRML code is most often generated by a 3D authoring program. VRML code can be written from scratch, like HTML, but most of the information contains coordinates and mathematical values that would be difficult for most non-programmers to code. It's possible to view the source of VRML code, just like HTML.

VRML is based on the Open Inventor ASCII File Format from Silicon Graphics. A subset of the Inventor File Format was agreed upon with added extensions to support networking.

Here's a look at a portion of a .wrl script generated by a VRML authoring program. Typically the scripts for VRML are much lengthier than HTML text files. There's not enough room to show this script in its entirety, so I've selected a portion that is representative of key issues and concepts.

The Webforce VRML browser's view source code feature.

.WRL Script

```
1  #VRML V1.0 ascii
2  Separator {
3  PointLight {
4  on TRUE
5  intensity 1
6  color 0.964706 0.964706 0.964706
   location 400 3240 100
   }
7  DEF R1 Group {
   Separator {
   Group {
8  Material {
9  ambientColor 0.0235294 0.0235294 0.0235294
10 diffuseColor 0.0941176 0.0941176 0.0941176
11 specularColor 0.0862745 0.0352941 0.458824
12 transparency 0
   }
   }
13 Coordinate3 {
   point [ 2380 -280.001 1830,
   -1820 -280.001 1830,
   -1820 -280.001 1910,
   2380 -280.001 1910,
   2380 -360.001 1830,
   -1820 -360.001 1830,
   -1820 -360.001 1910,
   2380 -360.001 1910 ]
```

note

Rendering Speed

One of the main misconceptions about VRML is that it is slow to download. Not true! It's slow for the end user's machine to render—if the models are not built well. One of the main disciplines Construct prides them-self on is to minimize the number of polygons in their scenes. This is a paramount design consideration, because the fewer the polygons the cleaner the interactivity. This means that sometimes the graphical elements suffer as a result, but Construct's attitude is that speed and performance outweigh prettier pictures.

tags

.WRL Deconstruction

1 This provides header information that identifies this as a VRML 1.0 document.

2 This isolates each command.

3 This sets the point light for the browser. A point light is one of three different types of lights: PointLight, SpotLight, or DirectionalLight.

4 This tells the point light to be on.

5 This sets the point light to full intensity. Here it is set to 1.

6 Color assigns RGB color values for the object.

7 This identifies whether the object is grouped or not. Grouping an object makes it possible to assign attributes to more than one model.

8 This sets material attributes.

9 This indicates the overall color of the light of the 3D space.

10 This sets the color of the object.

11 This sets the color of highlights in the object.

12 This dictates whether the object is see-through or not.

13 This specifies the object's position.

tip

How to Choose a VRML Authoring Program

If you're considering purchasing a modeling program for use on a VRML project, consider the following:

- Does it offer the capability to decimate, or reduce polygon counts without requiring a filter?
- Does it enable you to interactively preview color and lighting?
- Does it write .wrl files directly, or will you need an additional translator?
- Can you create animation in it for VRML 2.0 behaviors?
- Do other VRML authors use it and like it? Check in with some of the discussion groups and forums to see what others are using. See this site's summary for listing.

How to Set Up Links in VRML

Links can be set up two different ways in VRML projects. A 3D model can be set to link to another 3D object, environment, or page, or a 2D Web page can be set to link to a 3D VRML file. Let's look at both scenarios:

Example 1: Here's how to link to HTML within VRML:

```
DEF Guidebook WWWAnchor { name
"http://www.planetitaly.com/Culture/Nature/index.html"
description "Nature"}
```

- DEF Guidebook WWWAnchor { establishes the beginning of the link. The description is what the browser displays when the mouse is over the link. If more than one object were inside the WWWAnchor node, they would all be linked. The last } functions like a closed anchor tag—</A> in HTML.

Example 2: Here's how to link HTML to VRML:

```
<A HREF="http://www.construct.net/
worlds/spiral1.wrl.gz>Spiral</A>
```

- Basically, this takes a standard <a href></a> link, but the file type can be .wrl or .wrl.gz, which will produce a 3D navigable image if the browser supports it.

VRML Browsers

In order to view VRML pages, you will need a VRML-enabled Web browser. There are many browsers to choose from, all with varying degrees of support for VRML standards. Unfortunately, the 3D Web author and end user have just as much trouble with browser consistency as their 2D counterparts.

One of the most maddening things about the way different browsers handle VRML files is how they render color. To date, most VRML browsers only display 256 colors. This means that many of the same palette management horrors that 2D Web designers face are even worse for VRML creators. Most 2D Web browsers at least share the same fixed 216-color palette. With VRML browsers, each one has its own rendering technique, and unique set of 256 colors. This makes it impossible to author an object and have the assigned colors look identical between browsers. No good solution is really available, except to view your color choices on more than one platform within more than one browser and make necessary changes when unacceptable color variations occur.

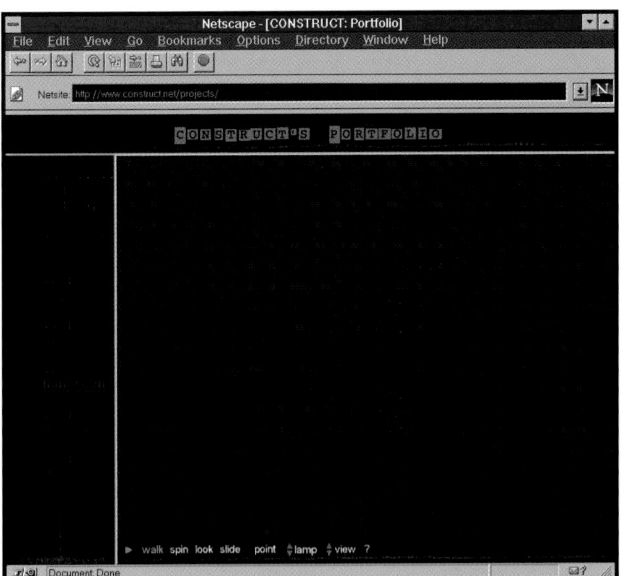

Here's an example of a model shown in the Live3D browser by Netscape.

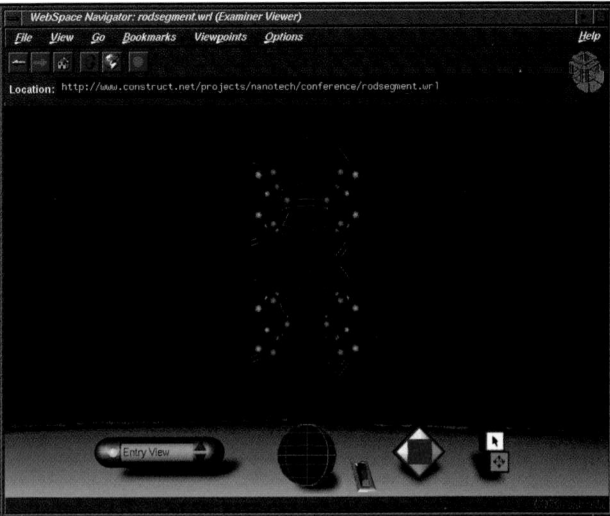

Here's the identical file shown within SGI's Webforce browser. Notice the difference in color!

VRML Tools: Browsers/Modeling Programs/Translators

Construct's Web site (■ http://www.construct.net/) is a great resource for gathering any kind of information about VRML. A list of VRML resources is reproduced here, complete with commentary from Construct's Webmistress extraordinaire Annette Loudon. She is candid about her personal opinions, preferences, and known and unknown quirks and bugs found within her list. You might also want to check this list from Construct's site as well (■ http://www.construct.net/tools/), because URLs change and newer VRML browsers are always on the market .

Browser Resources

Amber G

Dive Laboratories

■ http://www.divelabs.com/vrml.htm
Currently Supported Platforms:
Windows NT

This browser does not implement hyperlinking (WWWAnchor), or ASCIIText, and it has a limited navigation model. You can either orbit something in a fixed plane or fly around the model. There is no mode for moving the object being viewed.

i3d

Center for Advanced Studies, Research and Development in Sardinia

■ http://sgvenus.cern.ch/i3d
Currently supported platforms:
SGI under IRIX 5.2 or later

This is an SGI browser. It also supports the i3D format, which is specific to this browser as far as we can tell. It's interesting how many browsers support VRML and some other (proprietary) format. The nice thing about this browser is that it supports LCD shutter glasses (CrystalEyes) and Spaceballs. There are no plans to port this browser to the PC or Macintosh.

Live3D

Netscape (originally Paper Inc.)

■ http://home.netscape.com/comprod/products/navigator/ live3d/"
Currently supported platforms: Power Mac, Windows 3.1, Windows 95, and Windows NT

Live3D features 3D text, background images, texture animation, morphing, viewpoints, collision detection, gravity, and RealAudio streaming sound.

Live 3D is also available for Windows and Power Macintosh as part of Netscape Navigator 3.0:

■ http://home.netscape.com/comprod/products/navigator/ version_3.0/index.html".

And guess what folks, IT WORKS and IT WORKS WELL! Beta 4 for the Mac doesn't support links yet, and whilst using Navigator 3.0 and the Live 3D plug-in, my computer has been known to crash.

Pueblo

Chaco Communications

■ http://www.chaco.com/pueblo
Currently supported platforms:
Windows 95 and Windows NT

Pueblo is a VRML/HTML client that also hooks up to MUDs. MUDs, or multi-user domains, are servers that allow interactive behaviors. Hooking up VRML and HTML to a MUD is interesting because it allows these normally static and stateless media to have behaviors and memory. Chaco calls its version of VRML that supports these environments "I-VRML." It remains to be seen how successful this will be. The browser itself is implemented quite well, although the speed suffers because of the choice of rendering libraries. The inside word is that they are switching to a new, faster rendering library, which hopefully will mean it will get more usable in the near future.

Vrealm

Integrated Data Systems, Inc.

■ http://www.ids-net.com/ids/3dexp1.html" TARGET
Currently supported platforms:
Windows (95, NT)

This is an Open Inventor-based browser running on the PC. That probably means it's incredibly slow. This is another "VRML + something else" browser. In this case the something else is the IDS proprietary VR format. I don't know anyone using this browser.

Vrscout

Chaco Communications

■ http://www.chaco.com/products/# vrscout
Currently supported platforms:
Windows (3.x, 95, NT)

This is the stand-alone version of the fine Pueblo browser. Please see the Pueblo description for more information.

Vrweb

Gerbert Orasche and Michael Pichler

■ http://hgiicm.tu-graz.ac.at/vrweb
Currently Supported Platforms:
Windows (3.x, 95, NT), SGI, Solaris, SunOS, OSF, Ultrix, HP-UX, AIX, and Linux.

These guys win points just for the support of all those Unix platforms. If you run Unix, and it's not an SGI or Solaris ZX box, then you need this browser to see VRML files. The source code is also available, which scores still more points. Points are lost because they're using MESA on everything except the SGI platform. MESA is a free, GL-ish renderer that is unfortunately vvveerryy s - l - o - w.

WebFX

Paper Software

■ http://www.paperinc.com
Currently supported platforms:
Windows 3.x, 95, and NT

WebFX specializes in embedding the VRML browser into the primary Web browser. In addition, it is one of the fastest VRML browsers available for the PC. Some caveats are that the color model is limited, and that textures are not completely supported. However, in general, WebFX is the browser you've been waiting for if you have a PC.

WebOOGL 2.0

The Geometry Center

■ http://www.geom.umn.edu/locate/weboogl
Currently supported platforms:
SGI or Sun workstations

WebOOGL 2.0 is a "quasi-compliant" VRML browser: most of the VRML spec is implemented, but a few nodes are silently ignored (most notably texture mapping). The browser is built on top of the Center's 3D viewer Geomview.

WebSpace

Template Graphics Software and Silicon Graphics

■ http://www.sgi.com/Products/WebFORCE/WebSpace
Currently supported platforms: IBM, Windows (95 and NT), SGI, SUN Solaris ZX/TZX

WebSpace supports VRML as well as allowing the use of Inventor nodes. Notice a theme? On the SGI this is the browser of choice. On other platforms its reliance on Open Inventor means it runs very slowly. However, WebSpace is the de facto reference implementation for VRML Browsers. If you want to see many models in their full glory, you must use WebSpace.

Webview

San Diego Super Computer Center

■ http://www.sdsc.edu/EnablingTech/Visualization/vrml/webview.html"
Currently Supported Platforms:
SGI/UNIX systems<P>

Webview is a publicly available VRML browser for SGI/UNIX systems. Webview is released with full source code and is provided as a public platform for developing and testing experimental additions to the VRML specification. These guys win points for releasing their code. They're also doing some cool interactive stuff, some of which looks like it will be the basis for the VRML 2.0 spec. You can find more info on that proposal and others at The VRML Repository. ■ http://www.sdsc.edu/vrml/research. html

Whurlwind

by Bill Enright and John Louch

■ http://www.info.apple.com/qd3d/Viewer.HTML
Currently supported platforms:
PowerPC Macintosh

Whurlwind reads 3DMF and VRML models. It relies on QuickDraw 3D, so you must have QuickDraw 3D installed to use it (you can download QuickDraw 3D 1.0 at this page). Many people have difficulties with this browser, so don't be surprised if you do as well. The author has lately spoken up and said that a new version should be released "soon." I think it's funny how, no matter how fast this industry moves, "soon" is still this pseudo-infinite variable that can mean anywhere from three months to a year. All joking aside, this was the only even slightly usable browser for the Macintosh for quite some time, so the author wins points. He won even more points some months ago when he let folks know development had dropped off because he'd had health difficulties. Next time you folks complain about its performance, please note that you probably have yet to work yourselves into a heart attack trying to support all the cruel Macintosh 3D fanatics.

Worldview

Intervista

■ http://www.webmaster.com:80/vrml/
Currently Supported Platforms:
Windows (3.x, 95, NT)

Worldview was the first available PC browser, not counting WebSpace on Windows NT (we didn't count it, did you?). Anyway, this browser is still in beta, like most of them, but has recently added support for LOD, Textures, WWWInline, and a bevy of other beautiful nodes. We recommend that you give this browser and WebFX a try if you want to browse VRML on your PC. Worldview may soon be available on the Macintosh as well, but I wouldn't hold my breath if I were you.

Authoring Tool Resources

Ez3d VRML Author

Radiance

■ http://www.webcom.com/radiance/ vrml.html
Currently supported platforms:
Silicon Graphics (IRIX 5.3 or higher)

Ez3d VRML Author is a modeling tool that enables you to create VRML models using LOD, WWWInline, WWWAnchor, and polygon reduction tools. It also supports camera positions and enables you to preview your VRML model in a browser of your choice.

Gweb

■ http://www.demon.co.uk/presence/gweb.html
Currently supported platforms:
Silicon Graphics, Windows 3.1 and NT, Sun Sparc (SX /ZX)

Gweb has been designed as a modeling and prototyping tool specifically for virtual world builders who want to export their work to VRML. Unfortunately, "inlines, point sets, level of detail, fonts, info nodes, and orthographic cameras are unsupported in this release," which severely limits your ability to create VRML.

Homespace Builder

Paragraph

■ http://www.paragraph.com/vhsb/
Currently supported platforms:
MS-DOS 5.0 or higher, Microsoft Windows 3.1 or higher, NT, or Windows 95

Homespace Builder makes it easy for inexperienced modelers to create their own VRML spaces. It also boasts a fast rendering engine for middle and low-end computer users. Although very easy to use, Homespace Builder tends to encourage the creation of rectangular spaces that rely heavily on texture mapping for their atmosphere.

Pioneer

Caligari

■ http://www.caligari.com:80/com/products/ppfeat.html
Currently supported platforms:
Windows 95, Windows NT, Windows 3.11 (w/Win32S)

Pioneer (Fountain) is a VRML authoring solution that includes rapid modeling in perspective space, manipulation of texture-mapped VRML objects in real time and interactive lighting.

Modeling Resources

Different modeling programs tend to be suited for different things. We are attempting to get an understanding of what tools work best for what sort of modeling.

Karsten Isakovicc

Technical University of Berlin

■ http://www.cs.tu-berlin.de/~ki/engines.html

Here you will find a big overview of software 3D engines. It's not specific to VRML production, but still it can give you a good idea of the differences between modeling programs including Render-Ware, BRender, Mesa, Reality Lab, Virtek 3D Ware, Quickdraw3D, 3D Game Machine, blah, blah, blah, blah...

Cindy Reed

■ http://www.ywd.com/cindy/texture.html

Cindy explains in detail the ins and outs of texture mapping, both how it should work and how it really works, for your edification.

AutoCAD

Autodesk

■ http://www.arch.unsw.edu.au/helpdesk/software/autocad/

AutoCAD is a general purpose computer-aided drafting application program designed for use on single-user, desktop personal computers, and graphic workstations.

We used to proof and double-check lots of files that were converting improperly when working on the Interactive Media Festival models. This is a tight cousin to 3DS so the formats are more likely to match.

FormZ

AutoDesSys

■ http://www.formz.com/

This is Michael Gough's (a trained architect, who builds models for many of Construct's projects) favorite modeling program. He has recently tried Nichimen and 3Design, but has decided to stay with FormZ.

Open Inventor for non-SGI

■ ftp://ftp.sd.tgs.com/pub/template/OpenInventor/"
Currently supported platforms:
SUN, IBM, AIX

Template Graphics Software is evaluating a port of Open Inventor to OS/2 Warp.

Template Graphics Software is currently developing Open Inventor for Power Macintosh, DEC Alpha OSF/1 and NT, as well as Hewlett/Packard 9000/7xx. Please send email to info@tgs.com or call (619)457-5359 x229 for further information on this product.

Strata

Strata Incorporated

■ http://www.strata3d.com/mapserve/strata/ StrataProduct.html

This came in handy as a high-resolution modeler for objects during the Variety Arts Center project. We would take the resulting dxf files, assemble them in FormZ, and then translate them using 3Ds.

3D Studio

Kinetix

■ www.ktx.com

This is one of the main programs our volunteer team used to make the Variety Arts Center. Without 3D Studio we would have been be stranded. At that stage it converted through to VRML the most smoothly of any modeling programs we had used in those early days of VRML production.

trueSpace 2

Caligari

■ http://www.caligari.com:80/lvltwo/product/ts2.html

Caligari trueSpace is a 3D modeling and animation program currently available for the Windows 3.x platform (and runs quite nicely on Windows 95). trueSpace is primarily a "clay" type modeler, providing you with a number of different primitive objects that can be molded, stretched, lathed, scaled, and so on into whatever object you desire. It has extensive facilities for coloring and texturing your object, and is even able to deform and alter texture maps on the fly, enabling you to observe texture map deformations and alterations as they happen.

trueSpace can import DXF, 3D Studio binary, 3D Studio project, 3D Studio ASCII, LightWave, Wavefront, Imagine, VideoScape, Caligari Amiga, and Postscript files. Non-native export filetypes are DXF and 3D Studio ASCII.

Translator Resources

If you are using modeling programs that are unable to save directly to VRML you will need to use tools such as these to translate the output of your modeling program into VRML.

Alias To Iv

SGI

■ ftp://ftp.sgi.com/private/translators/AliasToIv.tar

Takes Alias files and spits 'em out as Inventor files.

Converters

■ ftp://sunee.uwaterloo.ca/pub/rend386/converters

Converters for this, that, and the other.

dxf 2 wrl

■ http://www.organic.com/vrml/

Organic offers a free dxf2wrl conversion service. Uploaded dxf files are converted on a batch basis with the resultant file put on the ■ http://www.organic.com Webserver.

Dx 2 vrml

■ http://www.tc.cornell.edu/Visualization/contrib/cs49094to95/ckline/dx2vrml/dx2vrml.html

Dx 2 vrml is an outboard module for DX 2.0 that translates DX objects into scene descriptions compliant with the VRML v1.0 specification. Using Dx2 vrml will make it easier for researchers to make their visualizations available to the public in their original three-dimensional representation.

dxf To Iv

SGI

■ ftp://ftp.sgi.com/private/translators/DxfToIv.tar

Takes the DXF files, reads the ASCII, and converts them to Inventor Format.

3ds To Iv

SGI

■ ftp://ftp.sgi.com/private/translators/3dsToIv.tar

Takes the 3DS files, reads the ASCII, and converts them to Inventor Format.

Iv To VRML

SGI

■ http://webspace.sgi.com/Tools/ivToVRML.tar.Z

Takes the Inventor files, reads the ASCII, and converts them to *.wrl.

obj 2 wrl

■ http://www.sdsc.edu/EnablingTech/Visualization/vrml/tools/obj2wrl/help/obj2wrl.html

Takes Wavefront obj file and outputs the geometry in VRML wrl file format.

Wadtoiv

■ http://www-white.media.mit.edu/~kbrussel/wadtoiv.html

Reads a Doom wad (or patchwad) file and outputs a specified episode and mission's map data in Open Inventor format.

txt 2 wrl

■ http://cs.uah.edu/~lthomas/vrml/txt2wrl.cxx

Translates ASCII text to wrl format.

wld2vrml

■ ftp://sunee.uwaterloo.ca/pub/rend386/converters/ wld2vrml.zip

Translates WLD files into VRML. wld2vrml runs under DOS. The WLD/PLG/FIG formats are used by a number of freeware VR programs, including REND386, AVRIL, VR-386, and Gossamer.

Wrlgrid

■ http://www.sdsc.edu/EnablingTech/Visualization/vrml/ tools/wrlgrid/help/wrlgrid.html

Outputs a colored, regular, or warped grid of line sets or face sets. This can be used to generate base grids for scientific visualizations, or to form "grout" lines for floor-tiled areas of virtual environments. In the latter case, we've found that the addition of grout lines helps create a sense of depth and provides a size-comparison visual cue that makes virtual environments seem more real.

wc 2 pov v2.6

■ http://www.europa.com/~keithr/wc2pov26.zip

wc 2 pov v2.6 is a Windows program that converts between various 3D file formats. These formats include 3D Studio, Wavefront, VRML, POVRay, NFF, DXF, TrueType Fonts, and others.

SDSC VRM

■ http://www.sdsc.edu/vrml/).

Most of these translation tools and the information about them were gathered from SDSC VRML Repository maintained by Charles Eubanks, John Moreland, and Dave Nadeau.

■ Miscellaneous Resources

DatafatMunger

■ http://www.construct.net/vrmltools/datafat.html

James Waldrop's DatafatMunger can squish your average VRML file to 5% of its original size by limiting the points of precision and then gzipping the result.

Lightscape Visualization System

■ http://www.lightscape.com/

Lightscape is the ultimate lighting tool! Lightscape's radiosity solution produces beautifully lit 3D scenes. Their home-page has some examples of just how amazing files can look when they're lit properly. Lightscape is currently available for SGI and NT platforms.

VR Player

■ http://www.spe.sony.com/Pictures/SonyMovies/10vr.html

VR Player is a viewer with a real-time cyberspace rendering engine for 3DS and DXF files courtesy of Autodesk, Inc.

Cyberspace Developer Kit Release 2

■ http://www.bluerock.com/cdkwv/

The CDK World Viewer is a simple program that can display in real-time any .DXF or .3DS file that contains 3D geometry and animations. To run the CDK World Viewer you need a 100% PC-compatible computer running Windows 3.1 or Windows NT (v3.1 or v3.5).

CubeWorld

■ http://cs.uah.edu/~lthomas/cw

CubeWorld is an alternate reality inhabited by Layne Thomas. You can find little VRML bits and pieces like the txt2wrl converter and the VRML maze generator (■ http:// cs.uah.edu/cgi-bin/lthomas/maze.pl). While you are there you should check out his plans for VR day (■ http://cs.uah.edu/~lthomas/cw/vr_day. html).

Authenticator Page

■ http://www.geom.umn.edu/~daeron/docs/vrml.html

So, you think you have a legitimate VRML object but aren't absolutely sure? Well no problem! Just submit the URL for your object to this authentication script. It will automatically check the syntax of your supposed VRML file and get back to you with the results. Be patient, because it may take a while depending on the size of your object.

Virtual World Factory

■ http://www.virtpark.com/theme/fact-info.html

Use the Virtual World Factory to create your own worlds, without having to program! All you need to do is fill-in-the-blanks, and out pops your world. Your world will be described in VRML, Virtual Reality Modeling Language, the international standard for virtual worlds. You will want to have a VRML browser to view and walk around in your world.

■ Thanks to Annette Loudon and James Waldrop of Construct for assembling this list.

■ note

.gz and .gzip File Formats

There are a lot of references to .gz and gzipped files in this chapter. gzip is a compression technique created by the Free Software Foundation for their GNU (Gnu's Not Unix) project. gzip was created specifically to allow the computing community access to an effective compression technology that is unencumbered by licensing and royalty restrictions associated with the more common LZW (Limpel-Zev-Welch) compression. On December 29, 1994, Unisys corporation decided to begin enforcing a patent that they have on LZW compression. They specifically targeted marketers of GIF encoding software (charging about $5,000 plus 15 percent of gross revenues), but they also targeted everyone marketing Unix-like operating systems (because Unix uses LZW in its standard "compress" utility). FSF responded by creating a better compression utility called "gzip." gzip is not at all related to the ZIP utility commonly used by PCs.

References:

■ http://www.lpf.org/Patents/Gif/Gif.html

■ http://www.gnu.ai.mit.edu/

■ site summary

Construct

There aren't many design firms creating 3D Web sites—yet. The learning curve is steep and the rules are different, but for the right subject matter and audience, the rewards can be worth it. Expect the tools to be shaky, the browsers to be buggy, and the technology to constantly evolve and grow. VRML is not for the fainthearted; it takes a lot of perseverance and determination to work in uncharted territory.

■ Identify your audience and your goals before you begin. If you add a lot of textures and lighting effects it may look gorgeous on networked SGI computers, but the home user on a standard PC might choke and crash on the same site.

■ The more polygons, the bigger the file, the slower the rendering speed. A standard acceptable cap is 5,000 polygons per scene, with the promise of 10,000 per scene within a year as browsers improve.

■ Check your VRML site on more than one platform using more than one browser. The color differences can be dramatic.

■ Be educated. Join mailing lists and discussion groups. Check out the links in this chapter to make sure you are using the best tools and browsers.

To join the VRML standards discussion, please subscribe to the www-vrml mailing list. Send mail to: majordomo@wired.com. No subject, message body: subscribe www-vrml your-email-address. Before posting, please read the etiquette guide at: ■ http://www.vrml.wired.com/ettiquette.html.

Browser-Safe Color Charts

CCFFFF R:204 G:255 B:255

What are browser-safe colors? These colors are used by most popular browsers (such as Netscape, Microsoft Internet Explorer, and Mosaic) whenever they serve Web pages to end users' systems that are limited to 8-bit displays (256 color video cards). If you use colors from the browser-safe color chart, they will not alter between most browsers, across multiple computer platforms, or within different operating systems.

009999 R:000 G:153 B:153

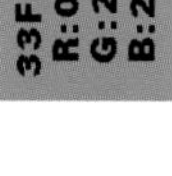

When should you use the browser-safe colors? Whenever you work with hexadecimal color—such as when you specify background colors, text colors, link colors, visited link colors, and active link colors. If you choose colors from the browser-safe color system, they will not shift between platforms. If you don't, the Web browser will change the color you did pick and convert it to one of these colors anyway. Only then, you won't have any control over the browser's conversion decision. Suppose the browser decides to convert your text color to the same color as your background? It has happened; I swear!

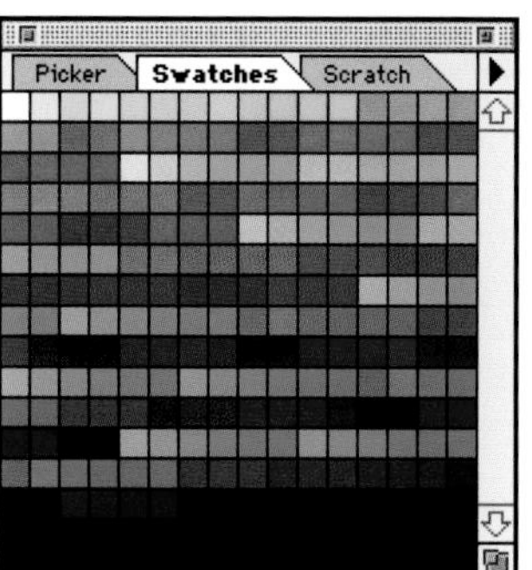

If you create any custom artwork, such as illustrations, logos, or cartoons, that involve large areas of a single color, you should work with these colors as well. If you follow this advice, your images will not dither or shift color. Chapter 1, "Hot Hot Hot," has a good example of "dithering" and how to avoid it using this color palette.

You do not need to worry about these colors when preparing photographs for the Web. The browsers do a great job of converting photographs to the browser-safe colors without your help. If you leave photographs in adaptive palettes (or better yet, as 24-bit JPEGs) your end viewers who can view more than 8-bit color have the added advantage of seeing better quality images.

For more information about browser-safe colors, visit:

- http://www.lynda.com/dwg/hex.html

<table>
<tr><td>990033
R:153
G:000
B:051</td><td>FF3366
R:255
G:051
B:102</td><td>CC0033
R:204
G:000
B:051</td><td>FF0033
R:255
G:000
B:051</td><td>FF9999
R:255
G:153
B:153</td><td>CC3366
R:204
G:051
B:102</td><td>FFCCFF
R:255
G:204
B:255</td><td>CC6699
R:204
G:102
B:153</td><td>993366
R:153
G:051
B:102</td><td>660033
R:102
G:000
B:051</td><td>CC3399
R:204
G:051
B:153</td><td>FF99CC
R:255
G:153
B:204</td><td>FF66CC
R:255
G:102
B:204</td><td>FF99FF
R:255
G:153
B:255</td><td>FF6699
R:255
G:102
B:153</td><td>CC0066
R:204
G:000
B:102</td></tr>
<tr><td>FF0066
R:255
G:000
B:102</td><td>FF3399
R:255
G:051
B:153</td><td>FF0099
R:255
G:000
B:153</td><td>FF33CC
R:255
G:051
B:204</td><td>FF00CC
R:255
G:000
B:204</td><td>FF66FF
R:255
G:102
B:255</td><td>FF33FF
R:255
G:051
B:255</td><td>FF00FF
R:255
G:000
B:255</td><td>CC0099
R:204
G:000
B:153</td><td>990066
R:153
G:000
B:102</td><td>CC66CC
R:204
G:102
B:204</td><td>CC33CC
R:204
G:051
B:204</td><td>CC99FF
R:204
G:153
B:255</td><td>CC66FF
R:204
G:102
B:255</td><td>CC33FF
R:204
G:051
B:255</td><td>993399
R:153
G:051
B:153</td></tr>
<tr><td>CC00CC
R:204
G:000
B:204</td><td>CC00FF
R:204
G:000
B:255</td><td>9900CC
R:153
G:000
B:204</td><td>990099
R:153
G:000
B:153</td><td>CC99CC
R:204
G:153
B:204</td><td>996699
R:153
G:102
B:153</td><td>663366
R:102
G:051
B:102</td><td>660099
R:102
G:000
B:153</td><td>9933CC
R:153
G:051
B:204</td><td>660066
R:102
G:000
B:102</td><td>9900FF
R:153
G:000
B:255</td><td>9933FF
R:153
G:051
B:255</td><td>9966CC
R:153
G:102
B:204</td><td>330033
R:051
G:000
B:051</td><td>663399
R:102
G:051
B:153</td><td>6633CC
R:102
G:051
B:204</td></tr>
<tr><td>6600CC
R:102
G:000
B:204</td><td>9966FF
R:153
G:102
B:255</td><td>330066
R:051
G:000
B:102</td><td>6600FF
R:102
G:000
B:255</td><td>6633FF
R:102
G:051
B:255</td><td>CCCCFF
R:204
G:204
B:255</td><td>9999FF
R:153
G:153
B:255</td><td>9999CC
R:153
G:153
B:204</td><td>6666CC
R:102
G:102
B:204</td><td>6666FF
R:102
G:102
B:255</td><td>666699
R:102
G:102
B:153</td><td>333366
R:051
G:051
B:102</td><td>333399
R:051
G:051
B:153</td><td>330099
R:051
G:000
B:153</td><td>3300CC
R:051
G:000
B:204</td><td>3300FF
R:051
G:000
B:255</td></tr>
<tr><td>3333FF
R:051
G:051
B:255</td><td>3333CC
R:051
G:051
B:204</td><td>0066FF
R:000
G:102
B:255</td><td>0033FF
R:000
G:051
B:255</td><td>3366FF
R:051
G:102
B:255</td><td>3366CC
R:051
G:102
B:204</td><td>000066
R:000
G:000
B:102</td><td>000033
R:000
G:000
B:051</td><td>0000FF
R:000
G:000
B:255</td><td>000099
R:000
G:000
B:153</td><td>0033CC
R:000
G:051
B:204</td><td>0000CC
R:000
G:000
B:204</td><td>336699
R:051
G:102
B:153</td><td>0066CC
R:000
G:102
B:204</td><td>99CCFF
R:153
G:204
B:255</td><td>6699FF
R:102
G:153
B:255</td></tr>
<tr><td>003366
R:000
G:051
B:102</td><td>6699CC
R:102
G:153
B:204</td><td>006699
R:000
G:102
B:153</td><td>3399CC
R:051
G:153
B:204</td><td>0099CC
R:000
G:153
B:204</td><td>66CCFF
R:102
G:204
B:255</td><td>3399FF
R:051
G:153
B:255</td><td>003399
R:000
G:051
B:153</td><td>0099FF
R:000
G:153
B:255</td><td>33CCFF
R:051
G:204
B:255</td><td>00CCFF
R:000
G:204
B:255</td><td>99FFFF
R:153
G:255
B:255</td><td>66FFFF
R:102
G:255
B:255</td><td>33FFFF
R:051
G:255
B:255</td><td>00FFFF
R:000
G:255
B:255</td><td>00CCCC
R:000
G:204
B:204</td></tr>
<tr><td>009999
R:000
G:153
B:153</td><td>669999
R:102
G:153
B:153</td><td>99CCCC
R:153
G:204
B:204</td><td>CCFFFF
R:204
G:255
B:255</td><td>33CCCC
R:051
G:204
B:204</td><td>66CCCC
R:102
G:204
B:204</td><td>339999
R:051
G:153
B:153</td><td>336666
R:051
G:102
B:102</td><td>006666
R:000
G:102
B:102</td><td></td><td>00FFCC
R:000
G:255
B:204</td><td>33FFCC
R:051
G:255
B:204</td><td>33CC99
R:051
G:204
B:153</td><td>00CC99
R:000
G:204
B:153</td><td>66FFCC
R:102
G:255
B:204</td><td>99FFCC
R:153
G:255
B:204</td></tr>
<tr><td>00FF99
R:000
G:255
B:153</td><td>339966
R:051
G:153
B:102</td><td>006633
R:000
G:102
B:051</td><td>336633
R:051
G:102
B:051</td><td>669966
R:102
G:153
B:102</td><td>66CC66
R:102
G:204
B:102</td><td>99FF99
R:153
G:255
B:153</td><td>66FF66
R:102
G:255
B:102</td><td>339933
R:051
G:153
B:051</td><td>99CC99
R:153
G:204
B:153</td><td>66FF99
R:102
G:255
B:153</td><td>33FF99
R:051
G:255
B:153</td><td>33CC66
R:051
G:204
B:102</td><td>00CC66
R:000
G:204
B:102</td><td>66CC99
R:102
G:204
B:153</td><td>009966
R:000
G:153
B:102</td></tr>
<tr><td>009933
R:000
G:153
B:051</td><td>33FF66
R:051
G:255
B:102</td><td>00FF66
R:000
G:255
B:102</td><td>CCFFCC
R:204
G:255
B:204</td><td>CCFF99
R:204
G:255
B:153</td><td>99FF66
R:153
G:255
B:102</td><td>99FF33
R:153
G:255
B:051</td><td>00FF33
R:000
G:255
B:051</td><td>33FF33
R:051
G:255
B:051</td><td>00CC33
R:000
G:204
B:051</td><td>33CC33
R:051
G:204
B:051</td><td>66FF33
R:102
G:255
B:051</td><td>00FF00
R:000
G:255
B:000</td><td>66CC33
R:102
G:204
B:051</td><td>006600
R:000
G:102
B:000</td><td>003300
R:000
G:051
B:000</td></tr>
<tr><td>009900
R:000
G:153
B:000</td><td>33FF00
R:051
G:255
B:000</td><td>66FF00
R:102
G:255
B:000</td><td>99FF00
R:153
G:255
B:000</td><td>66CC00
R:102
G:204
B:000</td><td>00CC00
R:000
G:204
B:000</td><td>33CC00
R:051
G:204
B:000</td><td>339900
R:051
G:153
B:000</td><td>99CC66
R:153
G:204
B:102</td><td>669933
R:102
G:153
B:051</td><td>99CC33
R:153
G:204
B:051</td><td>336600
R:051
G:102
B:000</td><td>669900
R:102
G:153
B:000</td><td>99CC00
R:153
G:204
B:000</td><td>CCFF66
R:204
G:255
B:102</td><td>CCFF33
R:204
G:255
B:051</td></tr>
<tr><td>CCFF00
R:204
G:255
B:000</td><td>999900
R:153
G:153
B:000</td><td>CCCC00
R:204
G:204
B:000</td><td>CCCC33
R:204
G:204
B:051</td><td></td><td>666600
R:102
G:102
B:000</td><td>999933
R:153
G:153
B:051</td><td>CCCC66
R:204
G:204
B:102</td><td>666633
R:102
G:102
B:051</td><td>999966
R:153
G:153
B:102</td><td>CCCC99
R:204
G:204
B:153</td><td>FFFFCC
R:255
G:255
B:204</td><td>FFFF99
R:255
G:255
B:153</td><td>FFFF66
R:255
G:255
B:102</td><td>FFFF33
R:255
G:255
B:051</td><td>FFFF00
R:255
G:255
B:000</td></tr>
<tr><td>FFCC00
R:255
G:204
B:000</td><td>FFCC66
R:255
G:204
B:102</td><td>FFCC33
R:255
G:204
B:051</td><td>CC9933
R:204
G:153
B:051</td><td>996600
R:153
G:102
B:000</td><td>CC9900
R:204
G:153
B:000</td><td>FF9900
R:255
G:153
B:000</td><td>CC6600
R:204
G:102
B:000</td><td>993300
R:153
G:051
B:000</td><td>CC6633
R:204
G:102
B:051</td><td>663300
R:102
G:051
B:000</td><td>FF9966
R:255
G:153
B:102</td><td>FF6633
R:255
G:102
B:051</td><td>FF9933
R:255
G:153
B:051</td><td>FF6600
R:255
G:102
B:000</td><td>CC3300
R:204
G:051
B:000</td></tr>
<tr><td>996633
R:153
G:102
B:051</td><td>330000
R:051
G:000
B:000</td><td>663333
R:102
G:051
B:051</td><td>996666
R:153
G:102
B:102</td><td>CC9999
R:204
G:153
B:153</td><td>993333
R:153
G:051
B:051</td><td>CC6666
R:204
G:102
B:102</td><td>FFCCCC
R:255
G:204
B:204</td><td>FF3333
R:255
G:051
B:051</td><td>CC3333
R:204
G:051
B:051</td><td>FF6666
R:255
G:102
B:102</td><td>660000
R:102
G:000
B:000</td><td>990000
R:153
G:000
B:000</td><td>CC0000
R:204
G:000
B:000</td><td>FF0000
R:255
G:000
B:000</td><td>FF3300
R:255
G:051
B:000</td></tr>
<tr><td>CC9966
R:204
G:153
B:102</td><td>FFCC99
R:255
G:204
B:153</td><td>FFFFFF
R:255
G:255
B:255</td><td>CCCCCC
R:204
G:204
B:204</td><td>999999
R:153
G:153
B:153</td><td>666666
R:102
G:102
B:102</td><td></td><td>000000
R:000
G:000
B:000</td><td></td><td></td><td></td><td></td><td></td><td></td><td></td><td></td></tr>
</table>

The browser-safe color palette organized by hue. This is how you can pick colors by whatever shade of a specific color you want. Keep in mind that the color of inks in a printed book are generated with CMYK values, and the browser-safe colors are RGB. Shifting will occur between print and screen. It's best to have these files handy as electronic files too, so you can judge the true screen colors. You can download the browser-safe color palettes, organized by hue or value, from ■ ftp://luna.bearnet.com/pub/lynda/.

FFFFFF R:255 G:255 B:255	FFFFCC R:255 G:255 B:204	FFFF99 R:255 G:255 B:153	FFFF66 R:255 G:255 B:102	FFFF33 R:255 G:255 B:051	FFFF00 R:255 G:255 B:000	CCFFFF R:204 G:255 B:255	CCFFCC R:204 G:255 B:204	CCFF99 R:204 G:255 B:153	CCFF66 R:204 G:255 B:102	CCFF33 R:204 G:255 B:051	CCFF00 R:204 G:255 B:000	99FFFF R:153 G:255 B:255	99FFCC R:153 G:255 B:204	99FF99 R:153 G:255 B:153	66FFFF R:102 G:255 B:255
99FF66 R:153 G:255 B:102	99FF33 R:153 G:255 B:051	66FFCC R:102 G:255 B:204	FFCCFF R:255 G:204 B:255	99FF00 R:153 G:255 B:000	33FFFF R:051 G:255 B:255	FFCCCC R:255 G:204 B:204	33FFCC R:051 G:255 B:204	00FFFF R:000 G:255 B:255	66FF99 R:102 G:255 B:153	FFCC99 R:255 G:204 B:153	66FF66 R:102 G:255 B:102	66FF33 R:102 G:255 B:051	00FFCC R:000 G:255 B:204	66FF00 R:102 G:255 B:000	33FF99 R:051 G:255 B:153
FFCC66 R:255 G:204 B:102	FFCC33 R:255 G:204 B:051	CCCCFF R:204 G:204 B:255	33FF66 R:051 G:255 B:102	33FF33 R:051 G:255 B:051	00FF99 R:000 G:255 B:153	FFCC00 R:255 G:204 B:000	33FF00 R:051 G:255 B:000	00FF66 R:000 G:255 B:102	00FF33 R:000 G:255 B:051	00FF00 R:000 G:255 B:000	CCCCCC R:204 G:204 B:204	CCCC99 R:204 G:204 B:153	99CCFF R:153 G:204 B:255	CCCC66 R:204 G:204 B:102	CCCC00 R:204 G:204 B:000
CCCC33 R:204 G:204 B:051	99CCCC R:153 G:204 B:204	FF99FF R:255 G:153 B:255	99CC99 R:153 G:204 B:153	66CCFF R:102 G:204 B:255	FF99CC R:255 G:153 B:204	99CC66 R:153 G:204 B:102	66CCCC R:102 G:204 B:204	99CC33 R:153 G:204 B:051	00CCFF R:000 G:204 B:255	33CCFF R:051 G:204 B:255	99CC00 R:153 G:204 B:000	FF9999 R:255 G:153 B:153	66CC99 R:102 G:204 B:153	FF9966 R:255 G:153 B:102	66CC66 R:102 G:204 B:102
33CCCC R:051 G:204 B:204	CC99FF R:204 G:153 B:255	00CCCC R:000 G:204 B:204	FF9933 R:255 G:153 B:051	FF9900 R:255 G:153 B:000	66CC33 R:102 G:204 B:051	66CC00 R:102 G:204 B:000	33CC99 R:051 G:204 B:153	00CC99 R:000 G:204 B:153	CC99CC R:204 G:153 B:204	33CC66 R:051 G:204 B:102	00CC66 R:000 G:204 B:102	CC9999 R:204 G:153 B:153	FF66FF R:255 G:102 B:255	33CC33 R:051 G:204 B:051	33CC00 R:051 G:204 B:000
CC9966 R:204 G:153 B:102	00CC33 R:000 G:204 B:051	9999FF R:153 G:153 B:255	00CC00 R:000 G:204 B:000	CC9933 R:204 G:153 B:051	CC9900 R:204 G:153 B:000	FF66CC R:255 G:102 B:204	9999CC R:153 G:153 B:204	FF6699 R:255 G:102 B:153	999999 R:153 G:153 B:153	6699FF R:102 G:153 B:255	FF6666 R:255 G:102 B:102	CC66FF R:204 G:102 B:255	999966 R:153 G:153 B:102	6699CC R:102 G:153 B:204	999933 R:153 G:153 B:051
FF6633 R:255 G:102 B:051	FF6600 R:255 G:102 B:000	FF33FF R:255 G:051 B:255	3399FF R:051 G:153 B:255	999900 R:153 G:153 B:000	669999 R:102 G:153 B:153	CC66CC R:204 G:102 B:204	0099FF R:000 G:153 B:255	FF33CC R:255 G:051 B:204	3399CC R:051 G:153 B:204	CC6699 R:204 G:102 B:153	669966 R:102 G:153 B:102	FF00FF R:255 G:000 B:255	339999 R:051 G:153 B:153	669933 R:102 G:153 B:051	669900 R:102 G:153 B:000
FF3399 R:255 G:051 B:153	0099CC R:000 G:153 B:204	9966FF R:153 G:102 B:255	CC6666 R:204 G:102 B:102	009999 R:000 G:153 B:153	CC6633 R:204 G:102 B:051	CC6600 R:204 G:102 B:000	339966 R:051 G:153 B:102	FF00CC R:255 G:000 B:204	FF3366 R:255 G:051 B:102	009966 R:000 G:153 B:102	CC33FF R:204 G:051 B:255	FF3333 R:255 G:051 B:051	339933 R:051 G:153 B:051	009933 R:000 G:153 B:051	9966CC R:153 G:102 B:204
FF3300 R:255 G:051 B:000	FF0099 R:255 G:000 B:153	339900 R:051 G:153 B:000	009900 R:000 G:153 B:000	6666FF R:102 G:102 B:255	CC33CC R:204 G:051 B:204	FF0066 R:255 G:000 B:102	996699 R:153 G:102 B:153	FF0033 R:255 G:000 B:051	FF0000 R:255 G:000 B:000	CC00FF R:204 G:000 B:255	CC3399 R:204 G:051 B:153	996666 R:153 G:102 B:102	6666CC R:102 G:102 B:204	996633 R:153 G:102 B:051	996600 R:153 G:102 B:000
3366FF R:051 G:102 B:255	CC3366 R:204 G:051 B:102	CC00CC R:204 G:000 B:204	9933FF R:153 G:051 B:255	0066FF R:000 G:102 B:255	666699 R:102 G:102 B:153	CC3333 R:204 G:051 B:051	CC3300 R:204 G:051 B:000	3366CC R:051 G:102 B:204	CC0099 R:204 G:000 B:153	9933CC R:153 G:051 B:204	666666 R:102 G:102 B:102	666633 R:102 G:102 B:051	0066CC R:000 G:102 B:204	9900FF R:153 G:000 B:255	666600 R:102 G:102 B:000
CC0066 R:204 G:000 B:102	336699 R:051 G:102 B:153	993399 R:153 G:051 B:153	CC0033 R:204 G:000 B:051	6633FF R:102 G:051 B:255	336666 R:051 G:102 B:102	006699 R:000 G:102 B:153	CC0000 R:204 G:000 B:000	993366 R:153 G:051 B:102	9900CC R:153 G:000 B:204	336633 R:051 G:102 B:051	006666 R:000 G:102 B:102	336600 R:051 G:102 B:000	6633CC R:102 G:051 B:204	3333FF R:051 G:051 B:255	006633 R:000 G:102 B:051
993333 R:153 G:051 B:051	993300 R:153 G:051 B:000	6600FF R:102 G:000 B:255	990099 R:153 G:000 B:153	006600 R:000 G:102 B:000	0033FF R:000 G:051 B:255	663399 R:102 G:051 B:153	990066 R:153 G:000 B:102	3333CC R:051 G:051 B:204	663366 R:102 G:051 B:102	6600CC R:102 G:000 B:204	990033 R:153 G:000 B:051	0033CC R:000 G:051 B:204	990000 R:153 G:000 B:000	3300FF R:051 G:000 B:255	663333 R:102 G:051 B:051
663300 R:102 G:051 B:000	660099 R:102 G:000 B:153	0000FF R:000 G:000 B:255	333399 R:051 G:051 B:153	3300CC R:051 G:000 B:204	003399 R:000 G:051 B:153	333366 R:051 G:051 B:102	660066 R:102 G:000 B:102		003366 R:000 G:051 B:102	0000CC R:000 G:000 B:204	660033 R:102 G:000 B:051		660000 R:102 G:000 B:000	330099 R:051 G:000 B:153	
003300 R:000 G:051 B:000	000099 R:000 G:000 B:153	330066 R:051 G:000 B:102	330033 R:051 G:000 B:051	000066 R:000 G:000 B:102	330000 R:051 G:000 B:000	000033 R:000 G:000 B:051	000000 R:000 G:000 B:000								

The browser-safe color palette organized by value. This is how you can choose colors by lights and darks. Keep in mind that the color of inks in a printed book are generated with CMYK values, and the browser-safe colors are RGB. Shifting will occur between print and screen. It's best to have these files handy as electronic files too, so you can judge the true screen colors. You can download the browser-safe color palettes, organized by hue or value, from ■ ftp://luna.bearnet.com/pub/lynda/.

How to Use the Browser-Safe Color Chart

You can easily use the colors from the preceeding page; just keep in mind that the colors will be different in print than they will be on your screen. You'll notice that each swatch has an RGB value and a hexadecimal value on it. Most imaging programs let you specify RGB values while HTML documents require that you enter hexadecimal values. See Chapter 5, "@tlas," to look at the HTML tags for specifying hexadecimal color.

You may notice a pattern for the RGB and hexadecimal values. The RGB values in the browser-safe color palette include 00, 51, 102, 151, 204, and 255. The hexadecimal values in the browser-safe color palette include FF, CC, 00, 33, 66, and 99. These are mathematically generated palettes!

You can use the Eyedropper Tool in many imaging programs to select colors from the browser-safe palettes, if you have the electronic versions in GIF format, which are available from: ■ ftp://luna.bearnet.com/pub/lynda/.

How to Use the Browser-Safe CLUT

If you own Photoshop, there is also a swatch palette available from the same ftp site, called "bclut2.act." If you open the Photoshop swatch palette and use the right arrow, you can load the CLUT file. This makes it easy to select from these colors when creating custom illustrations, logos, or cartoon-style artwork.

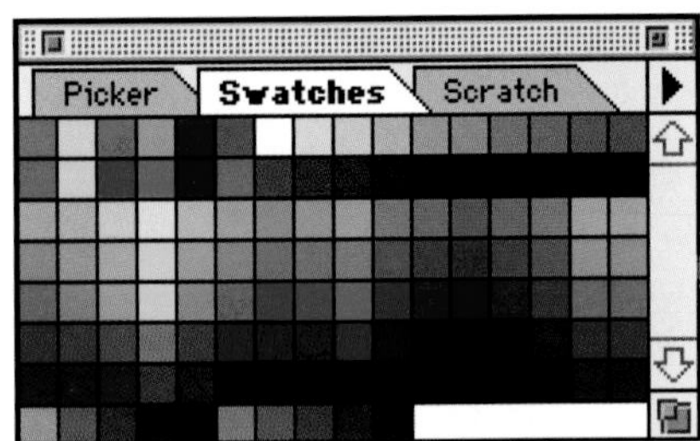

Step 1: In Photoshop, open the Swatches Palette.

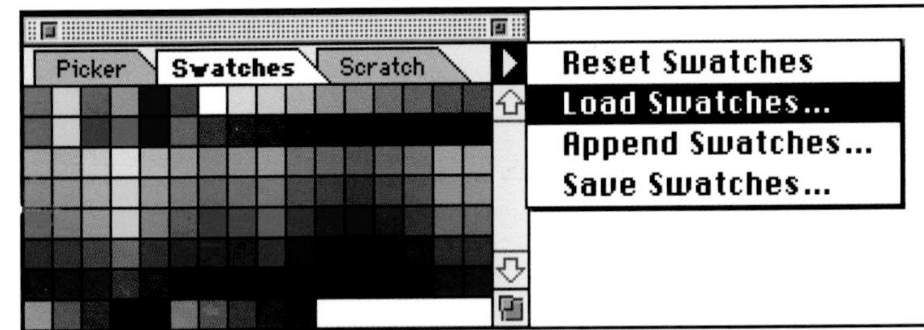

Step 2: Using the right arrow on the palette, choose Load Swatches.

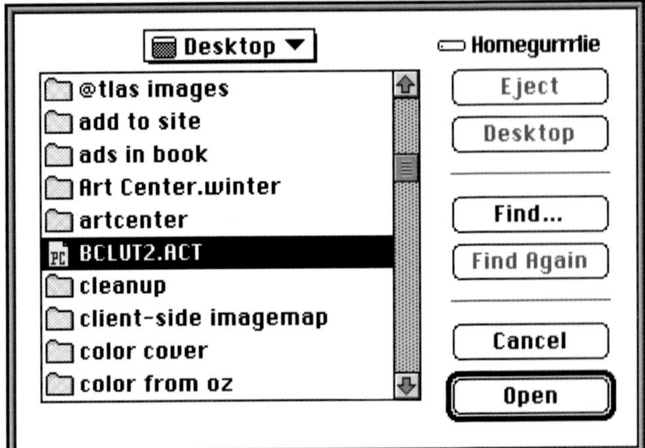

Step 3: Locate the "bclut2.act" file that you downloaded from ■ ftp://luna.bearnet.com/pub/lynda/. On Windows systems, use the pop-up menu in this dialog box to switch from the .aco exctension to .act.

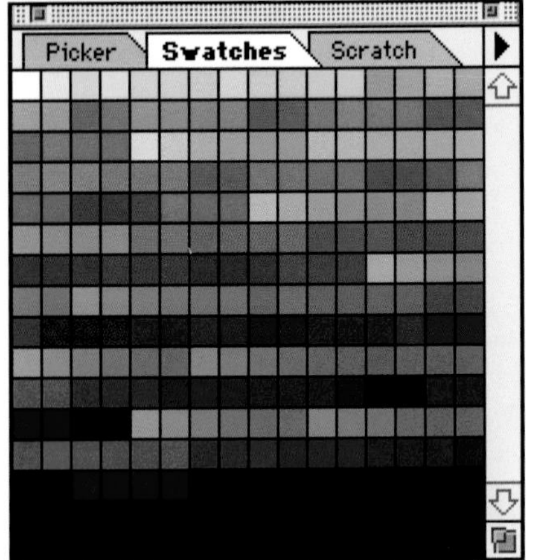

Step 4: The browser-safe colors will appear in your swatch set, and you can use the eyedropper to select Web colors for illustrations, logos, and cartoon-style artwork.

Glossary

8-bit graphics: Color or grayscale graphics or movies that have 256 colors or less.

8-bit sound: 8-bit sound has a dynamic range of 48 dB. Dynamic range is the measure of steps between the volume or amplitude of a sound.

16-bit graphics: Color images or movies that have 65,500 colors.

16-bit sound: Standard CD-quality sound resolution. 16-bit sounds have a dynamic range of 96 dB.

24-bit graphics: Color images or movies that have 16.7 million colors.

32-bit graphics: Color images or movies that have 16.7 million colors, plus an 8-bit masking channel.

adaptive dithering: A form of dithering in which the program looks to the image to determine the best set of colors when creating an 8-bit or smaller palette. *See dithering.*

active navigation: Point and click navigation, where the end user guides the information flow.

AIFC: A sound file format. AIFC is a new spec for the older Audio Interchange File Format (AIFF). Both AIFF and AIFF-C files can be read by this format.

aliasing: In bitmapped graphics, the jagged boundary along the edges of different-colored shapes within an image. *See anti-aliasing.*

anti-aliasing: A technique for reducing the jagged appearance of aliased bitmapped images, usually by inserting pixels that blend at the boundaries between adjacent colors.

artifacts: Image imperfections caused by compression.

attributes: Defined appearances or behaviors of 3D objects. For example, a lighting attribute would affect the color and lights of an object. A texture attribute would affect the surface texture of an object.

authoring tools: Creation tools for interactive media.

AVI: Audio-Video Interleaved. Microsoft's file format for desktop video movies.

behaviors: In VRML 2.0, behavioral information can be embedded into any object. A common type of "behavior" is animation.

bit-depth: The number of bits used to represent the color of each pixel in a given movie or still image. Specifically: bit depth of 2=black and white pixels. Bit depth of 4=16 colors or grays. Bit depth of 8=256 colors or grays. Bit depth of 16=65,536 colors. Bit depth of 24=(approximately) 16 million colors.

bit-depth or sampling resolution: Sampling resolution affects quality, just like dpi resolution affects the quality of images. Standard sampling resolutions are 8-bit mono, 8-bit stereo, 16-bit mono, and 16-bit stereo.

bitmapped graphics: Graphics that are pixel-based, as opposed to object oriented. Bitmapped graphics are what the computer can display, because it's a pixel-based medium, whereas object oriented graphics can be viewed in high resolution after they are sent to a printer. Graphics on the Web are bitmapped because they are viewed from a computer screen-based delivery system. *See object oriented graphics.*

browser: An application that enables you to access World Wide Web pages. Most browsers provide the capability to view Web pages, copy and print material from Web pages, download files over the Web, and navigate throughout the Web.

browser-safe colors: The 216 colors that do not shift between platforms, operating systems, or most Web browsers.

cache: A storage area that keeps frequently accessed data or program instructions readily available so that you do not have to retrieve them repeatedly.

Cinepak: Cinepak is a very high form of movie compression. The compression type is called "lossy" because it causes a visible loss in quality.

CGI: Common Gateway Interface. A Web standard for extending the functionality of HTML. CGI always involves the combination of a live Web server and external programming scripts.

client: A computer that requests information from a network's server. *See server.*

client pull: Client pull creates a slide show effect with HTML text or inline images. It is programmed within the <META> tag.

client-side: Client-side means that the Web element or effect can run locally off a computer, and does not require the presence of a server.

client-side image map: A client-side image map is programmed in HTML, does not require a separate map definition file, or to be stored on a live Web server.

CLUT: Color Look Up Table. An 8-bit or lower image file uses a CLUT to define its palette.

codec: Compressor/decompressor. A piece of software that encodes and decodes movie data.

color mapping: A color map refers to the color palette of an image. Color mapping means assigning colors to an image.

compression: Reduction of the amount of data required to re-create an original file, graphic, or movie. Compression is used to reduce the transmission time of media and application files across the Web.

data rate: Data rate relates to how fast movie data was captured.

data streaming: The capability to deliver time-based data as it's requested, much like a VCR, rather than having to download all the information before it can be played.

dithering: The positioning of different colored pixels within an image that uses a 256 color palette to simulate a color that does not exist in the palette. A dithered image often looks noisy, or composed of scattered pixels. *See adaptive dithering.*

dpi: Dots Per Inch is a term used mostly by print graphics-based programs and professionals, and is a common measurement related to the resoluton of an image. *See screen resolution.*

dynamic: Information that changes over a period of time. Typically refers to time-based media, such as animation or interactive documents.

extension: Abbreviated code at the end of a file that tells the browser what kind of file it's looking at. Example: a JPEG file would have the extension .JPG.

external graphic: Graphics that must be downloaded from the Web, instead of being viewed directly from a Web page. *See inline graphic and links.*

fixed palette: An established palette that is fixed. When a fixed palette Web browser views images, it will convert images to its colors and not use the colors from the original.

forms processing: Forms that enable users to enter information on Web pages are created using HTML and CGI, and their function is typically referred to as forms processing.

fps: FPS stands for frames per second. A movie contains a certain number of frames, and the fewer frames, the more jerky the motion and the smaller the file size.

frames: Frames offer the ability to divide a Web page into multiple regions, with each region acting as a nested Web page.

FTP: File transfer protocol. An Internet protocol that enables users to remotely access files on other computers. An FTP site houses files that can be downloaded to your computer.

gamma: Gamma measures the contrast that affects the midtones of an image. Adjusting the gamma lets you change the brightness values of the middle range of gray tones without dramatically altering the shadows and highlights.

GIF: A bitmapped color graphics file format. GIF is commonly used on the Web because it employs an efficient compression method. *See JPEG.*

GIF89a: A type of GIF file that supports transparency and multi-blocks. Multi-blocks create the illusion of animation. GIF89a files are sometimes referred to as "transparent GIFs" or "animated GIFs."

group: A VRML term. Grouping enables collections of objects to be treated as single objects. The group is a container for all the objects, so that nodes can be applied to multiple objects. If an object has two colors, chances are it has two groups.

hexadecimal: A base 16 mathematics calculation, often used in scripts and code. Hexadecimal code is requried by HTML to describe RGB values of color for the Web.

HTML: HyperText Markup Language. The common language for interchange of hypertext between the World Wide Web client and server. Web pages must be written using HTML. *See hypertext.*

HTTP: HyperText Transfer Protocol is the protocol that the browser and the Web server use to communicate with each other.

hypertext: Text formatted with links that enable the reader to jump among related topics. *See HTML.*

image maps: Portions of images that are hypertext links. Using a mouse-based Web client such as Netscape or Mosaic, the user clicks on different parts of a mapped image to activate different hypertext links. *See hypertext.*

inline graphic: A graphic that sits inside an HTML document, instead of the alternative which would require that the image be downloaded and then viewed using an outside system.

inlining: The process of embedding one VRML file into another.

interlaced GIFs: The GIF file format allows for "interlacing," which causes the GIF to load quickly at low or chunky resolution and then come into full or crisp resolution.

ISP: Acronym for Internet Service Provider.

JPEG: Acronym for Joint Photographic Experts Group, but commonly used to refer to a lossy compression technique that can reduce the size of a graphics file by as much as 96 percent. *See GIF.*

lighting: 3D artwork responds to lighting in a realistic manner, so lighting will affect overall appearance and color.

links: Emphasized words in a hypertext document that act as pointers to more information on that specific subject. Links are generally underlined and may appear in a different color. When you click on a link, you can be transported to a different Web site that contains information about the word or phrase used as the link. *See hypertext.*

LOD (Level Of Detail): A VRML term. The process of including more detailed models with higher polygon counts that are accessed based on the distance of the viewer. A low resolution object can appear at a faraway distance, and be replaced with a more detailed model at close-up distances.

lossless compression: A data compression technique that reduces the size of a file without sacrificing any of the original data. In lossless compression, the expanded or restored file is an exact replica of the original file before it was compressed. *See compression and lossy compression.*

lossy compression: A data compression technique in which some data is deliberately discarded in order to achieve massive reductions in the size of the compressed file.

mask: The process of blocking out areas in a computer graphic.

Materials: Material attributes affect the appearance of models, such as how shiny they are or their transparency level.

MIME: Multipurpose Internet Mail Extensions. An Internet standard for transferring non-text-based data such as sounds, movies, and images.

model: A 3D model is constructed with X, Y, and Z (width, height, and depth, respectively) coordinates. 2D artwork only has X and Y coordinates (width and height). 3D models are generally constructed with back, front, side, bottom, and top views, so that they can be viewed from any angle.

modeler: A person who builds models.

modeling: The process of creating a model.

MPEG: MPEG audio is a high-quality audio compression file format.

node: Theoretically, VRML objects can contain anything from 3D geometry to MIDI files or JPEG images. What the object contains is called a "node." VRML defines three different categories of nodes: shape, property, and group nodes.

object: The word "model" and "object" are sometimes used interchangeably. A model could be built from many objects. Sometimes the individual components within a model are called objects.

object-oriented graphics: A graphic image composed of autonomous objects such as lines, circles, ellipses, and boxes that can be moved independently. This type of graphic is used for print-based design because it can be printed at a higher resolution than a computer screen. *See bitmapped graphics.*

object resolution: Relates to how many polygons form a shape. High object resolution includes many polygons, looks the best, and takes the longest to render. Low resolution objects have fewer polygons and render faster.

passive navigation: Animation, slide-shows, streaming movies, and audio. Basically anything that plays without the end user initiating the content.

polygon: VRML data is constructed from polygons. The dictionary definition of a polygon is: a closed plane figure bounded by straight lines. Triangles, squares, geodesic domes, hexagons, and cubes are all polygons. Spheres, when created from polygons, will be made from many straight lines. If the amount of polygons in a sphere is small, it will have a lot of "steps" and won't look smooth. Most polygons are triangular; some are quadrangular.

Postscript: A sophisticated page description language used for printing high-quality text and graphics on laser printers and other high-resolution printing devices.

progressive JPEG: A type of JPEG that produces an interlaced effect as it loads, and that can be 30 percent smaller than standard JPEGs. It is not currently supported by many Web browsers.

provider: Provides Internet access. *See ISP.*

quick mask: A Photoshop technique for making masks. *See mask.*

QuickTime: System software developed by Apple Computer for presentation of desktop video.

render: The computer process of calculating 3D data and displaying the results on the computer screen.

sample rates: Sample rates are measured in kilohertz (KHz). Sound editing software is where the initial sample rate settings are established. Standard sample rates range from 11.025 KHz, 22.050 KHz, 44.10 KHz, to 48 KHz. The higher the sample rate, the better the quality. The sample rate affects the "range" of digitized sound, which describes its highs and lows.

screen resolution: Screen resolution generally refers to the resolution of common computer monitors. 72dpi is an agreed upon average, though you will also hear of 96 dpi being the resolution of larger displays.

server: A computer that provides services for users of its network. The server receives requests for services and manages the requests so that they are answered in an orderly manner. *See client.*

server push: Server push is a method of requesting images or data from the server, and automating their play-back. It involves CGI and the presence of a live Web server.

server-side: Server-side means any type of Web page element that depends on being loaded to a server. It also implies the use of a CGI script as well.

server-side image map: A server-side image map requires that the information about the imagemap be saved within a "map definition file" that needs to be stored on a server and accessed by a CGI script.

splash screen: A main menu screen, or opening graphic to a Web page.

sprite: An individual component of an animation, such as a character or graphic that moves independently.

tag: ASCII text indicators with which you surround text and images to designate certain formats or styles.

tables: Tables create rows and columns, like in a spreadsheet, and can be used to align data and images.

texture map: 2D artwork that is applied to the surface of a 3D shape.

transparent GIFs: A subset of the original GIF file format that adds header information to the GIF file, which signifies that a defined color will be masked out.

true color: The quality of color provided by 24-bit color depth. 24-bit color depth results in 16.7 million colors, which is usually more than adequate for the human eye.

μ-law: μ-law is a sound file format generated by Unix platforms. The sound quality is generally much lower than other sound formats, but the files are much smaller, too.

URL: Uniform Resource Locator. The address for a Web site.

Video for Windows: A multimedia architecture and application suite that provides an outbound architecture that lets applications developers access audio, video, and animation from many different sources through one interface. As an application, Video for Windows primarily handles video capture and compression, and video and audio editing. *See AVI.*

VRML: Stands for Virtual Reality Modeling Language, which is a protocol for distributing 3D data over the Web.

worlds: Instead of Web "pages" or "screens," VRML sites are called "worlds."

WYSIWYG: Pronounced wizzy-wig. A design philosophy in which formatting commands directly affect the text displayed on-screen, so that the screen shows the appearance of the printed text.

Talent Directory

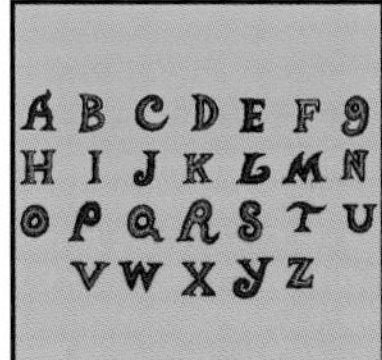

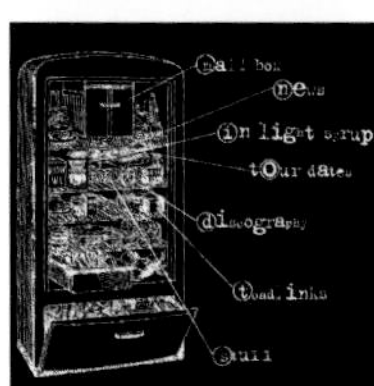

In an effort to promote the talented people who were profiled in this book, I created a contact list directory in this appendix. Feel free to let these people know what you think of their work, or better yet, hire some of these folks.

Hot Hot Hot

■ http://www. hothothot.com

Presence
175 S. Fair Oaks Ave.
Pasadena, CA 91105
(818) 405.9971

Tom Soulinille
Presence Founder
soul@presence.com

Mike Lazarro
CGI Programmer
mlazzaro@earthlink.net

Mike Kuniavsky
Webmaster
mikek@hotwired.com

Yeryeong Park
Designer
katrena@webstorm.com

DreamWorks Interactive SKG Prototype

■ http://www.dreamworksgames.com

Don Barnett
Designer/Illustrator
http://www.cris.com/~nekton/barnett.html
donb1967@aol.com

Bruce Heavin
Designer/Illustrator
http://www.stink.com
bruce@stink.com

Hollywood Records

■ http://www.hollywoodrec.com

Eric Hardman
Producer
eric_hardman@online.disney.com

Alex Lieu
Digital Designer
alex_lieu@online.disney.com

Johnny Rodriguez
Digital Designer
john_rodriguez@online.disney.com

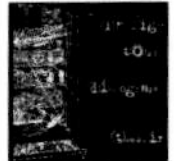

Sony Music Online

■ http://www.sony.com/Music/ArtistInfo/Toad/

■ http://www.sony.com/Music/ArtistInfo/AliceInChains/

Mary Maurer
Art Director
mary_maurer@sonymusic.com

Peter Anton
Webmaster
peter_anton@sonymusic.com

For the complete list of creative contributors check out the following urls:

dog's breath credits

■ http://www.music.sony.com/Music/ArtistInfo/AliceIn Chains/credits.html

house of toad credits

■ http://www.sony.com/Music/Artistinfo/Toad/stuff.html#credits

@tlas

■ http://atlas.organic.com

Michael Macrone
Webmaster
macrone@well.com

Amy Francheschini
Art Director
ame@sirius.com

David Karam
Art Director
Post Tool Design: Post/TV
http://atlas.organic.com/posttool
posttool@sirius.com

Olivier Laude
Content Acquistion
olivier@sirius.com

HotWired

■ http://www.hotwired.com/cocktail

Laura Moorhead
Concept and Information Content
laura@hotwired.com

Jonathan Louie
Design Director
jplouie@hotwired.com

Jill Atkinson
Programmer
jillo@hotwired.com

David Thau
Programmer
thau@hotwired.com

Brady Clark
Designer
http://www.hotwired.com/brady
brady@hotwired.com

Jon Lucich
Cocktail Photographer
(415) 642.9514

Marla Aufmuth
Photo Editor
marla@hotwired.com

Jeffrey Veen
Interface Director
jeff@hotwired.com
http://www.veen.com/Veen/Jeff/

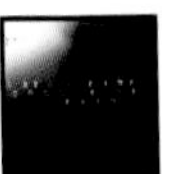

Art Center College of Design

■ http://www.artcenter.edu

Darin Beaman
Designer
dbeaman@artcenter.edu

Gudrun Frommherz
Designer/Webmaster
gudrun@artcenter.edu

Discovery Channel Online

■ http://www.discovery.com/DCO/doc/1012/world/science/muybridge/muybridgeopener.html

John Lyle Sanford
Design Director
John_Sanford@discovery.com

Sasha Knop
PhotoAssist
info@photoassist.com

Sue Klemens
Media Editor
Sue_Klemens@discovery.com

Peter Esmonde
Producer
Peter_Esmonde@discovery.com

Jim Jones
Internet Architect
jimj@nihilon

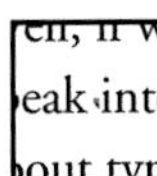

typoGRAPHIC

■ http://www.razorfish.com/bluedot/typo/

Razorfish, Inc.
580 Broadway, Suite 210
NY, NY 10012
info@razorfish.com
http://www.razorfish.com

Steven Turbek
Shockwave Programmer
sturbek@razorfish.com

Alex Smith
Art Director
(718) 638.2526

IUMA

■ http://www.iuma.com

Jeff Patterson
President, Technical Director
mugly@iuma.com

Evan Heidtmann
Production Manager
hero@iuma.com

Todd Williams
Vice President of Sales and Marketing
toddw@iuma.com

Brandee Selck
Art Director
brandee@choad.lvli.com

David Beach
Assistant Art Director
beach@lvl.com

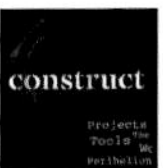

Construct

■ http://www.construct.net

Mark Meadows
Lead Designer
pighed@construct.net

Annette Loudon
Webmistress
annette@construct.net

Deconstructing Web Graphics Contacts

■ http://www.lynda.com/decon/

Lynda Weinman
Author
lynda@lynda.com
http://www.lynda.com

Bill Weinman
Tech Editor, Musician-Writer-Artist-Programmer-Technologist-etc.
wew@bearnet.com
http://www.bearnet.com/wew/

Ali Karp
Book Designer
alink newmedia
(213) 876.6212
alink@earthlink.net

Bart Nagel
Photographer
egon@aol.com

Douglas Kirkland
Photographer
dfkirkland@aol.com

Index

Symbols

A

B

C

D

E

F

G

Q

R

S

T

V

W

X

Z

HTML Tag Index

S

T

U

V

The Publisher and author would like to thank everyone who contributed their knowledge and talents to make this book possible, especially:

Presence Information Design

Copyright © 1996 Presence, All Rights Reserved

DreamWorks Interactive SKG

Copyright © 1996 DreamWorks Interactive SKG, All Rights Reserved

Hollywood Records

Copyright © 1996 Hollywood Records, All Rights Reserved

Sony Music Entertainment Inc.

Copyright © 1996 Sony Music Entertainment, Inc., All Rights Reserved. Reproduced with Permission

@tlas

Copyright © 1996 @tlas, All Rights Reserved

HotWired, Inc.

Copyright © 1994, 1995, 1996 HotWired Inc., All Rights Reserved

Art Center College of Design

Copyright © 1996 Art Center College of Design, a California nonprofit corporation, All Rights Reserved

Discovery Channel Online

Copyright © 1996 Discovery Channel Online, All Rights Reserved

Razorfish, Inc.

Copyright © 1996 Razorfish, Inc., All Rights Reserved

IUMA

Copyright © 1996 IUMA, All Rights Reserved

Constuct Internet Design Co.

Copyright © 1996 Construct Internet Design Co., All Rights Reserved

Coloring Web Graphics

This book is designed to help artists, programmers, and hobbyists understand how to work with color and image file formats for Web delivery. Artwork that looks good in print or on screen can easily end up looking terrible when viewed in a Web browser. Web browsers and different operating systems handle color images in specific ways that many Web designers and newcomers to Web publishing aren't aware of. This book offers in-depth answers about color, from both an aesthetic and technical perspective, and details what design constraints exist on the Web and how to work around them.

The CD-ROM includes custom browser-safe color artwork created by artist Bruce Heavin; browser-safe color swatches organized by hue, value, and saturation for imaging programs; and templates for color Web graphics. It also contains electronic files of recommended color groupings that offer hexadecimal and RGB conversions. The collection of buttons, horizontal rules, and background tiles is optimized for small size, cross-platform compatibility, and color accuracy.

Written by Lynda Weinman and Bruce Heavin, this book features practical, accessible, and down-to-earth advice that will help you greatly expand your color Web graphic design skills.

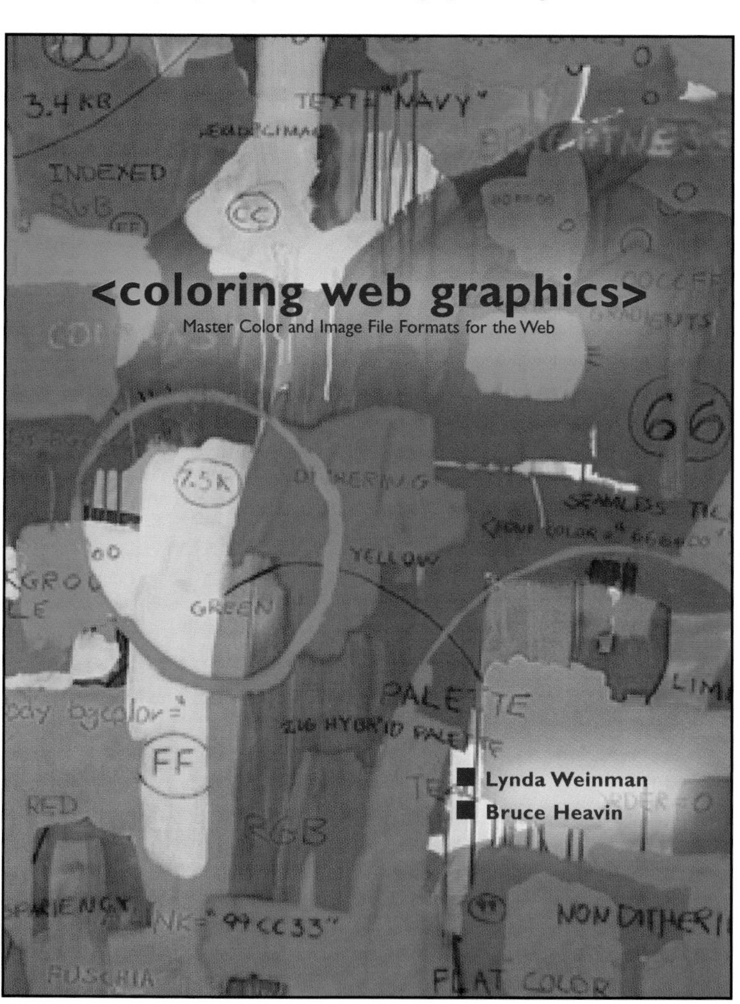

<coloring web graphics>
Master Color and Image File Formats for the Web
Lynda Weinman
Bruce Heavin

In this book, you'll learn to:

- Create colors in your artwork that won't shift or dither across multiple platforms
- Choose Web-appropriate color schemes for your page design
- Discover how to create thousands of browser-safe hybrid colors
- Gain access to the hundreds of browser-safe background tiles, rules, and buttons on the CD-ROM
- Use Photoshop™, Paint Shop Pro™, PhotoPaint™, and Lview™ to manage Web-specific color

The cross-platform CD-ROM includes:

- Browser-safe color palettes
- Browser-safe color swatches and scratch palettes for Photoshop and other imaging programs
- Browser-safe colors organized by hue, value, and saturation
- Browser-safe color clip art for Web use
- Electronic versions of color swatches grouped as they are in the book
- Sample HTML pages with recommended color groupings
- Sample patterns, backgrounds, buttons, and objects that can be customized with the color swatches on the CD-ROM

■ Product and Sales Information

Coloring Web Graphics by Lynda Weinman and Bruce Heavin $44.95 USA (book/CD-ROM set) 258 pages *Available Winter '96* ISBN: 1-56205-669-7 New Riders Publishing 1-800-428-5331 ■ http://www. mcp.com/newriders.

Designing Web Graphics

Designing Web Graphics is a full-color, step-by-step guide to preparing images and media for the World Wide Web. The book contains original research about how to make images small, understand compression, use colors that work accross multiple platforms, and to create images that will load quickly and look their best.

Written in a conversational, user-friendly tone, *Designing Web Graphics* has received rave reviews from both experienced Web designers and newcomers to the field. It's currently the best-selling book on this subject, and is being recommended and used by Web designers all over the world, including those from HotWired, Microsoft Internet Explorer design team, Adobe, and Discovery Channel Online.

The author maintains up-to-date Web pages, where you can read sample chapters, browse her list of Web design resources, or join her mailing list-based discussion group on Web design issues. Stop by and visit her site at: ■ http://www.lynda.com.

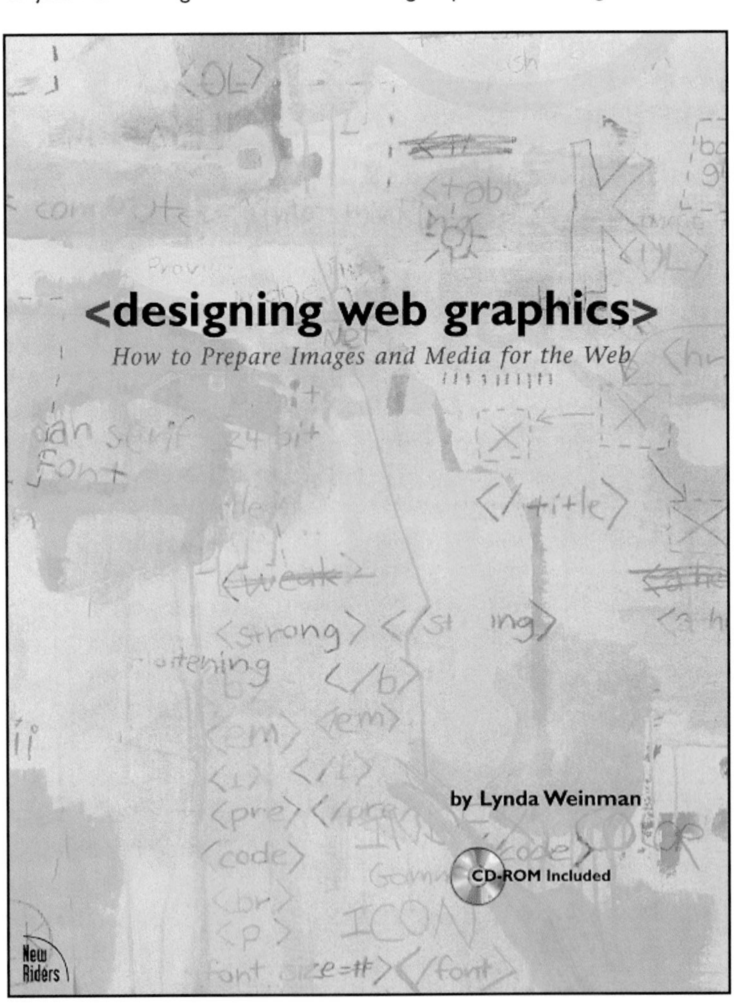

In this book, you'll learn to:

- Create graphics that are optimized for different browsers and platforms
- Design graphics that are appropriate in size and file format for the Web
- Maximize the speed and presentation of graphics on your Web site
- Create pattern backgrounds, colored text and backgrounds, trans-parent images, typography, tables, image maps, and dynamic documents
- Work with cross-platform, browser-safe colors
- Make seamless custom tiles
- Eliminate fringing from transparent GIFs

The cross-platform CD-ROM includes:

- Browser-safe color chart and color tools. Image, movie, and sound players
- Shareware and freeware utilities to create Web-specific artwork
- Web page templates, color palettes, and hexadecimal charts
- Shareware and freeware clip art for Web design icons, buttons, horizontal rules, background patterns, and symbols
- Demo software of Adobe Photoshop®, Adobe Premiere, Adobe Illustrator®, Fractal Design Painter, Kai's Power Tools, KPT Gradient Designer, KPT Power Photos, and DeBabelizer

Here's What People Are Saying About Designing Web Graphics:

"No Digital Fluff! Do you need to know it all and know it fast? Then *Designing Web Graphics* is the answer."
-Russell Brown, Sr. Creative Director, Adobe Systems, Inc.

"Your book has been incredibly useful for answering questions and providing inspiration. One of my team members made this comment: 'There are a lot of books out there that supposedly will answer all your questions about how to do things for the Web, but Lynda's book actually does!' I just love the logical and concise organization, and thorough discussion of each topic. And the 'Browser CLUT Palette' —that's worth 50 bucks all by itself!"
-**Dave Roh**, Simon & Schuster Elementary Group

"I just picked up your book *Designing Web Graphics*. Although I was already aware of about 75 percent of what your book covers, I still found it VERY, VERY helpful. It is well written and seems to keep in mind the fact that designers will be reading it. So in short, I'd like to thank you for providing me with a tool I can both learn from and hand off to others to help teach them the ins and outs of online design."
-**Dom Moreci**, Monnens-Addis Design

"I just want to let you know that I am sooo glad someone has finally assembled such a complete and useful reference on the subject. As a graphic designer who is increasingly finding himself asked to design graphics for Web sites, I have been feeling my way around in the dark on matters such as color palettes and cross-platform issues. Your book pulls everything together in one place and I will not hesitate to recommend it to colleagues in the same situation as myself."
-**Mark Fitzgerald**

"Your book is excellent!! It rocks!! It was a total lifesaver on my redesign project. Thank you, thank you, thank you!! It was so refreshing to read a book that isn't written by a 'tech-head' who is only interested in technology—you did a wonderful job of giving me not only the details, but also how they fit into the bigger picture and why they matter. I really appreciate writing that puts things in perspective. Your book does an excellent job. Your sense of humor definitely made it a fun read—I can't think of any better title for cross-platform issues than 'Platform Hell!'"
-**Dana Giles**

"I am a designer in the Philadelphia area—new to designing Web stuff—I just bought your book and WOW it is very good! Wish I had had a teacher like you in art school. Anyway, just wanted to say I am enjoying your book and home page—you have a refreshing style (open and fun)."
-**Victoria Land**

"You opened doors to so many problems I was encountering and had nowhere to go for the answers. Your book CLEARLY defines and illustrates every detail. I just can't thank you enough for taking the time for this project."
-**Joan Smith**

"Love the book! You made it easy and gave excellent samples that are easy to learn and expand on."
-**Julie A. Kreiner**, JAK Graphic Solutions, Chicago, IL

■ Product and Sales Information

Designing Web Graphics
Lynda Weinman
$50.00 USA (book/CD-ROM set)
258 pages Available Now
ISBN: 1-56205-532-1

New Riders Publishing
201 West 103rd Street
Indianapolis, IN 46290
1-800-428-5331
■ http://www. mcp.com/newriders